From a small bassoreliero in the possession of Archer Gifford Esq.

Your most obed^t Servant

Wm Franklin

LITH. OF SARONY & Co NEW YORK

CONTRIBUTIONS

TO THE

EARLY HISTORY OF PERTH AMBOY

AND

ADJOINING COUNTRY,

WITH

SKETCHES OF MEN AND EVENTS IN NEW JERSEY DURING THE PROVINCIAL ERA.

BY

WILLIAM A. WHITEHEAD.

AUTHOR OF "EAST JERSEY UNDER THE PROPRIETARY GOVERNMENTS," EDITOR OF "PAPERS OF GOVERNOR LEWIS MORRIS," ETC.

WITH MAPS AND ENGRAVINGS.

NEW YORK:
D. APPLETON & COMPANY,
346 & 348 BROADWAY.
1856.

JOHN F. TROW,
PRINTER AND STEREOTYPER,
377 & 379 Broadway.

TO THE MEMBERS

OF THE

NEW JERSEY HISTORICAL SOCIETY

THIS IMPERFECT ATTEMPT TO

"Copy Fair what Time hath Blurr'd,"

AND THEREBY AID THEM

IN ADVANCING THE OBJECTS OF THEIR ORGANIZATION,

IS RESPECTFULLY INSCRIBED

BY THEIR FRIEND AND ASSOCIATE

THE AUTHOR.

ERRATA.

		For		read	
Page	16, Line 16.	For	"ll se"	read	*sell.*
"	64, " 9.	"	"Dorkwra"	"	*Dockwra.*
"	68, " 16.	"	"Hamer ley"	"	*Hamersley.*
"	109, " 8.	"	"Jotham"	"	*Joel.*
"	110, Note 81,	"	"Lady Clinton"	"	*Lady Clayton.*
"	112, Note	"	"Risco's"	"	*Rusco's.*
"	122, "	".	"Chapter X"	"	*Chapter XI.*
"	136, Line 41.	"	"Wayne"	"	*Wolcote.*
"	146,	"	"Chapter IV"	"	*Chapter V.*
"	212, Note 7.	"	"John Fletcher"	"	*Seth Fletcher.*
"	240, Line 17.	"	"Gelding"	"	*Golding.*
"	329, Note 9.	"	"Elwers"	"	*Elmers.*

*** On Page 320, "February 24, 1820," is given as the date of the Act conferring freedom on every child born of Slave parents subsequent to July 4th, 1804. That, however, only *re-enacted* the provision referred to, among others, of previous acts relating to Slaves the original date being February 15th, 1804. The importation of Slaves into the State was prohibited as early as 1786.

PREFACE.

On a promontory of commanding height, overlooking the broad bay formed by the junction of the Raritan River with Arthur Kull Sound, and dividing their respective waters, stands Perth Amboy. Although the prominent position it once occupied among the towns and cities of the land, has long been lost, yet there are associations connected with it as the former seat of government and the place of residence of many of the most eminent citizens of New Jersey in other days, which must ever render its history worthy the consideration of the people of the State. To many, who cherish for the ancient city an attachment based upon personal acquaintance with its many pleasing scenes—for

> "The very Autumn of a form once fine
> Retains its beauties,"—

—a reference to those who long since gazed upon those scenes, and a recurrence to events to which they can give, so readily, "a local habitation," will afford more than ordinary interest.

No apology is therefore offered by the author, for presenting to his fellow Jerseymen these crude memorials of the past, which, favored by occasional leisure and opportunity, he has been enabled to collect. The result gives little evidence of the time and labor expended in his researches; and although he feels some satisfaction at the success of his undertaking, he regrets that abler hands, at an earlier period, had not entered upon it; while yet individuals were living, who, from personal knowledge, or traditions recollected, could have supplied so much of interest to the "snapper up of unconsidered trifles:"—those trifles which constitute so large a portion of the warp and woof of local history.

The illustration of the early history of Perth Amboy and the Adjoining Country, is not, however, the only purpose of the volume.

It serves as the thread on which is strung much miscellaneous matter bearing upon the general history of the State, accumulated while engaged in the preparation of other works, which is given to the public at the request of gentlemen whose genealogical and local researches have been facilitated by reference thereto; it having been suggested that such publication would render the information thus collected more available, and preserve, in a proper form, what was likely otherwise to be printed by others in a disconnected and unsatisfactory manner. The author's delay in so doing may lead to the supposition that, in some instances, he has failed to give credit to others, when, in fact, he has merely resumed possession of the results of his own researches. He has endeavored to make due acknowledgment in all cases, in connection with the specific topic, whenever indebted to books or written communications for the facts stated; not being disposed to adopt the practice, sanctioned by some recent writers of reputation, of summarily cancelling all obligations to others by giving *a list* of the works consulted. Niebuhr would not allow himself even to quote at second hand, without naming the author through whom he had obtained the reference, although he may have examined the work himself;—"He who acts otherwise," he says, "gives himself the appearance of greater reading than he possesses:" and the labor bestowed upon historical researches is assuredly deserving of the trifling recompense of an acknowledgment from those by whom the results are appropriated.

No attempt has been made to clothe with the importance of history, these desultory gleanings from the fields of the past; and collected, as the items have been, during brief periods, which, amid many cares and under the pressure of various pursuits, have now and then been presented, they have been allowed to retain in most instances the form in which they were at first arranged; no attempt being made, by skilfulness of combination, to supply any deficiencies in their interest or value. To bind together the scattered sheaves, however, has been a recreation rather than a task, and the author will consequently be doubly compensated should they prove acceptable to those for whom they have been gathered, and to whose service they are now dedicated.

NEWARK, New Jersey, *February*, 1856.

CONTENTS.

CHAPTER VIII.—Travelling Facilities.

CHAPTER IX.—Miscellaneous Topics.

CHAPTER X.—Events during the Revolution.

CHAPTER XI.—Woodbrigde.

CHAPTER XII.—Piscataway.

ILLUSTRATIONS.

EARLY HISTORY OF PERTH AMBOY

AND

ADJOINING COUNTRY.

Chapter I.—The Settlement.

"He view'd the woods that spread around,
The wide extent of various ground,
The verdant lawns, th' embosom'd glades
Which court the branchy sylvan shades.
*   *   *   *   *   *
Scarce need I say his eye pursued
With warm delight the place he view'd."

THERE are few places in the United States whose history, in its chief characteristics, corresponds with that which we are now about to consider. Generally, a retrospective glance at the existence of our growing and opulent communities, presents to the observer only a series of successful years through which they passed to ever-increasing eminence and prosperity: there may have been checks and misfortunes, but their progress was still onward,—the past shadowing forth the future—the improvement of one period giving sure promise of further improvement the next.

In the case of Perth Amboy a different view is presented. It has no crumbling castles, no time-worn battlemented walls, nor monuments of fallen greatness, such as excite the veneration and sympathies of the traveller among the dilapidated cities of the eastern hemisphere, but there are mementos of disappointed hopes, of defeated projects, of mistaken policy, and of the consequences of war, less striking to the eye, but equally as potent in their addresses to the understanding—telling of the instability of earthly enterprises, and the feebleness of man's exertions. We have not only to lament that its founders died without the realization of their hopes, but also that, while we see not, in its present condition, the object of their care, enjoying the eminence they imagined it would attain; we yet *look back* upon years already fled for the most renowned, perhaps the most prosperous period of its history, although the population at the present day may be greater.

Little did its fathers anticipate that the boasted "settlement on Ambo Point," the future capital of the Province, the intended London of America, would, after the lapse of one hundred and seventy years, come so far short of their expectations. Let us trace the events which have preceded this result.

The point at the mouth of Raritan River is first mentioned in the deed to Augustine Herman, granted by the Indians December 8th, 1651, by the name of *Ompoge*.[1] In the subsequent deed to Bailey, Denton and Watson, in 1664,[2] no particular name is given either to the point or country; but the next year, Bailey, on transferring his right to Philip Carteret, calls the country "Arthur Cull, or *Emboyle*"—which in 1666 was written *Amboyle*. From these names, most probably from the first, the name *Ambo*, conferred upon the point for some time after its settlement, was derived.[3]

The proprietaries, in their concessions, having directed that, "in laying out lands for cities, towns, villages, or other hamlets, the said lands should be divided into seven parts, one seventh part whereof to be by lot laid out" for them, it was provided, on granting the charter to Woodbridge, June 10th, 1669, "that Ambo Point be reserved towards the thousand acres of upland and meadow that is reserved, to be disposed of

[1] East Jersey under the Proprietaries, p. 19.

[2] Ibid, pp. 37, 42.

[3] Heckewelder in a catalogue of names communicated to the Philadelphia Philosophical Society, in 1822, gives *Emboli* as the origin of "Amboy," and, as its meaning, "hollow inside." This meaning, if correct, does not apply as well to the topography of Amboy Point as to the district of country included in the deeds mentioned in the text. *Ompoge* is the more probable derivation. See Note A in appendix.

by the lords proprietors, in lieu of the seventh part mentioned in the concessions ;" and that "the nine hundred acres of upland are to be in and about Ambo Point, as it is now surveyed by the surveyor-general, and the hundred acres of meadow is to be laid out by the said surveyor, in the most convenient place nearest adjacent to the said Ambo Point."

This reservation of "Ambo Point," at this early period, for the immediate advantage of the Lords Proprietors, is no slight proof of the sound discrimination and judgment of Governor Carteret. Its position, certainly, presents facilities for almost every pursuit that an enterprising people might adopt ; and the failure to make it a place of extensive trade takes nothing from his credit for selecting so eligible a situation for a town : for that such was his object in reserving it there can be no doubt, although immediate steps were not taken to effect a settlement.

In a letter to James Bollen, dated Elizabethtown, July 9th, 1680,[4] he mentions having made Amboy the subject of a special communication to Lady Carteret, and it is not improbable, that the establishment of the chief town of the province at this point was then in contemplation. The opposition to his authority which had been shown at Elizabethtown, may well be presumed to have had weight with the Governor, and induced him to recommend the removal of the seat of government to some place where the interests of the proprietaries would be more regarded.

The transfer of the province into other hands, and the subsequent death of Philip Carteret,[5] prevented his realizing the fulfilment of the plans he may have formed. The new proprietaries, however, appear to have been made fully aware of the advantages the point afforded, and of the intentions of their predecessors respecting it ; for the first twelve associates, on receiving their title, directly made known their purpose, "if the Lord permit, with all convenient expedition, to erect and build one principal town, which, by reason of situation, must in all probability be the most considerable for merchan-

[4] Grants and Concessions, p. 684.

[5] East Jersey under the Proprietaries, pp. 83, 85.

dise, trade, and fishery in those parts; to be placed upon a neck or point of rich land, called Ambo Point, lying on Raritan River, and pointing to Sandy Hook Bay, and near adjacent to the place where ships in that great harbor commonly ride at anchor."[6]

This was followed by their "proposals" for building and settling the town, as follows:—

"FORASMUCH as Ambo Point is a sweet, wholesome, and delightful place, proper for trade, by reason of its commodious situation, upon a safe harbor, being likewise accommodated with a navigable river, and fresh water, and hath, by many persons of the greatest experience and best judgment, been approved for the goodness of the air, soil and situation.

"We, the proprietors, purpose by the help of Almighty God, with all convenient speed, to build a convenient town, for merchandise, trade and fishery, on Ambo Point; and because persons that hath a desire to plant there, may not be disappointed for want of proposals, we, the proprietors, offer these following:

"First. We intend to divide fifteen hundred acres of land upon Ambo Point, into one hundred and fifty lots; which lots shall consist of ten acres the lot; one hundred of the lots we are willing to sell here, and fifty we reserve for such as are in America, and have long desired to settle there.

"Secondly. The price of each lot will be fifteen pounds sterling, to such who purchase before the 25th of December, 1682; and to such who purchase afterwards, before the 25th of December, 1683, twenty pounds sterling.

"Thirdly. Every lot is to be as equally divided as the goodness of the place doth require, and the situation can admit.

"Fourthly. The most convenient spot of ground for a town, shall be divided into one hundred and fifty equal shares, and set out into streets, according to rules of art; and no person shall be preferred before another in choice, whether purchaser or proprietor.

"Fifthly. We reserve four acres for a market place, town-house, &c., and three acres for publick wharfage.

"Sixthly. Each purchaser is obliged to build a dwelling house in the place designed for the town, and to clear three acres of upland, in three years, or else the proprietors to be reinstated in such lots wherein default is made, repaying the purchase money.

"Seventhly. We, the proprietors, do within a year hope, by God's assistance, to build for each of us one house upon Ambo Point; which we intend shall stand in an orderly manner, according to the best and most convenient model.

"And in pursuance of the design of the propositions abovesaid,

"Eighthly. And for the encouragement of carpenters, joiners, brick and tile makers, bricklayers, masons, sawyers, and laborers of all sorts, who are willing to go and employ themselves and servants, in helping to clear ground, and build houses upon the general account of and for the proprietors.

"The said proprietors will engage to find them work, and current pay for the same, in money or clothes, and provision, of which there is plenty (as beef, pork, corn, &c.), according to the market price at New York, du-

[6] Smith's N. J., p. 542. East Jersey, &c., p. 211.

ring the space of one year at least, next after the 25th of December, 1682; in which time (through God's blessing and their industry), they may have got wherewith to buy cows, horses, hogs, and other goods, to stock that land, which they in the mean time may take up, according to the concessions; neither shall such persons pay rent for their said land, so long as they are employed in the proprietors' work; and their wages shall at all times be so much as other such artificers and laborers, in the said province usually have; nor shall they be obliged to work for the proprietors longer than they find encouragement so to do.

"Ninthly. And for the more ready and certain employing those workmen and laborers that shall transport themselves to East Jersey, this is to let all laborers and persons that shall transport themselves know, they must upon their arrival upon that place, repair to the register of the abovesaid province, and enter themselves according to their respective qualities and designs, and thereupon they shall be entered into the service and pay of the proprietors."[7]

That "Ambo Point is a sweet, wholesome, and delightful place," cannot be denied, even at the present day; but, when reposing in all the freshness and beauty of a new creation, its trees, its vines, its soil, yet undisturbed by the intruder Man —how rich, how attractive to the lover of nature, must have been its aspect.

The proprietaries contributed twelve hundred pounds in furtherance of the project, to erect each a house,[8] and Thomas Rudyard, their first deputy governor, appears to have been instructed to carry out this, and other plans, respecting their new town. "Upon our view and survey of Amboy Point," he wrote under date of 30th May, 1683, "we find it extraordinary well situate for a great town or city, beyond expectation.* * * The point is good lively land, ten, some places, twenty feet above the water mark.* * * We are now building some small houses, fitting to entertain workmen and such, who will go and build larger. The stones lie exceeding well and good up the Raritan River, a tide's passage, and oyster shells upon the point, to make lime withal, which will wonderfully accommodate us in building good houses cheap, warm for winter, and cool for summer."

Samuel Groom, surveyor-general, who accompanied Rudyard to the province, wrote, under date of August 11th, 1683, that they had erected three of their houses, and had "three

[7] Smith's N. J., p. 543. East Jersey, &c., p. 211.

[8] MS. arguments of Counsel—Earl of Perth vs. Earl of Stirling, in my possession.

others ready to be set up ; but," said he, "workmen are scarce, and many of them base ; the best will work but when they can spare time out of their plantations ;" and he adds—mark the prophetic spirit—"if no help comes, it will be long ere Amboy be built as London is." It is to be presumed that help came not.

The houses then being erected were thirty feet long, and sixteen or eighteen feet wide ; "ten feet betwixt joint and joint," says Groom, "with a double chimney, made with timber and clay, as the manner of this country is to build." Such were the humble edifices at first contributed by art, to set off the natural beauties of the spot. Such the tenements which the proprietaries agreed should "stand in an orderly manner, according to the best and most convenient model."

Groom surveyed the harbor, and sounded the channel, from Amboy to Sandy Hook,[9] laid out the town into one hundred and fifty lots, and sent to England a draft of it, for the examination of the proprietaries there. Upon him, as well as upon Rudyard, the situation of Ambo Point, or *Amboy*, as it now began to be called, made a most favorable impression ; but it was not the happiness of either to witness the permanent foundation and growth of the new settlement.

In February, 1684, Gawen Lawrie arrived, as deputy governor, superseding Thomas Rudyard, and fixed his residence at Elizabethtown. By him came from the proprietaries the name of PERTH, for their new town, in honor of James, Earl of Perth, one of their associates ;[10] and the title of Amboy was, in a measure, dropped for some time, excepting when applied to the point.

Immediately after his arrival, Lawrie proceeded to adopt measures for the advancement of Perth. His instructions, referring particularly to the building of the town, were as follow :—

"As to the Lotts at Ambo Point, and the Towne of Perth,

[9] "I find it," says he, "to be a broad and bold channel, in no place less than three fathom at high water—in ordinary tides four, five, or six fathom, except in one short place."

[10] See appendix, Note B, for a notice of the Earl.

there to be built, wee Desire that due Care may be taken that it may be made regularly according to a scheme which is intended herewith to be sent. To be sure that the Streets be large. That the Houses be not Crowded one upon another, but that Each House have backwards a considerable voyd for a Yard and Garden, that so no street be laid closs to the Back of another without an Intervale of at least a Paire of Butts, and that the Key and Market Place be also immediately ordered."[11] To these instructions, dated July 20th, 1683, is the town probably indebted for its broad streets and ample gardens; but the care taken to prevent too close a proximity in the houses was, perhaps, unnecessary.

Under date of September 21st, Lawrie was directed what disposition to make of the houses erected for the proprietaries, and also to take the proper steps to effect the erection of a house for the governor. They say: "That it may appear how greatly desirous the Proprietors are of the expediting the work of building this town, they do unanimously consent and agree that there be a house built for the Governor, at the public charge, and, in pursuance thereof, do hereby order and impower you to set out such a portion of land, in such convenient place, as you shall think most convenient, to build the said house thereon; and to enclose so much ground as may be necessary and moderately useful, for garden, orchard, and other accommodations for a Governor."[12]

On the 2d March, 1684, Lawrie, after examining the province for several days, thus wrote to the proprietaries: "At last I pitched upon a place, where a Ship of three hundred Tun may ride safely within a plank length of the shoar at low water, and Joyning thereto is a piece of marsh ground, about twelve pearch broad and twenty pearch long; and high land on each side like our keyes by London Bridge:[13] This may be easie cut quite round, for small Vessels to come to the Key, and

[11] E. Jersey Prop. Records, A. p. 365. Grants and Concess., p. 175.

[12] Original MS. order in Author's possession.

[13] Known as "the Cove"—of late years, the property of the Lehigh Coal Co. Rudyard wrote also: "About it are several coves, where with small Costs may lay up Vessels as in a docke, besides great Ships of any burthen may all ryde before the town, land-locked against all winds."

lie safe. Round this island, I set out Lots one acre apiece, viz. four pole at the Key, and forty pole backward ; from thence along the river, near half a mile, I lay'd out the like lots very pleasant for scituation, where they can see the ships coming in the Baye of Sandy Hook for near twenty miles. The Ships may ride along by the Town, as safe as at London.* * * * There is no such place in all England, for Conveniency and pleasant scituation. There are sixty Lots upon the River, and forty backward between these and the River ;[14] and these backward have a high way one hundred feet broad, where I have laid out a place for a market, with cross Streets from the River to the Market, where the Town houses are to be built."

In the prosecution of his plans, Lawrie does not appear to have had reference to the draft sent out by the proprietaries, or to the lots laid out by Groom ; and his words would convey the idea that he claimed the credit of selecting the site of the town, which was certainly not his work, as we have seen.

He proceeds :—" I laid out four hundred acres to be divided in forty-eight parts, viz. thirty-six to each proprietor ; and those who have lots in the Town, I grant them half Lots in this ; to pay for the Lots in the Town twenty pound, or if a half Lot of thirty-six acres forty pound. I laid out four acres to lye untill the Proprietors agree to divide it, as people come over. There are sixteen Lots taken up by the Scottish Proprietors, and eight lots by the Proprietors that are here. There are twenty lots taken up in the Town, by other People. I engage all to build a house of thirty foot long, and eighteen foot broad, and eighteen foot high to the raising, to be finished within a year ;[15] To pay for laying out forty shil. a Lot, and four pence *per annum* Quit Rent : there are several begun already to build. I have laid out between forty and fifty Acres for the Governour's house. The highway and wharfe between the Lots and the River are one hundred feet broad, and to leave a row of trees along upon the River before the

[14] His meaning probably was, that besides the sixty on one river, *the Sound,* there were forty back of them, towards the other river, *the Raritan.*

[15] A year afterward, March 7th, 1685, Charles Gordon wrote: "There is about a dozen or fourteen houses in New Perth. The Governour's house and the Public Court-house are a building."

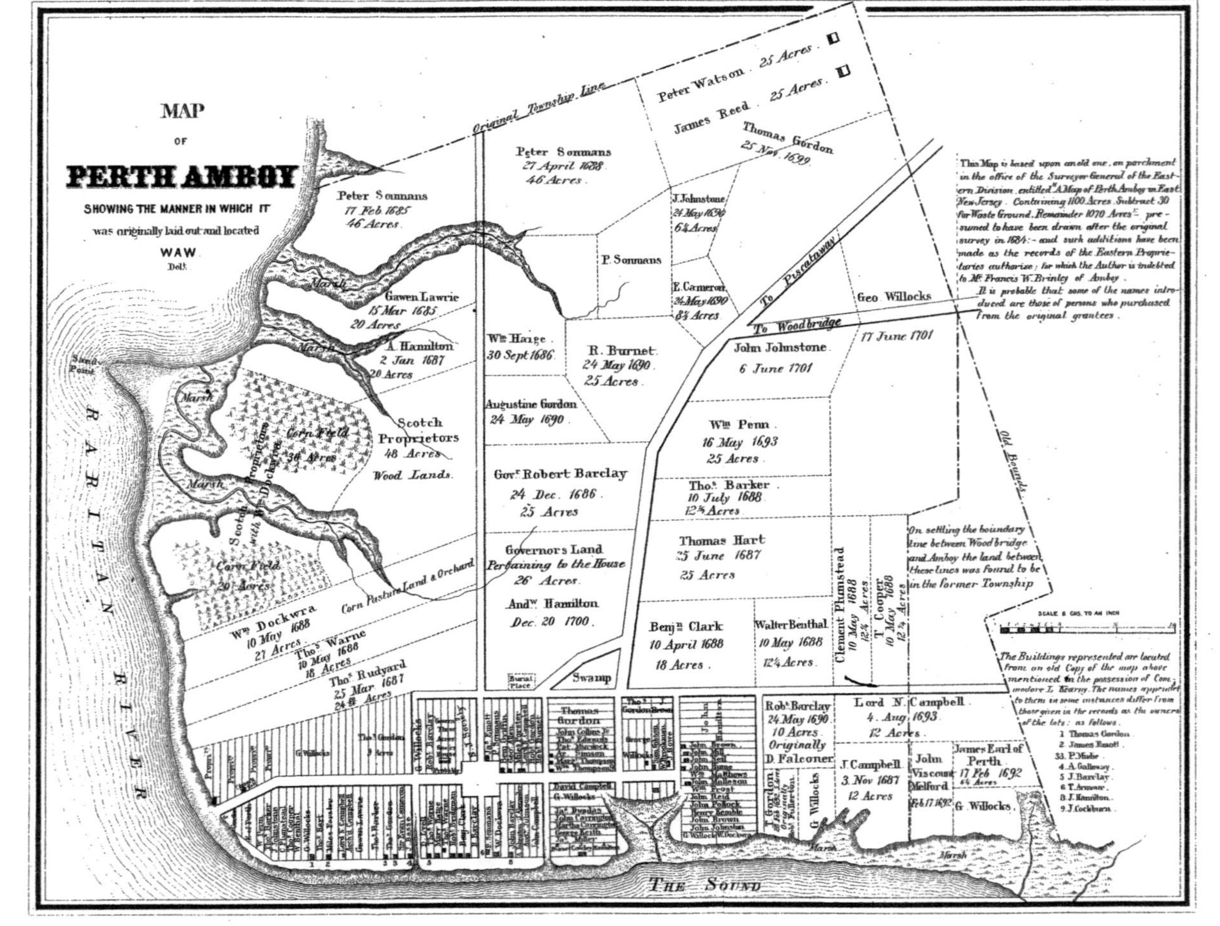
MAP
OF
PERTH AMBOY
SHOWING THE MANNER IN WHICH IT
was originally laid out and located
WAW
Delt.
Original Township Line
Peter Watson . 25 Acres .
James Reed . 25 Acres .
Thomas Gordon
25 Nov. 1699
Peter Sonmans
27 April 1688
46 Acres .
Peter Sonmans
17 Feb 1685
46 Acres .
J. Johnstone
24 May 1690
6¼ Acres
P. Sonmans
E. Cameron
24 May 1690
8¼ Acres
To Piscataway
To Woodbridge
Geo Willocks
17 June 1701
Gawen Lawrie
15 Mar 1685
20 Acres
A. Hamilton
2 Jan 1687
20 Acres
Marsh
Wm. Haige .
30 Sept 1686 .
R. Burnet .
24 May 1690 .
25 Acres .
John Johnstone .
6 June 1701
Augustine Gordon
24 May 1690 .
Scotch
Proprietors
48 Acres
Wood Lands .
Corn Field
30 Acres
Scotch Proprietors with Wm. Dockwra
Wm. Penn .
16 May 1693
25 Acres .
Govr. Robert Barclay
24 Dec. 1686 .
25 Acres
Thos. Barker .
10 July 1688
12½ Acres
Old Bounds
Sandy Point
RARITAN RIVER
Corn Field
20 Acres
Governors Land
Pertaining to the House
26 Acres .
Thomas Hart
25 June 1687
25 Acres
On settling the boundary
line between Woodbridge
and Amboy the land between
these lines was found to be
in the former Township
Corn Pasture Land & Orchard
Wm. Dockwra
10 May 1688
27 Acres
Thos. Warne
10 May 1688
18 Acres
Thos. Rudyard
25 Mar 1687
24 Acres
Andw. Hamilton
Dec. 20 1700 .
Benjn. Clark
10 April 1688
18 Acres .
Walter Benthal
10 May 1688
12¼ Acres .
Clement Plumstead
10 May 1688
12¼ Acres
T. Cooper
10 May 1688
12¼ Acres
SCALE 8 CHS. TO AN INCH
The Buildings represented are located
from an old Copy of the map above
mentioned in the possession of Commodore L. Kearny. The names appended
to them in some instances differ from
those given in the records as the owners
of the lots : as follows .
1 Thomas Gordon .
2 James Emott .
33. P. Mude .
4 A. Galloway .
5 J. Barclay .
6 T. Arnour .
8 J. Hamilton .
9 J. Cockburn .
Burial Place
Swamp
Thomas Gordon
John Hamilton
Robt. Barclay
24 May 1690 .
10 Acres .
Originally
D. Falconer
Lord N. Campbell .
4 . Aug 1693 .
12 Acres .
J. Campbell
3 Nov 1687
12 Acres
John Viscount Melford
Feb 17 1692
James Earl of
Perth
17 Feb 1692
64 Acres
G. Willocks .
G. Willocks
T. Gordon
Marsh
THE SOUND
This Map is based upon an old one, on parchment
in the office of the Surveyor General of the Eastern Division, entitled "A Map of Perth Amboy in East
New Jersey . Containing 1100 Acres . Subtract 30
for Waste Ground . Remainder 1070 Acres" - presumed to have been drawn after the original
survey in 1684 : - and such additions have been
made as the records of the Eastern Proprietaries authorize ; for which the Author is indebted
to Mr. Francis W. Brinley of Amboy .
It is probable that some of the names introduced are those of persons who purchased
from the original grantees .

houses, for shade and shelter exceeding pleasant." It is to be regretted that this sensible plan was not fully carried out, but, as with the similar scheme of Penn in Philadelphia, although with far less reason, beauty and comfort were made to give way to the sordid consideration of the value of the land or to measures for facilitating the commercial operations of the place.

"I have agreed," continues Lawrie, "for two houses of like dimensions, to be built for the Proprietors, and also a house for the Governour of sixty-six foot long and eighteen foot broad ; And if the quit rents come in, I intend three or four houses more for the Proprietors.[16] I can easily let them. * * * After I had finished this work I set the people to work, Scottish and English, about fifty persons, some preparing for building, others on clearing ground to get Corn sowne this spring, then came in a Boat, privately to Elizabethtown."

The quantity of land laid out for the town, governor's house and public highways was estimated at about two hundred acres. The map here inserted will explain to the reader the situation of the town and out lots as designated by Lawrie, and also show him who were the earliest owners. One hundred and fifty or two hundred acres of salt marsh, three miles up the Raritan, were at first retained in common to furnish grass for the settlers on the point.

In a letter to a friend, dated a few days subsequent to his despatch to the proprietaries, from which the foregoing extracts are taken, Lawrie reiterates his favorable impressions regarding the new city. He says : "Where the Town of Perth is now in building, a ship of three hundred Tun may easily ride close to the Shoar, within a plank's length to the houses of the Town ; * * * The bank of the River is twenty foot, in some places thirty, and in some forty feet high ; and yet hath

[16] "The plot of ground was divided into one hundred and fifty shares, for purchasers to build upon. Four acres were reserved for a market-place, and three for public wharfage—very useful things, if there had been inhabitants, trade and shipping. The town being thus artfully and commodiously laid out, some Scots began building, especially a house for a governor, which was then as little wanted as the wharf or the market." *Oldmixon's Brit. Emp. in America.*—More facetious than just, for certainly it was reasonable to provide these conveniencies for a town intended for the capital of the province.

many conveniencies for landing goods." And in connection with John Barclay and Arthur Forbes, who appear to have been specially delegated to make inquiries and convey information to the proprietaries, he states that "Among all the towns that are settled here, there is none lyeth so convenient for trade as *New* Perth, for ships of great burden may come up close to the houses, and may come up any time in the Winter. There came a Ship of three hundred tun in there this Winter, in the hardest frost we had, and lay hard by the town, so near that she was tyed to a tree." [17]

These letters exhibit plainly the strong interest taken by the writers in the advancement of Amboy, and the proprietaries in England aided to the utmost of their power and resources the endeavor to bring about the full realization of the hopes and anticipations of their representatives in the province.

On September 21st, 1683, Lawrie was directed "to remove the Governm^t of the Province to Perth Towne with all possible expedition, and that ye Council do sett there, and that ye Courts and quarter sessions be held there for time to come, till further orders, and as soon as may be, that the Assembly do also sett there, and that all such Publique business be brought thither, as may promote ye despatch of building the said Towne, and the trade thereof, to give encouragement to all such as shall come to settle there." [18] This the proprietaries followed up in December, with an injunction that it was not to be forgotten, that "as soon as can be, weekly markets and fairs, at fit seasons, be appointed."

The ensuing year, finding that the Deputy Governor was dilatory in carrying their wishes into effect respecting the removal of the offices of government from Elizabethtown, where he had established himself on his first arrival, they repeated their command in positive terms. "Wee doe Require this one thing Concerning the Court of Common Right, that it be

[17] Other extracts from these letters might be given, but as the re-publication of "Scot's Model of the Government of East New Jersey, in America," by the New Jersey Historical Society, has placed them all entire before the public, it is unnecessary to multiply quotations from them, further than may be necessary to illustrate particular points in the narrative.

[18] Original MS. order in my possession.

always held att our Towne of Perth, if it be possible, and that all other necessary Courts, as also the assembly (when Called) doe sett there, and particularly the Deputy Governor for the Tyme being doe Inhabit there and Convene his Councill in the s^{d} Towne of Perth"[19]— showing their determination to make their new town really the capital of the province. They also took the necessary steps towards procuring for it the rights and privileges of a Port of Entry, rightly judging that to advance its prosperity and facilitate its settlement, the removal of all restrictions upon its commercial intercourse with the other provinces and the mother country was a necessary prerequisite.[20]

Trifling as "every day occurrences" may appear to us as they transpire, after the lapse of years they assume a different character, and frequently prove to have been no unimportant links of that vast chain that binds man to man, under the ever-varying circumstances of life and through successive periods of time; from their tendency to modify the condition of individuals, and the action of communities, in matters of the greatest magnitude. It is to be regretted, therefore, that there are now no records in existence to throw light upon the incidents and counsels of this earliest era of the city's history. They might, perchance, guide the present generation in their exertions to advance its welfare, by exposing the errors committed, or the judgment and foresight exercised by its founders; and lead to the formation of a clearer conception of its improvement from year to year, during the period under review.

[19] E. J. Records, and see Grants and Concess., p. 199.

[20] See East Jersey under the Proprietaries, p. 111, &c.

Chapter II.—The Settlers.

> "* * * Chiefs, who under their gray stones
> So long have slept, that fickle Fame
> Has blotted from her rolls their names."

LITTLE information, comparatively, has come down to us respecting those enterprising spirits who merit the title prefixed to this chapter, of a character to enable the biographer to enlarge upon their individual history. The names of those who held some of the higher stations in society and occasionally a remark in relation to them and others, constitute most of the materials now to be obtained. They were allowed, with few exceptions, to go to their last homes with their virtues or their failings unrecorded, and soon, very soon,

> "To whom related, or by whom begot,"

became a matter of uncertainty and indifference.

The attempt here made to preserve some memorial of a few among the first who peopled this section of the State, is the result of much examination into records and ancient documents, which, to one not imbued with a fondness for such researches would have been labor too arduous to be undertaken with so little promise of reward. The notices are as full as as they can be made from existing materials.

THOMAS RUDYARD AND GAWEN LAWRIE.

The first two deputy governors, although residents of Elizabethtown; may yet, from the interest taken by them in the establishment of "New Perth," be properly enumerated among the settlers ; but nothing can be added to the information given of them in another work.[1] On reference to the map, it will be seen that both held land at Amboy, but it is not known that either of them placed any improvements upon their tracts.

SAMUEL GROOM.

This gentleman was one of the twenty-four proprietaries, and is styled "Mariner of Stepney." He was appointed Surveyor-general and Receiver-general in 1682, and accompanied Deputy-governor Rudyard to the province the same year. This connection with East Jersey grew probably out of an acquaintance with its advantages, acquired while on a voyage to Maryland in 1676, in a vessel of his own.[2]

His letter from the province,[3] from which some extracts have been given on preceding pages, exhibits his activity, energy, and industrious habits, and describes his pursuits at Amboy.

Rudyard having dispossessed Groom of his offices, in consequence of some opposition made by him to his wishes respecting some tracts of land on the Raritan,[4] the proprietaries, when expressing their disapprobation of the proceeding, thus allude to their surveyor-general—"Wee are very sensible of Samuel Groom's Honesty and Fidelity to our Interest, and therefore Cannot but very well Approve of his Proceedings, both in his Care in seeking Out and Discovering the best Land, and surveying it Out for our use, for his Endeavors to Clear it of the Indian Incumbrance, and for his refusing to Comply with the particular Interest of any there, by accommodating them with Lands or others, at their desire, to our General Prejudice, and this wee are willing to be signafied to him in our Name, and wee wish there may a way be found whereby he may still Continue to be Concerned with Us"—and they declared all surveys made by others invalid.[5] The proprietaries had previously shown their confidence in him, by placing in his charge

[1] East Jersey under the Proprietaries, pp. 123, 126, &c. Lawrie's will was dated August 15th, 1687, and letters of administration were granted his widow, October 20th. E. J. Records, B, 137.

[2] Ibid, p. 200.

[3] Ibid, p. 281.

[4] Ibid, pp. 99, 116, note.

[5] E. J. Records, A 366. Grants and Concess., p. 181.

when he came to the province, a cargo of goods worth seven hundred and fifty pounds, with which to purchase Indian titles. The death of Groom prevented his being reinstated.

His will was dated August 21st, 1682, and he died in the course of the following year, leaving on the stocks, unfinished, the first vessel built in East Jersey. He did not bring his family to the province with him.[6]

WILLIAM HAIGE.

When Rudyard suspended Groom from his offices of surveyor-general and receiver-general, he transferred them to William Haige, who was among the earliest settlers, and apparently a man much respected. The death of Groom having prevented his reinstatement, Haige continued to perform the duties conferred upon him until the arrival of George Keith, in 1685. In 1686 the proprietaries, "in consequence of the sudden disappoyntment in being so quickly Dispossest of the office of Surveyor-General, and for and in Regard of his Ready complyance with the succession of a new surveyor"—bestowed upon him five hundred acres of land in Monmouth County.[7] There was a William Haige in the Council of Pennsylvania, in 1683 and 1684, who frequently asked leave to be absent "about his business," who may have been the same person. The name is not met with in that connection after 1684.

The subject of this notice died about January 1st, 1688. His wife, Mary, who was the daughter of Deputy-governor Lawrie, survived him, but it is not known that he left children.

WILLIAM DOCKWRA.

Gawen Lawrie notices in one of his letters the exertions of "William Dockwra's people," in advancing the prosperity of the town, and he is therefore entitled to a place among the other settlers; although himself never in the province. He owned several town lots, and the valley of the Millstone River was his property. Dockwra was appointed Receiver-general

[6] East Jersey, &c., p. 201.

[7] The original grant is in my possession.

and Treasurer July 6th, 1688, on the death of Wm. Haige. Previously, on the 27th March, 1686, in consideration of his services, as their Agent in London, the Proprietors gave him a grant of 1,000 acres of land; and subsequently (April 29th, 1686), evinced their confidence, by authorizing him to sign various documents in their behalf, without consultation. On the 27th November, 1689, he was appointed Secretary and Register to the board of proprietors, performing his duties in the province by deputy, and continued to hold those offices until December 2d, 1702, when he was superseded by Thomas Gordon, having been guilty of some malpractices in issuing unauthorized orders, illegal grants, and other papers.[8]

When first mentioned in the East Jersey Records (July 20th, 1683), he is styled "Merchant of the parish of St. Andrew Undershaft, London," and he has secured for himself some fame, by having originated the "penny post" in that city.[9]

"The people" mentioned by Lawrie, were laborers sent over in order to obtain the grants for headlands, in accordance with "the Concessions,"—Dockwra receiving a portion of their earnings. The arrival of between thirty and forty of these laborers is recorded at different times; besides some on account of the Scottish proprietaries generally. Lawrie says that the Scots had taken a right course in sending over many servants and poor families, to whom they gave stock, and for a number of years they received half of the increase, excepting milk, which the tenant had to himself.[10]

Dockwra died about 1717, leaving several sons and daughters, but it does not appear that any of them ever came to America.

BENJAMIN CLARKE,

This man is styled "Stationer," and arrived with one son

[8] Proprietary Minutes, August, 1701, and December, 1702, and see Bill in Chancery, Robert Barclay vs. Earl of Stirling, p. 18.

[9] This fact is stated by both Smith and Oldmixon, but is more particularly referred to by Macaulay, who says:—"This improvement was as usual, strenuously resisted. The posters complained that their interests were attacked, and tore down the placards in which the scheme was announced to the public.* * * A cry was raised that the penny post was a Popish contrivance, &c. The utility of the enterprise was, however, so great and obvious, that all opposition proved fruitless."

[10] East Jersey, &c., p. 288.

(Benjamin), in 1683, and his wife followed in March, 1684. He secured headlands for eight others, besides himself and son.

It is presumed his house in Amboy stood on the south side of Market street, near its junction with Water street. His grant from the proprietaries stipulated that the building should be " thirty feet by sixteen ; eighteen feet high to the raising, with a window in each room to the front, three feet high, and three feet nine inches broad, and three lights, each light fifteen inches from rabit to rabit, uniform to the rest of the houses to be built."

Charles Gordon, writing to Edinburgh under date of March, 1685, says : " Neither are we altogther destitute of Books and Clergy, for George Keith,[11] who arrived three weeks since, with others (they were all winter in Barbadoes), hath brought *Mathematics*, and Benjamin Clarke, *a Library of Books to ll ;se* so that you may see New Perth begins to be founded upon Clergy ; "[12] and James Johnstone, in a letter to his brother, alludes to the " good Stationer's shop of books at New Perth."

Clarke died in the latter part of 1689, leaving his son Benjamin heir to all his property ; and as he does not mention his wife in his will, she probably preceded him to the ragve. Nothing is known of any descendants.

GEORGE KEITH.

Among those selected by the proprietaries in England to serve them in East Jersey was George Keith, a native of Aberdeen, an eminent Quaker, although originally a Scotch Presbyterian ; and among all, whose names subsequently became widely known, his was one of those which obtained the greatest renown. Those who first welcomed him to the province as a fellow-helper in subduing the wilderness, could hardly have prefigured for him the course which events opened to him in this and the adjoining province of Pennsylvania. The circumstance, which probably led to his acquaintance with the leading Scotch proprietaries was his having under his charge[13]

[11] See below.

[12] East Jersey, &c., p. 314.

[13] " Collections, testimonials concerning several ministers of the Gospel among the Quakers, 1760," p. 201.

in 1683, at a school which he taught in Theobalds, a son of Robert Barclay. He was appointed surveyor-general on the 31st July, 1684, but did not reach the province until the spring of the following year. On the 9th April he presented his credentials to the Council of proprietors, but, as the office to which he had been appointed was already filled by William Haige,[14] under a commission emanating from Deputy-governor Rudyard, they found themselves delicately situated and postponed the consideration of Mr. Keith's commission until their next meeting. It was unanimously agreed, however, that he should have one of their houses as directed by the proprietaries.[15]

The Council at the time appointed were urged by Keith to decide in his favor, and they finally desired both of the applicants to appear before them on the 12th June, when the office, in consequence of the absence of Mr. Haige, and the inability, from some cause,'of his deputy Miles Forster, was declared vacant, and Mr. Keith authorized to take the oaths and assume the duties.[16]

Besides performing the general duties of his office, for which he was well qualified, being "an excellent surveyor," he ran the division line between East and West Jersey in 1687; but in 1689 he left the province for Pennsylvania. Then residing in Freehold—of which settlement he was the founder, and where at the time of his removal he had a "fine plantation,"—he was induced, by the solicitation of the Quakers of Philadelphia to accept the superintendence of a school in that city, for which he received fifty pounds, a house for his family and whatever profits might accrue, with the promise of an increase to one hundred and twenty pounds after the first year,—the poor to be taught gratis. This is the first and only allusion to his family I have noticed. He did not long remain in this humble situation (vacating it the next year), and we are warranted in attributing its acceptance to other inducements more likely to affect a man of

[14] See page 14. East Jersey, &c., p. 99.

[15] Thomas Warne was directed to "clear out" of the one he inhabited, to make room for him.

[16] Proprietary Minutes, A B, p. 6.

his character than the pecuniary remuneration named. Having been eminent both as a preacher and writer among the Quakers for several years, he became a public speaker in their religious assemblies in Philadelphia. Possessing quick natural talents improved by considerable literary attainments, he was acute in argument, ready and able in logical disputations and discussions of nice distinctions in theological matters; but having great confidence in his own superior capacity he was apt to indulge in an overbearing disposition, not altogether in accordance with Christian moderation and charity.[17]

These peculiarities of mind and temperament naturally impelled him to assume the post of a leader, and he soon, through his talents and energy, gathered a party, inculcating increased attention to plainness of garb and language and other points of discipline: there being in his opinion "too great a slackness therein." Connected with these religious tenets were the political doctrines of the abandonment of all forcible measures to uphold secular or worldly government, and the emancipation of negroes after a reasonable term of service.[18]

Although his views and opinions met the approval of a large number of Friends, occasioning a serious division in that before united body—father and son, husband and wife, friends and relations who had usually worshipped together, though still professors of the same faith in the main, being seen going to different places of worship, "heats and bitterness" being engendered, occasioning "many labors and watchings, great circumspection and patience"[19]—yet, as they did not meet with the general acceptation he expected, Keith became captious, and indulged in censure and reproach; accusing some of the most esteemed and approved ministers with promulgating false doctrines,—although it is said the points he now condemned had been strongly advocated in his writings,—and declaring those only, who were associated with him, true Quakers.

[17] Proud's Penna., I. pp. 345 365. Saml. Smith's MSS. in N. J. Hist. Soc. Library.

[18] Gabriel Thomas, in Watson's Annals of Phila., p. 90. Proud. S. Smith's MSS. in N. J. Hist. Soc. Library.

[19] S. Smith's MSS.

He was charged with exercising an overbearing temper, and an unchristian disposition of mind in disparaging many of the society, and, at a meeting of ministers at Philadelphia in June, 1692, "a declaration or testimony of denial" was drawn up, in which both he and his conduct were publicly denounced.[20]

From this decision Keith appealed to the general meeting of Friends at Burlington, and, in the meanwhile, wrote an address to the Quakers, in which, as on different occasions verbally, he spoke in such a disparaging, if not calumnious, manner of the deputy-governor and other functionaries, as to bring upon him the ire of the civil magistrates (themselves Quakers), and he was in consequence proclaimed in the market-place, by the common crier, a seditious person and an enemy to the king and queen's government.[21] The general meeting confirming the declaration of the ministers, the separation became complete, but Keith continued preaching and writing in support of his views and for the establishment of his followers until early in 1694, when he appealed to the yearly meeting in London, and appeared there in person: but his behavior was such as led to the approval of the proceedings against him, and his authority and influence were at an end.

This controversy occasioned much disturbance in the province of Pennsylvania, and many of the pamphlets to which it gave birth are yet extant.[22]

[20] The following is an extract from this declaration:—"With mourning and lamentation do we say, How is this mighty man fallen? How is his shield cast away, as though he had not known the oil of the holy ointment? How shall it be told in Gath, and published in the streets of Askalon? Will not the daughters of the uncircumcised triumph, when they hear that he is fallen upon the soaring mountains, and from the high places of Israel? While thou walkedst in the counsel of God, and wert little in thine own eyes, thy bow did abide in strength, thy sword returned not back. His enemies were then vile unto thee, and His followers honorable in thy esteem. Oh! how lovely wert thou in that day, when His beauty was upon thee, and when His comeliness covered thee! Why should His ornaments exalt thee, which were given to humble thee before him! And how art thou fallen from thy first loves, and art become treacherous to the spouse of thy youth," &c. Proud, I. p. 365.

[21] Watson's Annals, p. 522.

[22] I would refer particularly to one, by Keith, entitled "A Further Discovery of the Spirit of Falsehood and Persecution in Sam. Jennings and his party that joined with him in Penna; and some abettors that cloak and defend him here in England: In answer to his scandalous Book called The State of the Case," pp. 52. London, 1694—and another containing "An account of the

Excited, it would seem, by the opposition he had met with, although for a time he retained a considerable number of adherents in England, and disgusted with the society from which he had received so little sympathy while aiming at its advancement in what he conceived essentials to true religion, Keith abjured the doctrines of the Quakers and became a zealous clergyman of the established church of England.

He officiated for some time in the mother country, and in 1702 returned to America as a Missionary from the Society for the Propagation of the Gospel:—sent out to travel through the different provinces, for the purpose of inquiring into their true condition, their wants in regard to their spiritual interests, and to arouse in the people "a sense of the duties of religion."[23] He preached in all the colonies from Massachusetts to North Carolina: and Amboy, among other places in New Jersey, profited by his ministrations.[24]

His labors are said to have been very successful, particularly in Pennsylvania, New Jersey, and New York,—to which he devoted more of his time than he did to the other provinces,—from his previous acquaintance with the people. In the first two especially, a large number of those Quakers who had adopted his views in the dissensions of 1691 and 1692, became converts to the doctrines and discipline of the Church of England.[25]

Keith published his Journal during this period, which,

Proceedings since and advice of the people called Quakers at the Yearly meeting begun in London, 28th of 3d month, 1694: with the proceedings of the Yearly meeting at Burlington and some queries to that party of the Yearly meeting at London who gave the aforesaid judgment, by Robert Hannay," pp. 16. London, 1694. There are many others that throw light upon the controversy, but all are exceedingly rare.

[23] He came passenger in the "Centurion," on board of which were, also, Governor Dudley, of Massachusetts, and Colonel Morris, of New Jersey. They sailed from England on April 24th, and arrived at Boston on June 11th. The Rev. John Talbot was chaplain of the ship, and associated with Mr. Keith in his missionary labors. Talbot rendered himself particularly acceptable to the people of Burlington, where he was for a long time stationed. Keith's allowance from the society was £200 a year. Humphries' Hist. Acc't of Society for Prop'g the Gospel. See chapter VI.

[24] Humphries. N. Y. Church Record, March 20th, 1841.

[25] So says Humphries, but compare Watson's Annals, p. 488. A letter from Isaac Norris, dated Nov. 8th, 1702, there given, says: "George Keith hath been twice here, but has not disturbed our meeting as hath been his custom at the eastward. He is now the talk and news of the town; but has little to boast of in all his progress hitherto. His own party here is like to fall with him. All his sermons are railings against the Friends."

however, contains little else than a statement of the texts preached from. Copies are still to be seen in some of the public libraries. He returned to England by way of Virginia, and received a benefice in Sussex, worth one hundred and twenty pounds per annum,[26] where he continued until his death to write against the doctrines of the Quakers.[27]

The importation of six servants by Keith, in 1685, is recorded, for whom he received headlands, and on reference to the map it will be seen he owned a lot of ground on Smith street, in Amboy.

THE CAMPBELLS.

In consequence of the unfortunate termination of the Earl of Argyle's expedition in 1685, the Campbells—already a family obnoxious to the government and all its branches, from their relationship to that nobleman and their political sentiments and affinities—became subject to much severity and persecution. The Earl's brother, Lord Neil Campbell, a gentleman universally esteemed, was especially the object of jealous supervision.

He had been cited before the council on the 1st August, 1684, but nothing save his relationship to the Earl of Argyle being brought against him, he was released on giving bonds for the sum of five thousand pounds that he would "confine himself to Edinburgh and six miles about, and compear before the council on a charge of six hours." But when, in 1685, animosity to the name was at such a height as to lead to the consideration of measures for its extinguishment, and when, by act of parliament, all protestant heritors were required to take the oaths of allegiance and supremacy, Lord Neil's only resource was flight.[28]

Leaving his wife and family he embarked alone for East Jersey in the autumn of 1685, having in August purchased the proprietary right of Viscount Tarbet, bringing with him,

[26] Sewall's Hist. of Quakers, pp. 659, 660.

[27] Proud says, from a well authenticated account it is asserted, he thus expressed himself on his death bed: "I wish I had died when I was a Quaker for then I am sure it would have been well with my soul."

[28] Wodrow IV. 48, 311.

or causing to be sent out immediately afterwards, a large number of settlers, for whom, subsequently, headlands were granted to him.[29]

The precise date of Lord Neil's arrival is not known, but he is mentioned in the proprietary minutes of November 27th, 1685, as having "newly come out.[30]" His presence in the province led the proprietaries to avail themselves of his services as their deputy-governor, circumstances inducing them to remove Lawrie from that post; he was commissioned on the 4th June, 1686, and entered upon his duties the ensuing October.[31] The change that occurred in the political condition of Scotland enabled him to return to his family, and he left East Jersey in March, 1687.

There were a number of individuals of the name of Campbell, more or less intimately related to the deputy-governor, who arrived in the province during the years 1684 and 1685. I have only succeeded, however, in identifying two with the settlement of "New Perth,"—John and Archibald, sons of Lord Neil, both obliged to seek in America a refuge from the hostility of the government. JOHN arrived in 1684, bringing his wife, three children and eleven servants to swell the population of the province. He died in December, 1689, leaving two daughters (Anne and Garraetta), and one son (John), of whose descendants I have no knowledge.[32]

[29] Their names are here given as correctly as James Emott's wonderful chirography in the old records will admit of. The list appears on the record in December 1685, and several of them were passengers on board the ship Henry and Francis, hereafter mentioned.

David Symson,
John Craige,
Archibald ——,
Bessie Richardson,
Wm. Dunlop,
Wm. Thompson,
Margary Thompson,
George Korrie,
Margarett Robertson,
John Chalmers,
Wm. Dunlop,
Agnes Dunlop,
Andrew Grantt,
Alexander Lermont,
Agnes Lawson,
Alexr. Wilson,
David Alexander,
John Campbell,
Wm. Sharpe,
Wm. Toish,
Janet Thomson,
Bessie Pollorse,
Arfella ——,
Grizzel Hog,
Tivella Lawson,
Margaret Edgar,
Robert Currey,
John Duncan,
John Chalmers,
Robert Chalmers,
Wm. Thompson,
Agnes Marshall,
David Herriott,
John Campbell,
Patrick Symson,
John Boyd,
Alexander Thompson,
Robert Campbell,
Dougald Symson,
James Craige,
John Hog,
James Sonzdone,
Sivella Sonzdone,
Gyles Duncan,
Janett Cunningham,
Marion Chalmers,
John Dunlop,
Magdalen Kattmaber,
Patrick Tait,
John Wilkey,
Thomas Theoron,
John Stonler,
John Pollorse,
Michael Marshall,

Making, with Lord Neil and Archibald Campbell, fifty-six persons: but it will be seen that several names are repeated.

[30] It is erroneously stated in East Jersey under the Proprietors (p. 117), that he did not reach the province until October, 1686.

[31] East Jersey, &c., p. 117.

[32] In Book B., p. 493 of the Proprietary Records is a memorandum of an agreement, to be extended in form

ARCHIBALD appears to have been in greater jeopardy than his father, having been taken prisoner and held captive for some time after the ill-fated expedition of his uncle was terminated—a reward of one thousand merks having been offered for his arrest. On the 1st August, 1685, he was brought before the Justices under sentence of death, but declaring himself willing to renounce all "rebellious principles," he was reprieved until December; but on the 18th August the capital part of his sentence was remitted by the king, and he was condemned to banishment and forfeiture of his estates.[33]

He seems to have arrived at the same time with his father, but no mention is made of any family. Both he and his brother held lots in the new settlement, and the first ravine north of the town was known at one time as "Campbell's Gully." Archibald died in May 1702, but whether or not he left children I have not ascertained.

In December, 1685, an arrival of more than ordinary interest added to the busy animation of the new settlement. A vessel freighted with Scots,—men, upon whom persecution had wrought its work of purification, and whose souls had been tempered for patient endurance by sore trials and misfortunes—anchored in the harbor after a long and disastrous voyage of fifteen weeks; the circumstances of which, with the events attending the embarkation of the emigrants, are deserving of special notice. For most of the facts the prolix narrative of Wodrow[34] has been taken as authority, for al-

afterwards, between John Campbell and Moneybaird, Laird of Toshach, by which, in consideration of Campbell's sending "a footman in velvet, to wait on Moneybaird as a proprietor when at Parliament in East Jersey * * * and to hold his stirrup during the foresaid time of Parliament * * * the livery to be the Campbell's livery," Moneybaird is to dispose of his interest in Amboy to John Campbell, and his heirs bearing the name and arms of Campbell. The meaning of the document can scarcely be conjectured so lamely is it worded, but footmen in velvet and Parliaments were such novelties in East Jersey at that period, that we might presume it to have been written in Scotland by some one ignorant of the state of the province, did it not bear date "At Amboy, the 16th Dec. 1684."

[33] Wodrow IV., pp. 311, 320. Fox's James II, p. 153.

[34] Wodrow's "History of the sufferings of the Church of Scotland." Glasgow, 4 vols., 8vo.

though his judgment of men and measures was ever influenced by his theological opinions, yet it is thought his statements of events are fairly made from such materials as he had in his possession, their deficiencies not being properly chargeable to him; and if disposed to present too prominently the darker shades of the picture, an excuse for him can readily be found in the fact that those were the shades which, alas for humanity! were entirely too predominant.

As early as 1662, we find among those who suffered for conscience' sake in submitting to the authority of Cromwell, Sir John Scot of Scotstarbet in Edinburghshire: Middleton, the lord-commissioner, inflicting upon him a fine of six thousand pounds. Such a parentage renders it less remarkable that, when on the 25th June, 1674, a decree passed against those who "kept conventicles," we should find the son of Scotstarbet among those who were amenable to its provisions.[35] Among those who appeared before the Council, and acknowledged that they had frequented the conventicles of Mr. John Welsh, Mr. Samuel Arnot and others, and who scorned to secure their liberty by taking the oath of supremacy, was GEORGE SCOT of Pitlochie, who was not only fined, in common with his companions, for the offence of which they were alike guilty—his penalty being no less than a thousand pounds—but for his "alleged impertinent and extravagant carriage before the Council" was further fined five hundred merks; and not until these fines were paid was he liberated from prison; and on the 23d July he was again fined a thousand pounds "for harbouring and resetting" the same John Welsh.[36]

[35] The bearing of these provisions may be gathered from the following. No "outed ministers or others," were allowed to preach or expound scripture, or pray any where but in their own families. A contrary course subjected both ministers and hearers to imprisonment or fines, even wives and children being made subject to the latter, and to imprisonment also, were the fines not paid; the master or mistress of the house where the conventicle was held being fined double the rates of the others. The "Field Conventicles," which were peculiarly obnoxious, were specified to be not merely meetings in the open fields, but "meetings in a house for prayer and preaching, where more meet than the house contains, and some are without doors." The minister and convocator of such a meeting "shall be punished"—so read the act, "with death and confiscation of goods"—and the fines imposed upon the hearers were double in amount to those named for attendants on house conventicles.

[36] Wodrow, I. p. 271. II. p. 238, 244.

On the 8th February, 1677, Scot was summoned before the Council, and sent to the Bass prison a second time, for, notwithstanding the experience he had already of the consequences, he again had been "at conventicles;" and on the 7th August following, his wife Margaret Rigg[37] (Lady Pitlochie), not appearing before the Council when cited for the same offence, was fined a thousand merks.[38] In October the Committee for public affairs advised the Council to liberate Scot and others from the Bass, upon their giving bonds to "compear" when called, and it appears that Scot did give bonds in the sum of ten thousand merks "to confine himself within his own lands, and not to keep conventicles," and was thereupon released.

On the 14th May, 1679, Scot was again brought before the Council, and having refused to depose as to his attendance or non-attendance at conventicles, the lords held him as having confessed, and directed his securities to pay three thousand merks, leaving the balance of the ten thousand to abide his future behavior, allowing him the next day to return to his estate. In February, 1680, he was fined seven hundred pounds for "absence from the King's host," and subsequently—but at what time, or for what special offence, has not been ascertained—was again, for the third time, imprisoned in the Bass.[39]

Well might he say, as he did afterwards, that there were "several in the kingdom, who, upon account of their not go-

[37] Margaret Rigg was grand-daughter of William Rigg, bailie of Aithernie, a very good, religious man, and wealthy merchant, who purchased the estate of Aithernie, in Fife, and other lands, her father being his second son Thomas. One of her aunts, Janet, married Sir Walter Riddell, and her children were Sir John and Archibald, who are elsewhere mentioned. Her sister, Catherine Rigg, became the wife of Sir William Douglas, of Cavers. Her brother, William Rigg, the last laird of Aithernie, had two children, William and Eupham, who with their mother were among the ill-fated passengers in the vessel referred to in the text.

[38] It was thought that "women were the chief fomenters of these disorders, and that nothing could restrain them except making husbands liable for their fines,"—but the Council, in January, 1684, petitioned the King that they might be authorized "to dispense with the fines of loyal husbands, as are no ways to be suspected of connivance with their obstinate wives, but are content to deliver them up to be punished."—Letter in Wodrow, vol. iv. p. 3. The application was made in consequence of a fine of £46,000 having been laid upon Sir William Scot, of Harden, for the nonconformity of his wife, p. 41.

[39] Wodrow, I. pp. 356, 357, 361. II. pp. 10, 179.

ing that length in conformity required of them by the law, did live very uneasie ;" and natural was it for him to turn his thoughts towards that land where he and they might "freely enjoy their own principles without hazard or the least trouble," longing for the wings of a dove that he might flee away and be at rest. From his confinement in the Bass he addressed a petition to the Council, praying for his release, engaging to "go to the plantations," and promising to take with him his wife's cousin, Archibald Riddell, one of the obnoxious preachers ;—offering to become his security in the sum of five thousand merks. This petition was acted on April 1, 1684, and the Laird of Pitlochie found himself once more at liberty."[40]

This liberty was employed by him in preparing "The Model of the Government of East New Jersey in America," to which we are indebted for a large portion of the information which has come down to us respecting the condition of East Jersey at that time, the character of the settlers, and the circumstances which attended their emigration from Scotland.[41] His position in society, his connection with many of the first families of the kingdom, and the persecutions to which he had been subjected, which, of course, increased his notoriety, all tended to secure for his work much more consideration from his countrymen, than would have been the case had the author been less distinguished ; and when, adding example to precept, he announced his intention of embarking with his family for the newly-discovered asylum for the oppressed, it is not surprising that many should have associated themselves with him in the undertaking.

The approbation of "those in authority" was obtained, and his arrangements based upon the following permission :—

"By the Right Honourable Earl of Perth, Lord High Chancellour of Scotland, &c. These are Permitting and allowing Mr. George Scot, of Pitlochie, with his Lady, Children and Family, and such other Persons as he shall ingage, to pass from this Kingdom either by Sea or Land, to any

[40] Wodrow, II. p. 57.

[41] Only three or four copies of this work are known to be in existence. It was reprinted, however, in the first volume of the Collections of the New Jersey Historical Society—in whose library one copy of the original work may be found.

of His Majestie's Forreign Plantations, providing such persons to be transported by him, be not declared Traitors, Rebels, Fugitives, and that without any Let, Impediment, or Molestation, from any person whatever: they always behaving themselves peaceably and according to Law. Given at Edinburgh the first of January, 1685.

"For all Magistrates, Officers, and Souldiers within the Kingdom of Scotland, whom these do or may concern. PERTH CANCELL."[42]

On the 11th February, the Council authorized Scot by warrant to transport "to the plantations" a hundred of the prisoners confined at Glasgow, Edinburgh and Stirling, if they were willing to go, excluding those who were "heritors above one hundred pounds of rent;" and such persons as were under bonds to appear before them when called, were to have those bonds returned should they join him.

Thus authorized, the Laird of Pitlochie proceeded to collect his company; and, under date of 7th August, he requests the Council to transfer to him a large number of persons who had been banished to Jamaica (of which number, however, only twelve were granted to him), having already obtained fifty prisoners, and engaged several workmen, to go with him to New Jersey.

Under dates of August 17th, 21st, and 25th, one hundred and five persons who had refused the oath of allegiance to the King,[43] or had been previously banished, and then in the tolbooth of Leith, were ordered to be delivered to Scot, to be transported to East Jersey, on his giving security to land them there, as, by a certificate from the governor or deputy-governor, might be made to appear, prior to September, 1686; the penalty to be five hundred merks in case of failure in any instance. Other persons were afterward assigned to him in like manner, and some, previously named, prohibited from embarking.[44]

Scot, as early as May, had chartered the "Henry and Francis of Newcastle, a Ship of three hundred and fifty Tun and twenty great Guns, Richard Hutton, Master," but it was

[42] Model, &c. p. 269. East Jersey, p. 332.

[43] "All the said persons, being men, having judicially in presence of the council, refused to take or sign the oath of allegiance, and the women abovesaid having altogether refused to own his Majesty's authority, or to take the oath of abjuration."—*Decree*

[44] Wodrow, IV. pp. 216,220,222,223.

not until the 5th September, 1685, that the vessel left the harbor of Leith, the banished persons having been on board for some time.

The names of all who finally set sail cannot now be given, the whole number being near two hundred. The list which follows comprises all mentioned by Wodrow,[45] those not named being of the number who embarked voluntarily, among whom were also those on the list marked †; and those distinguished by a * left a written protest against the measures which led to their banishment.[46] Those whose names are printed in italics are known to have died on the voyage.

Robert Adam,
Lady Aithernie, †
John Arbuckle, *
Rev. Wm. Aisdale, †
John Black,
George Brown,
Robert Campbell,
David Campbell,
Wm. Campbell,
John Campbell,
Christian Cavie,
John Crichton,
John Corbet,
Andrew Corbet,
John Corsan (Casson?),
Agnes Corhead,
Barbara Cowan,
Marjory Cowan,
Wm. Cunningham,
Patrick Cunningham,
William Douglas,
Charles Douglas,
Isabel Durie,
John Frazer,
Thomas Finlater,
Elspeth Ferguson,
Janet Ferguson,
Margaret Ferret* (Forrest?),
John Foord, *
James Forsyth, *
John Foreman,
John Gray,
Thomas Gray,
Thomas Graham,
Grisel Gemble,
William Ged, †
Fergus Grier,
James Grier (Grierson?),
Robert Gilchrist,
John Gilfillan, *
Bessie Gordon,
Annàbel Gordon, *
Katharine Govan,
John Harvie, *
John Henderson, *
Adam Hood, *
Charles Homgall, *
John Hutchison,
John Hodge,
Thomas Jackson, *
Wm. Jackson,
Annabel Jackson,
George Johnston, *
John Johnstone, †
James Junk,
John King,
John Kippon,
John Kincaid, *
James Kirkwood,

[45] His manner of rendering some of the names varies on different pages, as noticed in the list.

[46] Wodrow gives the following summary of this document: "That now being to leave their own native and covenanted land, by an unjust sentence of banishment, for owning truth, and holding by duty, and studying to keep by their covenanted engagements and baptismal vows, whereby they stand obliged to resist, and testify against all that is contrary to the word of God and their covenants; and that their sentence of banishment ran chiefly because they refused the oath of allegiance, which in conscience they could not take, because in so doing, they thought they utterly declined the Lord Jesus Christ from having any power in his own house, and practically would by taking it, say he was not King and head of his church and over their consciences; and on the contrary, this was to take and put in his room a man whose breath is in his nostrils, yea, a man that is a sworn enemy to religion, an avowed papist, whom by our covenant we are bound to withstand, and disown, and that agreeably to the scripture, Deut. xvii. 14, 15—'When thou art come unto the land which the Lord thy God giveth thee, and shalt possess it, and shalt dwell therein, and shalt say, I will set a king over me, like as all the nations that are about me; thou shalt in any wise set him king over thee whom the Lord thy God shall choose; one from among thy brethren shalt thou set king over thee; thou mayest not set a stranger over thee, which is not thy brother.'"—IV. pp. 331, 332.

John Kirkland,
John Kellie,
Katherine Kellie,
John Kennie,
Margaret Leslie,*
Janet Lintron,
Gawen Lockhart,
Michael Marshall,
John Marshall,
John Martin,
Margaret Miller,
George Moor* (Muir),
Gilbert Monorg, or *Monorgan*,
Jean Moffat,*
John Muirhead,
James Muirhead,*
Wm. McCalmont,
John McEwen,
Walter McEwen* (McIgne?),
Robert McEwen,*
John McQueen* (McEwen?),
Robert McLellan,
Margaret McLellan,
——— McLellan,
Andrew McLellan,
John McKenman,
Wm. McMillan,
John McGhie,*
Wm. Niven,†
Wm. Oliphant,
Andrew Paterson,
John Pollock,
John Ramn,
Rev. Archibald Riddel,†
Mrs. Riddel,†
Wm. Rigg,†
Eupham Rigg,†
Marian Rennie,
John Renwick,
James Reston,
Thomas Russel,
Peter Russell,*
Christopher Strang,*
Wm. Sprat,
Agnes Stevens* (Tannis?),
William Spreul,*
Thomas Shelston,
John Swinton,
John Smith,
John Sinton* (Seton?),
George Scot,†
Margaret Scot,†
Eupham Scot,†
Janet Symington,*
James Sittingtoun,
John Targat,
John Turpnie,
William Turnbull,
Partrick Urie,
John Vernor,†
Mrs. Vernor,†[47]
John Watt,
Patrick Walker,
James Wardrope,
Elizabeth Whitelaw,
Grizel Wotherspoon,
William Wilson,
Robert Young.*

The charge for transportation, as publicly announced, was five pounds sterling for each adult, and to each of those who were unable to pay for their passage, was promised 25 acres of land and a suit of new clothes on the completion of four years of service, to those who advanced the requisite amount.[48]

[47] Margaret Spence, "relict of John Vernor," on 1st November, 1685, made her will on board the vessel—"forasmuch as I am now presently lying under a grievous fever, and it being apparent that I am more likely to die than to live,"—thus ran the document—she left all she had on board to Christian Spence, daughter of James Spence, merchant, of Queensferry, Scotland—who was on board. On the 27th November, William Rigg made his will—leaving to Eupham Scott—her father and mother were already dead—all the jewelry on board, the clothes, &c., belonging to his mother and sister, deceased; as well as a joint interest they had with Eupham in a "common stock" laid out in Scotland.—Proprietary Records, B. 493, A. 238.

[48] "The charge of transportation, is, for every man or woman, five lib. sterling, passage and entertainment; for children under ten years of age, fifty shillings; and sucking children nothing; forty shillings for the tun of goods, and often under * * * For ordinary servants, who are willing to go over after four years' service from the time of their arrival there, during which time they shall be well entertained in meat and clothing, they shall have set out to each twenty-five acres to them and theirs for ever, paying twopence an acre, as much corn as will sow an acre, and a suit of new clothes. Now, considering that there is five pounds sterling paid for their passage, these are good terms, and then after the term of their service is expired, they will gain more in one year there than they could do in two at home."—Scot's Model, pp. 105, 106; and see East Jersey, &c. pp. 103, 104, 207, for other stipulations respecting settlers and their servants.

Many of the passengers of the "Henry and Francis" were consequently such as were known at a later period of American history as "Redemptioners."

Under these circumstances there is injustice in charging Scot, as Wodrow does, with "tampering" with some of the prisoners before they sailed, in offering, for five pounds sterling paid then, to set them at liberty on their arrival in East Jersey.[49] It was no more than those paid who voluntarily emigrated, and having rescued them from imprisonment, if not from death, under heavy responsibilities to land them abroad where peace and prosperity seemed to await them, with the expectation of being at the expense of their transportation and subsistence, a demand for some remuneration was not unreasonable. Feelings of commiseration for the oppressed, and of pain at the unfortunate character of the voyage, should not be allowed to warp the judgment when determining the propriety of the demand, especially so, as it appears from Scot's own statement to the council, that fifty of them at least, under the grant of the 11th February, willingly profited by an engagement with him to escape the rigor of their confinement. It should be remembered that Scot himself had been the victim of persecution; that the doors of the Bass had several times closed upon him, so that the pains of imprisonment, for conscience' sake, had by him been suffered as well as by his ill-fated companions; that it was "the evils of the times" which prompted him to emigrate, and that emigration in his case as well as in theirs—voluntary it is true on his part, while on theirs it was forced—was the alternative to a loathsome existence within the walls of a prison. To say, therefore, that he "proposed to be enriched by the prisoners," and that the result shows it to be "a hazardous venture to make merchandise of the suffering people of God"[50] is to ascribe motives and interpret judgments in a manner unwarranted by the facts. That Scot hoped for some remuneration for the expense he was in-

[49] Woodrow says, "Informations before me bear, that Pitlochy tampered with some of them," but he only mentions James Forsyth, who answered, "he would give him no money to carry him out of his native land, adding he had done nothing worthy of banishment." IV. p. 332.

[50] Wodrow, IV. p. 333.

curring is probable, as is also the supposition that assurances of some kind were given that he would not be unrewarded; else why burden himself with the transportation of those whose re-incarceration in Dunottar Castle depended upon his decision alone? Had the voyage been less disastrous, we should not probably have heard these accusations.

As has been already stated the vessel sailed from the harbor of Leith on the 5th September, 1685. We hear of no untoward event until after she had got beyond "the Land's End," when a fever began to prevail with virulence, particularly among the prisoners, many of whom were sick when they came on board, and the health of the others was endangered by the condition of the provisions laid in by the Captain; the meat, owing probably to the length of time which had elapsed since the vessel was chartered, becoming offensive, and uneatable. A month elapsed, and the fever assumed a malignant type. Few escaped it, and on some days as many as three and four bodies were committed to the deep. Not half of those who died are designated in the foregoing list, for the whole number was nearly seventy. Among them (as will be seen) was the Laird of Pitlochie himself, and his wife, with her sister-in-law Lady Aithernie, and her two children.

Death and unwholesome food were not the only evils the unfortunate emigrants had to encounter. Wodrow represents the conduct of the Captain as being most cruel; extending even to the devising of measures to interfere with their performance of religious services. The ship, too, sprang a leak twice, and calms and storms added to their anxiety and distress.

On the death of Scot, the direction of the voyage devolved upon John Johnstone, whom Wodrow calls Scot's "son-in-law"—which it is probable he was not at that time,—and we are told that he was urged by the Captain to change the course of the vessel towards Virginia, or to the island of Jamaica, either place presenting better opportunities for the employment of servants than New Jersey; Hutton offering, as an inducement, to charge himself with the disposal of the prisoners, and to account to him for them "in bulk."[51] What

[51] In cargo or productions of the country.

attention Mr. Johnstone paid to these overtures is not definitely stated, but there is an evident desire to impress the reader with the idea that he acceded to the project, for, "when they are thus treating," says our author, "and near an issue, very much for the advantage of the passengers and prisoners, the wind turns straight for New Jersey, and they were forced to sail with it." It is scarcely necessary, with a knowledge of all the circumstances which, from the first conception of the voyage, pointed out New Jersey as its termination, and of the heavy obligations entered into by Scot that such it should be, to proffer a refutation of the insinuated perfidy.

It is further stated by Wodrow that Mr. Johnstone endeavored to prevail upon the prisoners, before landing, to enter into a voluntary agreement to serve four years, in accordance with the terms before mentioned, in consideration of the expenses incurred by Scot for their transportation. This they would not do, but joined in another protest against their banishment, recounting at length the hardships of the voyage. He also says that "the people who lived on the coast-side" had not the gospel settled among them, were inhospitable, and showed no kindness to the destitute immigrants, but the inhabitants of a town "a little way up the country"—by which Woodbridge is supposed to be meant—were very kind to them : invited to their settlement all who could "travel ;"[52] sent horses for those who could not ; and contributed liberally to their support the remainder of the winter ; and that, when the spring opened, Mr. Johnstone had them cited before some legal tribunal, but, "after hearing both sides, the Governor called a jury to sit and cognosce upon the affair," who "found that the pannels had not of their own accord come to that ship, nor bargained with Pitlochie for money or service, and, therefore, were assoiled."[53] This statement is erroneous, although it purports to have been derived from some of the immigrants.

The records of the Court of Common Right which are yet

[52] "Travel"—Walk. [53] Wodrow IV. 333.

extant show that, at a session held at Elizabethtown on the 25th February, 1685–86, a suit was tried, in which Captain Hutton was plaintiff, and George Moore defendant: an action of debt for the sum of five pounds sterling, being the price of his passage in the Henry and Francis. Witnesses were examined on both sides, says the record, and the governor (Deputy-governor Lawrie) briefly summed up the evidence and charged the jury: to whom was submitted like issues against Christopher Strang and William Nivens. The verdict was—"We Jurours finde for the pl^{f} w^{h} five pounds sterling debt and costes of suite,"—and similar suits subsequently brought against Thomas Corbett and Robert Young were attended with a like result.

On the 13th May, further action of the Court favorable to Captain Hutton is met with, in an order that "a non-resident, arresting any person in this province not being a settled inhabitant, is not liable to give security to pay the defendant's cost." That numerous arrests had been made is evident from the court's naming a certain day in the succeeding June, "for the trial of all such actions as are depending in this court at the suit of Captain Richard Hutton, and that a jury be summoned from the town of Amboy Perth to try the same."

On the 9th June, the day named, one of the cases (Adam Hood's) was called, and Captain Hutton not appearing, the defendant was discharged on the payment of fees, and a similar order was issued in the cases of "all the other def^{ts} that were arrested to this Court of Common Right at the suite of the said Captain Hutton." What was the cause of his failing to appear is not stated. He may have left the province, but assuredly nothing had occurred in the prosecution of the suits to lead to their abandonment from doubts of success;—and the fact that the verdicts of the jury were rendered after a full examination of witnesses, goes far to prove that some understanding existed, even with those who remonstrated against their expatriation, that Scot, or the master, was to be remunerated for their passage. Upon what terms the vessel was chartered is not known, but the result of these judicial proceedings indicates a direct liability to the master, on the part of the passengers, or some of them, irrespective of any agency of Scot. They also exonerate Mr. Johnstone from the imputations cast upon him, for neither as plaintiff nor defendant does his name appear on the records of the court, before October, 1687. A claim by him for headlands on account of these unfortunate persons would appear upon the proprietary records, had he entertained at the time any expectation of deriving benefit from their services, and his character (as will be shown hereafter in these pages) was too humane to warrant any supposition of persecution or undue severity on his part.[53]

Besides those banished persons who were given in charge of Scot, the following were directed to be delivered to Robert Barclay, governor of the province, under date of 7th August, 1685, on condition that they should be transported to East New Jersey:[54]

George Young,	James Stuart,	John Campbell,
Robert Cameron,	James Oliver,	John Swan,
John Gibb,	Colin Campbell,	John Jackson,
Gilbert Ferguson,		

then in the Canongate Tolbooth:

John Gilliland,	William McIlroy,*	Thomas Richard,*
Archibald Jamieson,*	William Drennan,*	

then in the Laight Parliament house, or the Tolbooth, of Edinburgh:

William Thompson,	Donald Moor,	John McKello,
Malcolm Black,	John Nicol,	Duncan McEwen,
Alexander Graham,	John McAulin,	

prisoners in St. Paul's hospital. There is little doubt of their having been among the passengers in the Henry and Francis.

[53] Wodrow's assertion that "much of the money remaining [of Scot's estate after paying the expenses of the vessel] was spent upon the lawsuit in New Jersey," does not comport with our ideas of the simple proceedings of the times, or else proves that, in endeavoring to secure an asylum for himself and others, he had reserved little for the future.

[54] Wodrow IV. p. 221.

* Those thus marked were among a large number who, on the 31st July, were sentenced to have their left ears cut off by the common executioner on the ensuing 4th August; whether the sentence was carried into execution is not known.

It is difficult to determine how many of those who came to the province at this time remained in the vicinity of Amboy. A few will be found mentioned among the settlers of Woodbridge in a subsequent chapter, but most of them removed to New England, and not a few returned to Scotland.

WILLIAM JACKSON, one of the banished men, was a cordwainer; removed to New York; and it was at his house, in the lower end of Pearl street, that Makemie preached.[55]

JOHN FRAZER was a candidate for the ministry, and went up to London in 1678 or '9 for improvement, and, at the same time, to consult his safety. In 1684, being among the hearers of the Rev. Alexander Shiels who were seized by a party of soldiers in Foster Lane, near Guildhall, he was sent to Newgate and thence to Scotland, having been marched through the streets with his unfortunate companions manacled in couples. Arrived in Scotland, they were thrown into Dunnottar Castle, and underwent, with one hundred others, the horrors of imprisonment during the whole summer. Many, of course, died; some few escaped.[56]

Mr. Frazer did not long remain in New Jersey; he removed to Connecticut, and was ordained at Woodbury; but on the accession of William and Mary he returned to Scotland and became the minister of Alness. His son was the author of the well-known work on Sanctification.

WILLIAM NIVEN, "Smith in Pollockshaws," we first find mentioned as ordered to the plantations on 28th May, 1678, for refusing to state under oath who preached and who were present at a certain conventicle. He remained in prison with many others until November, when they were placed on board of a vessel at Leith, destined for Virginia; but on arriving at Gravesend, in consequence of the non-appearance of the charterer of the vessel, the master put them all ashore, rather than

[55] MS. letter from Rev. Richard Webster, of Mauch Chunk. I would here express my obligations to Mr. W. for many facts and details respecting the career of the immigrants of 1685, which his minute acquaintance with the theological history of the Middle States enabled him to communicate.

[56] Woodrow (IV. pp. 322, 323) gives these hardships in detail from the papers of Mr. Frazer and other prisoners.

retain the charge of them longer, and they generally reached their homes after an absence of about nine months.[57]

Niven continued to follow his trade, and lived quietly refraining from any objectionable conduct, save that he attended not the authorized religious services, until the 29th July, 1684, when he was taken from his bed at midnight, and carried to the Glasgow Tolbooth, where he laid in irons for three weeks; he was then examined, but nothing of a serious character was elicited. He refused, however, to take the oath of allegiance, and was sent into Edinburgh under guard, with five others fettered in pairs:[58] was there confined in irons night and day, until May, 1685, when, upon a charge of having some acquaintance with treasonable documents, he and others were sentenced to immediate execution. Circumstances occurring which led to a postponement, he was suffered to remain, subjected to all the miseries of imprisonment in Dunnottar Castle, of which, as so many of the emigrants were subjected to them, it will not be irrelevant to give some account.

The vault, in which about a hundred men and women were pent up all summer, was under ground, ankle deep in mire, with but one window overlooking the sea. They were without any conveniences for sitting, leaning, or lying, and, indeed, so full was the place, that little more than sitting room was afforded. Stifled for want of air, stinted for both food and water, and subjected to the direful influences of the impurities which necessarily collected, it was miraculous that they did not all die. Many did, and others became afflicted with diseases. An attempt was made by several of them, including Niven, to escape by the window which has been mentioned. They succeeded, to the number of twenty-five, in creeping along the face of a precipice at the hazard of their lives, to some distance from the fort, before the alarm was given, but fifteen of them were retaken and barbarously used. Beaten, bruised, and bound, they were laid upon their backs and obliged to undergo various processes of torture. Niven, who was among those retaken, as well as Peter Russel, another of

[57] Wodrow II. pp. 475, 476. [58] Ibid. IV. p. 151.

the emigrants, and others, were laid upon a form, their hands bound, and matches placed between their fingers; these were kept burning "equal with their fingers" for three hours without intermission. Some died under this torture—some were so badly burnt that the bones were charred, and Niven himself lost one of the fingers of his left hand.[59] Such, faintly sketched, were some of the trials which those in Dunnottar Castle were obliged to undergo, and it can cause no surprise that, to escape them, a voluntary expatriation was gladly acceded to, Scot's proposition to the Council was profited by, and Niven and others should have entered into an engagement whereby they were to be transported to New Jersey: upon what precise terms, as I have already stated, is not known.

I am ignorant of Niven's career after his arrival in the province, and his appearance before the Court of Common Right at Elizabethtown, in February, 1686, at the suit of Captain Hutton, which has been noticed. He subsequently returned to Scotland.

Christopher Strang is believed to have been the son of that Christopher who was executed on 7th December, 1666, for treason—his head being exposed at Hamilton, and his right arm affixed to the public posts of Lanark, "being the place where he took the covenant."[60] What became of the son after being brought by Capt. Hutton before the Court of Gommon Right, I have not ascertained.

Rev. David Simson, although not mentioned in immediate connection therewith, is presumed to have come to the province in Scot's vessel. The Council, on 14th August, 1685, ordering his bonds to be given up which had been required of him some months before on being liberated from prison, providing for his removal from the kingdom, and the cessation of his ministerial services, as he was going to New Jersey. His name will be found among those for whom headlands were claimed by Lord Neil Campbell. He is thought to have died here. A son, David, it is said conformed, but afterwards recanted, and died minister at Isla.

[59] Wodrow IV. pp. 322, 323.

[60] Sentence in Wodrow, II. p. 48.

It is not surprising, that, in such times as those which prompted this emigration to New Jersey, there should have arisen parties who met persecution with defiance, restraint with open opposition, opprobrium with kindred violence and abuse; and whose ravings and blasphemies were of a character to bring undeserved obloquy upon the Presbyterians as a body. Among these, John Gibb, once a shipmaster, Walter Ker, David Jamison, and John Young, were especially noted as the leaders of a Society claiming, or known by, the title of "Sweet Singers," who carried their madness to an extraordinary extent for a brief period. They published a manifesto or declaration of their sentiments, under date of April 27th, 1681, after they had been a few days in the Canongate, which is the most remarkable production of the kind, probably, ever penned; affording a sad illustration of how far astray men may go when they "take counsel, but not of the Lord."

It commences with a statement we, at least, cannot wonder at, that they had been called "madmen and devils," and subsequently, they say one of them had even been called a "blockhead," by the so-styled rulers. It had seemed good to the Holy Ghost and to them—so runs the blasphemous paper—to take from their Bibles the Psalms in metre—as being an unwarranted addition—to renounce the division of the Scriptures into chapters and verses, because done by human wisdom; and the received translations—the larger and shorter catechisms—the Confession of Faith—the Acts of the General Assembly, their covenants, manner of worship, preaching, &c. &c. "for all following that way go to hell together:"—and all their preachers, were alike renounced and abandoned for various reasons stated. They desired all to know and understand that they overturned and formally burnt all the former works of the clergy of Scotland, and throughout the whole world, which they conceived to be opposed to holiness.

They proceeded to renounce all authority throughout the world, all that were in authority, with all their acts and edicts, the names of the months, saint's-days, and holy days, and various other things, including "feastings," "sportings," "dancings," "laughings," "monk-lands," "friar-lands," "kirks and kirk yards," "market crosses," "registers of lands and houses," "bonds," "ships' passes," "story-books," "ballads," "romances," and "pamphlets;"—they disowned and burnt them all. So did they all the customs and fashions of that generation, their way and custom of eating and drinking, sleeping, and wearing, and all their former ways, as well religious as moral, in so far as they had been cast in that generation's mould: and they even denounced "all that were then in prison houses or correction houses, men and women," for say they, "when we sent them a copy of this, our renunciation, they called us devils."

With similar senseless outpourings and still more objectionable references to the Holy Spirit of God, by whom they say they "were pressed" to make the declaration, they continue at great length, pouring out their curses and denunciations upon almost every thing animate or inanimate, civil or religious, holy or common, with the spirit of demoniacs, and yet, with the greatest complacency, they say, "our joy no man can take from us, and our prison is so pleasant through the Lord, that we care for no company, for we know no company, but all are cursed, and we know not what it is to weary; but according to that scripture, 'Eat and drink my beloved, yea, eat and drink abundantly,' we are rather in paradise."[61]

This synopsis would not have been here introduced, but two, if not three, of the signers of the document came to New Jersey. One of them, Gibb, was among those granted by the Council to Governor Barclay, in August, 1685, and is presumed to have been a passenger on board "the Henry and Francis." An order was issued by the Council in August, 1681, for the liberation of himself and companions on their abjuring their disloyal principles, but they seem not to have complied with the requisition. Gibb was in confinement in the Canongate Tolbooth, when assigned to the governor.

Walter Ker is thought to have come to the province also, but at what time or under what circumstances is not definitely known. He must not be confounded, however, with Walter

[61] The document, at length, is in Wodrow III. pp. 348–353.

Ker, who was banished September 3d, 1685, and who may have been a passenger with Scot. He settled at Freehold, in Monmouth County, and was one of the founders and principal supporters of the Presbyterian congregation at that place.[62]

Jamison was also banished, and on his arrival became bound to Lockhart of Woodbridge, and by him was transferred to a Mr. Clarke of New York, who allowed him to teach school to redeem himself. He was employed in the office of the secretary of the province as a clerk, and acquiring a knowledge of law, was admitted to practice. He also held the office of clerk to the Council. On the arrival of Governor Hunter, in 1710, so well regarded was he, and so esteemed for his legal abilities, that he was selected to be Chief Justice of New Jersey.[63] Three years previously he had signalized himself by defending Francis Makemie, the Presbyterian clergyman, arrested by Lord Cornbury, for preaching without a license, whose case excited so much interest at the time, and appears to have justified Hunter's preference by a judicial career creditable to himself and satisfactory to the best portion of the community.[64] He had the reputation in both New York and New Jersey, of being zealous for religion and possessing "art and management," although it is not known that these last qualities are enumerated with the view of detracting from his character. Mr. Field[65] mentions one of his charges to a Grand Jury in 1716, exhibiting his acquaintance with the Bible, his authorities being drawn therefrom, and a considerable portion of the document being made up of passages from the Old and New Testament. He was one of the few who originated the first Presbyterian congregation in New York.

Although he continued to reside in New York, he was allowed to hold the office of Chief Justice in New Jersey, until 1723, when, on the ground of the inconvenience attendant upon his non-residence, he was superseded by Governor Bur-

[62] MS. letter of Rev. R. Webster. The Rev. Nathan Ker, of Goshen, N. Y., and the Rev. Jacob Ker, of Somerset Co., Md., were his grandsons. The son of the latter, Samuel Ker, M.D., was recently living at a great age, at Princess Anne, Md.

[63] Lord Bellamont, however, in 1700, pronounces him like *all* the lawyers in New York, "wholly unworthy." *Rev. Mr. Webster, from Brodhead Papers.*

[64] See Field's Provincial Courts, pp. 72, 91, 94.

[65] p. 103.

net, and William Trent appointed in his place. Of his subsequent career I know nothing. The name is not an unusual one in New York and New Jersey, but whether or not the "Sweet Singer" has any descendants among us is not known.[66]

JOHN FORBES.

This personage arrived towards the close of 1684. He was brother to the Laird of Barula. He had his plantation near the Gordons and Fullertons on Cedar Brook, but whether he remained in the province or not, is not known. An interesting letter of his is given in Scot,[67] in which he recounts the dangers experienced on the voyage, and describes the country, &c. From his letter it appears that he left Scotland, without the knowledge of his friends, on what may be termed "a voyage of discovery" to East Jersey.

Robert Hardie, John Doby, and John Cockburn, arrived in 1684. Cockburn was a mason, and was employed by David Mudie to build his renowned stone house.[68] He and Hardie have letters in Scot's Model.[69]

JAMES EMOTT.

It is not known when Mr. Emott came to the province, but it was probably before the purchase by the twenty-four proprietaries. The first public house in Amboy was kept by him, his name appearing in that connection as early as 1685. In 1686 he was appointed secretary of the province, although, as a scribe, little qualified for it, his handwriting so far as plainness is concerned, being almost undecipherable at the present day, even by the most expert. On the 10th December of this year his name appears in the first notice of the Amboy Militia, being appointed lieutenant of a "company of train bands, consisting of the inhabitants of Amboy Perth, under the command of the Right Honorable Lord Neil

[66] There was also an Archibald Jamieson banished in 1685, and granted to Gov. Barclay. See p. 34.

[67] See East Jersey, &c. p. 319.

[68] See a subsequent page for a notice of Mudie.

[69] See East Jersey, &c. pp. 305, 330.

Campbell." The same day he was appointed clerk of the County Court and Court of Sessions (he had previously held the same offices in Essex County), and is the only officer mentioned on the records as being specially re-commissioned by Andross, when East Jersey came under his authority in 1688.[70] He was also authorized by Andross to practise as an attorney at law, in August, 1688. Mr. Emott owned two lots in Amboy, as will be seen on reference to the map, and built a house on the one fronting the water.

No notice of his family has been discovered, but it is believed that descendants or near relatives resided in the vicinity of New York in subsequent years.

JOHN BARCLAY.

This gentleman was a brother of Governor Barclay, and came over to the province about the time of the purchase by the twenty-four proprietaries; and after examining into its condition, its advantages and capabilities, returned to England in 1683.[71]

In 1684 or 1685 he again came to East Jersey, and appears to have resided first at Elizabethtown; subsequently at Plainfield; and became a resident of Amboy about 1688. In January, 1688–9, he was appointed deputy surveyor under George Keith; and succeeded him as Surveyor-general, receiving the appointment, together with that of Receiver-general, April 6th, 1692, and was sworn into office the 1st November following.[72] On the 25th November, 1695, on Thomas Gordon's leaving the province for England, Mr. Barclay was appointed deputy Secretary and Register; on the 6th August, 1698, he was made Register of the Court of Chancery and one of the Commissioners of the Court of Small Causes; in 1700 he received the clerkships of the County Court of Common Right, of the Supreme Court, and Court of Sessions; and in 1704 he represented Amboy in the Assembly.

[70] East Jersey, &c. pp. 113, 121.

[71] He was the bearer of the letters of Rudyard and Groom to the Proprietaries. See Grants and Concess., p. 181.

[72] See East Jersey, &c., p. 133.

His continuance in public situations is some evidence of the respectability and popularity of Mr. Barclay; but it is doubtful if his offices were of much pecuniary benefit, for, losing most of them on the surrender of the government of the Province to the Crown, he was for some years before his death in humble circumstances, holding the clerkship of St. Peter's Church at the small salary of fifteen pounds per annum, and his principal creditor administered upon his estate.

He died in the spring of 1731, at an advanced age, with the character of a good neighbor and useful citizen,[73] leaving one son (John), of whom nothing is known, excepting that he was alive in 1768, and poorly provided with this world's goods.

Mr. Barclay's residence in Amboy was probably the old brick building, still standing, in the rear of the house for many years occupied by the Golding family, on High street, near the Square. Six servants are recorded as having been imported by him in 1685, but whether or not headlands were allotted him on their account is uncertain.

Mr. Barclay was one among the many who fell under the displeasure of Lord Cornbury when that nobleman ruled over the province; one of the matters of difference between the Assembly and the governor being the transfer of the proprietary records from his hands and those of Thomas Gordon into the possession of Peter Sonmans.[74]

Another brother of "the Apologist," DAVID BARCLAY, came to the province in 1684, and, in connection with Arthur Forbes, furnished the Scotch proprietaries with a description of the country, which has come down to us in Scot's "Model, &c."[75] He died at sea, about the end of August, 1685, on his return to East Jersey from Aberdeen, on board the ship Exchange, of Stopton, James Peacock, master; the cargo,

[73] Smith's N. J., p. 424.

[74] See a notice of Sonmans on a subsequent page. On one occasion Sonmans caused Barclay to be arrested on Sunday, as he came out of church, to the great surprise of the good people. This was made one of the special charges against Sonmans.

[75] See East Jersey, &c., p. 288. Smith erroneously makes John the author of this letter.

belonging to the proprietaries, being in his charge.[76] His brother John administered on his estate in January, 1686, and received several grants in his right.

JOHN LOOFBORROW, "Miller," arrived in 1685; and BENJAMIN GRIFFITH in 1687; the latter got to be a Commissioner of the Minor Court in 1696.

JOHN WATSON, "Merchant;" PETER WATSON, "Planter."—These names are found on the records as borne by two residents of Amboy between 1684 and 1696. Scot gives an interesting letter from Peter, dated soon after his arrival, in August, 1684, in which his wife and one son (Richard) are mentioned; but no further information has been obtained respecting them.

THOMAS KNOWLES, "Stationer," arrived in 1683; and ROBERT BRIDGMAN, "Merchant," arrived in 1684; but they are not subsequently mentioned.

STEPHEN WARNE.—THOMAS WARNE.

These were sons of Thomas Warne, one of the "twenty-four," who was a merchant of Dublin. They came to the province in 1683, and eleven persons are recorded as the number for whom they were entitled to headlands. They became owners of several lots at Amboy. Thomas, the younger brother, is styled "carpenter," and settled eventually in Monmouth County; but of their families or descendants nothing is known; the name is borne, however, by numbers in that quarter of the State.

THOMAS FULLERTON.—ROBERT FULLERTON.

The former of these, with his wife and ten servants, and the latter, with nine servants, arrived in October, 1684.

They were brothers to the Laird of Kennaber, and located themselves, with Thomas Gordon and others, on Cedar Brook, about eight miles west of Amboy. They seem, from their letters, a number of which are given in Scot's "Model," to

[76] E. J. Records, A 397. Stirling's Answer to Hunt in Chancery. MS. in N. Y. Hist. Lib. He was imprisoned in 1668 for some connection with the "Pentland rising." Woodrow II. p. 108.

have been intelligent men, and, like most others, enchanted with the province: "the weather here," says Thomas, "*is constantly clear;* the sun rises and sets free of clouds." What became of them has not been ascertained. Thomas was a brother-in-law of Dr. John Gordon, of Montrose.

JOHN REID.

This personage was sent over by the proprietaries in 1683, as a surveyor, and acted as deputy under George Keith (appointed October 13th, 1685) and John Barclay (December 17th, 1692).

In Scot's "Model, &c." he is said to have been gardener to the Lord Advocate. A letter is there given from him to a friend in Edinburgh, dated September 1st, 1684, in which he speaks very favorably of the province, and concludes thus:—"There are a great store of garden herbs here; I have not had time to inquire into them all, neither to send some of the many pleasant (tho' to me unknown) plants of this country to James Sutherland, Physick Gardener at Edinburgh, but tell him I will not forget him when opportunities offer. I had forgot to write of *Ambo*, or New Perth, therefore, I add, that it is one of the best places in America, by the report of all travellers, for a town of trade. For my part I never saw any so conveniently seated.[77]

Mr. Reid brought his wife with him, and resided at Amboy for some years after his arrival, becoming of some note among its inhabitants. After the surrender of the government to the crown, he was repeatedly a member of the Assembly, and on the 2d December, 1702, was appointed Surveyor-general.

In June, 1686, on account of his services in drawing maps of the province,[78] a grant of two hundred acres of land in Monmouth County was made to him. The tract was called "Hortensia," and was on the east branch of Hope River.

[77] See East Jersey, &c. p. 294.

[78] A fac simile of one of these maps is in the possession of the New Jersey Hist. Soc. It is entitled "A mapp of Rariton River, Milstone River, South River, Raway River, Boundbrook, Greenbrook, and Cedarbrook, with the plantations thereupon: also those of Chinquarora, Wiekatonk, the heads of Hop (Hope) River, Swimming River, and Manasquam River, likewise appends some on Hackingsack River."

He seems to have considered it his place of residence in 1686. His daughter, Anna, became the wife of Capt. John Anderson, of Monmouth.

MILES FORSTER.

The name of Mr. Forster first appears on the provincial records in the year 1684, as deputy to William Haige, the Receiver and Surveyor-general. In 1687, on the commissioners of the revenue opening the port of Amboy, he received the appointment of Collector and Receiver of the customs under Governor Dongan.[79] In 1689, he is mentioned as having his residence in New York, and in 1695 was a merchant in that city. Colonel Lewis Morris, father of Governor Morris, appointed him one of his executors in 1690—a proof of the consideration in which he was held. He owned several lots in Amboy, and resided here for many years before his death. In December, 1702, he received from the Board of Proprietors a grant for a town lot, in consideration of his having built the first sloop launched at Amboy.

Mr. Forster died in 1710, and William Bradford, the printer of New York, was one of his executors. His wife, Rebecca, was daughter of Gawen Lawrie, deputy-governor of the province, but the date of her death is unknown. They left one son (William), who lived in the island of Barbadoes in 1721, and was yet alive in 1729 ; and two daughters, Elizabeth and Mary : the latter was also alive in 1729, residing in Amboy, unmarried. Elizabeth had died previously.

A rude miniature likeness of Mr. Forster is in my possession, and one of his daughter Mary was lost recently, on its way to me, after enduring through the changes and chances of several generations, and outlasting herself and all her kindred.

"The lightest, frailest things we see
Are not so light, so frail as we."

[79] Appointed Nov. 26th, and sworn into office, Nov. 30th.

DAVID MUDIE.

This gentleman was one of the most valued residents of Amboy for some years. He was from the town of Montrose, Scotland, and arrived in East Jersey with four children and thirteen servants, in November, 1684.[80] This was only a portion of his family; several children and his wife being left behind in Scotland. One of his letters in Scot's Model, addressed to his wife, commences with the appellation "My Heart"—prepossessing us favorably at the outset. How could he be other than an affectionate husband?

During the year following his arrival he is styled "Merchant of Perth," and the same year (1685) was appointed a judge of the Court of Common Right, and was one of the governor's council during the administration of Lord Neil Campbell and Andrew Hamilton.

In November, 1686, he revisited the place of his birth,[81] but returned soon after to the province and continued a resident of Amboy until his death, which occurred in March, 1696. We learn nothing more of his wife. It is probable that, on his second arrival he was accompanied by two more children, as the whole of his family did not emigrate to America. Two sons, David and James, came with their father in 1684, but the first died before him, and, by his will, James shared equally with Isabel, Christian, Elizabeth, and John, in all his estate "anywhere in Europe." His property in New Jersey he left to Thomas Gordon, for the benefit of his five daughters, Margaret, Ann, Janet, Katherine, and Mary. Another daughter, Jean Strachen, is said to have been already provided for on her marriage.[82] Janet became the wife of Thomas Gordon, but nothing further is known of the descendants of Mr. Mudie.

From his letters we learn that, soon after his arrival, he commenced building at New Perth "a good handsome house,

[80] The name of "David Mudie" appears among a list of fugitives for political offences in May, 1684. (Wodrow IV. p, 19:) but I cannot identify with it the subject of this notice.

[81] He made his sons David and James his attorneys, during his absence, being bound "by the permission of God, on a voyage for the Towne of Montrose, in the Kingdom of Scotland."

[82] E. J. Records, E. 410. His will, dated February 18th, 1695–6: letters of administration granted, March 12th.

six rooms off a floor, with a Study, two stories high above the sellers, and the garret above." This was of stone, and at that time was an undertaking considered worthy of special mention by all the scribes among the settlers ; as was also his erection of a "horse-mill," which it was expected would be worth one hundred pounds per year. He says himself, "I am sure she will be better than fifty of clear money, for every Scotch *boll* of wheat or Indian corn pays here for grinding of it two shillings sterling." This mill he describes as thirty-two feet wide, forty feet long, and "the great wheel" thirty feet in diameter. It is a circumstance somewhat remarkable, that while the old and populous settlement at Newark did not secure a mill for the use of the inhabitants until four or five years after its settlement, and then by general action in the matter,[83] Amboy so soon after it was founded should have had one erected by individual enterprise.

Mr. Mudie selected his plantation on South River at a distance which took two hours to sail, and says of it in one of his letters, "I mind to settle some of my servants there against the middle of this month (March, 1685). I am provided with six coarse horses ; oxen and swine sufficiently in number for any plantation for the first year : the land I have settled on in my judgment is extraordinarily good."[84] All this indicates the possession of pecuniary resources such as the majority of the settlers did not enjoy.

Scot gives also a letter from Mr. Mudie's son James (apparently dictated by him to an amanuensis), to a cousin of the same name in Montrose, who seems to be the owner of the "Lairdship of Arbikie." The writer says, "there is abundance of much better land here than ever Arbikie was, and an Earldom to be bought far below in price the value of what such petty Lairdships as Arbikie are sold for in Scotland, without purging of the lands of any incumbrances."

GARRET AND WALTER WALL

Came early to this section of the province, but whether

[83] Town Records, Agreem't in Towne meeting, Aug. 24, 1670.

[84] East Jersey, &c. pp. 296, 317, 327.

from England or from one of the eastern colonies is uncertain. They both removed to Middletown previous to 1685.

Garret had a son John, who was the father of James Wall, who became subsequently a resident of Amboy ; and of John Galen Wall, who practised as a physician for several years, both in Perth Amboy and Woodbridge. His tombstone is yet standing in the Presbyterian cemetery in the latter place, bearing the following inscription :

> "In memory of Dr. John Galen Wall, 13 years physician in Woodbridge and Perth Amboy, born at Middletown, Monmouth, 17th December, 1759 ; died 14th January, 1798.
>
> "If physic's aid or friendship's balm could save
> From death, thou still had'st lived."

Dr. Wall's residence in Amboy, was that now in the possession of Mr. Wm. King, on the bank south of Market street. After his removal to Woodbridge, he married Nancy, daughter of Dr. Bloomfield, who, after his death, resided for some time with a sister, in Burlington County ; but subsequently returned to Woodbridge and became the wife of Mr. James Paton.

The Hon. Garret D. Wall, who, for so long a period bore a distinguished part in the public affairs of New Jersey, was a son of James Wall.

With the exception of a few, who are noticed as heads of some of the old families, the foregoing are all the settlers of whom any information has been obtained. It would have been a pleasing task to have embodied here more particulars of the lives and characters of these pioneers, and to have pointed out the destination and fate of their descendants, but the materials are wanting. Meagre as is the record, however, it may serve to preserve from oblivion the names of some, who had the improvement of their "New Perth" much at heart ; more so perhaps, than most of their successors in occupancy at the present day.

Chapter III.—The City.

"More than I seem, and less than I was born to."

"I love to dwell among these shades, unfolding to my view
The dreams of perish'd men and years, and by-gone glory too."

No special local government seems to have been established at first, for Perth Amboy; for its simple appellation of Perth was soon lost from joining with it the name of the point, *Ambo*. The various county officers and courts preserved order and regulated its police; and its existence as a town was soon recognized by admitting one or more representatives from it to the General Assembly, which held its first session in Amboy in 1686. In 1698 it was allowed two members, and that number continued to be its quota until the war of Independence.

The first charter was obtained from Governor Robert Hunter, August 24th, 1718;[1] the title of the incorporation being "The Mayor, Recorder, Aldermen and Commonalty of the City of Perth Amboy." The preamble to the grant is as follows:

"George, by the grace of God, King of Great Britain, France, and Ireland, Defender of the Faith, &c. To all persons to whom these presents shall come, greeting: Whereas our loving subjects, John Johnstone, Thomas Gordon, John Hamilton, George Willocks, John Barclay, William Eier, John Stevens, William Hodgson, William Frost, Henry Berry, John Sharp, Thomas Turnbull, Andrew Redford, and Alexander Walker, and many other inhabitants in our town of Perth Amboy, in our province of Nova Cesarea or New Jersey, by their humble petition presented unto our trusty and well beloved Robert Hunter, Esq., our Captain-general and Governor-in-chief of our said province of New Jersey, New York, and tracts of land depending thereon in America, and Vice Admiral of the same, &c., on behalf of themselves and others, the freeholders and inhabitants of the said town, have set forth, that the said town of Perth Amboy

[1] E. J. Records, Liber C.

is not only the best situation for a place of trade in our said province of New Jersey, and has a harbour for shipping preferable to those in the provinces adjoining, but that it is also the only port appointed for the collecting of our customs in the eastern division of our said province of New Jersey: that the said town hath many years languished under designed and unjust impositions to prevent its growth, to the loss and detriment of the province, until the government happily fell under the care of our said governor's just administration. The petitioners with a due sense of gratitude, thankfully acknowledging its new life and present prospects of becoming a place is to be wholly attributed to our said governor's expensive encouragement and favorable countenance, as also the repeated instances of his benignity during the course of his mild administration, is what gives the petitioners hope their present supplication may prove successful, tho' their request is not to be granted of right, but grace; therefore humbly pray for our royal grant by letters patent, under our great seal of our said province of New Jersey, to incorporate the freeholders, inhabitants of the said town of Perth Amboy, into a Body Corporate and politic, with perpetual succession by what name our said governor shall think fit; as also to grant such immunities and privileges as may be thought requisite for the well ordering and ruling thereof, &c. We, being willing to promote all trade, industry, rule, and good order amongst all our loving subjects, in granting their reasonable request in that behalf: Therefore, know ye, &c."

There is nothing particularly deserving notice in the provisions of the document, requiring its insertion at length.

The officers were to be a mayor, recorder, four aldermen, a town-clerk, four assistants, a sheriff, a chamberlain or treasurer, a coroner, a marshal, a sergeant at mace,[2] three constables, and two overseers of the poor.

The common council, of which the mayor and three aldermen constituted a quorum, were to hold their meetings in the court-house, or city hall, and their laws or ordinances were to be submitted to the Governor for approval within six months after their passage; but he does not seem to have been invested with any authority to veto them, their operation being limited to six months if they did not receive his approbation.

The mayor, clerk of the market, sheriff, and water-bailiff were to be appointed by the Governor; the recorder and town-clerk held their offices according to the tenor of their commissions, no particular term being specified. The aldermen, assistants, chamberlain, coroner, overseers of the poor,

[2] "The present and succeeding mayors of the said city shall, and may have a mace borne before him and them," said the charter.

and constables were elected by a majority of the freeholders; the assistants not to be chosen until it was known who were to be aldermen. The sergeant was to be appointed by the mayor with the approval of the common council, and, together with all the other officers, was required to be "of good capacity." The overseers of the poor and constables who should refuse to take the oath of office and enter upon their respective duties were to be fined five pounds, and others were to be elected in their stead, who should be held similarly liable should they decline the honors conferred. The mayor, recorder, and aldermen constituted the city court, and held a term once a month for actions of debt. None but free citizens were allowed to exercise "any trade, art, or mystery," saving during the times of fairs, which, with market days, were duly authorized.

A common seal was to be used, the device on which was prescribed: "On the dexter a hunting-horn, and over it *Arte non Impetu*; on the sinister a ship riding at anchor in the harbor, under it *Portus Optimus*." Such continues to be the seal at the present day, and a fac-simile of it is here inserted.

THE SEAL OF PERTH AMBOY.

The connection between the hunting-horn and its motto, and the past history or future destinies of the city, might afford matter for discussion to a whole college of heraldry, were not a clue presented in the Governor's own escutcheon. The well-turned compliments paid that functionary in the petition which preceded the granting of the charter, it appears, were not thought sufficient to insure his favorable consideration, but, in addition, the arms of his family were placed upon the seal of the corporation in testimony of its distinguished parentage.

The foregoing is a sketch of the municipal machinery intended and expected to work a great revolution in the circumstances of the city, improve its commerce, add to its population, and increase its dimensions ; but it need scarcely be added, the results fell far short of those anticipated.[3]

The "designed and unjust impositions," which are alluded to by the petitioners, as preventing the growth of the place, were probably those that a mistaken policy, as to the measures most likely to conduce to the advancement of the commercial interests of the province, had led previous assemblies to adopt. They will be more particularly referred to hereafter. The want of documentary evidence, which has already been alluded to, prevents any thing like a connected account of the events of this period. No attempt will therefore be made to construct a narrative out of the desultory gleanings of the past upon the various topics to which the author's researches have been directed.

There are very few notices of the place to be found, and none at all, having any pretensions to accuracy, upon which any estimate can be based of its growth, either in population or wealth : some improvement, however, was the result of the privileges secured to it by its charter, but from that time to the present, writers have been obliged, uniformly, to deplore

[3] The persons intrusted with the first official stations, are named in the charter to hold their offices until the annual election. They were as follows:

William Eier, *Mayor and Clerk of Market.*
James Alexander, *Recorder.*
Aldermen.—John Parker, John Rudyard, Sam'l Leonard, Wm. Hodgson.
Assistant Aldermen.—John Brown, Andrew Redford, Michael Henry, Jacob Isleton.
John Stevens.—*Chamberlain and Treasurer.*
John Barclay, *Town Clerk.*
John Harrison, *Sheriff and Water Bailiff.*
William Harrison, *Coroner.*
William Frost, *Marshal* or *Sergeant at Mace.*
Overseers of the poor.—John Ireland, Henry Berry.
Constables.—John Herriott, Fred. Buckaloo, Alex'r Cairns.

There is no register of the city officers existing, from which a perfect list could be made out of those who subsequently held these stations.

he disappointment which has attended the plans projected for its prosperity.

In 1738, it is stated, "planters had not resorted to it as was expected, notwithstanding its commodious situation,"[4] and the lapse of years brought no change.

In 1739–40, Governor Morris, although he expressed an opinion that the harbor is preferable to that of New York—"easier to be entered or departed from, and of the two, more safe,"—yet finds an argument for the establishment of another seat of government, upon the fact that it was "a poor inconsiderable place."[5] Hopes were still entertained, however, that in some way its peculiar advantages might be turned to better account, and at various times legislative action was put in requisition to enlarge its commerce, but the plans, which will be noticed in a following chapter, were attended by few beneficial results.

In August, 1747, on the arrival of Governor Belcher, the city authorities, in their address to him, say, "the city of Perth Amboy is not only most commodiously situated for a place of trade, but it has one of the best harbors for shipping upon the continent, and yet hath hitherto struggled with many difficulties :—nevertheless, by your excellency's favor and kind protection (which we humbly pray for), we hope trade will flourish amongst us."

In his answer the Governor said, "I have hardly ever seen a place more pleasantly situated for health, and more commodiously for trade, and you may depend on every thing on my part, to render it a flourishing city."[6] He disappointed the good citizens, however, by taking up his residence at Elizabethtown ; but his successors, who resided at Amboy, gave convincing evidence that the patronage of royal governors could not alone make a "flourishing city."

In 1759, Burnaby says Amboy had about one hundred houses (Mr. Burke, in his account of the American settlements" published in 1761, makes the number two hundred) ;

[4] Salmon's Modern Hist.

[5] Papers of Lewis Morris, pp. 69, 121.

[6] Virginia Gazette, Oct. 1st, 1747.

but, says Douglas, "notwithstanding its good deep water harbor and promising country—its being the capital of the province, &c., it has only the appearance of a mean village." And Oldmixon, in 1770, was sufficiently callous to the misfortunes and trials of the Earl of Perth to compare his *city* with his *Dukedom*, as being about alike valuable.

The provincial historian, Smith, whose work was printed in 1765, speaks of the pleasant situation and commodiousness of the harbor, but "by a fatality" attending such attempts, all endeavors to make it a place of extensive trade had been unavailing. It is convenient, at least, to place upon "the Fates" the burthen of our own mistakes in policy or legislation, or our own remissness in energy and enterprise.[7]

It is probable the city was at the "pinnacle of its fame" about the time the revolution commenced.[8] Its foreign commerce and domestic trade had perhaps both been greater in previous years, but it had then, doubtless, a larger population than at any time before ; and, as the seat of government, it held a rank far above what it has since possessed. The result of the struggle for Independence caused many of the inhabitants to remove—the operation of other systems of government drew off most of its little remaining commerce—and the restoration of peace found Amboy but feebly prepared to vie with other communities less unfavorably influenced by the changes the war had wrought.

An attempt to revive its importance and prosperity was made in 1784, by the renewal of its corporate powers, through an act of the Legislature, passed December 21st, which remained "the law of the land" *unimpaired* by any amendments until 1844 ; the fear of making it worse possibly deterring the good people from taking any steps to make it better

[7] "Alas!" says a modern writer, "clams and oysters and fish are quite too cheap at Ambo-point, and that is the reason that Ambo-point has not fulfilled the promise of its early prosperity."—(Paulding in Atlantic Souvenir for 1829.) That the fisheries may have interfered with the regular prosecution of other and more productive pursuits, is doubtless true; but as the *cheapness* spoken of has never existed, its *consequence*, as stated, may be questioned.

[8] Russell gives the number of houses at the commencement of the revolution at about three hundred, but that was probably an over-estimate. Vol. II. p. 272.

or more comformable to their situation, after the changes of half a century. The title of the act was "an act for erecting the north ward[9] of Perth Amboy and a part of the township of Woodbridge, in the county of Middlesex, into a city, and for incorporating the same, by the name and title of the city of Perth Amboy." The author of the bill must have been a warm friend to the young city, judging from the preamble, which was as follows.

"Whereas the improvement of trade and navigation in this State, is of the utmost importance to the well-being of the same: *and whereas* the prosperity of trade requires the collection of merchants together in sufficient numbers, in order that the union of their force may render them competent to great undertakings, and that the variety of their importations and their wants may always furnish to the purchasers and to the sellers a secure and constant market: *and whereas*, it is necessary in the present unprovided and disadvantageous condition of this State, to bestow on merchants, peculiar immunities and privileges, in order to attract them to its harbours, and to secure to them, for a sufficient and definite duration the entire profits of their commerce, without burden, abatement, or uncertainty, in order to excite in them a spirit of useful adventure, and to encourage them to encounter the risks and expenses of a new situation, and of important and beneficial undertakings: and inasmuch as commercial cities require a peculiar mode of government, for maintaining their internal police and commercial transactions; require more expeditious and summary tribunals than others: *and whereas*, divers good citizens of this State, residing in different parts thereof, by their humble petition presented to the Legislature, have set forth the great public utility of incorporating certain towns in the State, and of investing them with such powers, privileges, jurisdictions, and immunities, as shall conduce to the encouragement of its commerce; and have prayed that Perth Amboy aforesaid may be incorporated for the said purposes: *and whereas*, divers of the inhabitants of the said north ward of Perth Amboy, and others in the vicinity thereof, by their humble petition to the Legislature, have set forth, that for many years previous to the late revolution, the said north ward of Perth Amboy, under and by virtue of charters to them granted for that purpose, did hold, enjoy, and exercise, many powers, privileges, and immunities, which they found greatly beneficial to the inhabitants thereof, and have prayed that the said charter, or one of them so far as may extend to the said north ward and a part of Woodbridge, may be revised, corrected, and amended; or that a law for incorporating the said north ward, together with a part of the township of Woodbridge into a city and town corporate may be enacted: BE IT THEREFORE ENACTED, &c."

One would suppose the wealth of the Indies, if not the commerce of the world, would flow into the harbor after the obtainment of a charter which opened with so much promise.

[9] South Amboy, now a separate township, was the *south* ward.

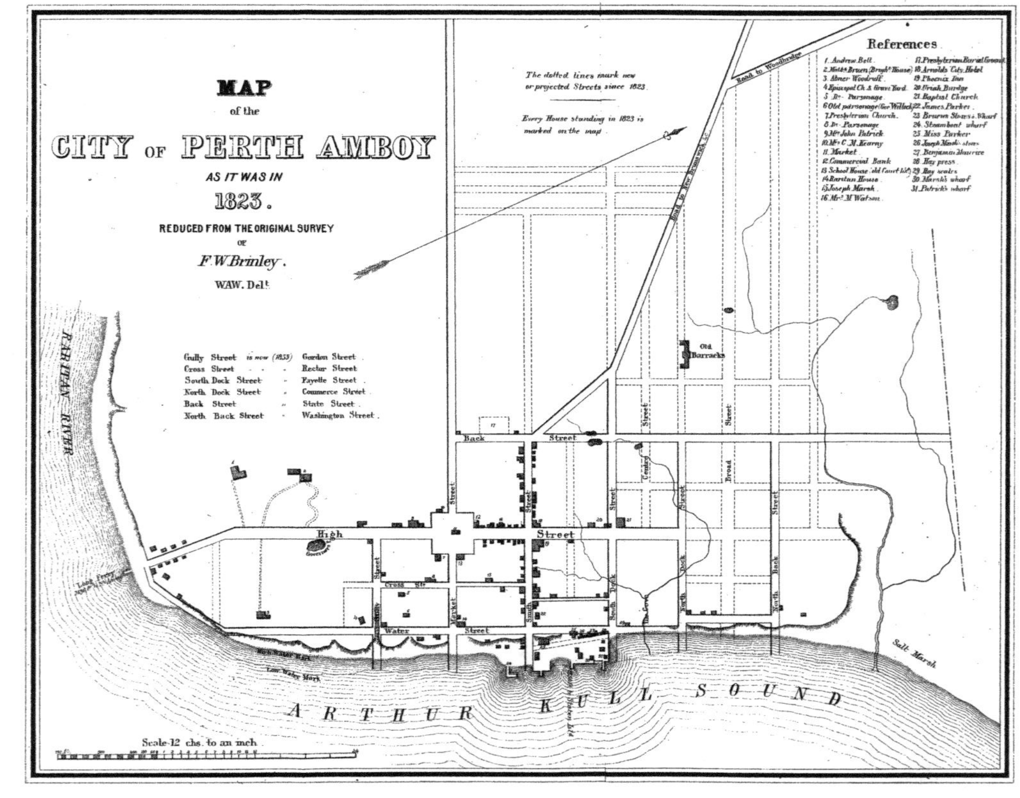
MAP
of the
CITY OF PERTH AMBOY
AS IT WAS IN
1823.
REDUCED FROM THE ORIGINAL SURVEY
OF
F. W. Brinley.
W.A.W. Del.t
Gully Street is now (1853) Gordon Street.
Cross Street - - Rector Street.
South Dock Street - Fayette Street.
North Dock Street - Commerce Street.
Back Street " State Street.
North Back Street " Washington Street.
The dotted lines mark new or projected Streets since 1823.
Every House standing in 1823 is marked on the map.
References.
1. Andrew Bell.
2. Matth.s Bruen (Brugh.t House)
3. Abner Woodruff.
4. Episcopal Ch. & Grave Yard.
5. D.o Parsonage.
6. Old parsonage (Gov. Willock)
7. Presbyterian Church.
8. D.o Parsonage.
9. M.rs John Patrick.
10. M.rs C. M. Kearny.
11. Market.
12. Commercial Bank.
13. School House (old Court H.e)
14. Raritan House.
15. Joseph Marsh.
16. M.rs M. Watson.
17. Presbyterian Burial Ground.
18. Arnolds City Hotel.
19. Phoenix Inn.
20. Uriah Burdge.
21. Baptist Church.
22. James Parker.
23. Bruens Stores & Wharf.
24. Steamboat wharf.
25. Miss Parker.
26. Joseph Marsh's store.
27. Benjamin Maurice.
28. Hay press.
29. Hay scales.
30. Marsh's wharf.
31. Patrick's wharf.
RARITAN RIVER
ARTHUR KULL SOUND
Salt Marsh
High Street
Back Street
Market Street
Water Street
Smith Street
Cross St.
South Dock Street
North Dock Street
Centre Street
Broad Street
North Back Street
Road to New Brunswick
Road to Woodbridge
Old Barracks
Scale 12 chs. to an inch.

But, however reasonable such expectations from the given premises might have been elsewhere, at Amboy they were not realized, and probably will not be until more innate energy is possessed. The genius of the place might say to us in the words of the renowned Dr. Syntax:

> "All those to whom I've long been known
> Must see I've habits of my own."

The map here inserted, shows the number and position of the dwellings standing in 1823. It was preferred thus to exhibit the place *as it was*, rather than *as it is*. The dwellings now are probably twice as numerous, and it will be seen from the tables below that the population has more than doubled.

The present act of incorporation was approved February 27th, 1844, by which the government of the city is confided to the following officers, mayor, recorder, three aldermen, six councilmen, clerk, assessor, collector, and treasurer.

The statistics of the population can only be given since 1810, the enumerations prior to that year, giving the number of inhabitants only by counties.

1810.—	White males	358	
	" females	372	
	All the free persons,	36	
	Slaves,	49	
	Total,		815
1820.—	White males,	346	
	" females,	372	
	All other free persons,	50	
	Slaves,	30	
	Total,		798
1830.—	White males,	404	
	" females,	400	
	Free colored,	63	
	Slaves,	12	
	Total,		879

1840.—White males, . . .	587
" females, . . .	678
Free colored, . . .	38
Total, ...	1303
1850.—White males, . . .	885
" females, . . .	918
Free colored, . . .	62
Total, ...	1865

Chapter IV.—The Citizens.

"* * * * * * * to what straits old Time reduces
Frail man, when paper—even a rag like this
Survives himself—his tomb, and all that's his—
And when his bones are dust, his grave a blank,
His station, generation, even his nation
Become a thing, or nothing! save to rank
In chronological commemoration,—
Some dull MS. oblivion long has sank,
Or graven stone found in a barrack's station
In digging the foundation of a closet,
May turn his name up as a rare deposit."

An investigation into the history of Perth Amboy, cannot fail to disclose one characteristic, almost peculiar to itself. Of the families residing within it during the provincial existence of New Jersey, there are but few representatives left, and of the original population, not even one *family name* remains as a memento of the race. Very few, even of those families who, as late as the war of Independence breathed the pure air of the point, and enjoyed the beauties of its situation, are now represented by descendants, who call the place their home. "Old things have passed away," in this respect if in no other, and it may prove not uninteresting to recall from the oblivion which has well nigh covered them a few of those to whom the place may have been indebted for benefits no longer remembered; nor unprofitable to notice briefly their characters and actions, as vaguely set forth in the unsatisfactory records of the past.

Before proceeding, however, with the subject of the chapter, it may as well be remarked that this great change in the population has arisen from several causes; but that two were particularly operative—the want of sufficient business to excite the enterprise and occupy the time of the youth of the city, and the removal, at the revolution, of a large number of the inhabitants.

The first has been always more or less in force since the settlement of the place, but became so especially on the subversion of the royal authority in the province; and the younger members of the different families having changed their residence in consequence of forming connections elsewhere, the family names have become extinct on the death of the parent stocks, and "the place that knew them, knows them no more."[1] The second of these causes was the natural result of the success of the American arms. Being the seat of the provincial government—a military post—and the place of residence of the principal officers of the crown, the interests of the lower, as well as of the higher classes, were too intimately connected with the cause which added so materially to their business facilities, their means of support, or the pleasures of society, to admit of their remaining neutral in the contest: and we consequently find the place noted for the disaffection of its inhabitants to the views and measures of the colonies. The adoption of the royal cause led, necessarily, to the abandonment of New Jersey when that cause failed.

The materials for the notices which follow, were gathered from a vast number of sources, and I regret that I have not been able to rescue more, respecting the worthies of past time, from the obscurity which enshrouds their names and generations.

THE GORDON FAMILY.

Among those emigrants from Scotland, who, in 1684, were induced, by the representations and influence of Governor Barclay, and the other Scotch proprietaries, to leave the country of their birth, and seek in the wilds of America that liberty of conscience and quietness of life which were there denied them, one of the most eminent was THOMAS GORDON, of Pitlochie.

[1] Of 150 persons on the assessors' books as residents, and most of these taxable, in 1802, the names of only 11 remained in 1832, and probably most of these have before this given place to others.

He arrived in the province in October, 1684, with his wife Helen, four children, and seven servants. The vessel on board of which they left Scotland had a tempestuous voyage, in which the bowsprit, and all three of the masts, were carried away, and she, for two or three days, left at the mercy of the winds and waves. By the aid of jury-masts, the Capes of Virginia were finally reached in nine weeks after leaving Aberdeen. The passengers, among whom were two brothers of Mr. Gordon, Charles and George, embarked on board of two sloops, and came up the Chesapeake; and thence "partly by land, and partly by water," to Elizabethtown. Another brother, Robert, came to the province about the same time.[2] George died in 1686, and the same year Charles returned to England, and died in 1698:[3] of Robert no information has been obtained.

It is presumed that these gentlemen were sons of Sir George Gordon, "Knight Advocate," whose name appears in some of the earliest records of the province in connection with theirs; and they are styled "brothers to the Laird of Straloch."

I have been informed[4] that Thomas Gordon was personally known to James II., and received from him various honors and advantages, notwithstanding his political opposition.[5] This aversion to the acts and policy of James finally became so great that he was induced to leave the Gordon clan in an insurrection consequent upon the troubles of 1680, or thereabout: the then Duke of Gordon being nearly related to him. The duke himself, it is said, was saved from attainder, and his property from confiscation at that time by his duchess;

[2] See East Jersey, &c., pp. 313, 319.

[3] Whether he died in East Jersey or Scotland does not appear. The letters from him while in the province, given by Scot, are written with vivacity, and show that he esteemed the country highly. Another brother, Dr. John Gordon, of Colliston, Scotland, was living in October, 1691.

[4] By Mr. L. C. Hamersley, of New York, a descendant.

[5] This must have been during the regency of James as Duke of York, when from motives of policy he endeavored to conciliate the chief individuals of the different clans, although they might be opposed to him and his religion. In 1666, a Thomas Gordon, "writer in Edinburgh," was appointed Clerk of the Court, commissioned to try those concerned in the rising at Pentland; and in 1680, the same individual is mentioned as Clerk to the Justice Court; and in 1682, is admitted Clerk to the Judiciary. Could this have been the Thomas Gordon of the text?

who locked him up in his bedchamber, and prevented his placing himself at the head of his clan when Thomas Gordon presented himself at the castle to resign the command. The unfavorable termination of the insurrection was the immediate cause of Mr. Gordon's emigration.

Mr. Gordon selected his plantation on Cedar Brook, about ten miles west of Amboy, in the vicinity of the present Scotch Plains;[6] and we find him thus writing to a relation at Edinburgh, under date of February 16th, 1685–6:—

"Upon the eighteenth day of November I and my Servants came here to the Woods, and eight days thereafter my Wife and Children came also. I put up a Wigwam in twenty-four hours, which served us till we put up a better house; which I made twenty-four foot long, and fifteen foot wide, containing a Hall and Kitchen both in one, and a Chamber and a Study, which we put up pretty well (with Pallissadoes on the sides and Shingles on the roof) against Yuill [Christmas], on which day we entered home to it: and have been ever since, and still are, clearing ground, and making fencing. So that I hope to have as much ground cleared, fenced, ploughed, and planted with Indian corn in the beginning of May (which is the best time for planting it) as will maintain my family the next year, if it please God to prosper it. Robert Fullerton and I are to Joyn for a Plough this Spring, consisting of four Oxen and two Horses; but if the Ground were once broken up, two Oxen and two Horses, or four Oxen alone will serve; so that the next Spring I intend (God willing) to have a Plough of my own alone. I intend to build a better House and larger, and to make a kitchen of this I am in; which I will hardly get done this Summer, because I resolve to build upon my lot at New Perth. I am settled here in a very pleasant place, upon the side of a brave plain (almost free of woods), and near the water side, so that I might yoke a Plough where I please, were it not for want of Hay to maintain the Cattle, which I hope to get helped the next year, for I have several pieces of Meadow near me." * * * * * "There are eight of us settled here within half a mile or a mile of another, and about ten miles from the Town of New Perth, or Amboy-point, so that I can go and come in a day, either on foot or horseback." * * * * "Blessed be God, myself and Wife, and Children, and servants have been, and are still in good health, which God continue." * * *[7]

His prayer was not granted. In less than two years thereafter wife and children were all dead, and he was left alone in the land of his adoption. This affliction, in connection with the death of his brother Charles, in 1686, which has been mentioned, must have sorely tried him.

[6] The Scotch Plains were so called from the fact that many of Thomas Gordon's countrymen accompanied him, and settled in that region.

[7] See Scot's Model, in East Jersey, &c., p. 336.

Mrs. Gordon died in December, 1687, and was buried in the old, or public burying-place. A large flagstone yet marks the spot, bearing the following inscription, in very antiquated characters, with a skull, crossbones, and hour-glass below it :[8]—

AN*ELEGIE*VPON*THE
DEATH*OF*THE*TRULY*VER
TVOVS*MRS*HELLEN*GORDON
SPOVSE*TO*THOMAS*GORDON
OF*THE*FAMILIE*OF*STRA
LOGH*IN*SCOTLAND*DIED
12*DECEMBER*1687*AGED*27
YEARS.

CALME*WAS*HER*DEATH
WEL*ORDERED*HER*LIFE
A*PIOUS*MOTHER
AND*A*LOVING*WIFE
HER*OFSPRING*SIX*
OF*WH—H*4*HERE*DO*LIE
THER*SOULS*IN*HEAVEN
WI*HERS*DO*REST*ON*HIGH.

The cause of this great mortality is now unknown, but the want of comforts and conveniences which usually attends the settlement of new countries may have had its full influence in producing the painful result. Very little is said any where of the health of Amboy after the settlement was effected, but had such sickness as prevailed in Mr. Gordon's

[8] There is a flaw in the stone, which probably, from the position of the small H in the word "which," was there originally. The last line of the inscription is almost illegible.

family been at all general, some notice of the fact would have come down to us.

Mr. Gordon became a proprietor before he left Scotland by the purchase of one twentieth of Governor Barclay's right, and after his arrival in the province acquired in various ways additional patents, which placed him among those most deeply interested in its soil.

In the year 1692, he was appointed Deputy Secretary and Register for the proprietaries, by William Dorkwra, their chief secretary in London; and the same year was made Clerk of the Court of Common Right, and Register of the Court of Chancery, and one of a commission (with David Mudie and James Dundas) for the trial of small causes, which was established at Amboy. The ensuing year (1693) he was appointed Judge of Probate; and in 1694, an officer of the customs being thought necessary at Amboy (whose duties were somewhat similar to those of a surveyor in modern times), he received the appointment.[9]

These honors, however unimportant the offices may have been in the early days of the province, speak well for the respect and confidence with which he was regarded by the people and proprietary government. The estimation in which he was held by the board of proprietors at this time was also manifested by the selection of him in 1695, when desirous to have some trusty person visit England for the purpose of giving the members there particular information respecting the condition and prospects of the province.[10] He remained there about three years, and received on his return, or soon after (January 22d, 1698) the appointment of Attorney-general of East Jersey. In December, 1700, he was again invested with

[9] He was "to take report of all vessels coming into, or belonging to this province; and to take entries, and give clearances, and to seize all vessels which shall trade (or not duly report) according to the several acts."

[10] A copy of the instructions of the proprietors to him when about to embark (in the handwriting of Andrew Hamilton, afterwards governor, with the signatures attached) is in the library of the N. Y. Hist. Soc., dated November, 1695. The document commences with an expression of their confidence in his ability and integrity, which had led them to choose him unanimously to undertake the voyage for the purpose named in the text. Appended to the instructions, but with lines drawn through it, as if omitted from the copy furnished him, is a passage recommending Mr. G. for the office of secretary, as he was willing to do all the public writing gratis.

the duties of Judge of Probate, a substitute having been appointed during his absence; and in 1702, Dockwra having been superseded, the proprietors appointed Mr. Gordon their chief Secretary and Register. In addition to these numerous offices of a local character, he represented Amboy and the county of Middlesex in the Provincial Assembly from 1703 to 1709, part of the time acting as speaker. In the last-named year, on the arrival of Governor Hunter, he was appointed one of the Council, and held the same situation under Governor Burnet at the time of his decease. From June, 1710, to March, 1719, he was receiver-general and treasurer of the Province.[11]

Mr. Gordon died in 1722, and was buried in the Episcopal churchyard. The following is a literal translation of the Latin inscription on the stone which marks his place of sepulture. The original inscription is much defaced by the hand of time, and a few more years will make it entirely illegible.

"IN HOPE OF A HAPPY RESURRECTION, HERE IS DEPOSITED WHAT IN THOMAS GORDON WAS FOUND MORTAL: WHO, BEING DESCENDED FROM AN ANCIENT FAMILY OF PITLOCHIE, IN SCOTLAND, COULD HAVE GLORIED, HAD THAT BEEN PROPER, IN HIS EXTRACTION; YET IN HIM WAS NOT WANTING THAT OF WHICH HE MIGHT JUSTLY BOAST, FOR AS THE SECRETARY OF THE PROVINCE HE EXERTED HIS BEST ABILITIES IN BEHALF OF THE COUNCILS OF THE STATE ACCEPTABLY TO ALL. DEAR TO HIS RELATIONS, A SINCERE WORSHIPPER OF THE ETERNAL DEITY, HE ENJOYED LIFE, AND DIED WITH RESIGNATION ON THE 28TH DAY OF APRIL, IN THE YEAR OF OUR LORD, 1722, IN THE 70TH YEAR OF HIS AGE.

"HIS MOURNING CONSORT, WHO ALSO DESIRES TO BE INTERRED HERE, HAS CAUSED THIS MONUMENT, SUCH AS IT IS, TO BE SET. HE LIVED AS LONG AS HE DESIRED—AS LONG AS THE FATES APPOINTED—THUS NEITHER WAS LIFE BURDENSOME, NOR DEATH BITTER."[12]

[11] His accounts, as submitted to, and allowed by auditors on his resignation, are in my possession, and are interesting from the light they throw upon the finances of the province at that time, and the evidence they afford of Mr. Gordon's business qualifications.

[12] For this translation I am indebted to the Rev. James Chapman, of Perth Amboy.

Too often, the partiality of friends renders the monumental inscription but poor authority for the general character of the dead ; in the present instance, however, we have no cause to doubt the justness of the terms in which his widow has transmitted to us the memory of Thomas Gordon.

He had married previous to his embarkation for England in 1695, *Janet*, daughter of David Mudie, a merchant of Amboy, who is mentioned elsewhere in these pages, and in his will alludes to her in very affectionate terms. Mrs. Gordon survived her husband for some years, but whether her request, to have her remains deposited near his grave, was complied with is not known—no stone or other memorial being now visible.

Thus to trace Mr. Gordon's career has required an extent of research disproportioned to the result, perhaps, but having formed a high opinion of his character and abilities, it has been to me sufficient reward to rescue from oblivion some of the incidents in the life of one so intimately connected with the early history of the province.

The confidence which appears to have been placed in Mr. Gordon soon after he became a resident of East Jersey, and throughout the period of the proprietary governments, was continued after the surrender to the Crown ; first, by his being selected to represent his fellow-citizens in the legislature, and afterwards by being appointed a member of the Council to two successive governors, as has been stated. And the selection of him by his fellow-members of the Assembly, to be their presiding officer, is a convincing proof of the respect felt for his character and reputation by those best acquainted with him, as it took place at a time when Lord Cornbury, then governor, was endeavoring to injure him in the estimation of the public by speaking of him in his communications to the assembly (although one of that body) in disparaging terms, styling him "one Thomas Gordon" and accusing him of embezzling a portion of the public records : making the accusation as an exculpatory plea for having dispossessed him of the office of register to the proprietors, contrary to the wishes of a majority of the board, and appointed Peter Sonmans to fill the vacancy.[13] In February, 1706, Mr. Gordon had several warrants against him issued, and was obliged to give bail—and in May, 1707, was suspended by Lord Cornbury from practising as an attorney at law—and during an adjournment in May, 1708, three days after his election as speaker of the Assembly, he was arrested by virtue of one of his lordship's own warrants, but was admitted to bail ; although Justice Pinhorne refused him a writ of habeas corpus. This persecution ended with the administration of Cornbury, and in December, 1708, Lord Lovelace reinstated him in his practice in the courts."[14]

Mr. Gordon's generosity to St. Peter's Church, by large donations, elsewhere referred to in this volume, evinced his regard for sacred things, and confirms the encomiums of his widow on his religious sincerity. He left six children.

ANDREW was a captain in Colonel John Parker's regiment, on the frontier, in 1721, and resided at Freehold. On the 5th April, 1723, in order to do away with any legal objections to his father's will, he generously made a declaration of his satisfaction with its tenor, relinquishing all claims to any portion other than that expressly left to him, and confirming all demises to his brothers and sisters, &c. His *grandson* and *heir-at-law*, was John Van Kirk of Cranberry, from which circumstance it is presumed he left no sons.

---

[13] See Smith's N. J., pp. 291, 300, 304, 306, 323, &c., for the messages and answers which passed between the governor and assembly in relation to this and other grievances. As the removal of Mr. Gordon constituted one of the principal complaints against Lord Cornbury, the following references to some of the events connected with it are inserted.

In October, 1704, Lord C. directed Mr. Gordon to deliver all the records to Jeremiah Basse (his private secretary, and former governor of the province), and on the 21st of the same month, Lewis Morris, then president of the board, was directed to write to the governor, and set forth the inconvenience, &c. which would attend obedience. On the 25th, as Mr. G. had not complied with the directions given him by the governor, an order was received by him from the governor and council to do so. Nothing further transpired, Mr. G. retaining the records, until, August 30th, 1705, when Mr. Basse meeting Mr. G. at Shrewsbury, made a formal demand for their delivery to him, and on Gordon's refusing to give a definite answer as to what he might do when in his office at Amboy, he was committed to the custody of the sheriff, and obliged to give bail in £2,000 for his appearance before the governor and council, in October. He did appear *as a representative of the people of Amboy*, and, with the committee of the board of proprietors, had a hearing. On the 27th the board of proprietors ordered that a copy of the records should be made under the direction of George Willocks, John Barclay, and Thomas Gordon, and counsel was appointed to attend the governor and council on the 3d December, to institute objections to the commission of Peter Sonmans—who was *then* substituted by Lord C. instead of Basse, as register. The difficulty lasted during the whole of Cornbury's administration.

[14] Stevens' Index.

THOMAS resided in Monmouth County at the time of his father's death, but afterwards removed to Hunterdon County where he was living as late as 1738. The time of his death is not known, but his descendants are numerous in that quarter of the State.

JOHN is styled "of Amboy," in 1735. His father, the day before his death, gave him half of his plantation on Raritan River, in lieu of all claims upon his estate.[15]

MARY and EUPHAM (Euphemia), are mentioned in his will, but of their destiny nothing is known.

MARGARET was married twice. Her first husband was a French gentleman named Louis Carrée, son of one of the Huguenots who came to America after the revocation of the Edict of Nantes. He was a shipping merchant. They had one child, who died in the West Indies. Mrs. Carrée subsequently married a Mr. Stelle, by whom she had two children, *Thomas Gordon Stelle*, who died unmarried, and *Margaret*, who married Andrew Hamer ley, about 1755. They had five children, William, Louis Carrée, Thomas, Lucretia, and Elizabeth.[16]

THE JOHNSTONE FAMILY,

In 1684, JAMES, and in 1685, JOHN JOHNSTONE, brothers, arrived in the province from Scotland. The first, settled in Monmouth County, near the present site of Spotswood—to which it is presumed he gave its name, as he had resided in Spotswoode, in Scotland. He is presumed to be the James Johnstone son of John Johnstone, of Ochiltree, whose name appears among the list of fugitives denounced in May, 1684, for having been in arms against the government, or been guilty of "resetting" those who had.[17] Scot, in his Model of East Jersey, gives letters from him,[18] stating that he had selected land for a plantation "nine miles from Amboy, and four from Piscataway." His prepossessions, like those of all the early settlers, were strongly in favor of the province, and he evinces a desire to benefit the spiritual interests of the colonists by urging the despatch, as soon as possible, of ministers of the Gospel, promising them "considerable benefices and good estates," and it was to his industry and enterprise the early settlers were indebted for the road between Amboy and Cross-

[15] There was a Peter Gordon in Amboy, in 1737, who may have been a son of John; but the name has long since disappeared from among those of the residents of the old capital.

[16] To one of them, Mr. Lewis C. Hamersley, the author was indebted for the above account of the descendants of Margaret Gordon. He was the last survivor, and died Nov. 4, 1853.

[17] Wodrow, IV. p. 18.

[18] East Jersey, &c. pp. 298, 306, 329.

wicks, it having been laid out and cleared by him.[19] He died about 1698.

JOHN JOHNSTONE, the head of the Amboy family, has already been named among the company on board the ill-fated "Henry and Francis," that arrived in December, 1685. He was a druggist in Edinburgh, and is designated in Scot's "Model, &c." as one of those to whom applications for passages was to be made "at the sign of the Unicorn."[20] He is said by Wodrow to have been married to Eupham Scot before embarcation ; but, while it is probable from the circumstances attendant upon the death of her father, which have been mentioned,[21] that some understanding existed between them as to their future relations, yet the family tradition has been that they were either married on the voyage, or soon after their arrival ; and an old record, the correctness of which there is no reason to question—confirms this last supposition, by giving, as the date of the marriage, April 18th, 1686.

The course of Doctor Johnstone—for he became immediately known by that title—under the responsibilities which devolved upon him subsequent to the death of the Laird of Pitlochie and the landing of the emigrants, has been already made the subject of remark, so that it is unnecessary here to advert to it more fully. Fortunate was it that the sole remaining representative of the enterprising and persevering Scot, possessed in him a kind protector,—one able to sustain her under the trials of the voyage, and the bereavements which enveloped her entrance upon the new world in gloom and uncertainty.

On the 28th July, 1685, the proprietaries in England granted five hundred acres of land to George Scot, on condition that he should reside in the province with his family, and build himself a house therein.[22] On the 15th January, 1685–6,

[19] Proprietary Records, C. p. 120.

[20] East Jersey, p. 333.

[21] See page 31.

[22] The reasons for the grant are thus set forth: "Whereas George Scot, of Pitlochie, in the Kingdom of Scotland, hath with much Industry and indefatigable Paines, Endeavoured the advantage and Promoted the Interest of East New Jersey by Giving that Collony a Character prefferable to Carolina and most other Countryes in America, not only by a certain Treatise he hath written and Published upon the subject for the Invitation of the subjects of Scotland to Transporte themselves

his daughter petitioned the board of proprietors to have the same confirmed to her; and on the 13th January following, her husband was put in possession of the tract, in Monmouth County.[23]

Dr. Johnstone established himself soon after his arrival, in New York, and it is uncertain in what year he first removed to Amboy; it must, however, have been before 1707, as in that year he is mentioned as "of the Jerseys," being the bail of the Rev. Francis Mackemie, when persecuted by Lord Cornbury. For several years prior to that, much of his time was spent on a plantation in Monmouth County, named in his patent (June 9th, 1701) "Scotschesterburg," part of the tract received as a remuneration for the losses sustained by him and Scot, in importing the emigrants by the Henry and Francis.

In 1709, and the following year, he was a member of the Provincial Assembly of New Jersey, but still was occasionally styled "of New York," and in 1720 was a member of Governor Burnett's Council for that province. The governor, however, in 1722, proposed his removal from that post, partly on account of his being constantly with his family in New Jersey.[24]

A few stones remained until recently on the banks of the Raritan, designating the spot where stood the mansion of Dr. Johnstone, which was not entirely destroyed until some years after the Revolution. It was a double two-story brick house, with a large barn and other out-houses near, and attached

thither, but also by Engaging diverse of the Nobility and Gentry (to whom he and his Lady are allyed), to Favour that Interest, and hath likewise undertaken to Freight out a considerable English Shipp, about three hundred Tunes, viz. the Henry and Francis, whereof Captain Richard Huttone is Commander, wherein himself, Lady, and Family, with the servants and Passengers on board that are about to be transported, will be about two hundred Souls in all," &c. E. J. Records, pp. 384–385. There is also on record (D. p. 113), an obligation from Lord Neil Campbell, to dispose of ten thousand acres of land in East Jersey, to George Scot, dated at Edinburgh, 14th August, 1685; and there are other grants at pp. 218, 253, 326. Liber C. p. 244.

[23] Proprietary Minutes, pp. 45, 48, 68, 76, 155. Some delay occurred in issuing the patent, in consequence of the omission of the words "heirs, executors, and assigns," in the grant to Scot. This, however, was overlooked, and in June, 1701, in consequence of a petition for headlands for the people brought over in 1685, the board of proprietors granted to Mr. Johnstone, the further quantity of 30,511 acres, "in consideration of ye great loss they did suffer by importing ye s^{d} people upon ye prop^{rs} incouragement, & w^{h} has Contributed very much to ye good of this province."

[24] Stevens' Index.

thereto was a spacious garden, stored with a well-chosen collection of fruit trees, and a fine orchard, of which a few aged trees yet mark the site.[25] It is thought that a house which stood on the site of the residence of Mr. William Paterson, was also his property.

His profession, in which he was considered skilful, gave Dr. Johnstone those opportunities which are the best calculated to exhibit goodness of heart where it is possessed; and his charity and estimable character earned for him a special notice by Smith, in his history; and on his death the following obituary appeared in the Philadelphia Weekly Mercury.

> "Perth Amboy, Sept. 19th, 1732. On the 7th inst. died here in the 71st year of his age, Doctor John Johnstone, very much lamented by all who knew him, and to the inexpressible loss of the poor, who were always his particular care."

Governor Hunter was warmly attached to him, and James Alexander, writing to Governor H. on 20th Sept. 1732, says:

> "Doctor Johnstone died the 7th of this month, being spent with age and fatigue in going about to serve those who wanted his assistance. I believe his family is left in tolerable good circumstances. I drew his will for him a few days before he died, when, although he was worn almost quite away, he retained his good sense and spirit, and so I am informed he did to the last."

It was not, however, only as an estimable man, and good physician, that Dr. Johnstone was known, he represented the people of Middlesex County, and of Amboy, thirteen years in the General Assembly of the Province, and for ten of them held the honorable situation of speaker. He was one of the commissioners in 1719-20 for settling the boundary between New York and New Jersey, and at different times held other offices with credit to himself.

Dr. Johnstone had several children. His sons were:

[25] This house was fitted up and repaired about the year 1774, for the reception of the family of Charles Pettit, Esq., secretary of the Province, and private secretary to Governor Franklin, who removed to Amboy at the same time from Burlington. Differing with the governor in the great political questions of those days, he removed to Philadelphia about the time the governor was made prisoner. It is probable that the *first* family mansion of Dr. Johnstone's was that hereinafter mentioned, subsequently occupied by his son Andrew, and called "Edinborough Castle."

John (born May 7th 1691), who married a daughter of David Jamison, settled in Monmouth County, and died in 1732. His wife survived him. They had five children, *John*, *Mary*, *David*, *Jamison*, and *Hannah*.

John was a Colonel in the Provincial forces, his commission bearing date, March 10th, 1758, and was second in rank on the Oneida station, in August of that year. He was killed by a cannon-ball at fort Niagara in the course of the war. He married his cousin Euphemia, daughter of Andrew Johnston.

David, who was the heir at law of his brother John, married Miss Walton, and lived and died at "Nine Partners," Duchess Co., N. Y. Their eldest son John, was for some years presiding judge of the Court of Common Pleas for that county, and died August 19, 1850. One of their daughters, "a young lady of great merit and beauty," married John Allen, Esq., of Philadelphia, April 6, 1775; another, the Hon. Gulian Verplanck, M. C., &c.; a third, became the wife of Dr. Upton, then a lieutenant in the English Army, and after his death married Thomas A. Cooper, the tragedian, leaving children by both husbands. Another son, David, died unmarried.

The descendants of *Mary*, *Jamison* and *Hannah*, are said to be numerous in Monmouth County, N. J.

Andrew (born Dec. 20. 1694), who until 1717 or 1718 was engaged in business as a merchant in New York. In Amboy he resided for some time in an old house, that stood back from the street, on the property now belonging to Mr. George Merritt, which went by the lofty title of Edenboro' Castle. This edifice was vacated, and soon after destroyed, on the erection of the brick edifice, now the residence of Mr. Merritt. Mr. Johnston[26] inherited the proprietary rights of his father, and at one time was president of the Board of Proprietors. He also succeeded his father in the Provincial Assembly, as a representative from Amboy, and like him was speaker for several years. In January 1748-9 he was chosen Treasurer of the College of New Jersey, then located at Newark, and held during his life various other offices. The following obituary notice is in the New York Mercury for July 5th, 1762: "Last Thursday se'ennight (June 24th), died at Perth Amboy, in an advanced age, the Hon. Andrew Johnston, Esq., one of His Majesty's Council for the Province of New Jersey, and treasurer of the eastern division of the Province. A gentleman of so fair and worthy a character, that truly to attempt to draw it would be throwing away words. He was really equal to what Pope means when he says: 'An honest man is the noblest work of God!'" "During the last fifteen years of his life," says the historian Smith, "he was in the Council,[27] and a diligent attender on the business there; he had great equality of temper, circumspection of conduct, an open, yet grave, engaging mien, much goodness of heart, and many virtues both public and private." A pencil sketch of him by John Watson is in my possession. Mr. Johnston died in his sixty-seventh year. He married Catharine, daughter of Stephanus Van Cortland of New York, by whom he had two sons and six daughters, viz:

John, who married Isabella, daughter of Robert Lettice Hooper of Trenton, in February, 1768. He was a merchant in Amboy until 1775, in partnership with Peter Barberie; his store standing where one has been kept in late years by Mr. Lewis Golding. In 1767 he was a member of Assembly, and was appointed one of the Committee to correspond with the agent of the Colony in Great Britain, the other members being Cortland Skinner, John Lawrence and David Cooper. He

---

[26] The children of Dr. Johnstone dropped the final *e* from their name.

[27] His commission is in the Rutherford MSS. dated Sept. 21st, 1745.

left several children. Two daughters are thought to be yet living in Nova Scotia, and a son at the West; two other sons and a daughter removed to Ohio, where they left descendants.

Stephen died about 1790. His granddaughter became the wife of General Morgan of South Amboy, and had several children.

Anne became the wife of John Terrill; died before her father, leaving one son, William.

Gertrude married John Barberie, elsewhere noticed.

Catharine became the wife of Stephen Skinner.

Margaret married John Smyth, treasurer of the Province at the time of the Revolution.

Elizabeth and *Mary* died unmarried, and *Euphemia* married her cousin Col. John Johnston.

WILLIAM (born 1696) died April 7th, 1698.

JAMES (born Oct. 3d, 1700) died young.

GEORGE (born Sept. 3d, 1702) died before his father, leaving children whose destination is not known.

LEWIS (born October, 1704) resided in the house then standing near the site of the present mansion of Mr. Paterson, to which it gave place in 1795.[28] He adopted the profession of his father, and was much respected, both as a man and a physician. His education was principally received at Leyden in Holland, then the resort of all who sought the highest scholarship, and after his return to this country he kept up a literary correspondence with several eminent men of Europe. Some interesting letters to him from Gronovius the botanist, written in 1735-6-7-9, are in my possession, extracts from which are given in the appendix to this volume.

Dr. Johnston died November 22d, 1773, at an advanced age, and the annunciation of his death is made in the papers of the day, with the remark that he was "a physician of the highest reputation, and very greatly beloved by all who knew him." He married Miss Martha Heathcote, daughter of Caleb Heathcote of New York.[29] They had two sons and two daughters.

---

[28] It stood a short distance west of the present building, and was advertised for sale by his executors, August, 1775.

[29] Col. Caleb Heathcote occupied an important position both public and private in the province of New York. He was one of seven brothers. Their father, tradition says, was a man of fortune, and mayor of Chester in England. The eldest of the brothers was Sir Gilbert Heathcote, one of the founders and governors of the Bank of England, and lord mayor of London, in 1711. Caleb had formed a matrimonial engagement with a lady of great beauty, but unfortunately took one of his brothers or a nephew to see her, with whom she became so fascinated that he was enabled to supplant Caleb in her affections. This caused him to seek refuge with an uncle, George Heathcote, in New York,* who died unmarried, and left his property to his nephew. Caleb arrived in America about 1692, and married Miss Martha (Patty) Smith, of Long Island.

The New York Gazette of May 30th, 1737, contains the following article, under date of London, March 22d, 1737:

"A curious fine monument is now finished by Mr. Rysbrack, in Oxford Road, and speedily will be erected in the church at Chesterfield, in Derbyshire, on which is the following inscription:

"To the memory of Sir *Gilbert*

* A George Heathcote "mariner of Stepney," was bearer of Carteret's letter to Bollen, from Elizabethtown in 1680, and Groom's attorney, in 1688.

Ann, the eldest daughter, married Captain (afterwards General) John Burnet of the British army, "a fine, gentlemanly fellow," says Mr. Dunlap, in a letter to the author, "remembered in New York." She accompanied him to England, where she was left a widow with one daughter, who died young and unmarried.

Margaret, the youngest daughter, married Bowes Reed, a lawyer of Burlington County, sometimes called Colonel Reed, from his holding that rank in the militia. He was secretary of the State from the Revolution to the time of his death (July 11th, 1794), when he was also register-general and mayor of Burlington. Bishop McIlvaine, of Ohio, is their grandson, and other descendants are living in the western part of the State.[30]

John Lewis, the eldest son, married Susannah, daughter of John Barberie, and settled in Spotswood. They had several children.

Heathcote, the youngest son, was remembered by Mr. Dunlap as a spirited young man, the companion of British officers stationed at Amboy before the Revolution; and engaging in their schemes of pleasure

---

Heathcote, Kn't and *Bart.*, a Person of great natural Endowments, improved by long Experience; Ready to apprehend, Slow to Determine, Resolute to act—a Zealous Friend to the Rights and Liberties of Mankind. In offices of Power and Trust, True to his own and Country's Honour. A great instrument in founding and governing the Bank of England. In the year 1711 was Lord Mayor of *London*: which City he governed with Courage and Temper, after having represented it in four successive Parliaments with Dignity and Integrity from the year 1731.

"A kind Landlord, a steady Friend, an affectionate Relation:
In his character unblemished,
In his extensive Trade without a lawsuit.

"Sir *Gilbert Heathcote*, born at *Chesterfield*, in *Derbyshire*, married *Hester*, Daughter of *Christopher Rayner*, of *London*, merchant: Dyed Jan. 25, 1732-3: Ætat 82. Left Issue, Sir *John Heathcote*: *Anne* married to Sir *Jacob Jacobsen*, of London, Kn't. *Elizabeth* married to *Sigismund Trafford*, of Lincolnshire, Esq. Had six younger Brothers, eminent merchants, happy in his friendship."

A family story respecting Sir Gilbert, represents him to have been called upon one evening by a young spendthrift who wished to learn from him how he had acquired his wealth, or by what course secured it. Sir Gilbert complied with his request, impressing upon him in the first place the necessity of strict economy, enforcing the precept by putting out the lights in the apartment, saying, "We can talk over this matter just as well in the dark."

I have in my possession a copy of the will of Wm. Heathcote, one of the brothers, by which he bequeathes upward of 20,000 pounds besides annuities and his real estate. A copy of Caleb Heathcote's will is also in my possession. He left two sons, *Gilbert* and *William*, and four daughters, *Anna, Mary, Martha*, and *Elizabeth*. One of those became the wife of Lieut. Gov. James De Lancey. His son Gilbert inherited the bulk of his property, and went to England in 1727. There was a Gilbert Heath ote, Lord Mayor of London for part of the year 1742, but whether he was the one or not is unknown. An original letter is before me, addressed to him, on his departure for England by Samuel Clowes, of Jamaica (the first lawyer settled on Long Island), one of his father's executors, giving him advice in relation to his living and company in England. For further information the reader is referred to Bolton's History of Westchester County, N. York.

[30] Mr. Bolton, in his pedigree of the Heathcote Family (vol. 2, p. 102), makes Mr. Reed Governor of New Jersey. He never attained that honor. He also states that John Burnet (or as he erroneously names him, William) was a son of Governor Burnet—which is also a mistake.

and gayety—fond of dress, good living, horses and dogs. He was elected captain of a militia company in Amboy, on the withdrawal of the British troops to join General Gage at Boston. "I, with other boys," says Mr. Dunlap—"all eyes and wonder, looked on in Love Grove, when Heathcote Johnson was saluted captain, I presume, against his wish, but he accepted, and very soon after absented himself. He was in New York during the war."[31] His services were rather brief, considering that he had, in common with the other officers of the regiment, promised and engaged "under all the ties of religion, honor, and regard, to the country," to observe and carry out the orders, &c. of the Provincial Congress.[32] He subsequently went to England, and received an appointment in the general post office. He never married, and died very suddenly, Dec. 13th, 1798, of what was presumed to be "gout in the heart."

The daughters of Dr. JOHN JOHNSTONE were :

EUPHEMIA, born Jan. 18th, 1687, died unmarried, 1723.

ISABEL (born 1688) and KATHERINE (born 1689) died in infancy.

MARGARET, born Feb. 12th, 1693, became the wife of Lawrence Smyth, and the mother of several children.

JANET, born April, 1699, married John Parker, whose descendants are elsewhere noticed.

ISABEL, born July, 1707, who died in infancy;

And MARY, born Oct. 12th, 1710, who died unmarried.

THE SONMANS FAMILY.

The creek or brook which flows into the Raritan from the ravine at the western termination of Market street, is designated on the map of the township as "Sonman's Creek"—deriving its name from PETER SONMANS, who owned the adjoining lands.

[31] Graydon, in his admirable Memoirs, says "I cannot omit to note the attention I received from Mr. Heathcote Johnston of Amboy [Graydon was then a prisoner of war, in New York]; meeting him one day in the street, he stopped me, and in a very friendly manner invited me to spend a few weeks with him at Amboy. This I could on no account have consented to, had I been at liberty to leave New York; but that not being the case, I availed myself of this restriction in declining his invitation. He replied that it might be got over, and that if I would favor him with my company, he had no donbt but that he had sufficient influence to obtain an extension of my limits. I was now obliged to decline his civility in more positive terms, though with a due impression of the liberality and kindness which had prompted it."

[32] This pledge is in my possession, together with other documents relating to his command; showing that he executed an order of his colonel to draft four men from his company, in March, 1776, to make up the number directed to be held in readiness to proceed to New York, when that city was thought to be threatened by the British. *Peter Kenan* was sergeant of this company, and a worthy of the town known as *Ned Aswell*, acted as "*fugleman*" during the week, and on Sunday assisted in the services of the church by responding with stentorian lungs in the office of clerk.

His father, Arent Sonmans, was a Hollander—residing at Rotterdam, and subsequently at Wallingford, Scotland—and one of the twenty-four proprietaries of East Jersey. On becoming interested in the province, he made arrangements for visiting it, but on his way to Scotland from London, in August, 1683, in company with his wife, Robert Barclay, and one other person, when passing through Hunterdonshire, he was shot by a highwayman, in his thigh.[33] In the course of a few days the wound proved fatal, and he was buried in Friends' meeting burial-ground, at Hinton. His wife was named Frances Hancock, and they had three children ; *Peter*, above mentioned, *Rachel*, the wife of Joseph Ormston, and *Joanna*, wife of Joseph Wright.

PETER SONMANS inherited the greater part of his father's property and came over to New Jersey as early as 1688, but probably returned to Europe the same year. In 1705, however, he appears to have arrived again in New Jersey with the intention to remain. He had received his education at Leyden,—had held several offices in England under King William, and, although we shall have occasion to remark that his character was not above reproach, after his establishment in New Jersey he was selected both by the people and the government to fill important stations.[34]

For some time he was one of the Council, and afterward a member of the Assembly, from Bergen County. He was receiver of the proprietary quit-rents, ranger of the forests, surveyor-general, and agent for some of the non-resident proprietors. Lord Cornbury, during his administration, also

[33] In the printed answer in Chancery "Hunt *vs.* Stirling," it is stated that he was robbed of his papers, but it was thought by some that he was killed by an emissary from Holland, on account of political matters.

[34] The Boston News Letter of 12th -19th August, 1766, contains an advertisement which followed him to this country—stating that the queen had granted all the proprietary quit-rents &c. belonging to Arent Sonmans to "Joseph Ormston of London, merchant, and Rachel his wife, and their heirs for ever, in trust for Peter Sonmans, Rachel Ormston, and Joanna Wright, and their heirs for ever,"—and warning all persons from purchasing any portion thereof from Peter Sonmans, who claimed the right to dispose of them. This difficulty was settled by an order in council, February 2d, 1717-18, by virtue of which Sonmans became possessed of all lands already patented in behalf of his father's rights, and Joseph Ormston of the residue, Prop'y Records.

placed in his hands the records of the province, a circumstance loudly complained of by the people, and the Assembly, in not very gentle terms, called in question the honesty of Mr. Sonmans, in their "representations of grievances" handed to the governor at various times: he retorting the accusation upon Thomas Gordon, from whom the records had been taken.

In an address presented in March, 1708, to Governor Lovelace, they accuse him of malversation in office, as one of the judges of the Court of Sessions, and a grand jury, aggrieved by some of his acts, did not hesitate to notify the Assembly in an official manner that he had been indicted at the preceding term of the Supreme Court for perjury and great immorality. And although Mr. Sonmans noticed these accusations at length,[35] it does not appear that he was able to rescue his name from the opprobrium cast upon it; similar accusations renewed at a subsequent period before Governor Hunter, leading to his dismissal from the Council, and probably from his other offices also. It is somewhat remarkable that notwithstanding the strong and apparently well-founded prejudices against him, he should have possessed sufficient influence to have secured among those offices that of Associate Justice of the Supreme Court of the province, to which he was appointed two months before the arrival of Governor Hunter.[36]

The board of proprietors who had intrusted him with the collection of their quit-rents withdrew their authority, and conferred it upon another, but Sonmans still continuing to act, Governor Burnet, in 1726, issued a proclamation pronouncing his conduct illegal and unwarranted.[37]

[35] The document may be found in the State Library, bound up with other miscellaneous matters in the volume entitled "Votes and State Papers, Vol. I."

[36] William Pinborne, was the acting executive for some time before Hunter's arrival, and being unpopular himself, he may have been disposed, in consequence, to regard Sonmans in a more favorable light. We cannot otherwise readily account for his obtaining so responsible an office.

[37] One of the original proclamations is in my possession. The affair was not settled until 1728. James Alexander writing to Cadwallader Colden under date of Nov. 25th, of that year, says; "At Perth Amboy we had hard struggling against Sonmans, and on the information against him for a cheat in receiving improper quit-rents without power, a special verdict was found—which finds that he gave himself out to be receiver, produced a proclamation of Lord Cornbury, &c."

Among the charges brought against Sonmans, as judge, was his prohibiting Quakers from sitting as jurors, which he endeavored to prove was proper. The acts which had been passed for relieving them from some of their legal disabilities, allowing affirmations instead of oaths, &c., did not admit them to the privileges of jurymen, or to any office or place of profit,—and although, in the instructions to the governor, he was authorized to waive these disabilities, in view of the small number of qualified persons that might be in the province on the first settlement of the government, yet, he argued, as there were at that time a sufficient number able to fill such offices, the Quakers should be passed over.

The prejudice continuing—and especially with reference to the act of the Assembly relative to the affirmations of the Quakers—doubts of its validity and force generally prevailing, —Governor Hunter, in 1716, officially, in a proclamation, answered the arguments advanced against their eligibility to office, &c., judging it necessary, he said, "for the satisfaction of the minds of the scrupulous, and stopping the mouths of the clamorous and seditious, until a more effectual method may be pursued, if necessity so require, to set the matter in so clear a light that the half-sighted may see, and the half-witted be convinced of the unreasonableness and absurdity of that objection. The rest can see and understand without any help." And he shows conclusively that the admission of the Quakers to all the rights and privileges of other citizens was clearly in conformity with the instructions of the crown and the laws of the colony.[38] Failing to vindicate his character, Sonmans was obliged at last to leave the province. Whither he removed is uncertain, but probably to Philadelphia. In December, 1712, Governor Hunter informed the board of trade that he was then in Pennsylvania, where he "printed and dispersed his libels against the government." He died in March, 1734, and from the following obituary notice—here inserted as embodying the testimony of a friend in his behalf,—it appears that his remains were deposited in Eliza-

[38] Votes and State Papers, Vol. I.

bethtown. It is from the Philadelphia Weekly Mercury, of April 11th, 1734, and given as an extract from a private letter, dated Elizabethtown, April 1st.

"On Saturday, 29th of March, was here inter'd the Body of *Peter Sonmans, Esqr.*, Chief Proprietor of *East New Jersey.*[39] He was Son to *Arents Sonman*, late one of the States of Holland, which Government, after having finished his Study at *Leyden*, he quitted and came to *England*, where he had the Honour to hold some considerable offices under his late Majesty, *King William*, 1705; Coming a second Time into this Country, where he had so considerable an Interest, He was appointed of her late Majesty's Hon. Council, Agent to the Proprietors, Surveyor General, General Receiver of the Quit Rents, and Ranger of the Forests, as well as Sea coasts. He was, in two succeeding Elections, Chose Representative for the County of *Bargain*, in which Station he manifested himself a true Patriarch to his Country. He was justly esteemed for his Charity and Clemency, his sincerity in Friendship, Patience in oppressions, and undaunted Spirit in Dangers, manifested his first Merit of the Motto of his Arms—*Patientia est Fide.* In *Augustis interpridus*, much more could be said, but for Brevity Sake is omitted."

Mr. Sonmans was married twice—his second wife being Sarah, daughter of John and Mary Nevill, of Stafford, England, and a sister of Judge Nevill, of Amboy, whom he married October 17th, 1723. He left her his sole heiress and executrix, although he had a son—*Peter*,—a practising physician in Philadelphia. Mr. Sonmans appears to have been one of those fortunate personages who enjoy contentions, and would rather attain their end by some tortuous course, abounding in difficulties to be overcome, than by a straightforward procedure, requiring some concessions and accommodation to circumstances. The same amount of energy, exhibited by him in his various conflicts with all parties, directed in other channels, might have made him a prominent benefactor to the people of the province.

Mrs. Sonmans dying in December, 1735, the settlement of the estate devolved upon her brother, who came to America for the purpose, giving him for years much labor and anxiety. The son set up a claim for a portion of the property, and in 1745 Mr. Nevill obtained a release of all his pretensions. In 1747, writing to his friend, Mr. Alexander, he says: "I have made a peaceful end with the *Jews*, and

[39] There was no authority for applying to him the title of Chief Proprietor.

heartily wish it had been done some years ago. Had my unhappy brother Sonmans labored for peace and good neighborhood so much as I do, I should not have had these difficulties to struggle with."[40]

It is thought the son died shortly after the settlement with Mr. Nevill, but whether he left descendants is not known.

THE WILLOCKS FAMILY.

JAMES WILLOCKS, "Doctor of Medicine in Kennay, Scotland," became possessed of a proprietary right to East Jersey in 1683, but died soon after, and his property was inherited by GEORGE WILLOCKS his brother. This gentleman arrived in the province with two servants in 1684, and after remaining here for some years, during which no particular mention of him or of his pursuits is made in the early records, he returned to England; and in 1697 was appointed attorney for his brother proprietaries to collect the quit-rents due to them from the settlers which the disturbed state of the province had caused to accumulate. In furtherance of this arrangement he sailed from England about April, 1698, in the "Despatch, William Fidler, master," and arrived safely at Amboy. On board of this vessel, was a cargo on account of the proprietaries of the value of £500 sterling, with the procurement and disposition of which, it is thought, Mr. Willocks had been also intrusted.[41]

Soon after his arrival in the province he was appointed "Chief Ranger,"—an office with the duties of which I am unacquainted, but which seems, from its title, to have been

[40] Full evidence of the disinterestedness of Judge Nevill is afforded by the fact that, although the heir-at-law of his sister, and, therefore, rightfully entitled to all she had derived from her husband, yet, on his arrival in East Jersey, he entered into articles of agreement with his brother, John Nevill, and Peter Sonmans, jr., to the effect that, so soon as the debts of the estate were paid, an equal division should be made of all the property among the three.

[41] The proprietaries directed the governor to examine the invoices, &c., to see if the goods delivered on shore at Amboy, were bona fide of the value specified in the text. I do not advance this as a proof of a want of confidence in Mr. Willocks, but taken in connection with the fact that Charles Gordon, then in Scotland, in August, 1687, authorized his brother, Thomas, of Amboy, to "call George Willocks to account for all his intromissions as his attorney," it must be allowed to bear somewhat that character. See E. J. Records, Liber B. p. 303.

well suited to his roving disposition, as evinced in his repeated change of residence. He was also appointed one of the Commissioners for the Court of Small Causes.

It appears that he established himself first at Amboy, but soon afterward removed into Monmouth County, and took up his abode at a place then called Rudyard, settled and named by Deputy-governor Rudyard; and his residence there led to a matrimonial connection. In consequence of a refusal on the part of the persons named in the will of the Deputy-governor to serve as his executors, Mr. Willocks became one of the administrators of the estate; a circumstance which brought him into intimate connection with all the family, and Margaret, one of the daughters, having lost her husband, Samuel Winder,[40] was living, a widow, in the vicinity of Mr. Willocks' new abode. It would be assuming too much, to say, from the records, that she was the attraction that drew him to Monmouth, but in a very few months, early in 1699, he became the husband of the widow.

In 1701, Mr. Willocks again made Amboy his place of residence, being appointed, in March, Deputy-surveyor of the Province under John Reid. How long he exercised the duties of this office is not known, but the next year he is represented as living in Richmond County, N. Y., (Staten Island):—is styled "of Amboy," again in 1703, "of Elizabethtown" in 1711, and "of Philadelphia" in 1724.

With the exception of an appointment, March 1720, as one of the Commissioners for settling the boundary between the Province and New York, the offices which have been named were all Mr. Willocks filled, and they were not of sufficient importance to base upon them any estimate of character; but tradition has not coupled his name with any special commendations. Letters which have come under my inspection, indicate considerable business talent, a sufficient cause for his selection to fill the various stations to which he was appointed.

[40] See East Jersey, under the Proprietaries, p. 125. Samuel Winder's mother (Sarah), previous to her marriage with his father, was the widow of John Palmer. Samuel had three brothers, James, Thomas and Charles, the last two dying without issue.

His time appears to have been employed principally in attending to his large landed estate, having become deeply interested in the soil of East Jersey, and this may have occasioned those repeated changes of residence which have been noticed. In 1719 he held the exclusive right of the ferries from Perth Amboy to Staten Island and South Amboy.

In the autumn of 1724, Mr. Willocks took passage at Philadelphia for Europe, but after proceeding down the river as far as Newcastle, he was obliged to return in consequence of some infringement of the Revenue Laws of the Province, by the vessel in which he had embarked.[41] The voyage was subsequently made, however, and it is probable that he resided in London until 1726, when he returned to Amboy, and continued there until his death, in January or February, 1729, after a long and distressing illness. Mrs. Willocks preceded him to the grave, having died in 1722. Of this lady a most favorable account has descended to us: among other good deeds, being the exercise of her influence over her husband to induce the gift of a portion of the land now occupied by St. Peter's Church and Cemetery, during her life, and of other property at his death;—including his own residence, which for many years thereafter was occupied as the parsonage. It continued to stand, though shorn of some of its dimensions, until 1844, when it was taken down. The accompanying sketch represents its appearance in 1832. In "olden time," as late as 1790, it was three stories high, with a four-sided roof.

GEORGE WILLOCKS' HOUSE: THE OLD PARSONAGE.

[41] The letter conveying this information to his Amboy friends, is in my possession. The *Collector*, for some reason, refused to seize the vessel, and the *Governor* caused it to be done by his special authority, which caused a rupture between those two functionaries in Philadelphia.

Mr. Willocks expressed great contrition in his will, or rather acknowledged his great sinfulness, which, whatever may have been his life, we may charitably consider indicative of a change in his sentiments and feelings; particularly as his selection of the Reverend Wm. Skinner, of Amboy, and the Reverend Edward Vaughan, of Elizabethtown, to be his executors, and several donations to churches and charitable purposes, show different associations and dispositions, than under other circumstances could have been expected. He directed a tract of land in Monmouth County to be sold, and the proceeds divided equally between the churches at Shrewsbury, Burlington and Hopewell; and also gave one third of the value of 320 acres to the Episcopal Church at Aberdeen, in his native country, then "just erected," — and an equal sum to be distributed among the poor of the parish of Kennay. He desired that a monument of white marble of the "value of £70, more or less," should be procured in Philadelphia, and placed above the remains of himself and wife; but this does not appear to have been done. A vault, now in ruins, in St. Peter's Cemetery, is known by tradition as "Willocks' Vault," and it may be that the amount devised by him for a monument was expended in its construction. Certain it is, save the tablet erected in 1825 to commemorate their liberality to the Church, there is nothing which records the deaths of George and Margaret Willocks.[42]

Mr. Willocks left no children. The bulk of his property was inherited by a nephew and niece, George Leslie, and Anna, wife of John Ritchie, children of a sister who was yet living in Scotland at the time of his death. Mr. Leslie came to the Province some years before his uncle's death (was with him in Philadel-phia in 1724), and resided for a long time after that event at South Amboy, where he died in 1751. A considerable portion of the property inherited by him was sold in 1742 or 1743, under pecuniary necessity; but at the time of his death he

[42] See subsequent chapter on Religious Denominations.

still held, adjoining the ferry at South Amboy, ten or twelve hundred acres of land.[43]

It was made obligatory on Mr. and Mrs. Ritchie to remove to East Jersey in order to inherit the portion of the estate left to them, and they accordingly did so, bringing with them two daughters, Elizabeth and Magdalen. They experienced some difficulty in obtaining possession of their property, but after a delay of some years succeeded.[44] What became of them, or their descendants, is not known; a miniature likeness of Mr. Ritchie is in my possession.

THE LYELL FAMILY.

David Lyell, whose name is found among the early proprietors of the Province, was a goldsmith by trade ("of St. Martins-in-the-field"), a dependent, tradition says, of a wealthy family in England, named Lorraine, with a daughter or near connection of which he formed an attachment, which proving reciprocal, the lady gave up all for love, and fled with him to a new home in America. He became a proprietor in April, 1697, by the purchase of a forty-eighth part of the Province from Andrew Hamilton, for which he gave £220; and came to New Jersey towards the close of that, or the beginning of the eighteenth century.

He appears to have resided part of his life both in New York (1701-3) and in Monmouth County; and is styled "of Monmouth" at the time of his death. He had a permanent residence, however, in Amboy, his house standing directly upon the shore of the harbor, a short distance north of the Episcopal Church. Under Governor Burnet, from 1719 to 1723 he was a member of the Council. He died in 1726. His wife

[43] His widow, Elizabeth, as executrix advertised his property at South Amboy, Feb'y 24th, 1752. She says there is upon it "a prospect of a sea-coal mine, some whereof has been tried."

[44] I have in my possession a letter from them to the executors, complaining that although five years had elapsed since the death of Mr. Willocks, they had not yet been put in possession of their property, and threatening legal proceedings. This letter is dated Sept. 30th, 1734, but subsequently there are documents on record, showing that they were finally successful, and had control of their lands.

(Sarah) survived him several years, dying November 4th, 1756, aged 86.[45] In Mr. Lyell's will, the following children are mentioned: *David, Catharine, Fenwick, William, Jane, Robert* and *Mary*, but information respecting them is scanty.

Fenwick died in 1742. From letters in my possession, I am led to form a favorable opinion both of his intelligence and education. He filled the honorable station of Councillor under Governor Burnet, as his father had done before him, and was also appointed one of the Council of Governor Morris, who recommended him in 1739 as Deputy Advocate-general in Admiralty for New Jersey, as "a good lawyer, * * * and a person very capable."[46]

David held the office of Postmaster at Amboy, receiving it from Governor Morris, in 1739, but died not long after.

"Miss Caty," and "Miss Jane" are remembered by the aged inhabitants of Amboy, as two unmarried ladies, living in the house at the southeast corner of High and Smith streets. They prided themselves much upon their descent, through their mother, from several noble families of England, and had in their possession, kept with the greatest veneration, a small embroidered pocket-handkerchief — that had come into their possession through the Fenwick family, with whom they were connected — which, they stated, had belonged to, and been spotted with the blood of Charles I., who, on the scaffold, fell a victim to kingly prerogatives, and ill-judged encroachments on the liberties of his subjects.[47] Catharine, as her tomb-stone tells us, died some time before her sister Jane, who lived to be 85 years of age.

One of the brothers had a son *Thomas*, a sea captain, who lived at one time in Willocks' lane. He commanded a Brigantine in the employ of Messrs. Skinner and Kearny, who were engaged in commerce before the revolution; he traded to Madeira and Lisbon, usually making two voyages each year, importing wine, &c., from both places. He had several children. One of his daughters is yet living on Long Island — the widow of James Lent, not long since a member of Congress from New York — and one of his sons (Thomas) removed to North Carolina, where he died in 1796.

---

[45] Three hundred acres belonging to David Lyell, "called Middletown Point," together with two houses in Amboy, &c., were advertised for sale by his executors in January, 1730. His widow then resided "at her house, near Capt. Harmanus Rutgers', in New York."

[46] Morris Papers, pp. 65-66.

[47] This handkerchief remained for several years in possession of the family of Samuel Moore, of Rahway, who administered upon the estate of Jane Lyell, and is now in the possession of Mr. E. B. Thompson, of New York; having within a few years been noticed in the newspapers at different times, as an interesting relic of Charles I. I was always disposed to regard its history as somewhat apocryphal, until some degree of confirmation was given to it, by information received from the late Col. Robt. G. Johnson, of Salem; to the effect that he had in his possession, at one time, an order from Cromwell to Major John Fenwick, to superintend the execution of the King, which service, if performed, would have given him an opportunity to have secured the handkerchief; — rendering its possession by the Fenwick family, and its transmission to the Lyells, less improbable.

THE HARRISONS.

This family seems to have come to the Province from Long Island in 1699 or 1700.

JOHN HARRISON, the senior, it is presumed, established himself either in Monmouth or Middlesex County; which, is uncertain, as he appears to have repeatedly changed his residence. Another, John, thought to have been a son, settled at Elizabethtown, and subsequently removed to Amboy, and was the individual who joined Thomas Gordon, and others, in their liberal donations to the Episcopal Church, which are elsewhere mentioned.[48]

One of the name was a member of the Provincial Assembly, as a representative from Middlesex County, from 1703 to 1716, with some intermissions, but whether it was the father or son, has not been determined. In 1723 the latter was a Master in Chancery, but he could not have received an education,—judging from his letters,—fitting him, properly, for any legal office. In 1709 he was attached to the Northern Army as a Captain of a company, and acted as a Commissary; and several letters, interesting from the details given respecting the troops, the climate, and the condition of the country at that time, presenting a marked contrast to the luxury and convenience that now abound in the same region, are in my possession. They were addressed to Captain Elisha Parker at Amboy, who was charged by the Provincial Government with the duty of supplying the troops on the frontiers, and some extracts from them may be admissible.[49]

"ALBANY, ye 10 of August, 1709.

"CAPT. PARKER,

"Sir:—This Comes to Let you know our wants are great, the weather Cold and Rainy, and we nothing But the Bare ground to Lie on, no tents nor Blankets, which is enough to kill us all, The Indians are Better provided for than we. This is ye first Complaint, which I hope you will speedily take Care of that I may not trouble you any more upon this head. But now Comes another Which this Day I must answer for, Before ye General and

---

[48] See Chapter on Religious Denominations.

[49] The orthography and grammar of the letters, were both so widely *different* from our standards that it was thought expedient to correct the extracts.

ye Commissioners of Albany, to give in a true List of all my men, and also a just account of all ye Provision I have for 72 men, which the General has told, that he may Lay ye same Before the Governor of Boston, and also Before the Governor of Connecticut, and ye Governor of Rhode Island, that they may have a true state of all ye Provision that Is Laid in from Every Province with the number of men. I Dare give in no more men than I have so that I may stretch out that Little provision for forty days, for 72, which is all I Can do, and that will not answer, for the General will have provisions for 60 days from this day. You may know what will Be wanting when you know how many men Captain Lucker has, and how many men Comes from West Jersey. I pray you do not let us want. * * * I pray yōu to let us have good store of good Bread, for to be sure, Every man will have his full allowance of that, which is a pound a piece. We want Bowls or trays to eat out of, but we have nothing; and as for Scales to weigh our provisions we have none nor Can get none upon any terms. You never see such a Country in your Life as this, for there is nothing to be had but Indian trade. Captain Schuyler is extraordinary kind, and will Let me have any thing he has, he has promised to get me some peas as soon as he can get them thrashed, he will supply me with Blankets, But I am loth to meddle with any until I hear from you. The General Is as kind to me as I Can Wish, for he Comes almost Every day to me to Invite me to Dinner with him, and has sent Mr. Reid and myself Each of us a Barrel of Noble Beer to my Lodgings. * * * The Albany people have great faith in our Jersey Commissioners. I am proffered goods By all the Shop keepers In Albany to Let me have what goods I will, and have fitted all my men out Like gentlemen for the warrants I gave them for the seven pound ten a man. * * * I would not for any thing, that the Jerseys should Lose the Credit they have, for they desire no other pay than our money Bills of Credit. Sir, a great many things more I could add, but Comply with every thing I have here writ for, and formerly, and you will much oblige, Sir, your most humble Servant,

"JOHN HARRISON.

"Before I had sealed up your Letter I had one from Lieut. Rudyard, who gives me a very sad account of his March to the Camp. How the wagoners pilfer and steal Both Bread and flour, and Every thing that they Can Come at. I have enclosed his Letter, that you may be the Better satisfied. But for God's sake either send me Blankets, or give me orders to buy them, or we shall starve all our men, you do not think what a noise I have every day about my Ears, first ye General, then ye Commissioners, and the men daily sending for Blankets, for the weather Is three times as Cold here as it is with you. * * * Farewell once more.

J. H.

"But before I take my Leave of you Let me Desire of you to send tents for the Officers, or Else we shall be shouted out of the Camp, and not be able to hold up our heads, for the Indian officers are allowed tents. Let us not Be counted the worst of men when we Look as well as the Best of them all — farewell once more."

"ALBANY, ye 19 of Sept., 1709.

"I Received yours Dated the 25 of August, wherein you seem to be sorry I Bought the Blankets, Rum and Bread of Mr. Wandel, which I think you have no Reason for. * * * Consider with yourself what you would do in frost and snow, and nothing but the Cold ground to Lie on, and but poorly Clothed as it was when I Bought the Blankets; you write me to sell them—Could you believe I kept them a day after I Bought them when the people were ready to tear me to pieces; and if every man had four Blankets a piece, it would not be too much. * * *

"The last week I was at the great Camp, and was entertained by the General very kindly; upon the 14th day of this instant I Left the great Camp, and came to fort Nicholson where my Company is posted, and works Every day as hard as negroes in Clearing of ground, and Building of houses. I stayed but one night there, but was forced to post to Capt. Spicer's company, which is posted at the Little falls, from thence to Fort Ingoldsby, to see what was wanting there, for one half of Capt. Spicer's men are there, and one half of Lucker's, and from thence to the half moon and Sprouls, where the Rest of the men that belong to the Jerseys are posted; you may think with yourselves what trouble I have to travel from place to place, to see that every body is satisfied, which is almost impossible, for they are always grumbling, do I what I can. * * *

"I am put to a very great Charge in travelling up and down, and Likewise forced to endure a great deal of hardship, having nothing but the bare ground to Lie on, with a few bushes about me, which is very hard: but I go through it with a great deal of Cheerfulness, and I bless God I have my health, which is a great happiness.

"This Comes in haste By an Express from the Camp to Bring News of the death of Major Shanks, who died yesterday suddenly. This with my hearty Love and Service to you all, wishing you health and happiness, I Remain, Your Most Humble Servant,

"John Harrison.

"John Reed had like to have been shot by a Mauhauk Indian, but it missed his body and took his horse; he will be at home in a few days, to tell the story himself."

"Fort Nicholson, Sept. y[e] 28th day, 1709.

"Sir:— * * * * You say I should write to you Every week, which I would gladly do, if you would settle the post office here as well as it is with you; however, I have not Been Backward in writing, when any opportunity presented. This is my 17th Letter, as will appear By my Copies, and never Received But three, and them never gave me any answer to mine. * * * * You say we have money and honor, pleasure, and abundance of fine things; I could heartily wish you was But for one week to have the trial; I cannot choose but have a very fine time of it if you do but Rightly Consider, almost Every day travelling a-foot from one place to another, to stop the mouths of so many people who are always Exclaiming against me for one thing or another, Let me do what I Can. I buy Cattle for them, and drive them from place to place where they are posted, and leave here a fat ox or a fat Cow, and so to another place, for our Jersey men are posted at six several places; some ten miles, twelve miles, and some twenty miles asunder, and as fast as I can get them Cattle they Eat them up, or let them run away before they kill them, so that my pleasure is no Rest nor Quiet. I wish you or any body else had my post and all the profit I shall get Besides my Lodging in the woods almost every Night without Clothing, for I Cannot Carry my Lodging upon my back with heavy musket. * * * * My men are all in good health, But forced to work every day Like horses. New England men die like Rotten Sheep, and Come from the Camp every day sick, by ten or eleven of a day, in horse litters. Capt. Lucker's men are one half Run away before Ever they felt any hardships. My men—I mean my one particular Company, is posted at Fort Nicholson. We are employed about enlarging the fort. * * * * I thought you would have sent me some sugar, lime-juice, and Rum for my own use, as you wrote in your Last Letter you would, to Comfort me with In all my troubles and adversities, Being urgent, and the weather very cold. However it is with you I know not, but this part of the world is the coldest and worst that Ever I saw in all my Life; but if it was ten times worse I will not Leave it without the General Leaves, but I do believe in fourteen or fifteen days, you will find enough that wish this. Without any Bitterness or Reflections, I conclude with my Love to you and all our friends in Jersey.

"Your assured friend and humble servant,

"JOHN HARRISON."

"To Capt. Elisha Parker, or Capt. Thomas Farmar, at Amboy, in New Jersey."

Mr. Harrison died suddenly in 1724, from hemorrhage of the lungs, leaving a wife (Elizabeth), and one son (Benjamin). From the inventory of his estate he appears to have been in humble circumstances; but existing documents testify to the regard for him, entertained by his neighbors, and Colonel John Parker acted as his executor.

The following memorandum of the expense attending his funeral and the "going into mourning" of the widow and son, affords an insight into the customs of that day:

	£.	s.	d.
1 doz. Men's Wash Leather Gloves,	1	8	0
1 doz. do. White top't Gloves,	1	10	0
½ doz. woman's white Gloves,	1	10	0
¼ lb. Cinnamon,		10	0
¼ lb. Cloves,		6	0
¼ lb. Nutmegs,		6	0
5 y'ds Black Cloth, of about 24*s.* per yard, or between that and 30*s.*	6	0	0
Lining and trimming,	2	5	0
A crape hat band,		6	0
1 pair men's black leather gloves,		3	0
5 y'ds black Shalloon	1	0	0
24½ y'ds of Lutestring, not exceeding 8*s.* per yd.	9	16	0
5½ y'ds Crape, for a hood and scarf,	1	4	9
1 pair black leather women's gloves,		3	0
1 pair black men's stockings,		12	0
1 pair black women's do.		9	0
1 black handkerchief,		6	0
	£27	14	9

It is presumed the *accompanying* ingredient for the cinnamon, cloves, and nutmegs, was furnished from the cellars of the deceased.

In his will, Mr. Harrison mentioned three sisters ; *Anne*, the wife of Richard Allison ; *Mary*, the wife of Samuel Moore ; and *Sarah ;* and three brothers, *William*, *Henry*, and *Edward*—the last already dead—and desired to be buried by the grave of his daughter.

In 1722, there was an innkeeper in Amboy named William Harrison, who was probably one of these brothers.

THE KEARNY FAMILY.

In 1716, MICHAEL KEARNY, then residing in Monmouth County, purchased a lot of ground in Perth Amboy, on the hill south of St. Peter's Church, and soon after removed thither.

He was originally from Ireland, and his first wife came with him from that country, but died in Philadelphia.[50] Before coming to Amboy, he had married Sarah, daughter of Lewis Morris, afterwards governor of the province. She died at Morrisania, having, so tradition says, foretold the day of her death some time before.

Mr. Kearny had not been long a resident here before various offices were bestowed upon him—among others were the Secretaryship of the province—the office of Surrogate (Oct. 24th, 1720), the Clerkship of the Assembly (Dec. 16th, 1720), and of the Court of Common Pleas (April 23d, 1731).[51] He was yet living in July, 1738, but more than this has not been learned respecting him personally.

For many years before the Revolution the mansion house of the family, standing on the lot which has been mentioned,[52] was occupied by his eldest son, and only child by his first wife.

[50] Her mother's name was Elizabeth Brittain.

[51] He was succeeded by Jeremiah unbar, in Oct., 1734.

[52] It was advertised in March, 1735–6, as "the property of the late Governor Hunter." Philip Kearny, however, *then* lived in it, and probably bought it at that time. When Gov. Hunter obtained possession of it is uncertain, but probably on his accession to the government. The well upon the premises was dug in 1732. Michael Kearny describes it July 22d, 1738, when recommending it for the residence of Gov. Morris, that it had the "best conveniences of any house in town, besides a good stable for three or four horses, and there is a good cellar big enough to hold all his liquors, with lock and key to it."—*Rutherfurd MSS.*

PHILIP KEARNY: he was eminent as a lawyer, and died July 25th, 1775, "universally lamented." He had filled several public stations, been member of the Assembly, &c. He was twice married. His first wife was *Lady Barney Dexter*, whose maiden name was *Ravaud*. His professional services being required by the lady, then in Philadelphia, the consequent intercourse that arose between them changed the client into the wife, and the lawyer into the possessor of the property he was employed to protect.

They had two sons and two daughters; *Philip*, *Elizabeth*, *Susannah*, and *Ravaud*. Becoming a widower, Mr. Kearny subsequently married Isabella, a daughter of Robert Lettice Hooper, of Trenton, Chief Justice of the province, by whom he had issue: *Sarah*, *Michael*, *Francis*, *Joanna*, and *Isabella*. Of these children the following information has been obtained:

PHILIP resided in the house in late years occupied by the Hon. James Parker. He removed to Newark, and left children whose descendants are living in New York. General Kearny, late of the U. S. army, was his grandson.

ELIZABETH became the wife of Cortlandt Skinner, as is elsewhere stated.

SUSANNAH married Richard Stevens, elsewhere noticed.

RAVAUD was educated for a lawyer, and inherited the law library of his father.[53] He lived at one time near South River, and also at Morrisdon, Monmouth County. He married *Ann*, daughter of James Hude, of whom many of the present generation cherish a pleasing recollection, from having witnessed that suavity of manners, and that mild, amiable, Christian deportment, which in old age she retained to a remarkable degree. Mr. Kearny died Sept. 3d, 1806, aged 68, and she remained a witness to the change of times and circumstances, until April 3d, 1828, when at the advanced age of ninety, she followed him to the grave. Their remains moulder in the soil of St. Peter's cemetery. Their children were:

Philip, who went to sea, and died early in life,

James Hude, who died in 1811, leaving a widow and two daughters, yet living at Amboy, *Ann Hude*, married to the Rev. Alexander Jones, D.D., and *Gertrude Parker*, married to Dr. Charles McKnight Smith, and having issue.

Susan Ravaud married the Rev. Dr. John R. B. Rodgers, of New York, and left several children, and

Ann Hude, who married Mr. John G. Warren, of New York, and left several children.

SARAH married Major John Skinner, elsewhere noticed.

MICHAEL married a daughter of Judge Lawrence of Burlington, a sister of Capt. James Lawrence, of the "Chesapeake." They resided in the

[53] He advertised it for sale, February 1782. He then resided at Morrisdon

"Kearny cottage" (still so called), standing on High street, where the father died, and where the widow afterwards lived for many years, having seven sons—John, Michael, Robert, James, Philip, Francis, and Lawrence,—the latter of whom, a gallant officer in the navy, is yet living: one son, William, died young.

FRANCIS entered the Royal service, was a captain in the corps of Colonel Beverley Robinson in New York, and in 1782 was a major in Allen's corps of Pennsylvania Royalists. He rose to a lieutenant-colonelcy, and married in Ireland, whither he went after the war.

JOANNA died unmarried: and

ISABELLA became the wife of a Captain Rogers, of the British army, and was not long since living in Ireland.

The children of Michael Kearny (first named), by his second wife, Miss Morris, were:

MICHAEL, who entered the British navy, and died unmarried.

ISABELLA, who never married—

MARY, who became the wife of James Van Horne,

SARAH,

ARABELLA EUPHEMIA, who married a Mr. Leonard and had one daughter, successively the wife of a Mr. Lawrence, and Mr. John Jacob Faêch—and

GRAHAM (a daughter), who married the Rev. Samuel Cook, and had several children.[54]

THE FARMAR FAMILY.

At the west end of Smith street, in a house now occupied by Mr. Andrews, resided, previously to the revolution, the Farmar family; the children of THOMAS FARMAR, who removed to Amboy from Bentley, Richmond County, Staten Island, about 1711. Both parents, at the time referred to, had been some time dead. Soon after his arrival in the province, Mr. Farmar was appointed, October, 1711, Second Judge of the Provincial Supreme Court, and from March, 1728, to November, 1729, was the presiding Judge of that Court; being succeeded by Robert Lettice Hooper, who had also preceded him in the office.[55]

[54] Ann Kearny, widow and Executrix of John Kearny of New Brunswick, advertised for a settlement of his estate Sept. 29th, 1746; and a Major James Kearny lived near Middletown Point, before and during the Revolution—"a large elegant house," his residence, was burnt down in May, 1772. The relationship, if any, between them and the persons mentioned in the text, has not been traced.

[55] There were several of the name of Farmar in New York connected with the Amboy family. *Samuel*, *Peter* and *Jasper* are thought to have been brothers of *Thomas*. They were all merchants. *Peter* was taken prisoner in 1759, on his way to Louisburgh and Quebec, by a Privateer, and after some delay was sent to Halifax. His return to the city was publicly announced in the papers in September. *Jasper* com-

He represented Middlesex County, in the Assembly, from 1740 to 1743, during Governor Morris's administration, being one of that functionary's supporters in that body. At one time he kept a country store in Amboy, and for some time before his death was insane. He had several children.

ROBERT, who is presumed to have been his eldest son, entered the Provincial Military service in 1740, on the fitting out of the expedition against the Spaniards; raising a company of men which he commanded.[56] He embarked in September at Burlington, but did not finally sail until the following month. He served in the West Indies in Col. Gooch's regiment, and so much to the satisfaction of his superiors that he was ordered, in 1742, by the commanding general, Wentworth, to return to New Jersey, intrusted with the difficult duty of raising recruits. Success seems to have attended his exertions, and he was yet in the province in December of that year, but of his subsequent career nothing is known.

JOHN, said by Governor Morris to be the youngest son of Thomas Farmar,[57] but which he could not have been, followed the example of his elder brother, and, furnished with a letter

manded an Artillery Company in the city, and is therefore generally styled "Captain." On the receipt of the intelligence of the surrender of Fort William Henry, in August, 1757, he gallantly set off with his men for the seat of war. He did not, however, get farther than Esopus, having been ordered back to Col. De Lancey. It is probable that he was previously a prisoner—a Captain Farmar of New York being mentioned as detained at Quebec. He died April 24th, 1758, in the 51st year of his age, after a short illness, and his remains were deposited in Trinity Church. "He was a gentleman," says a newspaper of the day, "remarkable for a noble spirit of patriotism; no fatigues, difficulties, or dangers, when his country's good required it, could in the least discourage it. The various instances he has given of his uncommon loyalty are too numerous and too deeply impressed on the minds of all those that knew him to require a present recapitulation. His honesty in trade, his affable, humane and generous disposition, procured him not only the good will and affection of his intimate acquaintance, but likewise of all such as had the least knowledge of his character, which nothing could more sufficiently evince than the universal sorrow and dejection displayed by the inhabitants of this city on the news of his death. The second Independent Artillery Company, which he himself raised and commanded, testified their high respect towards him by a voluntary appearance under arms at his funeral; marching before his corpse to the grave, and performing the military ceremonies with unusual solemnity." [Twelve lines on his death follow this obituary ending,]

"Let this be said, this never be denied,
Farmar beloved lived, lamented died."

[56] "He is a vain young man, but to do him justice has been very diligent in getting his company together." So wrote Governor Morris to Adjutant-general Blakeney. See Morris Papers, p. 102 and p. 157.

[57] See Morris Papers, p. 148.

of introduction from Gov. M., sailed for the West Indies in July, 1742, as a volunteer, but nothing is known of him subsequently.

CHRISTOPHER, another son, took the name of BILLOP, which was the maiden name of his wife, and with it inherited a large estate on Staten Island, part of which—the southern termination of the island—is yet known as Billop's Point.[58] His residence, yet standing, although antiquated and neglected in its appearance, is a prominent object in the view of the traveller between New York and Philadelphia by the Camden and Amboy route. While occupied by him it was surrounded by fruit trees and cultivated grounds, and wore the aspect of gentility and comfort. The dilapidated condition of the house adds not a little to the interest it possesses as a memento of the ante-revolutionary period, and also from its having been the place of conference between the American Commissioners and Lord Howe in 1776.[59] Mr. Billop, or, as he was generally called, Colonel Billop—from his holding that rank in the Richmond County Militia, and subsequently in the British army—was a man of courage and energy, of high standing in the province of New York—of the Assembly of which he was a member for some years. On the commencement of hostilities, Mr. Billop warmly engaged on the side of the royalists and aided in raising what was called 'the New Corps,' in which he received a

[58] The first of the name of Billop noticed, was Christopher Billop (son of "Christopher Billop, Gent., of London"), who was commissioned Lieutenant of the New York troops in 1674, but was subsequently, for some misconduct, superseded. What became of him is not known, but it is presumed that it was his son, a Capt. Christopher Billop of the British Navy, who married a sister of Judge Thomas Farmar, and obtained a patent for one thousand or fifteen hundred acres on Staten Island. A tradition, preserved in the family, makes the patent to have been a gift from the Duke of York for bravery displayed in a naval engagement in which the vessel he commanded was blown up. Charnock in his *Biographie Navalis* mentions a Christopher Billop, who was a Lieutenant in the British Army in 1671, appointed Captain in 1673, and in 1692 was in command of a ninety gun ship, and the year following commanded a first-rate. He was living in London unemployed in 1699. As the time of his death was not known, it is not improbable that he was the Capt. Billop who married Miss Farmar. He had two daughters—the youngest of whom married the Rev. Mr. Brook, Missionary in New Jersey, and after his death became the wife of Rev. Wm. Skinner, of Amboy, but died without issue—the eldest married her cousin, Christopher Farmar, noticed in the text, and she being the sole heiress of her father, the estate was left to her husband, on the condition that he should assume the name of Billop.

[59] See Newark Daily Advertiser, July 23d, 1851, and John Adams's Diary.

Colonel's commission. It is thought that his services, which were of an active partisan character, were confined to Staten Island. Being well known in the eastern section of New Jersey, the possession of his person was frequently attempted to be gained by the spirited "rebels" of the neighborhood, and at last on the 23d June, 1779, he was taken prisoner by a small detachment of continental troops, commanded by Capt. Nathaniel Fitz-Randolph (or Randall as he was more generally designated) of Woodbridge, the party surprising him in his own house and bringing him over to New Jersey.

In what place he was first confined is not known, but in November, Col. Billop was sent to the Burlington Jail;—the sergeant of the guard escorting him, being the bearer of the following mittimus:—

"*To the Keeper of the Common Jail for the County of Burlington—Greeting:*

"You are hereby commanded to receive into your custody the body of Col. Christopher Billop, prisoner of war, herewith delivered to you, and having put irons on his hands and feet, you are to chain him down to the floor in a close room in the said jail; and there so detain him, giving him bread and water only for his food, until you receive further orders from me, or the Commissary of Prisoners for the State of New Jersey for the time being. Given under my hand at Elizabethtown this 6th day of November, 1779.

"ELISHA BOUDINOT, Com. Pris. New Jersey."

Not long after Col. Billop fell into the hands of the Americans, the fortune of war had placed his captor, Capt. Fitz-Randolph, in the power of the enemy,[60] and it is rather remarkable that they should in consequence have become the

[60] He was taken prisoner in February, 1779, by a party commanded, it is said, by one Smith of Staten Island, but Smith was probably the guide, the newspapers of the day stating that the party was commanded by Captain Ryerson; and was exchanged, it is thought, for Captain Jones of the British Army, who was captured for the purpose by some of Fitz-Randolph's followers at what was known as the "Half-way House," between the New Blazing Star and Ryerson's Ferry, on Staten Island. Previous to his capture (December, 1778,) the Legislature voted Fitz-Randolph a sword. He was exchanged in May, 1780, but died of a wound received at or near Elizabethtown, in the skirmishes attending the expedition of the British to Connecticut Farms and Springfield, in June the same year.

His remains were deposited in the Presbyterian Cemetery in his native village, and a simple headstone marks the spot, bearing the following inscription:—

SACRED
to the memory of
Capt Nathaniel Fitz Randolph, who died
July ye 23d A D 1780,
in the xxxiii year of
his Age.
Here lies beneath this Stone repos'd
Patriot Merit straitly hous'd
His Country call'd he lent an Ear
Their battles Fought and rested Here.

"He was active, bold and intelligent," says Mr. Dunlap in a letter to

sufferers by the retaliatory measures adopted by their friends as the means of effecting a melioration in their respective conditions. There can be no doubt of Capt. Fitz-Randolph's having suffered greatly in New York, but the treatment received from the English by him and other Americans affords but a poor apology for the inhumanity directed to be exhibited towards Col. Billop.

Accompanying the document given above, was the following letter addressed to the Colonel himself, stating the grounds upon which his treatment was based :—

"Elizabethtown, Nov. 6th, 1779.

"SIR,—Sorry am I that I have been put under the disagreeable necessity of a treatment towards your person that will prove so irksome to you; but retaliation is directed, and it will, I most sincerely hope, be in your power to relieve yourself from the situation by writing to New York, to procure the relaxation of the sufferings of John Leshier and Capt. Nathaniel Randall. It seems nothing short of retaliation will teach Britons to act like men of humanity.

"I am, sir, your most obedient servant,

"ELISHA BOUDINOT, Com. S. Pris.

"Col. Christopher Billop,
"Burlington."

It was not until the 26th December, that Col. Billop was released from his ignominious confinement ; Colonel Hendrickson of the American army arrived at Burlington at that time, on his parole, for the purpose of effecting an exchange.[61] After the war, Col. Billop removed with some of his family to the Province of New Brunswick, where for many years he filled important offices and took an active part in public affairs. In 1823, as a member of the Council, he claimed the Presidency of the Government on the death of Governor Smythe, but did not succeed in securing it. He died at St. John in 1827, in his ninetieth year. His wife, Jane, died there in 1802.[62] He had five daughters, two of whom married gentlemen of the name of *Seaman*, whose descendants are numerous in New York and on Staten Island, and the others married

me, "and had a contrast in a brother, Ezekiel, a butcher, who was dull, forgetful and sleepy, remarkable for leaving to his horse the guidance of his butcher's cart."

[61] Simcoe's Journal, pp. 268 to 285.

[62] She is said to have been aged forty-eight. If so, it must have been a second wife.—*Sabine's Royalists.*

distinguished individuals in New Brunswick. One son entered the counting house of an uncle in London, and another was at one time in business in New York, but having joined in the expedition against the Spaniards in South America, under Miranda, he suffered death at Porto Cabello with several of his companions.

THOMAS FARMAR, unlike his brother Christopher, was a stanch whig, and joined the colonists in their struggle for liberty. He turned out in the militia with his musket as a private, but it is not known that he was in active service. He married a cousin, the daughter of Samuel Farmar of New York, and after her death the widow of his younger brother. He died August 27th, 1822. A tablet is erected to his memory in the walls of St. Peter's Church, Perth Amboy, and his remains moulder in its cemetery. He left no children. In 1782–3 he resided on a farm situated on the Raritan, but removed to New York and engaged in mercantile business. His widow survived until 1849.

JASPER, thought to have been the youngest son, entered early into the English army. He was extremely prepossessing in his appearance, and Mr. Dunlap says, "one of the few pictures by Reynolds in this country is of Jasper Farmar in his youth," in whose possession he does not state. He married the eldest daughter of Cortlandt Skinner, elsewhere noticed, and had several children, one of whom, a daughter, who became the wife of a Mr. Murphy of Nova Scotia, left several children; she and one son perishing by shipwreck on the coast of Long Island in 1850. After the death of her husband Mrs. Farmar became the wife of her husband's brother, as above stated.

There were several daughters in the Farmar family.

One married Effingham Lawrence, commander of a merchant vessel out of New York, and afterwards a successful merchant in London. They had three sons, William Effingham, Effingham, and Edward Billop, and one daughter, Catherine Mary, who in 1816 married Sir John T. Jones, Bart., of Cranmer Hall, Norfolkshire, England, Aid to the Duke of Wellington.

Another became the wife of a Captain Davis, who also resided in London.

A third, Rachel, married Peter Goelet of New York, and left two sons. After her death, Mr. Goelet married another sister.

The youngest, Sarah, who was celebrated for her beauty, married Dr. Alexander Ross of New Brunswick (originally from Jamaica); but the physician could not cure himself, and died; his widow having a liking for the profession, removed to New York and married a Dr. Howard of the British army, and left children.

The names of Farmar and Billop are no longer familiar words in the vicinity where once they were heard, and as "the stranger parts the flaunting weeds" from the neglected spot where

THE GRAVES OF THE HOUSEHOLD

were made, with no stones nor monuments (save of two connections) to perpetuate their "name and generation," and marks the aspect of all things around what was their temporal habitation, thoughts sad, though perchance instructive, are aroused; but "there may be," in the language of Dickens, "people in the world at this instant, far away from here, whose good actions and good thoughts are the deeds in which those dead may be best remembered."

ELIAS BLAND.

Mercy, daughter of Thomas Hart, one of the twenty-four proprietaries, married Walter Benthal,—subsequently, also a proprietor,—and their daughter, Priscilla, became the second wife of John Bland, goldsmith (son of Elias Bland, carpenter), who had, by a former marriage, two sons, Elias and John, the former of whom is presumed to have been the gentleman several times mentioned in these pages, as living at the southern termination of High street, opposite the Long-ferry tavern.

He has been described to the writer as an eccentric individual, who came to this country—called probably by a landed interest derived from his mother-in-law—leaving his wife behind him.

His establishment was an exceedingly comfortable one, and with no other inmates than his servants, he resided in Amboy several years. Tradition represents him as having been very fond of children, doing all in his power to induce them to visit him, by making them presents, and giving them entertainments at his house.

It is probable he returned to England, as the name of Elias Bland, banker, of London, is met with in connection with the affairs of Amboy, in 1771; subsequent to which time nothing is known of him. A memorial of his taste for pictures —a copy of Earl's engraving of "Elijah Raising the Widow's son," by Rembrandt—is in my possession. There was a wharf before his house, and a ferry thence across the Raritan, which went by his name.

THE SKINNER FAMILY.

Among the most influential families of the ancient capital, were the Skinners, descendants of the Reverend William Skinner, the first rector of St. Peter's Church. This gentleman was a MacGregor, and among those of that clan proscribed after the rebellion of 1715, having taken an active part in the restoratory struggles of the Stuart family. He had received a superior education at one of the first literary institutions in England (thought to have been Oxford University), and possessed mental endowments of a sterling character. Obliged to leave Scotland after the battle of Preston Pans, in which he was wounded, and prevented from bearing the name of his clan, he assumed that of a friend in Edinburgh, from whom he received favor and protection.

As William Skinner, he left England for Holland, in company with Lord Belmerino, and subsequently, by way of Barbadoes, or Antigua, came to Philadelphia, where he had, or made, a friend in a Mr. Logan,—one of the family of so much notoriety in the annals of Pennsylvania,—with whom he found a home ; probably in the capacity of tutor, as it is understood the sons of that gentleman received from him instruction in the languages, which he was well qualified to impart.[63]

Mr. Skinner probably pursued theological studies while residing in Philadelphia ; for after a few years he returned to England, and received ordination from Robinson, Bishop of London. While there (in 1721) he was appointed missionary to Perth Amboy, from the "Society for Propagating the Gospel in Foreign Parts," and entered upon his labors in September, 1723. The following year he was called to the rectorship of St. Peter's Church, and for thirty-five years continued to discharge his duties faithfully and acceptably, occasionally officiating in the neighboring towns ; death putting an end to his earthly career in 1758, in the 71st year of his age. His remains were deposited in the rear of the Church, but the precise spot not having been marked by any monument, is now unknown.

Mr. Skinner is said to have been exceedingly kind-hearted, generous and hospitable; and—almost a necessary consequence from the possession of these virtues—very regardless of money; living unostentatiously himself, in order that his resources might be greater for his charities ; fully complying with the

[63] He had other pupils also, for the Rev. Mr. Talbot who arrived with Mr. Skinner at Philadelphia in 1722, advocating the establishment of a free school or college at Burlington, says, "several of Mr. Skinner's scholars at Philadelphia are fit for the Academy."

directions to all their missionaries by the society, in whose service were his first ministerial labors; "that as they be frugal in opposition to luxury, so they avoid all appearance of covetousness, and recommend themselves according to their abilities by the prudent exercise of liberality and charity."[64]

He was twice married. His first wife was a daughter of Christopher Billop, of Staten Island, and the widow of the Rev. Mr. Brook, one of the society's missionaries, whose indefatigable labors in New Jersey are elsewhere alluded to.[65] His second wife was *Elizabeth*, youngest daughter of Stephanus Van Cortlandt of New York.[66] His children, all by this lady, were—one daughter, *Gertrude*, who became the wife of James Parker, and was the mother of the present elders of that family;—and four sons, 1 *Cortlandt*, 2 *Stephen*, 3 *William*, and 4 *John*—who will be noticed in succession.

CORTLANDT, the eldest son of the Rev. William Skinner, was educated for the bar, studying the profession in the office of David Ogden, an old and distinguished practitioner at Newark, at which place he also, for some time, was established after his admission to practice.

In 1652 he married *Elizabeth*, daughter of Philip Kearny of Amboy, and shortly after, if not before, took up his residence permanently in the place of his birth. Although not of studious habits, he became eminent in his profession, his natural abilities being good, and his oratorical powers consider-

[64] See Rules and Regulations of the society for the government of the missionaries and schoolmasters.

In July, 1749, when 62 years of age, he thus wrote to the secretary of the society. The extract shows some of the privations and trials which encompassed the early missionaries to New Jersey:

"Now is my time of trial. In this extraordinary dry and hot summer, hitherto, since Whitsuntide, I have gone, and to the end of October, must go, to South River every Sunday. In doing which I must cross a river almost two miles broad, and that done, ride twelve miles in the sand, equally scorching with those of Arabia, and not a house by the way, excepting one by a saw-mill, and that good for no thing.

"This is hard service at the present time of day with me, for I am old, and also much worn out. * * * * My lot has been hard, for I have these twenty-seven years had the most laborious, and least profitable mission to the society, * * * * and it is too late to sue for a separation." See Chapter on Religious Denominations, and the notices of Piscataway, in Chapter XI. for a more particular account of Mr. Skinner's services. His letters contain abundant proof of his efficiency and of his self-denying labors.

[65] See Chapter on Religious Denominations.

[66] For genealogical table of the Van Cortlandt family, see Bolton's Westchester.

ably above mediocrity. He was soon appointed the King's Attorney-General for the province, and continued to hold that office until the Revolution put an end to the authority whence it was derived. In 1761 he was elected to the Provincial Assembly from his native city, in the place of Andrew Smyth, deceased, and continued thereafter to be a prominent member of that body while it existed : in 1765 (Nov. 28th) receiving a convincing proof of the esteem and confidence of his associates in their choice of him to be Speaker.

During the early stages of the struggle for independence, Mr. Skinner, like many others who in the end became royalists, was strongly opposed to the encroachments of the British Ministry upon the liberties of the colonies ; and his being chosen speaker, to succeed Robert Ogden,—whose course as a delegate from the province to the New York Congress had so displeased his constituents as to lead to his resignation,—together with his appointment, at the same session, as one of the Committee to correspond with the agent of the colony in England, shows conclusively that he was considered to be a friend to the colonial cause at that time.

We are admited, however, into a closer communion with him, on the exciting subjects of the time, by finding the following passages, in a letter to Governor Boone, dated October 5th, 1755.

"Every thing here is in the greatest confusion, and the first of November dreaded. The laws of trade hâd ruined the merchants, and drained the colonies of their silver. Little was left after paying the duties, to pay their debts in England. Without money no clothing can be got, and woollens must be had in this climate; great attention was therefore given to manufactures on which considerable advances are made, but the want of wool and manufacturers, are difficulties not easily removed. Discontent was painted in every man's face, and the distress of the people very great, from an amazing scarcity of money, occasioned by the sudden stagnation of trade. At this time (and a more unlucky one could not have been chosen) the Stamp Law and Mutiny Bill found their way through parliament.

"Upon these laws all restraints were broken through, and the papers will abundantly show you the violence and fury of the people. Great pains have been taken by some writers to expose the laws, and show the people that they are deprived of all liberty, and contributed not a little to the outrages that have been committed. The increased jurisdiction of the Courts of Admiralty, and the restraint on the press by the Stamp Law, have been the subjects and employment of their pens, which they have taken care to dip, if not in gall, yet abundantly in scurrility and abuse, if not in *treason.* With great difficulty the people have been restrained in this province, but how long it will be in the power of the magistrates to prevent disorder I know not. As the day approaches on which the Stamp Law is to take effect, fresh causes present themselves to fear great disturbance. * * * * It is hoped that with the new ministers will follow a change of measures, and that the interest of Britain with respect to her colonies will be better understood, and the colonies relieved both from duties and stamps. I wish it may prove so; for if the interest of Britain is adhered to, it will be best advanced by encouraging the colonies in their trade to the West Indies. While that continues, agriculture will be their only employment, and they will not then (as it will not be their interest) think of manufactures; but solely attend to the improvement and settlement of lands. Without trade they have no money, and every body knows that all the money they can get will not pay for the necessary clothing from Britain; consequently they cannot pay taxes. But the wealth flowing from trade will be more for the interest of Britain than all the taxes that can be imposed on the colonies. * * * * The protection of the colonies is made the pretence for taxing them. This is assistance indeed. Garrisons may be necessary at Quebec and Montreal, but what occasion is there for garrisons and forts hundreds of miles in the Indian country. These are so far from protecting, that they are the very cause of our Indian wars, and the monstrous expenses attending them. Before we had these forts we had no wars with the natives, they were our friends, and will be so again when we withdraw the French settlers and our garrisons from their country. Their quarrel with us is, that we will take their lands, and treat them as a conquered people. All we want with them is their trade, which we can never enjoy with any advantage until we remove their jealousy. When this is done we shall live in all the security we have heretofore enjoyed, when a few independent companies were sufficient for the continent. And why cannot we do without so many regiments when every enemy is removed at least a thousand miles from our borders?

"But independence is suggested and made the pretence, more than a fear of Indian inroads. Those who make these suggestions are enemies to their country, and are most likely to put the thought into the heads of the colonists by the very means they take to *prevent* dependence. Separate governments and an encouragement to agriculture and settlement, will effectually fix it. Taxes and a restraint on the West India trade are most likely to force the colonists into manufactures and put independence into their heads. *They are in the high road to it now, and though 'tis true that they have not strength to effect it, but must submit, yet 'tis laying the foundation for great trouble and expense to Britain, in keeping that by force which she might easily do without, and alienating a people which she might make her greatest prop and security.*"

To another correspondent he wrote:—

"Winter with us, you know, is a season when the farmer has little to do. Snow enables him to travel cheap and with expedition. The times will furnish him conversation, and disorder, I fear, will be the production of this winter's meetings. Nothing can prevent it but a repeal of the laws that occasioned it, in which Britain is more interested than her colonies. Temporary distress is all the colonies can fear; a very short time will enable them to clothe themselves, and they can live well without any West Indian produce or that of any other country. When necessity has made them accomplish these two points, the consequences are not to be thought of without horror."

The sentiments thus expressed to his private correspondents were also conveyed, but in a formal manner, in his official letters to the Colonial Agent at this time; and all his influence, which was very considerable, was exerted to bring about a restoration of the harmonious relations which had previously existed between the mother country and her American dependencies.

Such continued to be his position until the first blood was shed at Lexington, and the more decided measures of the colonists prompted thereby caused a marked distinction to be drawn between the friends and the, so-considered, enemies of the country. From Mr. Skinner's official relations to the government it was to be presumed that his conduct would be scanned with a watchful eye and his words studiously criticised, and subsequent events proved that it was no ill-founded foreboding that led his wife to write to him—he being then at Burlington—on receiving the news of the engagement at Lexington; "I could not help being alarmed. God protect and defend *you*."[67]

It is not surprising that Mr. Skinner should have found it difficult to discern in the *acts* of the provincials any thing confirmatory of their repeated expressions of abhorrence to independency which were so frequently uttered; there were many others equally blind; but he appears to have prudently abstained from all proceedings calculated to embroil him with those who thought differently from himself upon the great questions at issue. The only instance discovered of his incurring the displeasure of the numerous committees of observation by which he was surrounded, consisted in his being found guilty by the Committee of Morris County, on Sept. 28th, 1775, of having 'spoken disrespectfully of the Continental Congress, reproaching the minute-men, and charging them and the county with protecting a supposed criminal from justice.' To this charge he made such explanations and apologies as were deemed satisfactory by the Committee; but soon

[67] She adds "a letter just received from * * * * gives a circumstantial detail of the affair, and assures them that the provincials fired first, and that the troops did not fire till so harassed they could not avoid it."

after he was obliged to seek, in an open avowal of his loyalty and refuge beneath the English flag, that personal safety which he could no longer enjoy within the bounds of New Jersey.

In December a letter of his was intercepted, addressed to his brother, Lieut. Col. William Skinner, in England, which contained the following language:—

"* * * * I have always fondly, I may say foolishly, hoped that the unnatural dispute now subsisting would have an amicable conclusion. I find myself sadly disappointed. The tea duty began the controversy: it has branched out into divers others, and now the contest is for dominion. For the rise of the dispute we are indebted to smugglers; for the present state of it, to the pride, ambition, and interest of those who, enemies to the ecclesiastical establishment of their country, have long plotted, and to others who have become of consequence in the struggle. They who began had their interest in view, and feared the ruin of their smuggling; here they, I believe, were willing to leave the dispute. The others, with deeper views, keep it up, and, building on the foundation, are attempting a superstructure (a republic) that will deluge this country in blood. This is not new. All history, as well as our own, shows great convulsions, rebellions and revolutions, from mad enthusiasm and designing men; and the last spring up like mushrooms. We are now upon the eve, I may say, have actually begun a revolution. The Congress are our King, Lords, and Commons. They have taken Canada, with the consent of its grateful inhabitants; they block up the Royal Army in Boston; they say they have secured the Indians; have appointed an Admiral; are fitting out a fleet, and are universally obeyed. Is this, or is it not, independency? They say it is not! and we must believe even against our senses. An edict, manifesto, or what you may please to call it, has been issued from the Congress: in which they say, "We have taken into consideration a proclamation issued by the Court of St. James"—meaning the late Royal Proclamation. You will soon see it. I fear bad consequences will attend the mistaken people who are so obstinately loyal as to favor the Royal cause. Where or what will be the end I know not. The mistakes of Generals and Admirals, and the strange security in sending succors, ammunition, &c., to this country, amazes me, while success here in every mad measure vexes me. The saints say, Heaven is on their side: I rather think the old saying more applicable, "The devil is kind to young beginners." We must have in every war a campaign, at least, of blunders. This may be called so, from the ill-timed march to Lexington to the losing of Canada. Another year may set us right; but not, if we only succor Boston. A few regiments and fleets to different Provinces will set us right; at least bring us to our senses, and support the friends of Government. But I have said enough on this disagreeable subject; you will know every thing from the papers, though, now Rivington is suppressed, you can hear only one side of the question." [68]

This letter was sufficient to condemn him. On the 9th January, 1776, it was laid before Congress, and it was

"Ordered, That a certified copy of the intercepted letter of Mr. Cortlandt Skinner be sent to the Committee of Safety for New Jersey."

[68] American Doc. Hist., 4th Series, Vol. 4, p. 363.

"That orders be sent to Lord Stirling to take with him a sufficient force and immediately apprehend and keep in safe custody the said Cortlandt Skinner of Amboy, till further orders from this Congress."

"That he carry said Cortlandt Skinner before the Committee of Safety of the colony of New Jersey for examination."

"That the said Committee be directed to present his examination to Congress."

A copy of the intercepted letter was received by the Provincial Congress from Lord Stirling on the 5th February, but no action was had by that body upon it until the 2d March, when, in consequenee of the "many sentiments and expressions prejudicial to the peace and welfare of the united colonies" which it contained, the Treasurers of the colony were requested not to make any farther payments of salary to the Attorney-general: this being all that the Congress could do, Mr. Skinner having "left the colony."

In the office of Mr. Skinner, as students of law, there were, on the breaking out of the Revolution, two young men whose courses throughout the struggle were very dissimilar. One of them, the son of a British officer, the late highly esteemed and venerable Andrew Bell, of Perth Amboy, from previous education and associations was led to embrace the royal cause with his legal preceptor, went to New York and became one of the Private Secretaries of Sir Henry Clinton.[69] The other was Joseph Bloomfield, who espoused the Colonial cause, and subsequently served his native State both in military and civil stations.[70] On the 7th February, Mr. Bloomfield was appointed by the Provincial Congress, a Captain in the third battalion of provincial troops, and the first duty he undertook, or upon which he was sent, is believed to have been the arrest of his former friend and adviser, Mr. Skinner. It is to be hoped that the duty was delegated—not assumed. We will not venture to analyze the feelings with which the house in which he had ever found a home was *carefully searched* in the hope of securing the convicted loyalist. Fortunately its

[69] He was with the English Army in its retreat across New Jersey, prior to the battle of Monmouth, and a Diary kept by him during the retreat will be found in the Proceedings of the New Jersey Hist. Soc., Vol. VI., p. 15.

[70] He was Governor of the State from 1801 to 1812, and in the war of that year was a General of the State forces.

mistress was absent: but it was, under any circumstances, a trial of no ordinary character to have one who had dwelt beneath their roof, and been warmly cherished, thus diligently seeking to entrap the object of her highest regard:[71] particularly as there was no reason for presuming Mr. Skinner to be in Amboy: for having received information of the danger which threatened him he had escaped the day after his letter was intercepted—before measures could be adopted by Lord Stirling to prevent it—and taken refuge on board the "Asia" man-of-war, then lying in the waters of New York.[72]

He was, of course, received as an efficient and active auxiliary, and General Howe evinced his regard and consideration by appointing him, soon after, a Brigadier-General, with authority to raise five battalions from among the disaffected in New Jersey: but the evils to which they had been subjected in common with their neighbors, during the occupancy of the country by the British during the winter of 1776-7, had led them to regard a closer connection with the royal army as a circumstance not specially desirable, and consequently the battalions of Mr. Skinner were not easily filled; in fact, of 2,500 privates, of which the five regiments were to consist, he succeeded in obtaining only 517.[73]

General Skinner's head-quarters were on Staten Island, and it is not known that he served with the army in any other section of the country. Although unable to induce many to join his standard, yet he had friends among the provincials, who, when his personal safety was concerned, were ready to give him intelligence of the movements of the colonial forces. An instance of the kind occurred in November, 1777, when General Dickinson projected an expedition against Staten Island, with two thousand men. Knowing the neccessity for secrecy, he concealed his object even from his field officers, until the

[71] A letter to Mr. Skinner from Joseph Bloomfield, written two years previously, is before me, expressive of the most cordial sentiments. It concludes, "Wishing you health and a speedy return home, in which Oliver (Oliver Barberrie, another student,) and Andrew join me, with our best respects, remain your most dutiful and humble servants."

[72] See Doc. Hist. of U. S., 4th Series, Vol. 4, pp. 586, 595.

[73] Gordon's Hist. of America, II., p. 200, quoting Lord Howe's despatch.

night in which it was to be executed, yet by 3 o'clock the next morning, General Skinner had been made aware of his intentions, and saved his brigade by taking shelter in some works too strong to be carried by assault. The expedition consequently was a failure.[74] Two of his battalions were in the detachment which, on 7th June, 1780, under General Knyphausen, crossed over to Elizabethtown, and penetrated as far as Connecticut Farms, and subsequently remained encamped at the Point until the 23d, when the march to Springfield, and the engagement there occurred ; but it does not appear that General Skinner himself was with them. His family in the month of February, 1776, was broken up, some of his children taking up their abode with his son-in-law, Mr. Terrill, at Piscataway, and Mrs. Skinner and one daughter going to her brothers, in Monmouth County. After some time, however, the General took a house at Jamaica, Long Island, and gathered his family again within it, giving them as much of his time as his official duties would permit.

After the Revolution General Skinner went to England with his family, and received from the government compensation for his forfeited estate, and the half-pay of a Brigadier-General during his life. He died March 15th, 1799, aged 71. It is said in letters written at the time, that he was there universally known and beloved, and the attention paid to him during his illness truly remarkable, hundreds of people that his family had never known, or scarcely heard of, sending daily to inquire about his health. His wife survived him, after a union of 47 years, and continued to reside among her children, in England and Ireland, until her death.[75]

Mr. Skinner's residence in Amboy stood on the bank, on the south-west corner of South and Water streets, opposite the

[74] Marshall's Washington, 2d Edit., I. p. 181.

[75] The following is the inscription on General Skinner's tombstone in St. Augustine's Church, Bristol: "Near this place are deposited the remains of Brigadier-General Cortlandt Skinner. Born in New Jersey, North America, where he was many years his Majesty's Attorney-General. Died at Bristol, 15th March, 1799, aged 71. Descended from an honorable family in Scotland, of distinguished loyalty, he proved the inheritor of their virtues, in the steady performance of all the duties of life, which will make his death ever regretted by his family, most of all by his afflicted widow, Elizabeth Skinner, who erects this monument to his memory."

house of late years occupied by the Hon. James Parker. It was of stone and brick, and not many years since a portion of the foundation remained to identify the spot. His office was the one now occupied by Mr. Parker, on the opposite corner. The gardens attached to Mr. Skinner's house extended along Smith street to what is now Rector street (no buildings then occupying the ground), and where the stable stood, is now the dwelling occupied by Mr. Jotham Smith. Cortlandt Skinner had several children:

William was placed in the English navy, and died young.

Philip Kearny entered the Army, and died in London in 1827 or 1828, unmarried. He was taken prisoner on one occasion by the French, and detained for some time at Lisle. On his release and return to England, in 1799, he found he had been promoted to an Adjutant-generalship, and before his death was Lieutenant-General, commanding at Bombay.

John was a Lieutenant in the young company called the "Governor's Guards," elsewhere mentioned.[76] Soon after a memorable review day he was required to doff his cap, with its motto "Liberty or Death," and was sent on board the Phenix frigate, at Sandy Hook, and entered as a midshipman.[77] Soon after this, the Phenix on passing up the North River came within range of the guns at Fort Washington, and young Skinner had the misfortune to have his right hand shot off by a ball, which did no other injury on board. He had previously, while playing in the market Square, at Amboy, lost the sight of one eye from a cork-dart;[78] and thus mutilated he passed through life, a bachelor, ever active and cheerful, benevolent to a fault, an affectionate son and valued citizen.

As a post-captain, he for many years commanded the Holyhead packet, and while in the discharge of his duty was accidentally drowned in 1830; being swept overboard in a sudden squall. A monument, erected by public subscription, attests the estimation in which he was held.

Cortlandt was left by his father for several years in this country, with his brother-in-law, Mr. Terrill, but afterward went to England, and eventually established himself in Ireland, and died in Belfast.

He held different offices, and for several years was Comptroller of the

---

[76] See Chapter on Revolutionary Events.

[77] It is probable that he commanded a small cruiser before the war was over. R. Laird in his Journal, recounting his escape from Yorktown, in March, 1782, p. 412, and journey northward, mentions his having been taken on board a vessel in Amboy Bay (after embarking in a boat from Monmouth County for Staten Island) commanded by "Capt. Skinner," who put him and his party ashore, and gave them a note of introduction to his father, General Skinner.

[78] "While playing with me, and other urchins," says Mr. Wm. Dunlap, in a letter to the author, and he adds, "What a strange thing is *identity*, that I should call myself an *urchin*." Mr. D. was then in his 70th year.

[79] "What most interested me at this place (Holyhead), was a lofty and tasteful monument on a neighboring height, to the memory of Captain Skinner, the son of an American Refugee, who formerly commanded a packet out of this port, and was accidentally drowned a few years since. It was built by subscription, and so widely and favorably known was the subject of it, that contributions were received from all quarters in the north of Wales, the west of England, and in Ireland."—Correspondent of N.Y. Com. Advertiser, London, Sept. 4th, 1843.

Customs, being highly respected and esteemed. After the death of his father, his house became the residence of the widow, who described his premises in her letters to her friends in this country, as being highly improved, and pleasantly situated. He subsequently resided at Dungannon Park, the property of Lord Dungannon, who was his personal friend. He was twice married. His first wife was Miss Kingsmill, the second Miss Isabella McCarty, and he left several children.

Downs, named probably by Mrs. Governor Franklin, as that was her maiden name, went from England to the Island of Jamaica, whither his brother-in-law, Sir George Nugent, was sent soon after as Governor, and married there. He returned to England for his health in 1801, but finally died in Jamaica, previous to 1803. He left but one daughter, named after his mother, Elizabeth Kearny, who married a Rev. Mr. Simpson of England, and has two children, William and Adelaide, twins, born on the day Queen Adelaide was crowned.

General Skinner had seven daughters :

Susan married Major Jasper Farmar of the British Army, and after his death his brother, Thomas Farmar, who are elsewhere noticed, and descendants bearing the name of Murphy are living in Nova Scotia.

Elizabeth married William Terrill, of New York, and had four daughters, who never married, and one son, John, who is yet living in England and has children,—one of his daughters married Henry Meigs, of the Metropolitan Bank, New York, and left one daughter.

Euphemia became the wife of Oliver Barberie, who studied law with her father, and is noticed on another page.

Catharine married Sir William Henry Robinson, son of Col. Beverly Robinson, of New York. She died at Marlow, England, in 1843, aged 75, and left several children.[80]

Maria married, in 1797, Captain (afterward General) Sir George Nugent, G. C. B. D. C. L., and accompanied her husband both to India and Jamaica, whither he was sent by his government to discharge important trusts; and a diary kept by her has been printed for private distribution since her death, which took place in 1834. At one period they resided in great splendor at Dublin. Sir George Nugent died March 11th, 1849, aged 92, leaving four children.[81]

Isabel married a Doctor Frazer, while the family were on Long Island. He subsequently went to England, and she followed, with her father, at the close of the war. They had several children. One son (Thomas) be-

---

[80] See Sabine's Royalists. A daughter, with her husband, Commissary General Robinson, of the British Army, was recently residing in Canada.

[81] At the time of his death he was the oldest general officer in the English Army, his first commission, as Ensign, bearing date, July 5th, 1773. He served in America, from 1777 to 1783, was in the expedition that proceeded up the North River for the relief of Burgoyne's army, and was at the taking of Forts Montgomery and Clinton. He subsequently served with credit on the continent, and in 1811, was Commander in Chief of the troops in India, and he held high civil trusts, both in Ireland and Jamaica. He attained to a colonelcy in 1794, and was promoted to the rank of General in 1813.

His acquaintance with Miss Skinner commenced in America. His heir is Sir George Edmund Nugent, born in 1802, who in 1830 married the daughter of Lord Colburn. He is a captain in the Grenadier Guards. There is another son, and two daughters—Lady Freemantle and Lady Clinton.

came a physician; another is, or was, a captain in the British Army, and a third a clergyman.

Gertrude married (June, 1780, at Jamaica, L. I.) Captain Meredith, of the 70th regiment of foot, who died previous to 1800, leaving her with four children, one of whom (Richard) is a captain in the British Navy.

STEPHEN, the second son of the Reverend William Skinner, was for many years previous to the Revolution engaged in mercantile pursuits, in 1758–9 making a trading voyage of several months' duration among the West Indian islands, and up to August, 1767, keeping at Amboy what was then called "a general store," which he then sold out. His residence was on the bank, on the north side of Smith street, where during the present year (1855) some buildings have been erected, adjoining the Bruen stores.

After relinquishing his mercantile pursuits, Mr. Skinner, as treasurer of the province for East Jersey, was for several years a very prominent character. On the 22d July, 1768, the public money-chest in his possession was robbed of between six and seven thousand pounds, and the circumstances of the case were such as to lead to much angry discussion between the Executive and Legislative departments of the province. The Governor and his Council threw the odium of the robbery upon one Samuel Ford, a notorious rogue and counterfeiter, while the Assembly attributed it to the negligence of the treasurer, at least, if they did not directly impugn his integrity, and desired to hold him accountable for the loss. The matter agitated the province greatly, but cannot in this place be more fully noticed. Mr. Skinner finally (Feb'y 23d, 1774) resigned his office, and his successor was authorized to institute a suit for the recovery of the money. This, however, was never brought to a legal termination; the political events which soon after occurred, sending the ex-treasurer into banishment, and putting an end to the provincial government. After his resignation, Governor Franklin, very unwisely for his own popularity, appointed Mr. Skinner one of his Council.[82]

Although chosen by the good people of his native town to represent them in the Provincial Congress, in April, 1775, in

[82] See Proceedings of N. J. Hist.Soc., Vol. V. page 49.

conjunction with James Parker and Jonathan Deare, there is nothing known of his sentiments, rendering it probable that he was favorably inclined to the colonial cause. Certain it is that soon after the commencement of hostilities he removed his family to New York, and thence to England, the property left behind him in New Jersey being confiscated to the use of the State. His house was accidentally set on fire on 28th December, 1776, and entirely consumed; the New York papers of the time stating that, by fire, and "the depredations of the rebels," Mr. Skinner had suffered within the month a loss of full £3,000.

He married *Catharine*, daughter of Andrew Johnston, by whom he had nine or ten children, but they all died without issue, either in England, or Nova Scotia, to which province the family eventually removed, having received a grant of land there, as compensation for his losses in New Jersey.

William, the third son of the Rev. Mr. Skinner, entered early in life the provincial service, and served as a captain against the French in Colonel Schuyler's regiment,[83] participating in all the trials and dangers of the campaigns of 1755 and 1756.

A letter from Captain Skinner in my possession, dated Oswego, September 7th, 1755, says:

[83] One of his muster rolls is in my possession, giving the names of all his company, during April, 1756. His company numbered besides the Captain, Lieutenant (who was his brother John), and ensign (Daniel Clark), four sergeants, four corporals, two drums, and ninety privates. The pay of the captain was £10 1*s*., of the Lieutenant, £7 10*s*., 9*d*., of the ensign, £6 14*s*., 8*d*., of the sergeants and corporals, £2 10*s*. 3*d*., and of the privates, £1 13*s*. 6*d*. each, per month. On May 11th, 1755, a letter now before me, dated at Amboy, says: "Billy Skinner's company was mustered yesterday, and is complete. John Parker's will be on Tuesday next, and also Capt. Risco's. I was at Elizabethtown on Friday, to muster Risco's company, but what with people under age, and more unfit for service, he had but seventy-nine, which he said he would make up by Monday night. Colonel Schuyler's company we hear has about sixty, and Woodward's will never fill, but I believe that his company will be given to one Dr. Ogden, who, many say, has got fifty or sixty men. We propose having them move, and every thing ready by the 25th." From the accounts of Col. Schuyler, from June 6th, to Sept. 7th, it appears from the amount of pay, that the companies ranked in June—1 Risco's, 2 Skinner's, 3 Parker's, 4 the Colonel's, 5 Woodward's:—and in September, 1 Woodward's, 2 the Colonel's, 3 Skinner's, 4 Risco's, 5 Parker's.

"We are now building a fort on the east side of the river, upon a hill which commands the lake, and overlooks all the land about it, so that it will be impossible to hurt us, when that is finished;" and contains the following items relating to the operations of that period:—"We have now in our regiment the following officers, not capable of duty: Capt. Woodward, who, since he has been here, has seldom or never appeared in Camp: his ensign very bad: my ensign, an old grumbling scoundrel, and always complaining: Capt. Parker's ensign, sick these six weeks past, and I don't think he'll recover: the colonel's ensign very bad—so that you may judge how hard our camp duty is: the rest of us very hearty and well, and have not above forty men in our regiment sick."

He had previously stated that Captain Ogden had sold his commission (in consequence of sickness), to a Mr. Whittemore for £10 proc. and had left for home, as had also Capt. Rusco, who had been ill for three weeks.

"By yesterday's orders we are in hopes of going upon action, for the batteaux are repairing, and every thing is to be got in readiness, and we expect to go from here in four days at furthest, but whither is not mentioned. So you may expect to hear something worth while, by the next letter I write to you provided I get safe back."[84]

"There has been a good deal of disturbance in Shirley's regiment, which consists of the greatest villains I ever knew, five and six deserting of a night, some of whom were brought back by the Indians, and tried by a general court-martial; five were condemned to be shot, three of whom were afterwards reprieved; the other two executed, which I hope will put a stop to it."

"I am glad to hear our Assembly has granted thirty thousand pounds for this expedition, and should be glad if they would send us a pipe of wine to make amends for the smallness of our pay, for our stock is out, and what we shall do for a little comfort I don't know. If we dine at the sutler's, and keep officers' company, our day's pay is gone."

Captain Skinner was at Oswego, in August, 1756, when the fortress was surrendered to the French under General Montcalm, and as a prisoner of war was sent to France, where he remained until the following May (1757), when he was permitted to pass over to England on his parole to await an exchange, which was effected in the course of a few months through his intimacy with the family of Sir Peter Warren, whose widow was his first cousin.[85]

[84] A letter from Dr. Stakes in the Rutherfurd MSS. dated Oswego, Sept. 9th, 1755, says, "we have now about two hundred sick a week, so that our effective men I imagine to be about 1,600, of which say 1,000 are to go on this expedition. Our officers and soldiers long to be in action, and the Indians are absolutely mad to proceed."

[85] Lady Warren was a daughter of Stephen De Lancey of New York, who married Anne Van Cortlandt, sister of Elizabeth, wife of Rev. Wm. Skinner. Another sister, Margaret, mar-

From letters written at this period the following items are extracted :

Under date of May 17th, 1757, he thus wrote :

"I have the pleasure to acquaint you that we [himself and brother John] are now in London, having come over from France (about ten days past), with the officers who were there, upon our paroles: to return in three months if we can't find officers, prisoners in England, of equal rank, to send to France in our room; which we find attended with a great deal of difficulty, for there are not a sufficient number of French officers here for us, so that we shall be obliged to return to France, if we cannot get our time prolonged, which I am in hopes we shall." * * * * —giving as a reason the influence of Lady Warren, and the steps taken by the proper department to effect the exchange— * * * * "I waited on Mr. Partridge (the agent of our province), and told him the situation I was in. He told me he would introduce me to Lord Halifax and many others, who he thought would be of service to me in regard to what I had done, but at the same time told me nothing could be done till I am exchanged, which I find to be the case."[86] * * * *

---

ried Stephen Bayard, and their daughter married Peter Kemble. Sir Peter Warren died at Dublin, July 26th, 1752, after three day's illness of inflammatory fever, leaving four daughters, aged respectively, fourteen years, six years, three years, and three months.

[86] In this letter he mentions the liberality of Col. Schuyler, in furnishing himself and brother with a letter of credit for £200 sterling, that they might be supplied while in England—one of many like instances of generosity by this true-hearted old provincial.

The following Memorial, or Deposition, alluding to this trait in his character, in the handwriting of William Alexander, is among the Rutherfurd MSS.

"Col. Schuyler was taken prisoner at Oswego, August 14th, 1756, and continued in Canada until October the 29th, 1757, when he was permitted to make a visit to his family upon parole. He returned again to Canada in July, 1758, and on the 8th of November following was released by the capitulation of Fort Frontenac.

"During his captivity, which was at the different periods eighteen months or thereabouts, there were in Canada a great number of captive soldiers belonging to the troops of this colony, taken at Oswego and Sabbath-day Point: who were thrown into goals, and allowed only two ounces of pork, or four ounces of salt fish and half a pound of bread per day, for their subsistence. The small pox and fluxes raged much among them; and as the subsistence allowed them was insufficient for the support of the healthy, and unfit for persons laboring under diseases, Col. Schuyler, not doubting but he should meet with the approbation of the government, supplied the sick and imprisoned captives with such provisions and necessaries as were absolutely wanted for their support, which is the charge he makes of expenses in his accounts.

"That this charge is high, hath arisen from—1st, the number of persons he had to supply; 2d, the sickness that prevailed among them—and 3d, the extravagance of the prices of all kinds of provisions.

"As to the number of prisoners, we cannot particularly ascertain. Doctor Stakes says that those taken at Oswego were sent to Europe by detachments, and that near or upwards of 200 men were brought in, being taken at Sabbath-day Point; that there were constantly a number of sick, and at one time thirty belonging to the Jersey regiment. To all which Col. Schuyler daily administered; and as to the prices of provisions he can declare; beef and flour was at 10½*d.* sterling per pound, which is nearly equal to 1*s.* 7*d.* this currency—a shoat of about forty or fifty pounds weight, sold for £5 12*s.* Wine for the sick, cost from 12 to 20*s.* sterling per gallon, and all other articles in the like proportion

"June 6th. Since my last, I waited on Lord Barrington, who told me he would do me all the service that lay in his power, and desired me to draw out a memorial which I shall present to his Lordship the next levee day, and get it backed by Admiral Boscawen and Lord Powerscourt, two great friends of her Ladyship—the event of which I hope to acquaint you very soon. * * * *

"Sept. 8th. In all probability, some of my people will get to America soon, for they are exchanged, and now in England. I have applied to my Lord Barrington for their subsistence, and an order to send them to America, but he told me he had nothing to do with them, but advised me to write to Mr. Pitt, Secretary of State, which I have done, but have not as yet had an answer. The people are now at Plymouth, with Capt's Rusco, Becker, Walters, and Ogden, of Col. Schuyler's regiment, and are subsisted by the government, through a mistake made by the Secretary of War's clerk, who, taking them to be regulars, ordered them to be subsisted, which is not contradicted as yet. * * * * I have the pleasure to tell you that I have my exchange, which I received yesterday." * * * *

His exertions for the welfare of his companions in arms who were less favorably situated than himself, did not end with the application to the Secretary of State. In a letter dated October 7th, he wrote:

Dr. Stakes paid himself for a very ordinary bed and diet, which was only soup, 18s. this currency per day.

"The moneys charged as paid to Capt. Woodward and Ensign Webb, will not appear to be high, when it is considered that those gentlemen were left in Canada, when Col. Schuyler was suffered to go to his family upon parole, and continued there until his return, which was about nine months; during which time they could not avoid supplying the wants of the suffering distressed prisoners of this province, and upon a calculation it will appear they only expended, including their own charges, about 34s. per day.

"William Crips, ferryman at Amboy, of Capt. Parker's company, taken at Sabbath-day Point, says, after he was taken he was carried to Montreal, and thence to Quebec, with about 300 men of his regiment, part of whom were taken at Fort Wm. Henry, and part with this deponent—where they were put into goal. The next morning Col. Schuyler came to them, to inquire their situation. He says there were many of them sick, and some had the small-pox. That Col. Schuyler ordered fresh provisions for the sick—that this deponent went very often with four or five more of his fellow prisoners, to Col. Schuyler's lodgings, to fetch fresh provisions for the sick; and that he verily believes many of the sick would have died if Col. Schuyler had not supplied them in the manner he did. This deponent also declares that when there was not a sufficiency of fresh provisions at Col. Schuyler's lodgings, the Col. would give the men money to buy provisions themselves—that the sick in general complained to him of the want of fresh provisions, and that they could not bear to eat the salt fish given them as their allowance—that Col. Schuyler assured them he would take care of them, and accordingly sent them fresh provisions, and this deponent declares that he himself went sometimes every day, at other times every other day, with four or five more men to the Col.'s lodging to fetch fresh provisions for the sick.

"That the expenses attending the supplying the sick were very high, but that he was certain the Assembly would readily allow them, as they were absolutely necessary for the preservation of the lives of the poor sufferers."

"All the officers and men of Col. Schuyler's regiment are arrived at Plymouth, excepting Col. Schuyler and Doctor Stakes, who are kept at Quebec for reasons unknown to every body." * * After narrating what he had done in anticipation of their arrival, as above, he added: "Mr. Pitt wrote to Mr. Partridge, Agent for the Province of New Jersey, who wrote to Mr. Pitt, that he could do nothing for them without orders from the Province. Upon which I wrote another letter to the Secretary of State, and told him that it was very cruel that so many fine fellows who had served their country for two years past, should be so neglected by the mother country as to want common necessaries of life, and at the same time told him that if the government of England would not subsist them and send them back to America upon their expense, I did not doubt but that the province of New Jersey would pay it: upon which I got an order for their subsistence, and also to send them to America." And on the 25th November, he wrote: "To relate all the trouble I have met with in getting subsistence for the provincial troops as they landed from Old and New France would be too tedious; but I can't help telling you that Mr. Partridge, the Agent for our Province, is a d——d scoundrel; all that he would do was this: if Mr. Pitt (to whom I had written several letters on the subject) would advance money to the provincial officers for their subsistence, he would give his note for the sum to be paid out of the next cash he had in his hands belonging to the Province, but would not advance it himself, 'though he is worth at least £30,000 sterling. He is such another as old John Watson,[87] therefore not fit for the post he is intrusted with.'[88]

The application of Capt. Skinner to Lord Barrington for promotion into the regular service proved unavailing, his Lordship releasing himself from all obligations to advance his views on account of his being only a Provincial officer; but on applying by petition to the King, his application was granted, and on 7th October he thus wrote:—

"I have the pleasure to acquaint you that I received a letter from my Lord Barrington yesterday, in which he told me that I was appointed a Lieutenant in General Cornwallis's Regiment, and take place of all the Lieutenants appointed in consequence of the present augmentation, which is an additional Lieutenant to every company in His Majesty's service. General Cornwallis's Regiment consists of two Battalions—the first is gone upon a secret expedition, the other is quartered at Gosport. I consulted with my friends whether I should accept of it or not, who all advised me to take it. The Duke of Grafton, my Lord Harford, and many others, tried to get me a company before they went out of town, but there were so many trying for companies (who had a better right to expect them than I had) and were obliged to accept of Lieutenancies, that I thought it

---

[87] John Watson, the Painter and "Miser," of Amboy. See page 126 of this volume.

[88] Upon what grounds the Government could base their refusal to provide for troops who had been made prisoners of war while fighting the battles of their country and were on their way to their homes, is not known. Mr. Partridge would certainly have been imprudent to have incurred the expense without instructions from the Province.

better to accept of my Lord Barrington's offer, and trust to the interest I have for my further promotion."

The course pursued to obtain his commission he thus graphically describes :—

"Being determined to try every method, and, luckily for me at that time, getting acquainted with Mr. Fitzroy, brother to the Duke of Grafton, who was courting Miss Warren, I was resolved to petition the King, which I did at a time when the Court was in mourning for the Queen of Prussia, and as every officer that had a petition to deliver goes in his regimentals, I did the same. When I entered into the first room whom should I meet but the Yeoman of the Guards, who came up to me in a rough manner and told me the Court was in mourning, and that my dress was not suitable to the times, and I could not be admitted :—the answer I gave him was very short, being that I had a petition to deliver the King and was determined to see him. I then passed him and got into a room where there was a large levee of most of the nobility in England. I looked about for my good friend Fitzroy, and spoke to him: he went directly to my Lord Harford, the Duke of Newcastle, Lord Lenox, and many others, and told them that I was a relative of Lady Warren's and a friend of his, and introduced me to them, which made every one in the levee room inquisitive to know who I was and my business, which my good friend told them.[89] The next thing was to know where I should place myself and in what manner I should present myself to the King, which my Lord Halifax was so kind as to instruct me in, and took the trouble to place me himself, which was by the door that the King passes through to his bed chamber, and ordered me, when the King returned that way, to kneel upon my right knee and present it to him, which I did with great resolution and a genteel posture, *considering where I was born.* When I presented it, the King stopped and looked at me, took it out of my hand, went into his bed chamber, and did me the honor to read it himself: upon which my Lord Halifax came to me and said that he did not doubt but that it would succeed, for, said he, the King has read your petition, which I never knew him to do before, for the Lord in waiting always does it for him. This reception gave me great encouragement, and I went home well satisfied."

"Three days afterward, I attended my Lord Barrington's levee, and asked him whether the King had spoken to him about me. His Lordship told me that he had, and repeated the words as the King spoke them, which were that "one Capt. Skinner, an American, belonging to a Provincial Regiment, had delivered a petition. 'I like the man's looks—he is fit to serve me—provide for him.' "

Lieutenant Skinner's promotion was rapid ; he was gazetted Captain, August 4th, 1759, and, as Major of Royal Volunteers was in the Expedition to Belle Isle, in 1761. The following letter gives an interesting account of the attack upon that post :—

[89] It may be remarked here, that Capt. Skinner was a remarkably fine looking man, such as would be likely to attract attention any where, although a stranger. A portrait of him is in the N. J. Historical Society's Collection.

BELLE ISLE, ye 24th May, 1761.

"I think in my last letter to you I acquainted you that I was going upon an Expedition to the East Indies, but was agreeably surprised when we anchored in Belle Isle Road. Our Army consisted of about 9,000 men, mariners included, under the command of Generals Hodgson, Crawford and Rufane; the Navy under the command of Commodore Keppell. On the 8th of April, we made an attempt to land, but were repulsed with the loss of about 400 men killed, wounded, and taken prisoners, which, added to the natural strength and innumerable fortifications in every part of the island where there seemed to be the least possibility of landing, made every body imagine it impossible to make our landing good. Despatches were immediately sent home with an account of our bad success, but before we got an answer to that Express, we made another attempt, on the 22d of April, and made good our landing, with the loss of about 300 men, and 400 of the enemy.

"Our principal attack was intended to be made at Fort Andrew, with the choice of our troops, under the command of General Crawford; another body of men, consisting of Beauclerk's Grenadiers, 500 of our Regiment, Grey's and Stewart's Independents, and about 500 mariners, under the command of Col. Lambert, were designed to make a feint at another part of the island. Col. Lambert did me the honor to give me the command of the first division that landed, in which I succeeded, with the loss of about 300 men; we were opposed by about 500 men, who, if they had behaved as they ought to have done, might have killed every man of us, for we were obliged to scramble up an eminence, while the enemy were upon the top of the hill discharging their pieces at us, and pelting us with stones; however, we succeeded in our landing, and drove the enemy before us.

"The General did me the honor of thanking me in public for my behavior, and mentioned me to Mr. Pitt; and has promised me that if a vacancy of Lieut. Col. happens he will recommend me to the King for it.

"We have since made our approaches, and opened our batteries of 32-pounders this morning in order to make a breach, but our wise Engineers have been mistaken in their distance, and find it impracticable till we get 200 yards nigher; till then we shall do nothing. We have a line of circumvallation about the Citadel, so that not a man can come out, and hope in about ten days time we shall be in possession of it. We have lost, since we came to the Island, near 900 men, and the French 1,000, which reduces their number to 1,200, by the accounts of deserters. This is all that has happened since we landed, excepting an unlucky accident that happened to General Crawford, who was taken prisoner in a sortie the enemy made upon our lines in a dark night; but they met with so warm a reception that they have not attempted it since.

"We are alarmed here with a report that the Spaniards have assisted the French with 12 sail of the line, in order to relieve this place, but how true it is we do not know."

The following year he accompanied the Army, under Lord Loudoñ, to Portugal, and Lord Viscount Pulkney, his superior, having been placed temporarily in command of another corps, Major Skinner held the rank of Lieutenant-colonel; and the following April (1763) received the promotion regularly, in consequence of the death of that nobleman. Shortly after this, he returned to England. In a letter written at this time he expresses an opinion that his regiment would be broken, and he hoped in a few months to see his American friends; but this wish was never gratified. Previous to the Revolution he had risen to the rank of Colonel. He died in England about 1778.

Colonel Skinner married a daughter of Lady Warren, and his only child (Meauna Maria)[90] married Henry, 3d Viscount Gage, and her son, Henry Hall Gage, is now the possessor of the titles and estate of the family.[91]

JOHN, the fourth son of the Rev. Mr. Skinner, entered the Provincial service at the same time with his brother William, as Lieutenant in his company; was taken prisoner with him at Oswego, in 1756, and was his companion during his sojourn in France and on his transfer to England.

While waiting the result of an application for a commission in the regular army, he volunteered his services in a secret expedition then fitting out, and during the cruise (in the Mediterranean) performed duty in the Grenadier Company attached to Lord Loudon's Regiment. The fleet returned to England in October, 1757, and so well pleased were his superiors with Mr. Skinner's conduct, that they petitioned the Secretary of War in his behalf, and he received a regular commission as Ensign in that regiment.

[90] So in the "English Peerage," but the relations of the family here say she received at baptism the simple name of *Susannah*.

[91] THOMAS GAGE, Commander in Chief of the English Forces in North America during the first part of the War of Independence, was second son of Thomas, first Viscount Gage. He married, in 1758, Margaret, daughter of Peter Kemble, of New Jersey, (she died in 1824, aged 90,) and died in 1788, leaving several children, among them *Henry*, 3d Viscount Gage, who inherited the title October 11th, 1791, in consequence of the death, without issue, of his uncle, Wm. Hall, 2d Viscount. He was born in 1761, and married Miss Skinner in 1782. He became a Major-general in the British Army, and left two sons—Henry Hall (4th Viscount) and Thomas William.

Henry Hall Gage (4th Viscount) was born December, 1791, and succeeded, on the death of his father January 29th, 1808, to the titles of the family, which are, Viscount Gage of Castle Island and Baron Gage of Castlebar, Peerage of Ireland; Baron Gage of High Meadow, Peerage of England: and a Baronet of England of date 1622. He married, March, 1813, Elizabeth Maria, eldest daughter of the Hon. Edward Foley, second son of Thomas, first Lord Foley, and has issue: *Henry Edward Hall* (born 1814, married, in 1840, to the only daughter of Sir Charles Knightley, Bart., who was in her 13th year, and in 1844 he was a Lieutenant in the Rifle Brigade); *Elizabeth Maria; Anna Maria; William* (born in 1820, was a Lieutenant in 83d Foot, in 1844); *Caroline Harriet; Edward Thomas; Fanny Charlotte.* The seats of Lord Gage are: Firle Place, Sussex; Westbury House, Hants; Town Residence, Gullais Hotel, Albemarle street.

In 1759, he had risen to a Lieutenancy in the regiment of Colonel Grey, and his brother writing at that time, gives us an insight into his character. "His pride," says he, "will hinder his promotion. He thinks it beneath a man of honor, and one entitled to promotion for his services, to ask a favor of any one, or even wait upon people whose interest would prefer him immediately." The regiment to which he was attached being ordered to America, he had the pleasure of again meeting his family and friends. He was promoted to a Captaincy, June 10th, 1768, and in September of that year he attended Governor Franklin to Fort Stanwix, to assist at the Council held there with the Indians. He rose to be a Major in the 70th Regiment, and returned with it to England, in 1770, and continued there during the revolution. He subsequently sold his commission, returned to America, and took up his residence again in Perth Amboy, entering into mercantile business. He married (Feb'y 16th, 1774,) Sarah, daughter of Philip Kearny, and died in December, 1797, leaving one son, *James*, who died at Amboy in 1827, leaving a wife and daughter—that daughter, previous to her marriage to Mr. Laforge, was the last of the descendants of the Rev. Wm. Skinner, in this country, bearing his name.

THE NEVILL FAMILY.

It has been stated in the notice of the Sonmans family, that the wife of Peter Sonmans was named Sarah Nevill, and, as his widow, inherited his property. In September, 1735, she married again; her second choice being Mr. Christopher Gildemeister. But she was permitted to enjoy the new connection but a short time: he died the November following, and on the 1st December she also died. Upon her death her property became vested in "Samuel Nevill, of London, Gent.," her eldest brother and heir at law. Another brother, John Nevill, was then in New Jersey, of whom, although it seems he was a resident of Perth Amboy, little is known, save that he held at different times various offices under the Provincial Government, and at one period was the lessee of the Ferry across the Raritan. His brother, however, occupied a more important station in society.

Samuel Nevill, so soon as he heard of his sister's death, embarked for East Jersey, reached the province towards the end of May, 1736, and established himself at the capital. He had received a liberal education in England, and was a lawyer by profession. He had been Editor of the London Morning Post, and even the few memorials of him that are now to be found indicate the possession of character and talents much above mediocrity. He soon rose to eminence, and became a Judge of the Court of Common Pleas, Mayor of Perth Amboy (then no trifling station), second Judge of the Supreme Court of the Province, and filled several other important offices, to the credit of himself, and, it is believed, to the satisfaction of the government and the well disposed among the people.

The following is an extract from a charge by Mr. Nevill to the Grand Jury of Middlesex County, September, 1747 :—

"The law being always desirous diligently to find out the truth in all causes called in question in the Courts of Judicature, to the end impartial judgment may be given and strict justice executed accordingly, hath in all ages esteemed it to be the best method to search out this truth by the oaths of honest, lawful, and indifferent persons; and certainly that man who doth profess God to be his Creator, by whom alone he hopes for salvation, when he doth solemnly swear in the presence of that God and his people, that he will present the truth, and nothing but the truth, according to his knowledge of the matter in question, as God shall help him, that is, as he expects the Blessing of God in this life and eternal happiness in the life to come: I say certainly that man will, in all respects, be void of partiality and private affection. For an oath is fitly termed a holy band or sacred tie, a godly vow, and the foundation and ground of truth: a ceremony instituted by God himself, wherein he is a party, and will see it verified or sharply punished. Therefore, as the law doth reverently respect the oaths of men, taketh her intelligence of matters in faith from them, and giveth such credit and approbation unto them, as to found and build her judgments in most cases of the greatest importance upon them; so she has always intended that those oaths shall be taken by men of sincerity of life and mature judgment, men indifferently affected, and such as will respect the truth of their knowledge and not the face of the person."[92]

Mr. Nevill was a member at various times of the Provincial Assembly,[93] and prominent in the dissensions which occurred during Governor Morris's administration; he was

[92] Speeches of Mr. Nevill may be found in the Elizabethtown Bill in Chancery.

[93] From 1743 to 1749, and from 1754 to 1764. In 1744 and 1745, and from 1748 to 1751 being Speaker.

equally energetic in upholding the Eastern Proprietors in their difficulties with the rioters at Elizabethtown and Newark; and so exasperated were the latter against him, in consequence of the ability displayed in protecting the rights of the proprietors, that threats of vengeance against him and his property were publicly made—failing in execution—we have every reason to believe—not through any want of will on the part of those who made them.[94]

In 1752, while holding the office of second Judge of the Supreme Court, Mr. Nevill published the first volume of an edition of the laws of the Province, in 2 vols. folio, under the auspices of the Provincial Assembly—the second volume not appearing until 1761. This was a valuable service to the Province, simplifying greatly the labor of subsequent compilers. In January, 1758, under the *soubriquet* of "Sylvanus Americanus"—in imitation, probably, of "Sylvanus Urban" of the Gentleman's Magazine, which had then been published in London twenty-seven years—he commenced editing a monthly periodical, published at Woodbridge, by James Parker, called "The New American Magazine." It was the first periodical of any kind printed in New Jersey, and only the second Monthly Magazine on the continent. Each number contained about 40 pages octavo, and in variety and interest it will compare with many modern publications in good repute. A History of America, and a Travellers' Diary, were published in connection with each number, paged separately, in order to form distinct volumes at the end of each year. The appellation "New," was to distinguish it from its only predecessor, at Philadelphia, which, however, it superseded—the publication being immediately relinquished on the appearance of this new competitor. It continued to be issued monthly until March, 1760, when it was discontinued for want of patronage, and some years thereafter many copies were sold in sheets, by the printer, as waste paper.[95] I have never met with

[94] Elizabethtown Bill in Chancery.

[95] Thomas' Hist. of Printing, II. p. 211. The Printer of this Periodical (James Parker) was so intimately connected with the establishment and progress of periodical literature on this continent, that he deserves the notice of him which will be found in Chapter X.

any of these magazines save in the New York and New Jersey Historical Libraries, and one volume which is in my own possession; probably but few others exist.

On the death of Chief Justice Morris, in January, 1764, Nevill would probably have been raised to the vacant bench, but the infirmities of age rendered the performance of its duties impracticable.[96] He died soon after (October 27th, 1764,) in the 67th year of his age, leaving a name unsullied, it is believed, by the slightest stain. His wife preceded him to the grave, dying in 1755, and their simple headstones yet mark their places of sepulture in the graveyard of St. Peter's Church. They left no children. Though a stranger to his blood and family, out of respect to the memory of one whom he conceived worthy of a place among the most eminent of other days, the author, a few years since, caused the spot where his remains were deposited to be rescued from the neglect and decay to which time had consigned it.

Mr. Nevill resided on the farm which had been Mr. Sonmans', at the termination of Market street, but in 1752 offered

[96] A more fitting place, probably, will not be presented for the insertion of the following extract from a letter among the Stirling Papers in the New York Historical Society Library:—

From the Earl of Stirling to Governor Franklin.

"New York, January 30th, 1764.

"DEAR SIR,—By the death of Chief Justice Morris another seat in your Excellency's Council has become vacant; upon which I beg leave to offer you my sentiments. The office of Chief Justice is a dangerous one to leave open; for its being so will be an inducement to the Ministry to fill it up. They will think it incumbent upon them to fill up an office they are informed is vacant; and if they do fill it up from thence, it is a thousand to one if it be tolerably filled—for who will leave Britain for this appointment? And yet the office is of the utmost importance to the Crown, as well as to every individual in the Province.

"On the other hand, if your Excellency fills it up during pleasure, and recommends your appointment for confirmation, it is most likely it will obtain it; and if you determine on this measure, the person who most naturally occurs to me is Charles Reade.* But the superannuated state of Mr. Nevill leaves Mr. Reade alone on the bench, and makes it necessary that some other person should be thought of to fill up one, if not both, the other seats. Fit persons are difficult to be found in New Jersey. Few, if any, of the gentlemen of the country, have read Law enough to qualify themselves for the bench, and as few of the lawyers fit for it will give up their business. The only one I can think of is Mr. Kearny.† I believe he inclines to retire from business, and your Excellency's offer of the office to him, with a seat in the Council, may, perhaps, induce him to accept it. If he should not incline to be in the Council, the next that occur to me are James Parker,† and Cortlandt Skinner,† both residing at Amboy, which is a convenient circumstance, added to their other qualifications."

* He was appointed.

† These gentlemen will be found noticed in this volume.

it for sale, "being determined to leave off the farming business and to live retired;" and the following August he also advertised to be sold at auction a house and lot in Amboy "near the parsonage"—thought to have been the same, at present the property of Mr. William King—where he had resided at one time. It is probable, however, that the farm was not sold until after his death.[97]

THE BARBERIE FAMILY.

Among the thousands of Protestants who left France to escape the evils imposed upon them by Lewis XIV., were the ancestors of the Barberies. They settled at New Rochelle, in the State of New York. The burial-ground of St. Peter's Church contains the only visible memorial of the residence in Amboy of any descendant of the family. A plain stone bears the inscription "JOHN BARBERIE, aged 50 years, died July 23d, 1770."

The name first enters upon the records in March, 1702–3, in a petition to the proprietors for a house-lot—the prayer of which was granted on condition that the house should be built within a year. The petitioner is presumed to have been the father of John Barberie above mentioned, and the same gentleman whose name is met with as one of the Council of New York or New Jersey, during the administrations of Governors Hunter, Burnet, and Montgomerie.

There is a traditionary statement that the subject of this sketch—the possessor of the tomb-stone—was the eldest of four brothers (none of the others, however, resided in Amboy) who, through some folly or superstition of their parents, shared but *two* names among them: the first being called *John*, the second *Peter*, the third *John-Peter*, and the fourth *Peter-John.*

[97] Philip Kearny, in his will, dated 1770, mentions this farm as having been "lately" bought by him at Sheriff's sale. In October, 1754, Mr. Nevill having been elected to the Assembly (then holding the office of Judge) a petition was presented, proclaiming him ineligible. A New York Editor remarks thereon, "it would seem very strange that an office which the house has not thought deserving of more than £25 salary *per annum* should deprive a gentleman of another place, because similar to the Judgeship of King's Bench in England." Apparently no action was had upon the petition.

Mr. Barberie was a gentleman of pleasing manners and address, occasionally marred by exhibitions of temper, and extremely proud of his birth and family connections. His residence was the house of late years known as the Lewis Place. At the time of his death he was Collector of Customs for the Port, and "well respected in that office." He married *Gertrude*, daughter of Andrew Johnston, elsewhere mentioned in these pages; they had five sons and four daughters.

PETER was a merchant in Amboy, in partnership with his uncle, John Johnston, and afterward removed to New York, where he died, leaving a widow and children.

JOHN was a Captain in the 2d Battalion of Cortlandt Skinner's Brigade, raised during the revolution, and after the war retired to St. Johns, in the Province of New Brunswick, where he died in 1818, aged 67. He was Colonel of Militia and a Magistrate of the County. A son, Andrew, became a Member of the Provincial Assembly of New Brunswick.

OLIVER commenced the study of Law in the office of Cortlandt Skinner, subsequently entered the British Army, and became a Lieutenant in the Loyal American Regiment. He married a daughter of his legal preceptor, and one of his sons now holds an honorable post in the Army or Navy of England. He died in the Province of New Brunswick.

LAMBERT died unmarried.

ANDREW was placed in the Navy, and was shot on board of an English vessel of war during the revolution.

SUSANNAH married her cousin, John L. Johnston, of Spotswood, and had several children.[98]

FRANCES married James Throckmorton, of Monmouth County.

CATHERINE became the wife of Mr. Henry Cuyler. Mr. C. died in Newark, in May, 1774, aged 28, and was buried under a pear tree in what was afterward the orchard of Col. Samuel Ogden, north of what is technically known as "the Stone Bridge." Mrs. Cuyler is thought to have died at Amboy. They left several children.

GERTRUDE died young, and unmarried.

THE WATSON FAMILY.

On what is now the site of Mr. John Manning's house, in the ancient metropolis, a site commanding an extensive view of the broad bay, formed by the confluence of Arthur Kull Sound with the Raritan—of the shores of Monmouth County and Staten Island, and, far beyond, of the Atlantic Ocean—a site such as a painter might naturally be disposed to select for his residence, there lived before the Revolution, the first limner of whom the American annals of art make mention.

[98] See pedigree of Heathcote family in Bolton's Westchester.

John Watson came to this country from Scotland about the year 1715, and died August 22d, 1768; aged 83 years. His remains lie interred in the rear of St. Peter's Church.

"After his first visit to America," says Mr. Dunlap in his History of the Arts of Design, "the painter returned to Europe, and brought thence to his adopted country many pictures which, with those of his own composition, formed no inconsiderable collection in point of numbers, but of their value we are ignorant. It is, however, a fact that the first painter, and the first collection of paintings of which we have any knowledge, were planted at Perth Amboy."

There were two houses standing near each other, both belonging to Mr. Watson, one of them being appropriated to these paintings, which it is said covered the walls; but before the Revolution, this house had decayed and been demolished. The other, occupied by the painter himself, and which disappeared during the struggle, was of wood, having its window-shutters covered with "heads of heroes, and of kings with awe-inspiring crowns"—owing their existence to the taste and talents of the painter.

When he became a resident of Amboy, he was extremely poor, but his circumstances improved from the exercise of his profession and from a small legacy left him, and with increasing riches came their too frequent attendant, a thirst for more. His penurious habits, and his love for unlawful interest, gained for him, even among his neighbors, the titles of miser and usurer, and an extremely irascible disposition prevented the growth of any attachment to him, in those around. He was unmarried, and his family consisted of himself, a nephew, and a niece, for whom he had sent to Scotland soon after his establishment at Amboy.

What became of Mr. Watson's collection of paintings is not known, and as none of his own of any size have come down to us, we are left comparatively in ignorance of his proficiency in the art. I have, however, in my possession a number of miniature sketches in India-ink, made by him, which are tolerably well executed, and among them a series of drawings of himself, at different ages, from one

JOHN WATSON.

Portrait Painter, 1715,–1768.

LITH. OF SARONY & Co. NEW YORK.

of which the likeness accompanying this notice of him was taken.[99]

"Alexander Watson, the nephew, who had been a midshipman in the British Navy"—the quotation is from Mr. Dunlap's work—"superintended his business when the uncle became too infirm to paint or even examine bonds and mortgages, and shared his frugal fare with the cheering hope of a blessed change when the old man should 'shuffle off his mortal coil.' But 'hope deferred maketh the heart sick.' The painter became blind, and deaf, and bed-rid, but still he lived. In this condition the old man remained several years. The nephew, anticipating the hour in which he was to become lord of money, houses and lands, used to speak of it as that which must soon come 'in the course of nature,' but in the meanwhile had no power over the revenue.

"During this period, which is called proverbially the time of 'waiting for dead men's shoes,' the house wanted repairing; but the bed-rid man turned his deafest ear to any proposal involving the expenditure of money for that or any other purpose. The hand grasped the world's idol with the greater intenseness as the hour approached on which its hold must be relaxed for ever. The nephew, *trusting* to the uncle's incapacity of moving or hearing, and finding tradesmen willing to *trust* to the kind course of nature, determined to prevent the decay of the property he felt an heir's affection for, and concluded his bargain with the carpenters for a new roof.

"Accordingly the house was unroofed and re-roofed, while the owner was living in it, perfectly unconscious of the important operation which was in progress over his head. The strokes of hammers, however, occasionally reached his ear, penetrating the obstacles interposed by art and nature, and the heir was startled by the question 'What is the meaning of that pecking and knocking that I hear every day?' The nephew, taken by surprise, answered: 'pecking? pecking? Oh! ay! 'tis the woodpeckers; they are in amazing quantities this year—leave the trees, and attack the roofs of the houses—there is no driving them off.' When the roof was finished, the saucy birds ceased pecking."

The old man at last died, and the nephew inherited his property. So soon as it came into his possession, he started off "in search of a wife," and although a short, red-haired man, of very unprepossessing appearance, with no mental qualifications to counterbalance those outward defects, his travels were not in vain. He returned to Amboy, bringing with him a very amiable and interesting woman as his wife, whom he had met with at Westchester, New York. They resided after their return to Amboy, in the house now occupied by Mr. William King, nearly in front of old Watson's premises.

[99] Among these sketches are likenesses, apparently original, of Gov. Burnet, Gov. Keith, of Pennsylvania, Governor Spotswood, of Virginia, Judge Bunnel, and other distinguished men, showing that some notoriety was enjoyed by the painter.

Mrs. Watson died very suddenly, being struck with death while riding with her husband in 1774.[100] After her death, Mr. Watson resided on a farm, above the "great gully" bordering on the Raritan, in those days called "Florida," and left it in 1776, to flee from the storm which threatened the adherents to the royal cause in New Jersey. The property of his uncle he had wasted in ill-judged schemes, and by injudicious management, and what he left behind him was confiscated. He finally died in New York. Mrs. Watson bore him two sons, who removed to Westchester.

Miss Watson, the niece of the painter, became the wife of Dr. John Waterhouse, whose grave is yet to be seen in the rear of St. Peter's Church, and after his death she married John Terrill of New York. Mrs. Sophia Brown, remembered by most of the present population of the place—having died as recently as August, 1837, aged 80,—was her daughter by her first husband. She had several children by Mr. Terrill.

THE PARKER FAMILY.

Between the years 1670 and 1680, several individuals by the name of Parker established themselves at different places in East Jersey, and it is probable they were nearly related to each other, if not members of the same family. In Elizabethtown, were Benjamin[101] and John Parker;[102] in Monmouth County, we find Peter, Joseph[103] and George Parker; and in Woodbridge, was ELISHA PARKER, the ancestor of the present Amboy family of that name—one of the few remaining of those inhabiting the place previous to the war of independence.

The first grant of land to "Elisha Parker, senior, Yeoman,

[100] "As I remember the story," says Mr. Dunlap, in a letter to the author—"She was riding out with her husband, being in perfect health, and when returning through Woodbridge, she suddenly exclaimed, 'I see two suns!' and fainted. She was brought home, and died." The New York Gazette, however, of March 10th, 1774, says: "Last week, died *at the Blazing Star, on her way to this city*, Mrs. Watson, wife of Alexander Watson, Esq., of Perth Amboy."

[101] Admistration on his estate granted to Martha Parker, March 10th, 1683.

[102] His last will dated in 1702.

[103] Administration granted on his estate to Jediah Allen, May 15, 1685.

of Woodbridge," was for 182 acres on the highway leading to Piscataway, under date of April 19th, 1675; and it is presumed that shortly afterward he removed to Woodbridge, from Staten Island, where he had previously resided. In November, 1694, he was appointed High Sheriff of the County of Middlesex; in 1707 he represented the county in the Provincial Assembly, of which body he continued a member for two years, and in 1711 was appointed a member of Governor Hunter's council. His residence is said to have been the house which, until a few years back, was for a long period the parsonage of the Presbyterian Church in Woodbridge. He died June 30th, 1717, and his memory is associated with the characteristics—as enumerated by his contemporaries—of a good father, a kind master, and a sincere Christian. Mr. Parker appears to have been three times married, and had several children. Those by his first wife (Elizabeth ———) were as follows:

I. Thomas, who resided in Woodbridge, early in life;[104] but probably removed to Staten Island; as one of his name, residing on the island in 1687, sold some lands in Woodbridge; and nothing is known of his descendants in the vicinity of the place of his birth. His children, by Mary ——, were *David*, born May 1st, 1676; *Thomas*, born March 9th, 1682–3; *Elisha*, born August 20th, 1684; *Joseph*, born Sept. 18th, 1690; *Benjamin*, born January 4th, 1692–3; and *George* and *Eliza* (twins), born March 30th, 1695.

II. Elisha,[105] who, in 1681 was styled "Weaver," and afterward, in 1701, "Merchant, of Woodbridge," was, in 1709, captain in the provincial forces, and attached to the commissariat, being charged with the duty of furnishing supplies to the troops then engaged on the Canadian frontier. About 1712, or 1715, he removed to Perth Amboy, and died, April 16, 1727, unmarried and much regretted, being eminent for his piety. He left his property in equal proportions to his three half-sisters, *Elizabeth*, *Ursula*, and *Mary*.

III. Samuel, born March 1st, 1669, died Dec. 27th, 1672.

IV. Mary, born December 3d, 1672, married Daniel Robins, Nov. 27, 1691.

V. Samuel, born June 1, 1674.

By his second wife, Hannah Rolph (died October 14th, 1696), whom he married March 26th, 1691, he had:—

I. Elizabeth, born Dec. 23d, 1691, died March 13th, 1692.

II. John, born Nov. 11th, 1693. He was the grandfather of the pre-

[104] In October, 1680, his father gave him 60 acres of upland, and 15 acres of Raritan meadow.

[105] He purchased from his father, Sept. 7th, 1680, seven acres in Woodbridge, part of his "home lot, lying on the west side of the highway that goeth *from the prison to the meeting-house.*"

sent elders of the family. He married, Sept. 16th, 1721, *Janet*, daughter of Dr. John Johnstone. He held the rank of Colonel in the provincial forces the same year, but I am not aware that he was ever called into service. From 1726 to 1728, he was engaged in business in New York, as a merchant, but appears to have always resided at Amboy, and to have been one of its most valued citizens. The stone part of the old Parker mansion, familiarly termed "the Castle," was built by him. Besides several minor offices which he held at different periods, he was appointed by Governor Burnet, in October, 1719, one of his council, and continued a councillor from that time until his death in 1732. In his will he left two hundred pounds "for extraordinary schooling and teaching one or more of my sons the Latin and French tongues, regard being chiefly and in the first place had to the eldest." His widow lived until Feb. 16th, 1741.

Their children, besides one son who died in infancy, were:

Elisha, who was bred to the profession of the law, under James Alexander, was licensed May 3d, 1745, and attained to some eminence. He married Catharine, daughter of James Alexander, and died of consumption, March 14th, 1751, in his 47th year. He left no children. His widow married Walter Rutherfurd, then an officer in the army, and was the mother of the late John Rutherfurd, of Belleville.

James, who will be more particularly noticed on a subsequent page.

Mary, who died unmarried February 25th, 1813, in her 86th year, and was buried in St. Peter's Cemetery; where most of the family were interred, although no monuments mark their graves as in her case.

John, who is more particularly noticed below; and

Lewis Johnston, born Dec. 9th, 1731, who died February 2d, 1760, in his 29th year, of consumption, while preparing himself for the bar; having sought for health in vain by a sea voyage, and residence in another climate. Several poetical effusions, in which he bewails the loss of strength and vigor in melancholy strains, are preserved.

By his third wife, Ursula Crage (Craig), to whom he was married Sept. 27th, 1697, and who survived him, he had :—

I. *Elizabeth*, who was born March 21st, 1698–9, and married James Johnston, of Monmouth County.

II. *Ursula*, born Dec. 21st, 1700, died unmarried.

III. *Mary*, born Dec. 22d, 1702, died unmarried.

IV. *Edward*, of whom no information has been obtained, excepting that he was baptized by the Rev. Jedediah Andrews, of the first Presbyterian Church, Philadelphia, April 30th, 1716.

JOHN PARKER, the last above mentioned, was born November 7th, 1729; received a mercantile education, and from October, 1745, to May, 1750, served as a midshipman on board H. M. ship Chester, Capt. Spry. In 1751 he went on a voyage to Jamaica, as supercargo of a vessel; from June to September, 1752, was in Virginia, and in April, 1754, went to Newfoundland, on similar commercial enterprises. In the campaigns of 1755 and 1756, against the French, he commanded a company in the 4th battalion of the Royal Americans, and after the capture of Colonel Schuyler, at Oswego, being the senior officer, the command of such of the New Jersey forces as were not involved in that disaster, devolved upon him.

Captain Parker was then in his 27th year, a bold and energetic officer, and the surrender of Oswego seemed to him uncalled for. In a letter to his brother, at Amboy, dated "Fort Eagle, August 18th, 1756," he says:

"I am busy preparing for an attack hourly expected. * * * * My love to all friends, and you may venture to tell them, that Jack Parker will never be taken in this poor, little, *footy* fort, without losing more than five, if all the force that was at Oswego comes against him; how that affair was managed I don't know, and therefore suspend judgment.

"Col. Schuyler, Capt. Skinner, his brother Jack, and all the officers that were there are well and untouched, except Col. Mercer, who was killed; Capt. Patten of Shirley's, Ensign Walter of Schuyler's, wounded; five men killed."[106]

The remainder of the year was spent by Capt. Parker amid the excitement, the hardships, and sufferings of the border warfare; and the ensuing August (1757) found him holding the rank of Colonel, at Fort William Henry, the melancholy fate of whose garrison, was one of the most remarkable events of the campaign; and there he came near losing his life, even before the capitulation, the dangers of which he also shared; having been born, as his brother observes in a letter in the author's possession, "under an unlucky planet." The circumstances of this affair were as follows: On the 21st July, Colonel Parker, with a detachment of about 350 men, officered by three of his captains (Woodward, Shaw and ———) and six or seven of his subalterns, together with Captains Robert

[106] The following extract is from a letter, written by Capt. Parker's brother, James, dated Albany, August 25th, 1756.

"Every thing is kept a secret at head-quarters, and it is only supposed by persons that know but little about the matter, that if Gen. Webb should receive accounts that it (Oswego) is not taken he will strip the carrying place of as many men as possible and march immediately to relieve it, after being joined by Sir William Johnston, with about 500 militia, and 300 Indians, which numbers it is said he has got together, which in the whole, including Battoe men, 'tis supposed will make up about 2,500 men:—quite sufficient, in my opinion, under a good officer to answer that end." He says that the Earl of Loudon had received a letter two days before from Capt. Parker, which had pleased him, and mentions a probability, which was, however, never realized, that Capt. P. would obtain the command of a company of Rangers in the Regular Service.

Maginnis and Jonathan Ogden, and Lieutenants Campbell and Cotes of the New York regiment,—went out in boats to attack the advanced guard of the enemy at Ticonderoga.

Having encamped for the night on an island in the lake, three batteaux were sent out towards the main land to reconnoitre, which were taken by the enemy, and the intentions of the detachment, in consequence, discovered.

On the morning of the 22d the boats moved forward towards a point where they expected to meet the advanced party, and decoyed by three batteaux, which were placed there by the enemy, the whole detachment eagerly landed, where an ambush of about 300 men had been stationed ; and at the same time forty or fifty boats came out from behind the point, effectually cutting off theirretreat. A desperate conflict ensued, which resulted most disastrously for the Americans. Colonel Parker and Capt. Ogden, with seventy or eighty men, being all that escaped death or capture. The three Jersey captains were killed, one of them, Woodward, having jumped overboard after being severely wounded.[107]

The success was so complete that the ardor of the French army revived, and they renewed their exertions toward the capture of Fort William Henry. Thrice had Montcalm been obliged to draw off his forces from before it, but he now returned to the attack under the most favorable circumstances, and the fort fell on the 9th of August.

Colonel Parker having escaped the dangers which attended the capitulation, returned to New Jersey, the provincial forces having been disbanded in consequence of the terms agreed upon, which prevented their serving against the French for eighteen months. But he was too fond of a military life to remain inactive when his services could be rendered available. He consequently returned to the frontier in the spring of 1759, and participated in the events of the campaign of that year, having purchased a company in the 60th Royal American regiment. He was also attached to the expedition which, in the beginning of 1762, sailed to the West Indies, with the view of reducing the French islands ;

[107] N. Y. Mercury, August 1st, 1757 ; Mante's Hist. of Late War, 1772, p. 85 ; Smollett's England, &c.

being then in command of a company in the 27th regiment, which he had purchased for £1,300 sterling, selling his previous commission for £1,100. He was at the taking of Martinico, but exposure in that climate, and the fatigue connected with the service, affected his health, and he fell a victim to disease, February 15th, 1762, and was buried at Port Royal.

Having ever led an unsettled life, consequent upon his military career, Mr. Parker never married. He was bold, courageous and active, but his public services secured to him but little fame, and less wealth.[108]

JAMES PARKER was the only child of John Parker, senior, who left issue. He married Gerturde, only daughter of the Rev. William Skinner, and was the father of the present elders of the Parker family.

Like many others of the young gentlemen of Perth Amboy, he entêred the provincial military service, and in August, 1746, embarked for the northern frontier, as captain of one of the six companies raised for the expedition of that year. His orders from acting Governor John Hamilton, and other papers connected with his command, are in my possession. It is thought, however, that his military services terminated with the campaign[109] (unless a residence of some duration in Albany in 1756 may have had some connection with the army movements), and he afterward engaged in mercantile business in New York, with Mr. Beverly Robinson,—his transactions being principally with the West Indies, some of them in partnership with Andrew Johnston; and in 1750–51 he made a voyage to Jamaica, upon affairs connected with these commercial projects.

Soon after this he took up his abode permanently at Amboy. His time was much engrossed in attending to the large landed

[108] It is somewhat singular that the surrender of Oswego, which he considered so unfortunate for all concerned, was the cause of promotion to two of his companions—the Skinners—(see pages 113 119) while his own success in escaping a similar disaster resulted in no benefit to him whatever.

[109] Among the Rutherfurd MSS. is an account of his command, dated March 9, 1747: 72 Privates on duty, 1 absent on furlough, 2 in fort at Albany, 1 discharged, 6 dead, 16 deserted—3 Commissioned Officers.

interest possessed by the family, and in executing the duties of various local offices conferred upon him : among others being that of Councillor under Governor Franklin, to which he was appointed in October, 1764, to supply the vacancy occasioned by the death of Chief Justice Morris. Mr. Parker took a prominent part in the proceedings of the Council, and many of the addresses and other documents emanating from that body during his connection with it, were written by him. In 1771, and in other years, he was Mayor of Amboy, and in April, 1775, was appointed with Stephen Skinner and Jonathan Deare, a delegate from Amboy to the Provincial Congress, but he did not attend its sessions. The deep interest he had at stake led him to pursue a course different from that adopted by most of his family connections, by preserving a strict neutrality in word and deed, between the royalists and provincials. He took no office, and endeavored to keep himself aloof from the party dissensions of the time, removing his family in November, 1775, to a farm in Bethlehem, Hunterdon County, where they resided until the peace in 1783,[110] when they removed to New Brunswick, and two years thereafter returned to the family mansion at Amboy.

Although Mr. Parker's neutrality was undoubted, yet, as all his connections were on the royal side, it was considered proper by the provincial authorities to place him under restraint, in retaliation for a similar course pursued by the enemy towards some suspected individuals, and he was consequently for some time, in 1777, in confinement at Morristown. As he took no part in the war, his property escaped confiscation. In 1789 he was solicited to become a candidate for Congress, but did not give his consent until it was too late to succeed. In a letter written to his brother-in-law in England at this time he says :

"We are all very anxious in this quarter of the world, and looking forward to our new Constitution. Many are doubtful whether it will take place as it is, or be subjected to be amended by another convention ; if

[110] The "Convention troops," in their march through New Jersey, in 1778, were quartered upon him. From the 5t tho 13th Dec. different divisions were provided for on his premises, and in 1779 (Nov. 24), General Philips, General Reidesel, with several officers of their suites, breakfasted at his house (under the inspection of Colonel Hooper of the American Army), on their way to New York, after being exchanged.

the latter, we shall have no Constitution without bloody noses. Eleven States have agreed, some of them conditionally, and the dominion (Virginia) is ready to join those who have made the conditions. There are many anti-federalists amongst those who are to go to Congress, who have many behind them of the same political sentiments. General Washington will undoubtedly be President, by a great majority, if not unanimously. John Adams, Vice-President. The fourth instant was appointed for the day of meeting, but they will not get together until atleast a month after, if so soon.

"Our election for Representatives began the 11th Feb'y (which day, 63 years ago, I was born), and it is not yet ended. The five western counties below Asanpink, determined to put in their men, it is said don't intend to close the poll till Wednesday next. All the other counties, except Essex, closed ten days ago; this will keep up that jealousy that has ever been between the two divisions.

"The great struggle is whether the temporary seat of Congress shall be New York, or Philadelphia. The Governor and Privy Council, who are to declare the elected, say they will not receive the returns from the different counties after the time mentioned in the law; if so, West Jersey will be disappointed, and the State in an uproar, however consistent this resolution may be.

"I was ong solicited,land as long refused my consent to a nomination; but at length declared, but so late that it answered no other purpose than to show what I might have done, had I declared in time. I lost every chance in West Jersey, where the suffrages would have been much in my favor, and plans early formed shut me out where my interest was very considerable."

And in another letter he says:

"Should they appoint another convention to amend the exceptionable parts [of the Constitution] it is thought dissension and bloodshed will ensue. Should it be carried into execution with all its energy, the citizens at large will feel what they have ever been strangers to, and it is more than probable that the Horse hitherto rode with a slack rein, when he comes to be held up and spurred, will kick. In short, our situation is such that we require an energetic government at the same time that we cannot submit to it; and I fear there are too many amongst us that have other views than the good of the public at heart." Alluding to the question of the removal of Congress from New York to Philadelphia, he says:—"this has already had such an effect upon the citizens of the two places that they seem to bear the greatest enmity to each other, and it has raised such an opposition in the election of representatives for this State, that East and West Jersey were never more opposed than at the present moment. * * * * It is amazing to think what numbers go back to the western world, and now to Genesee and Niagara, and still we are overstocked with people for our mode of farming. I think the year 1789 the most alarming, both to America and Great Britain." [111]

Mr. Parker was a man of tall stature, and large frame, possessing a mind of more than ordinary strength and vigor;

[111] James Madison, under date of 19th March, 1789, wrote to Gen. Washington:

"In New Jersey the election has been conducted in a very singular manner. The law having fixed no time expressly for closing the polls, they have been kept open three or four weeks in some of the counties, by a rival jealousy between the eastern

and his lady was remarkable for her piety and excellence of character; her many virtues remaining vividly impressed on the memories of her contemporaries, and shining out in a few literary memorials of her, which are preserved. If the "blood of the martyrs was the seed of the church," a praying mother is, in all ages, the well-spring of spiritual life in the family. Mr. Parker died October 4th, 1797, aged 72, and she followed him to the grave, on 10th Feb'y, 1811, aged 71. They rest side by side in the cemetery of St. Peter's Church.

Their children were :—

JOHN, who married Ann, daughter of John Lawrence, and left two daughters: *Maria*, married to Edward W. Dunham, who died in 1834, leaving several children, and *Gertrude Aleph*, yet living, unmarried.

ELIZABETH, who died unmarried, October 27th, 1821.

JANET, who married Edward Brinley, of Newport, R. I., and left four children—*Gertrude Aleph*, who became the wife of the Rev. Edwin Gilpin of Nova Scotia, and left children; *Elizabeth Parker*, who married the Rev. Job F. Halsey of New Jersey, and has one daughter; *Catharine Sophia*, who died unmarried; and *Francis William*, who has several children.

GERTRUDE, who is yet living.

SUSAN, who died unmarried, April 23d, 1849.

MARIA, who married Andrew Smyth, and died without issue.

WILLIAM, who died young.

JAMES, who was born March 3d, 1776, and is yet living, having filled many important public offices and trusts, been a member of the State Legislature and of Congress, a Commissioner to settle the Boundary Line between New York, New Jersey, &c. His first wife was Penelope, daughter of Anthony Butler; his second Catherine Morris, daughter of Samuel Ogden, of Newark. By his first wife he had (besides two children who died in infancy):—

James, married to Anna, daughter of Cleaveland A. Forbes, and residing in Cincinnati, Ohio (being one of the Judges of that State), and has several children.

William, married to Lucy C. Whitwell, of Boston, and now a resident of that city, having several children.

Margaret Elizabeth, married to William A. Whitehead, of Newark, and having issue.

Gertrude, and

Sarah Coates Levy, died unmarried.

Cortlandt, who married Elizabeth Wayne, daughter of Richard W. Stites, of Morristown, and resides in Newark, having children; and

Penelope, who married Edward Dunham, of Brooklyn, L. I.

---

and western divisions of the State; and it seems uncertain when they would have been closed, if the Governor had not interposed, by fixing on a day for receiving the returns, and proclaiming the successful candidates. The day is past, but I have not heard the result. The western ticket, in favor of Schureman, Boudinot, Cadwalader, Sennickson (if this is the name), is supposed to have prevailed; but an impeachment of the election by the unsuccessful competitors has been talked of."—*Sparks' Correspondence of Revolution*, Vol. 4, p, 253.

CATHERINE MONTGOMERY, who married James Hude Kearny, and is yet living, a widow, having two daughters married.[112]

CORTLANDT LEWIS, who married Elizabeth Gouverneur, was bred a merchant, and died in the island of Curacoa, in 1826, while holding the office of American Consul; leaving several children, of whom two sons, *James Cortlandt* and *John*, and three daughters, are living in New York or its vicinity.

THE CASTLE—REAR VIEW.

The old mansion of the family was enlarged before the revolution, by the addition of the front or wooden building which is seen in the accompanying sketch, towering over the earlier and more primitive portion of the structure, which, at the same time, was reduced in height one story.[113]

It is a disadvantage under which family associations labor in this land of ours, that the same house should continue so seldom to be occupied by different generations of the same family. The inclination for change which is so prevalent, and the diversified fields for industry and enterprise which are here opened, would naturally sever the ties which bind the children to

[112] Vide page 91.

[113] The Gardens are on the other side of the street which runs in front of the building.

the paternal mansion, did not the abolition of all laws of entail effectually operate to disperse the different members of the family. Seldom does the man close his pilgrimage beneath the roof which sheltered him when a boy, and rare are the instances where the child sports upon the grounds which his father's father secured for his inheritance—occupies the dwelling which a still more distant and honored ancestor may have erected—walks the same streets—fills the same responsible stations in the same precincts, and at last finds his grave among the crumbling memorials of many progenitors in the same consecrated ground.

But such a mansion is the one here represented. Six or seven generations have issued from its portals to mix in the active business of life. The soldier, the lawyer, the merchant, the legislator, have been trained to usefulness within its walls, and many have been the daughters, wives, and mothers who have there imbibed those principles of virtue which, carried thence, have diffused their healthful influences far and wide, like ever-spreading circles on the surface of the tranquil lake. Who does not cherish veneration for such ancient halls, where true hospitality and charity ever abounded, where cheerfulness at all times lent its charms to attract both young and old, and where religion ever sanctified the active duties of the world?

THOMAS BARTOW.

In the house standing on the south-west corner of Market street and the Square, of late years occupied by Mrs. C. M. Kearny, resided, prior to the Revolution, an old and solitary man, who, by feebleness and rheumatic affections, was prevented from any active participation in the proceedings of the colonists, although their cause had been by him warmly espoused. Consequently, when collision with the mother country could no longer be avoided—when the storm of war burst upon the country, and the fair fields of New Jersey were about to become the possession of British troops—he left his home, and sought, with a son in Philadelphia, that shelter and protection of which his declining years stood so much in need.[114]

This lone individual was THOMAS BARTOW, and, as he was unconnected with any of the political events of the day, whether general or local in their nature—the only individual of the name, with one exception, whose residence in the ancient Capital has come to my knowledge, and one with the events of whose life I have but a slight acquaintance—the introduction of his name with any particular notice in these pages would hardly be looked far. But the recollection of youthful exploits, and of the scenes which were their theatre,—remembering with a gratification which time will not lessen, the delight which in my boyhood I ever found in the house I have referred to,—I was induced first to inquire after, and inquiry has led me to esteem, the amiable, quiet old gentleman, who, seventy years ago, was the proprietor and occupier of the premises.[115] He was the grandson of General Bertaut, a French Protestant, who fled from France to England in 1685; his father being the Rev. John Bartow, the first Rector of St. Peter's Church, Westchester, New York, and his mother, a Miss Read, or Reid, a Scotch lady, who had a brother residing in New Jersey.[116] He was their eldest son.

Mr. Bartow had no other inmates of his mansion than his housekeeper and a male assistant. The only companion for whose society he appeared to look was the late William Dunlap, to whom reference has several times been made—then a child from six to ten years of age—and to him the old man laid open the stores of his own mind, while he kindly directed the opening faculties of the boy in his first essays for the acquirement of knowledge. "Thus," says Mr. Dunlap, in a letter to the author, "commenced my acquaintance with

[114] Such was the emigration into New Jersey from New York on account of the expected invasion of the British in 1776, that the Provincial Congress, doubting the *cause*, passed an ordinance to repress it, obliging those capable of bearing arms to return to the defence of places threatened with an attack, unless authorized to remove by the Committees.

[115] Mr. Bartow built the house.

[116] They were married in 1705. Bolton, in the genealogical table contained in his History of Westchester (p. 209), says that Mrs. Bartow was the sister of Colonel Read, *Governor* of New Jersey. New Jersey never had a governor of that name. He was, probably, John Reid, the Proprietors' Surveyor. See page 45.

Homer in his English dress, with Pope, with Milton, with Troy, Greece, and Rome. I learned to love books and pictures, and my love for them has continued." With a just estimation of the benefits he in this way derived from his communion with the recluse, the author of the "History of the American Theatre," and of the "Arts of Design," has introduced Mr. Bartow's name into those works, with an acknowledgment of his indebtedness, creditable alike to pupil and preceptor.

Thomas Bartow was a small, thin man, whose pale and time-worn countenance was rendered highly impressive by long, gray locks, which, divided from his forehead to the crown of his head, hung down on either side "in comely guise." Rheumatism had affected his walk, age had enfeebled his frame, and these, with mildness of expression and demeanor, his hoary head, and neatness of person, for which he was remarkable, made him strikingly venerable in appearance. His books were the principal source of his amusement, and, apparently, his only company, excepting the youthful visitor who has been named. With him the neighboring villages were occasionally visited in a one-horse chaise in summer,[117] and a sleigh in winter, and these excursions were the extent of the old man's travelling. His property had been accumulated through a long series of years by speculation in land, and by the employment of his pen in different clerkships: having been, in 1735, Clerk of the Supreme and Chancery Courts; in 1741, of the Assembly; in 1762, of the Surveyor-General's office, and, during the absence in England of Wm. Alexander, Surveyor-General for some years subsequent to 1756, he acted as Surveyor-General of the Eastern Division. In 1740 he also held the appointment of Commissioner of Probate with John Bartow—presumed to have been a brother.

His son—with whom Mr. Bartow took refuge from the tur-

[117] Among the Stirling Papers in the N. Y. Historical Library are two amusing letters from *John Harris*, at Perth Amboy, dated January and April, 1762. He appears to have had charge of horses belonging to Lord Stirling, and in April 11th he says: "Mr. Bartow yesterday was saying to me y[e] Doct[rs] tells him he must wride, so he[s] going to keep a Horse, and he also signified to me his Wanting his Stable and Pasture. I made bould with y[r] Lordship[s] submition to offer him one of yr little Bay's till he can suite himself, &c."

bulence of the times—married a daughter of Anthony Benezet. He was a Moravian by religious profession, and it is probable that Mr. Bartow was himself a dissenter from the established church; for, although his Bible was read at home, he attended not the ministrations of "Parson Preston" in public. He owned no slaves, which in those days, when all the menial offices were filled by negroes, was a singular circumstance, and his was the only dwelling in Amboy where a black face was not to be seen.

Here leave we this worthy old man, in doubt as to his subsequent career, save that he died at Bethlehem, Pa., about 1780, never having revisited his peaceful residence in Amboy.

After Mr. Bartow's departure, the house was occupied for a short time by Andrew Elliott, of New York, a gentleman holding several offices under the Royal Government, who had left that city to avoid the Americans, a cause, the converse of that which had driven from it the previous occupant—but he returned to New York as soon as he could with safety. The house then became the residence of Mr. Ravaud Kearny, afterward of his son James Hude Kearny, whose widow now inhabits it.

THE SARGANT FAMILY.

Of the same opinion in politics as the venerable old man who has just been noticed, but one who was permitted by his age and constitution to take a more active part in the views and measures of the colonists, was SAMUEL SARGANT, the head of the family whose name is at the head of this article.

His energy of character once aroused, he embarked his own fortunes with those of the multitude upon the broad ocean of revolutionary excitement, either to attain the haven of just and equal privileges or perish in the attempt. He had been commander of a merchant vessel in the European trade, and had acquired sufficient property to retire from the sea some years previous to the revolution, and enjoy the fruits of his industry on land; the receipts of a small country store to which he attended when called upon (which was not often) contributing to the support of his family.

His residence was near the west termination of Smith street, in the house for many years, until recently, occupied by Mr. Charles Ford. His wife was a Miss Leonard, of New York (a sister of Mrs. Thomas Farmar, elsewhere mentioned), but she had died before the period of his life of which some knowledge has been gained. She was buried in the Episcopal churchyard, where her headstone is yet to be seen, recording her death on the 20th December, 1761. They had one son, who died young, and three daughters, who lived with their father at the time of which we are treating.

Mr. Sargant was of reserved habits, and, until roused into action and induced to identify himself with the cause of the colonists, lived, apparently, an isolated being; like old Mr. Bartow, engaged, when at home, with his maps and books, but, unlike him, sharing with no one their treasures. A private room was connected with his store, within which he was ever shut up, excepting when absent enjoying his solitary rides on horseback, or when his customers required his attendance. The commencement of the war, however, seems to have infused into him a new spirit, or to have acted as an electric spark, giving life and efficiency to the faculties which had previously lain dormant. Notwithstanding the strong *tory* bias of almost every rich, influential, or respectable family in Perth Amboy—notwithstanding that all the relatives of his deceased wife, with one exception, were connected with the royal cause —notwithstanding the marriage of his eldest daughter to an English officer,[118] which must have operated strongly to embarrass and distress him—his patriotism triumphed, and with philosophic firmness he entered at once upon the arena of colonial opposition, and became chairman of one of those "Committees" which tended so materially to advance the American interests in the early stage of the struggle.

Mr. Sargant lived not to enjoy the fruits of his exertions in the cause of liberty, or even to get a glimpse of the happiness which was to be secured to the country. When the English

[118] Lieutenant (afterward Captain) Poole England, of the 47th Regiment. He returned to Amboy after the revolution, and resided there until 1789—when he removed his family to Nova Scotia.

took possession of New Jersey, he retired with his two remaining daughters into Pennsylvania and served for a time as a Commissary, but his health declined, and he died about the summer of 1778.

The eldest daughter, whose marriage has been mentioned, accompanied her husband, Lieutenant England, to the British camp, and while at Boston, had the pain of receiving him and one of his brothers, severely wounded, from the sanguinary fight of Bunker's Hill—their wounds received from hands in whose deeds her father felt so deep an interest.

The second daughter married a gentleman of the name of *Vanleer*, and left children.

The third daughter became the wife of Captain (afterward General) John Heard, of "Sheldon's Dragoons," and had several children. Their only daughter, *Margaretta D.*, died at Mount Carmel, Ill. (the wife of A. Slack, Esq.), on 4th March, 1839, leaving four children.

Mr. Sargant was an uncle of Mr. William Dunlap, who thus alludes to him:—"I remember him with that kind of reverence, approaching to awe, which is inspired by a being of whom every recollection is of something good or something mysterious. His image dwells in my imagination hallowed and enlarged by indistinctness. Every thing I know of him presents him to my mind as a superior being; yet he had no connection with my father or his British military friends, or with any of the officers of the King's government" [not remarkable, considering his political views], "in short, he is remembered by me as an isolated being, until the wrongs of his country brought him into action."

THE STEVENS FAMILY.

Among those who in other days lived and died in Perth Amboy, Richard Stevens is one of the few of whom we have a memento in a monument covering his grave, recording his death on the 4th July, 1802, in the eightieth year of his age.

He was of small stature, had red hair, and all the vivacity of a Frenchman. Being largely interested in landed property, he was constantly travelling through the province, and died in consequence of injuries received by being thrown from his gig on his way to New Brunswick—living only one day thereafter.

His wife was Susan, daughter of Philip Kearny. She followed him to the grave the ensuing year (1803), lying an entire winter speechless from the effect of paralysis. They lived in the house of late years the residence of George Merritt, Esq. They were both violent whigs, differing in that respect from the greater number of their friends.

They left one daughter, who married John, son of the Rev. Mr. Roe, of Woodbridge. They had several children, who lived in New England.

JOHN STEVENS, brother of Richard, was a prominent citizen, represented Amboy in the Assembly at different periods, and in June, 1763, was appointed one of the Council. He is said to have been remarkable for his courteous and refined deportment. His wife was Elizabeth, daughter of James Alexander, and sister of Lord Stirling. He died in Hunterdon County, in 1792: leaving two daughters, one of whom (Mary) married Chancellor Livingston, of New York, and one son, *John*, renowned as the originator of many modern improvements in travelling, and from whom the gentlemen have descended who, of late years, have been so extensively engaged in promoting the convenience and comfort of those traversing the distance between Philadelphia and New York.[119]

Mrs. Stevens, after her husband's death, resided with her daughter, at Clermont, Livingston Manor, until the year 1800, when she died.

There was a John Stevens in Amboy in 1722, then an innkeeper, and in 1735, Clerk of the Court of Chancery, who died in 1737; and another John, possibly his son, resided there in 1741, but whether or not they were the ancestors of the gentleman first named has not been determined.

[119] He died March 6th, 1838, aged 88, leaving four sons (Edwin A., John C., Robert L., and James H.), and four daughters (Elizabeth J., married to Thomas A. Conover; Harriet, married to Joshua R. Sands; Esther B., and Sophia C. Van Cortlandt).

THE BRYANT FAMILY.

In the rear of St. Peter's Church, Perth Amboy, stands a dilapidated headstone—the upper portion having been shot away by a cannon ball during the revolutionary war—erected to the memory of WILLIAM BRYANT. It bears the following inscription :—

> "Sacred to the memory of William Bryant, who in 55 voyages in the merchant service between the ports of New York and London, approved himself a faithful and fortunate commander. Of integrity and benevolence to man, he lived a singular example. Of piety and resignation to God, he died an amiable pattern, 14th July, A. C. 1772, ætatis 88. Sax inornat pat sui dignum memoriæ sacrum fil anor posuit." [120]

Being one of the very few regular commanders trading between the old and new worlds, Captain Bryant for many years was quite a distinguished personage in New York. His ship, the "Joseph," is frequently mentioned as the bearer of important intelligence to or from the colonies, and about the time of his death a vessel was in the trade called the "Bryant," in his honor. Part of the time he united the business of a regular merchant with his pursuits as a mariner.

At what time he removed to Amboy has not been ascertained. His widow, Mrs. Ellenor Bryant, from some manuscripts in my possession, appears to have survived him a few years, but she too died at Amboy, and probably her remains repose beside those of her husband, although no memorial exists to mark the spot.[121] It is presumed that they left two

[120] His obituary notice in the New York papers of July 17th, 1772, confirms the monumental record, he "being in an eminent degree possessed of the virtues of sincerity, temperance, integrity and benevolence, and a true and unaffected piety"—and the following epitaph is thought by a friend to be appropriate—

> "Tho' Neptune's waves and Boreas' blasts
> Have tossed me to and fro;
> In spite of these, by God's decree,
> I harbor here below,
> Where safely I at anchor lie
> With many of our fleet,
> One day we shall again set sail
> Our Admiral Christ to meet."

[121] She died in February, 1776. I have the original of the following bill of expenses attendant upon her funeral:—

			£	s	d
"Cash paid	for 7 pr. Gloves		£1	6	3
do	"	1 Nutmeg	0	0	5
do	"	1 Gall. Wine	0	14	0
do	"	1 Gall. Rum	0	7	6
do	"	4 pr. Gloves	0	12	0
do	"	1 Load of Wood	0	9	6
do	"	2 lbs. Loaf Sugar	0	4	0
do	to the Sexton		0	7	6
do	for the Coffin		1	15	0
Jersey Money at 8s. pr. oz.			£6	6	2
is equal to Proc.			£5	6	11

children—one son, Dr. William Bryant, who was living at Trenton in 1776, and thence supplied his mother's wants; and one daughter, Mary, who crossed the Atlantic with her father in early life, and resided some time in London, where she became acquainted with the Rev. Dr. Watts, under whose instructions she received those religious impressions which in after life "brought forth fruit abundantly," being eminent for her piety and benevolence. She became the wife of the Hon. Wm. Peartree Smith, of New York and, subsequently, of New Jersey,—a scholar and a Christian. He was one of the projectors, and for many years a trustee, of the College of New Jersey; was an educated lawyer, and, with Wm. Livingston and others, one of the writers for the Independent Reflector, published in New York in 1752–3–4. He resided at Elizabethtown, in the house previously the seat of Governor Belcher; was Mayor of that borough for several years; a member of the Committee of Safety, and, after the revolution, one of the Judges of the Court of Common Pleas for the County of Essex. He also resided for some years in Newark.

Mr. Smith died, Nov. 20th, 1801, aged 78, and his widow, August 16th, 1811, aged 92.[122] They were both interred at Newark. Of twelve children, two only lived to become heads of families—one of whom, Catherine, was the first wife of Elisha Boudinot, of Newark, and the other, William Pitt Smith, was a distinguished physician of New York, who left one son and two daughters.

The information obtained relative to other families or individuals is of a character too fragmentary and traditional to be inserted, and this portion of the volume is, therefore, left to be added to and filled up by others, who may have it in their power to contribute further to the illustration of the lives of the early citizens of the central portion of the State.

[122] Notices of both are in Alden's Collection of Epitaphs, Vol. I., pp. 81 and 204

Chapter IV.—Resident Governors.

LITTLE is known respecting the actual residence in Perth Amboy of Thomas Rudyard, Gawen Lawrie, Andrew Hamilton, Lord Neil Campbell, and Jeremiah Basse, while they filled, respectively, the chief office in the province. Hamilton and Campbell may have been permanently established, the latter during his entire but brief term, and the former, prior to 1689, and again from 1692 to 1698.

After the surrender of the government of the province to the Crown, in 1701, and subsequently for several years, while New York participated in the honor flowing from the joint possession of a Governor, that province was conceived to be most worthy of the personal presence and attention of the several incumbents of the office ; and New Jersey, in consequence, was only visited during the sittings of the Assembly, and at such other times as convenience or pleasure prompted : its most urgent affairs being attended to by a Lieutenant-Governor, or the President of the Council acting as such.

Richard Ingoldsby was Lieutenant-Governor under Lords Cornbury and Lovelace, but no trace of a residence in Amboy has been discovered, either by him or by any of the Presidents of the Council who succeeded him, down to 1736.

GOVERNOR HUNTER.

ROBERT HUNTER was the first of the royal governors of New Jersey who regarded the province with sufficient favor to secure upon its soil any thing like a permanent home. He was born in Scotland, but of his parentage, or of the incidents of his early life, nothing is known, save that he was apprenticed to an apothecary, and subsequently entered the army.[1] In what capacity he first served is not stated, but it is evident that he possessed sufficient interest to procure advancement, which a prepossessing appearance and ready wit without doubt facilitated.

We find him, in 1707, bearing the title of "Colonel," the personal friend and associate of Swift, Addison, Steele, and other literary and distinguished men of that day, among whom his attainments seem to have secured for him a prominent position. For although no intimation is given of his having enjoyed any peculiar advantages, it is evident from the style of his despatches, and the frequent quotations in his letters from the Latin and other languages, that he had received more than an ordinary education, or had improved himself by self-culture beyond most of those connected with the colonies in that era.

Having been appointed, in 1707,[2] Lieutenant-Governor of Virginia—Addison being then Under-Secretary of State—he embarked for that colony; but was captured by the French, and for some months detained a prisoner in Paris. While there, Swift corresponded with him; and from his letters we learn that the witty Dean had been expecting the influence of Hunter to obtain for him a bishopric in Virginia. Under date of 12th January, 1708-9, Swift wrote:—

> "I am considering whether there be no way of disturbing your quiet by writing some dark matter, that may give the French Court a jealousy of you. I suppose Monsieur Chamillard, or some of his commissaries, must have this letter interpreted to them, before it comes to your hands; and therefore I here think good to warn them, that if they exchange you under six of their lieutenant-generals they will be losers by the bargain. But, that they may not mistake me, I do not mean as *Viceroy de Virginie, mais comme le Colonel Hunter*. * * * * Have you yet met any French Colonel whom you remember to have formerly knocked from his horse, or shivered, at least, a lance against his breastplate? Do you know the wounds you have given, when you see the scars? Do you salute your old enemies with
>
> 'Stetimus tela aspera contra,
> Contulimusque manus?' "...........

---

[1] Smith's New York, I., p. 177.

[2] Smith's New Jersey says 1705, but in the absence of the precise date, 1707 is thought the most probable.

And under date of March 22d, he wrote:—

"I find you a little lament your bondage, and indeed, in your case, it requires a good share of philosophy; but if you will not be angry, I believe I may have been the cause you are still a prisoner; for I imagine my former letter was intercepted by the French, and the most Christian king read one passage in it (and duly considering the weight of the person who wrote it), where I said, if the French understood your value as well as we do, he would not exchange you for Count Tallard and all the *debris* of Blenheim together." [3]

The date of Colonel Hunter's release and return from France I have not ascertained, but in September, 1709,—Addison still continuing one of the Secretaries of State—he was appointed Governor of New York and New Jersey.[4] He arrived at New York 14th June following, and commenced an administration more successful than any which had preceded it, and which, in substantial benefit to the province, no subsequent one exceeded.

Dr. Colden, eminent for his sound discrimination and discernment, thus alludes to Hunter's course in comparison with his predecessors', in a letter to James Alexander:—

"Slaughter, ye first governor, fell in with the landed men, and his administration was as inglorious as it was short. Col. Fletcher fell in with the merchants. He had a perpetual struggle all his time, and was at last recalled in disgrace. The Earl of Bellamont employed the third sort, or the most numerous, and succeeded in all his devices. The Lord Cornbury turned to the landed men and the merchants, who led him into such measures that the Queen, his own cousin, was obliged to turn him out. After such examples, Brigadier Hunter followed ye Earl of B. in joining with the more general interests of the country, and he went through a long administration with more honour and advantage to himself than all his predecessors put together"—the only course he conceived likely to ensure success. [5]

This is not the place for discussing the political events transpiring during Governor Hunter's stay in New Jersey. He arrived at a most inauspicious period for his own ease, immediately succeeding the unpopular and disorganizing administration of Cornbury—Lovelace, his predecessor, not living long enough to perfect any changes—but he addressed himself at once to the task of harmonizing, so far as was in his power,

[3] Swift's works.

[4] For his Commission at length, see New York Colonial Documents, Vol. V., p. 92, and for his Instructions, see same volume, p. 124.

[5] Rutherfurd MSS.

the discordant elements around him; success being rendered more difficult by the fact that the majority of his council were opposed to the measures which the people generally called for, and which he was disposed to favor; so that between the "humors of the Assembly" in New York, on the one hand, and the determined opposition of his Council in New Jersey, on the other, his post was by no means one of ease.

"If honesty is the best policy," said he, in his first message to the Assembly, "plainness must be the best oratory; so to deal plainly with you, so long as these unchristian divisions, which her majesty has thought to deserve her repeated notice, reign amongst you, I shall have small hopes of a happy issue to our meeting. * * * * Let every man begin at home, and weed the rancor out of his own mind, and the work is done at once. Leave disputes of property to the laws, and injuries to the avenger of them, and like good subjects and good Christians, join hearts and hands for the common good."

Such and similar pregnant sentences had their effect in inducing more cordial feelings between the executive and the representatives of the people than had prevailed in the province, and prepared the way for such a co-operation as naturally tended to overcome opposition; but it was a work of time.

The Governor adopted the views of Lewis Morris, Dr. John Johnstone, and others associated with them, including the Quaker interest, known as the "Country party," and necessarily brought upon himself the opposition of those who had, from the time of the surrender of the government to the crown, been earnestly striving to obtain the control of affairs, and who had been countenanced and sustained by the dissolute Cornbury; and he soon found himself obliged (May 7th, 1711), to ask for the dismissal of Pinborne, Coxe, Sonmans, and Hall, who represented that faction in the Council;[6] the Assembly in a memorial addressed to him, in 1710, not hesitating to say that so long as they, and two or three others, remained in places of trust in the province, justice could not be duly administered, nor could they consider their liberties and property

[6] New York Colonial Documents, Vol. V., pp. 190, &c.

safe; a sentiment which he fully endorsed while asserting that having "noe personall dislike of any man," and having "noe ends to pursue but Her Majesty's service," he had avoided party prejudices and had acted by noe passions in any part of his administration.

In this connection I am tempted to introduce an extract from one of his despatches, conveying to the Lords of Trade his views of the scope and tendency of the colonial governments, which contains a nascent prophecy, subsequently by others more definitely uttered, of the fulfilment of which we are witnesses:—

"The Proprietary Governments, which were modell'd according to y[e] humours of their respective Proprietors, consist of y[e] Governour and y[e] Representatives, the Councill in most being a mere cypher, haveing no share of y[e] legislature; by which means y[e] Governours depending upon y[e] good will of y[e] people for their dayley bread have beene obliged to make such concessions and past them into laws, that if these governments be purchased and continued upon the foot they now stand, her Maj[y] pays deare for much trouble and noe dominion. This is y[e] plan of the government, however, they all aime at, and make noe scruple to own itt.

"The Legislature of the governments immediately under her Maj[ty] is in y[e] Governour, councill and assembly by her Maj[ties] gracious concession; for y[e] time was when in this very Province [alluding to New York] the Governor and Councill were y[e] sole legislature; but y[e] assemblye's claiming all y[e] priviledges of a House of Commons and stretching them even beyond what they were ever imagined to be there, should y[e] Councill by y[e] same rule lay claime to y[e] rights and priviledges of a House of Peers; here is a body politick co-ordinate with (claiming equall powers) and consequently independant of y[e] Councill of y[e] realm.

"A greater assertor of liberty, one at least that understood it better than any of them, has said: That as Nationall or independant Empire is to be exercised by them that have y[e] propper ballance of dominion in the nation; soe Provinciall or dependant Empire is not to be exercised by them that have y[e] ballance of dominion in the Province, because that would bring y[e] government from Provinciall and dependant, to Nationall and independant. Which is a reflexion that deserves some consideration for y[e] sake of another from y[e] same person, to witt: *That ye colonies were infants sucking their mother's breasts, but such as, if he was not mistaken, would weane themselves when they came of age.*"[7]

The difficulties attending the Governor's administration, in both his governments, were not a little enhanced by differences with the clergy of the established church. His relations with some in the Province of New York, from causes not attributable to him, and contrary to his wishes, had not been

[7] New York Colonial Documents, Vol. V., pp. 255–6.

from the first of a friendly character, and Coxe and Sonmans being, nominally at least, members of the church, enlisted the influence of the missionaries in New Jersey on their side; and it was soon announced to the authorities at home, that Hunter was the protector of dissenters and quakers, the enemy of the established church, and the upholder of men of low and depraved character; but his calumniators were unable to impair his standing with the ministry.[8] On the contrary, when in 1715, he was induced to retaliate by reporting to the Board of Trade, that the Rev. Mr. Talbot had incorporated "Jacobites in the Jerseys under the name of a Church," the Board at once transmitted his letter to the Bishop of London, with an intimation that the missionaries sent to America ought to be of unspotted character;[9] and in February, 1718, after the Rev. Mr. Vesey, as the Bishop of London's Commissary, had visited New Jersey, and inquired into the truth of the allegations against Mr. Talbot, the Board informed the Governor, that he need not apprehend any ill results from the endeavors of his opponents to injure him; rather a remarkable instance of confidence, as the Lords of Trade were not wont to be very lavish of their commendations upon the functionaries in the colonies. Mr. Talbot and the Governor appear to have been on amicable terms subsequently, and even Mr. Vesey, who had been an active promoter of the ill feelings entertained by some against the Governor, either through policy or a conviction of injustice done him, manifested less hostility. Hunter's course throughout the controversy appears to have been dignified and consistent, and there seems to have been no good grounds for any of the accusations urged against him. He says, in one of his despatches, and there is nothing known to create a doubt of his sincerity,—"I must begin with attesting

[8] The Rev. Jacob Henderson, of Dover (Delaware), communicated the intelligence, and was after censured by a convocation of Clergy in New York, [illegible]ng the character of sundry church members.—*New York Colonial Documents*, *Vol. V. pp.* 335.

[9] Stevens' Analyt: Index.—Coxe, whom he elsewhere styles a noisy fool, Griffith, and Basse, "that vile and impudent tool of Cornbury," are said to be Talbot's "main props," It is somewhat amusing, that the Board on transmitting his letter to the Bishop should have said in this connection, that "*the Indians* in America require *Protestant* missionaries."

the all-discerning Searcher of hearts, for the sincerity of mine in my good wishes and best endeavours for propagat[g] the true Interests of our Holy mother, in whose communion, ever since I was capable of sober thoughts, I have lived, and by the blessing of God am resolved to dye: and in the next place I appeal to the evidence of all sober men, clergy, or Laity, for a testimony of my conduct in my station with relation to that interest." [10]

Governor Hunter's house in Amboy was on the knoll south of St. Peter's church, commanding a fine view of the harbor, and of the bay and ocean beyond. Whether built by him, or purchased, is undetermined; but there was his official residence while on his tours of duty in New Jersey, and thither also did he retire when desirous of recreation or relief from the weighty cares which his administration of the affairs of New York frequently brought upon him,[11] imbibing fresh vigor from the healthful breezes of the Atlantic, and securing the respect and esteem of those about him by his intelligence and engaging manners.

On one occasion, depressed by the weight of his cares and responsibility, in a letter to his friend Swift (March 1st, 1713), he compares his condition to that of Don Quixote's renowned squire, and quotes in the original Spanish, Sancho's complaint.

"I thought in coming to this government I should have hot meals, and cool drinks, and recreate my body in Holland sheets upon beds of down; whereas, I am doing penance as if I was a hermit; and as I cannot do that with a will, believe in the long run the devil will fly away with me,"—and adds: "This worthy was indeed but a type of me, of which I could fully convince you, by an exact parallel between our administrations and circumstances. * * * * The truth of the matter is this: I am used like a dog, after having done all that is in the power of man to deserve a better treatment, so that I am now quite jaded." Again on the 14th March, in a letter borne by Mr. Sharp, his chaplain, he said: "Here is the finest air to live upon, in the universe; and if our trees and birds could speak, and our assemblymen be silent, the finest conversation too. *Fert omnia tellus*, but not for me. For you must understand, according to the custom of our country, the sachems are of the poorest of the people. In a word, and to be serious, I have spent three years of life in such torment and vexation, that nothing in life can ever make amends for it."

No particulars are given in any of the books, or papers of

[10] N. Y. Colonial Documents, Vol. V. p. 313.

[11] He sought a retreat there also, in Sept., 1714, from the smallpox, which then prevailed in New York.

that period respecting the Governor's family. While in the army he married Lady Hay, the relict of Lord John Hay, and daughter of Sir Thomas Orby, Bart., and had several children. She came with him to America, and died in August, 1716.

In addition to his property at Amboy, he purchased of the West Jersey Society, in 1710, Mattenecunk Island in the Delaware, near Burlington, and retained possession of it for some years after he left the province. In June, 1721, James Alexander wrote to him, that Governor Montgomerie was much delighted with the island—and added: "he got vistas cut from a point upon it to Burlington, the point house, Brick Creek, John Hummels, up the river, Bristol, and down the river, and to some other houses on the side of the river, which from that point gave a most agreeable prospect. I believe it will be a considerable satisfaction if you'll make the title of it to him." [12]

In 1719, the Governor's health not being good, and his interests seeming to require his presence in London, he left his governments, never to return. For on his arrival in England, he effected an exchange with William Burnet, taking an office held by him in the customs, and resigning in his favor the governments of New York and New Jersey. This post in the Customs he retained for several years, but in 1727 was appointed Governor of Jamaica, and sailed for that island in November. He took with him his two sons, but left his unmarried daughters (Henrietta and Charlotte), in charge of the mother of Mr. Wm. Sloper, who had married his eldest (Catharine) a few days before he sailed. He was attacked with rheumatism on the voyage, put in at Madeira the last week of December, and arrived at St. Jago on 29th January, 1728. One of his sons (Thomas Orby), he sent shortly afterward to sea at his own request, the other (Charles), whom he mentions in his letters with high commendation, remaining with him.

Hunter's interest in New Jersey, was not lessened by this change of residence. Distance did not estrange him from the many friends he had here secured, and an active correspond-

[12] Rutherfurd MSS.

ence, kept him acquainted with the political and personal events as they transpired. On the departure of Governor Burnet for Massachusetts, he repurchased the house in Amboy, in which he had resided, and seems to have been disposed to make other investments in landed property. Thus in January, 1730–1, he expresses a desire to purchase five or six hundred acres at Inians Ferry (New Brunswick), if they could be obtained at a reasonable rate ; but I have not ascertained that the purchase was made. His correspondent, Mr. Alexander, thus describes the prospects of the settlement, in his answer dated in August of that year :

"As to New Brunswick at Inians Ferry, it grows very fast, and the reason is the country grows very fast back of that place; for when I came to this place in 1715, there were but four or five houses in the thirty miles between Inians Ferry, and the Falls of Delaware; but now the whole way, it is almost a continued lane of fences, and good farmers' houses, and the whole country is there settled, or settling very thick; and as they go chiefly upon raising of wheat and making of flour, and as New Brunswick is the nearest landing, it necessarily makes that the storehouse for all the produce that they send to market; which has drawn a considerable number of people to settle there, insomuch *that a lot of ground at New Brunswick is grown to near as great a price, as so much ground in the heart of New York*."[13]

Age began to wear upon the Governor. He wrote in September, 1731, that he was tired of public life, and added with feeling : "I have lived for others, and to some purpose hitherto ; I would fain live a little for myself before I die." In the summer of 1732, he was subjected to a heavy trial in the death of his son Charles, and his bereavement appears to have made his years weigh more heavily upon him—while apprehensive that the permission granted to him to visit England, he should not be able to profit by,—his thoughts revert with pleasure to his former associates, as he expresses his wish to revisit New York :—but subsequently his failing health rendered the voyage impracticable, and before the end of the year, he desired that his affairs might all be brought to a close.

His death did not occur, however, until 1734. He had

[13] Rutherfurd MSS.—In a previous letter, dated in January, Mr. Alexander says that "plantations north of the Raritan had risen extravagantly high," even to 3, 4 and 5*l*. per acre, and that for a tract of 500 acres, unimproved land, belonging to Hunter, south of the Raritan, he had refused 1,200 pounds.

amassed enough property, to leave his children comfortably provided for, [14] "having," as the provincial historian, Smith, quaintly remarks, "a ready art at procuring money, and,"—I give the conclusion as I find it,—"few loved it more." [15] Yet he manifested less anxiety than many of his contemporaries and successors, about his support while in the province. Whatever his failings may have been, there is abundant evidence of his possessing high integrity, and other qualities characterizing the gentleman; while the success which attended his administration, despite the unfavorable circumstances under which it was carried on, is ample proof that he was intelligent, able, and persevering.

GOVERNOR BURNET.

William Burnet—deriving his Christian name from William, Prince of Orange, who stood sponsor for him in baptism—was ready and sagacious, a man of good understanding and cultivated mind. An education secured under the supervision of his father—the celebrated Gilbert Burnet, Bishop of Salisbury—and Sir Isaac Newton, had been improved by travelling; and advantages, resulting from a happy combination of studiousness and affability, had given him a knowledge of men and books which enabled him in a remarkable degree to assimilate himself to those among whom he was thrown. And yet from his own account, his talents seem to have remained undeveloped to so late a period, that he was nearly twenty years of age before his father perceived any promise of his attaining to distinction. Books were his delight—his most highly-prized companions—and their acquisition was ever with him a cherished purpose, leading to the reception of more than one rebuke from the relative charged with the purchase of new works, for his frequent and expensive orders: amounting in some years to one hundred pounds sterling—a sum that, as he

[14] He left his daughter, Mrs. Sloper, 400*l*., anually; his other two daughters, 5,000*l*. sterling each, and the residue of his estate to his son "on condition that he should not marry Sarah Kolly, widow of Charles Kolly."

[15] Smith's New Jersey, p. 431.

had become greatly involved soon after he left England by the explosion of the South Sea scheme,[16] was greatly disproportioned to his income, which, independent of his salary in the province, was only about £250 per annum. Drafts, in consequence, were at first freely made upon his brothers, rather to their annoyance.

His contemporaries all accord to the Governor the possession, in a high degree, of those frank and open manners and pleasing qualities which seldom fail to secure the regard of associates. He was "the delight of men of sense and learning," says the historian Hutchinson, and is represented as having nothing of the moroseness of a scholar, but gay and condescending, affecting no pomp, visiting every family of reputation, and devoting himself with unrestrained converse with ladies, by whom he was much admired. Some of Hunter's "gravest correspondents" in the province wrote to him that they did not know how the fathers and husbands would like the new governor, but they were sure the wives and daughters did so sufficiently. And his brother Gilbert wrote :—"I know your temper to be so much inclined to familiarity, that I wish it may not be turned to your disadvantage." [17]

[16] His brother Gilbert, and brother-in-law Mitchell, suffered to a still greater extent.

[17] I am greatly indebted to the Misses Rutherfurd for the use of the valuable and interesting correspondence from which the extracts in the text are taken. This correspondence gives some interesting information respecting the publication of Bishop Burnet's History of his Own Times, to which, although foreign to the scope of this volume, it may be well to refer in this place, as it has never before appeared in print.

In January, 1721-2, Gilbert wrote: "None of our friends think it is time yet to publish my father's history, unless we would blow ourselves up. I don't think the gain worth that risk. Stay till we are all a little settled in the world and people gone off the stage." These objections seem to have been overcome, and Governor Burnet is informed, in September, 1723, that Ward, of the Inner Temple, had undertaken the publication of the work, he to be at all the charges, and the sons to receive half the proceeds of sales. "He has printed," he writes, "6,000 copies, which brings us in clear, if all sold, about £3,000. * * * He has to do only with this edition; not so much as an engagement to be employed on a second edition, if there be one." By February, 1723-4, 4,500 copies of the history were sold, and the Governor's share of the receipts, which is stated to be one third, amounted to £697 9s. 6d. The remainder of the edition was expected to be soon disposed of, when a new one would be put to press. "The history takes prodigiously," says Gilbert, "and though at first some people were out of humor, they now hold their peace and acquiesce. The Jacobite party, who at first lay still, and did not know what to make of it, have now broke out with such fury against it as does us great service."

Governor Burnet received his appointment April 19th, 1720, sailed from Portsmouth about 20th July, 1720, and assumed the government of New York on the 17th September. A few days after, he visited New Jersey, and went through the usual forms of proclamation at Perth Amboy and Burlington.

The acquaintance of Governor Hunter with the leading men of New Jersey, from his longer connection with the province, had been more intimate than that of previous governors; and the intercourse between him and Burnet in England, prior to the latter's embarkation for his government, was decidedly advantageous, as it enabled him to enter society with some knowledge of the characters, as well as of the social and political relations of the individuals composing it; and it would seem that the impressions thus derived were sufficiently favorable to lead him to look forward to more frequent and longer visits to New Jersey than had been the custom of previous executives, and with that view he purchased the house which has been mentioned as Hunter's residence in Amboy. Burnet's tastes and sentiments, however, upon many subjects, differed widely from those of his predecessor, and it is not, therefore, surprising that some of Hunter's warmest friends were never taken particularly into favor. Hunter, although a churchman, was extremely liberal in his views, and not disposed to make religious sentiments in any measure the test of friendship; but Burnet's "eccentrical genius"[18]—although he was so moderate that he could find among some of Hunter's friends those whom he thought proper to designate as "Jacobites,"[19]—disposed him to repose confidence more particularly in those who generally agreed with him in doctrine.[20]

[18] His "eccentrical genius," says Dr. Chandler, "was not to be confined within the limits of orthodoxy."—*Chandler's Life of Dr. Johnson*, p. 41.

[19] He applies the epithet particularly to George Willocks, of whom, as we have already seen, tradition has preserved few traits that would characterize him as a religionist of any kind.

[20] In 1725 the Board of Trade transmitted a series of inquiries, to which answers were requested. One of them referred to "the number of planters," &c., to which Burnet replied that "the people of New Jersey (being generally of New England extraction, and therefore enthusiasts), would consider the taking the number of Planters, &c., as a repetition of the same sin as David committed in numbering the people."

The census was, however, taken, and the result is made accessible to

The course taken by the Governor with the Assembly which he found in existence, was rather calculated to impair the favorable impression which his character and good sense had made upon the people of New Jersey, for dissatisfied with the extent of the support accorded to the government, he dissolved the House: a measure which appears to have been contrary to the wishes of the Lords of Trade, and to have excited some apprehensions among his friends in England.[21] Had the governor regarded policy more than intelligent, independent action, he would probably have reasoned as they did for him, and before venturing upon any decidedly hostile steps, have established himself more firmly in the affections of the representatives of the people. No bad result, however, seems to have flowed from the course pursued, and the tenor of his communication to the new Assembly on their convening in the spring of 1721, was calculated to remove any unpleasant feelings which may have been excited, directing attention, as it did, less to his own emoluments than to those holding subordinate stations. "I must recommend to you," was his language, "not to think of me so much as of the inferior officers of this government, who want your care more, and whose salaries have hitherto amounted to a very small share of the public expense." The session thus happily commenced, ended harmoniously, and the Governor seems thereafter to have secured a fair share of the confidence of the Assembly. Some

Jerseymen through the liberality of the Legislature of New York.

The number of Whites was -	29,861
" " Negroes " -	2,581
Whole number of Inhabitants	32,442

Monmouth was the most populous County. Essex stood second, Burlington third, and Middlesex fourth.—(*N. Y. Colonial Documents*, V., 819.)

When will the Legislature of New Jersey be induced to attach sufficient importance to the archives of the State in the possession of Great Britain, to place them within reach of its citizens?

[21] "All your friends," wrote his brother Gilbert, "think you should have given way to their humor, and taken what they would give you, and managed matters so softly as to have got more next time. * * * Regulate yourself in this matter prudently and cautiously, for God's sake, that you may not lose one way the honor you get another." This proceeding was likely to be more noticed from his allowing the Assembly of New York to continue in existence, and that for a much longer period than was desired by the people. His brother wrote to him: "Take care you don't find it (the new Assembly) harder to deal with than the former. The government of provinces goes on the same maxims with that of Kingdoms, and you know how Princes get little by dissolving a parliament and calling a new one. * * * If you can't do what you would, do what you can."

of the members of his Council, however, were ranged in opposition, and one of them, George Willocks of Amboy, was suspended by him in the spring of 1722; he being, as the Governor informed the Board, at the head of a cabal of intriguers! The Governor's addresses and communications to the Assembly were generally brief and explicit, evincing the disposition—for which his correspondents censure him—to be always "in a hurry," not giving them, in consequence, as they thought, sufficient information respecting his affairs.

It is evident that the Governor's friends were not over confident in his being able so to conduct himself as to insure stability to his government, and confirm himself, by a wise administration, in the good opinion of the people. Considerable advice was given from time to time about attention to business, the cultivation of business habits, of regularity and precision. Even his own confidence in the propriety of his measures was a source of uneasiness to them. "You seem never to think solidly and soberly," wrote his brother Gilbert, "and to lay every thing together, but to be guided by fancy and imagination, which you change every day, as appears by your letters; for you forget what you say, and so altering your way of thinking, often flatly contradict yourself." And yet we learn from another source that he frequently made use of the saying "let us mind small matters, for great matters will make us mind them,"[22] which could scarcely have been popular with one so regardless of method and rule as his English friends would lead us to suppose him to have been. This is not the place for the narration of the public events transpiring during his administration, but neither in New York nor New Jersey was it characterized by any weakness on the one hand, or oppression on the other; and although the influence of a powerful faction in New York, inimical to him for his strong opposition to certain commercial projects affecting their interests, which he deemed injurious to the colony and particularly favorable to the French, did, eventually, secure his transfer to another government, on the plea of thereby preserving the

[22] Pocket Commentary of the First Settlers of New Jersey, in Philadelphia Library, p. 16.

public tranquillity, yet in both provinces his administration commended itself to the approval of the people generally.[23]

The charge of an undue indulgence of his fancy and imagination, preferred by his brother, may have been prompted by a knowledge of the fact that the governor was engaged in doing what many wise men before and since have proved their weakness in attempting—namely, explaining and illustrating the Apocalypse of St. John.

It is said[24] that the Governor, early in life, was inclined to infidelity, but the character of subsequent associations, as well as the beneficial instructions of his father and Sir Isaac Newton, had led him to exchange the erroneous opinions he may have entertained, and so far as can now be ascertained he was a consistent Christian before coming to America. The examinations which these youthful errors induced, may have laid the foundation of that fondness for the study of divinity which he manifested, and which rendered him, at least in his own estimation, a theologian of some distinction. This continued to be a favorite occupation after his arrival, although in some respects it was rightly characterized by one of his correspondents as "not the thing in the world most for his advantage," as it led him to adopt such a course towards the ministers of

[23] The reason for his transfer given to his friends in England by the Lords of Trade, was the desire felt to have a man of ability in Massachusetts, and the belief that he would be particularly acceptable to the people.

As a specimen of some of the contemporaries of Burnet, the following letter—never before in print—from Sir Richard Everard, Governor of North Carolina, is given from the Rutherfurd MS. *verbatim et literatim*:—

Edenton 19 br 2d 1726

Dear Bro

I'm most sincerely ashamed I hant paid you your thirty pounds you were so kind an oblidging to lend me at New York the true Reason is our Receiver Genels running away wth all our monys that we have been Forced to live meanly on our Creditt Pitch and Tar are now such poor Comodities they are not worth Sending as For Whale bone or Oyl I shall have enough this Spring and we have one Waldron an Amboy man a Whaler that will bring it to you Pray Favour me wth your Answer I thank God I have pacified and made easier our Sovereign Lords the Mobb Mr Burrington is gon to England or Ireland and if he returns he is an Outlaw and his Bully Porter is indicted For his Insolence to me and assaulting and stabbing my Secretary, these Prosecutions has so dispirited the Faction that wth my Lenity I shall bring this Province to be easie and Quiet and also a Florishing Province. If your Breed of Pea Fowl are in being I beg you'l oblidge me wth a Cock and Hen Pray make my Humble Service acceptable to Mrs Burnett and All Friends—

I'm Sr Your most oblidged
Brother & Faithfull
Humble Servt
RICHd EVERARD.

[24] Elliot's Biographical Dictionary.

the Church of England as incurred the displeasure of the ecclesiastical authorities at home.

The Bishop of London complained that clergymen already provided with his license to preach in the colonies, were subjected by the Governor to a subsequent examination by himself; and the manner in which it was conducted was particularly objectionable:—

> "Your method," wrote Richard West,[25] in 1724, "is to prescribe him a text, to give him a bible for his companion, and then lock him into a room by himself, and if he does not in some stated time produce a sermon to your satisfaction, you peremptorily refuse to grant him your instrument (permission to preach): the consequence is that the man must starve. * * * * I have seen a great many complaints against Governors, but then, nobody was surprised, because I could always give some pecuniary reasons for what they had done. You surely are the first who ever brought himself into difficulties by an inordinate *care of souls;* and I am sure that makes no part of your commission."

The Governor's work was a small quarto of 167 pages, entitled, "An Essay on Scripture Prophecy, Wherein it is Endeavoured to Explain the Three Periods Contain'd in the XII Chapter of the Prophet Daniel. With some Arguments to make it Probable that the *First* of the *Periods* did Expire in the year 1715.[26]

> Jam non ad Culmina Rerum
> Injustos crevisse queror, tolluntur en Altum
> Ut Lapsu graviore ruant
>
> Claudian, in Rusinum Lib 1 Lin 21."

It did not bear the author's name, neither is the place of publication given, the imprint being simply "Printed in the year MDCCXXIV." The only copy I have seen, or that is known to exist, is in the Library of the Massachusetts Historical Society.

The first allusion to the book met with is contained in a

[25] The Governor's brother-in-law, Solicitor-General to the Board of Trade. He died in Ireland, Dec. 3d, 1726.

[26] Having satisfactorily determined that the first period expired in 1715, the second was expected to expire in 1745, and the third in 1790. "And that this may not seem presumptuous," he concludes, "though in general it is not safe to guess at what is yet to come, we may remember that our Saviour allows and commands us in St. Luke, when these things begin to come to pass then look up, and lift up your heads, for your redemption draweth nigh. If, therefore, I have made it probable that the first period is come to pass, we may be justly entitled to hope that the rest, which end in the Kingdom of God, are nigh at hand, even at the doors."

letter from his brother Gilbert, under date of 11th August, 1722.

"I wish," says he, "you would not write to any body about the Revelations. They only laugh at you, and I must tell you one in your station should not be laughed at." On the 28th of the same month he again refers to the subject, and adds, "I see people whom I told you of before, who endeavored to represent you here as going wrong in the head, and will take advantage of this, which, in every body's eyes, will be allowed to be madness, and perhaps knock you down by it. For God's sake be more reserved, therefore, on these points. * * * * This is the serious thought of all your best friends here, who all join in urging you to keep your hopes to yourself, and not to be gazing up to heaven so as to fall into a ditch upon earth."

"I would much rather wish you," wrote another relative, "instead of publishing any thing upon the Revelations, as I am told you talk of, to keep a daily register of your own transactions, that you may be able to defend yourself if ever your management should be called in question."

Notwithstanding these earnest appeals, the work continued to grow. Its publication became more and more the fond dream of its author, and his letters conveyed to his brother many of his peculiar views, and developed some projects which excited no little apprehension for his sanity. In September, 1723, Gilbert wrote to him: "What you drop of going to France to prevail with great men there to destroy the Popedom, frightened me. I told it to nobody. For God's sake don't say things that, if your letters miscarry or are opened, will make you pass for a man of a disturbed understanding. * * I assure you I would not show your five sheets about it for a great deal." Some months after, the publication of the work is again warmly denounced, and Sir Isaac Newton's opinion is introduced as being decidedly adverse to its publication.

But, nevertheless, the book was completed—and the book was printed, where, as I have said, does not appear—and in October, 1724, sundry copies made their appearance in England. Gilbert acknowledges their receipt, and states that he had distributed them without making known the author's name. West, who has been mentioned as commenting on the Governor's treatment of the Missionaries, tells him very frankly that he had better have spent the time the work had occupied over the chess board or backgammon, and adds, in connection with what has been already stated relative to his theological examinations :—

"I cannot but think that, if upon the prescription of some prophetical text (it is two to one it is so) any poor devil should be so unfortunate as to fix the expiration of your *first period* in the year 1640, in defiance of your Excellency's having so judiciously determined it to be in 1715, he would be in great danger of being looked upon as a most incorrigible unqualified blockhead, and that, consequently, his instrument would be denied."

Surely the Governor's good nature can be vouched for, if unmoved by such epistles. But what says Gilbert now that the deed is done and the work given to the world, which was to condemn his brother to be classed among those "gone wrong in the head," or of "disturbed understanding." We can fancy the emotions of doubt and apprehension with which the Governor broke the seal of the letter which would make known to him the decision of one, of whose intelligence and judgment he seems to have entertained a high opinion, and scarcely need we the artist's pencil to depict the change which passed over his features as he read, "I like your Essay mightily, finding few mere imaginations in it, but a world of parallels that clear up passages. I own most of them were quite unknown to me before." A candid admission to be made to a layman by a regularly ordained clergyman. And then the zeal with which he enters upon a discussion in relation to some of the texts is quite remarkable, considering that only a few months before he had said of the Governor's theory, "I can't see that it even approaches to truth, or even probability." He subsequently awarded the Governor great credit for the interest with which he clothed the subject, and, as is frequently the case, from being a hearty disbeliever in the value of such researches, became an earnest inquirer ; pages of foolscap at each opportunity being filled with discussions, which, had they not been so much to the taste of his correspondent, would probably have prompted a warning to beware himself of "the ditch" in whose depths he had once feared his upward gazing would cause the Governor to be lost.

Both the Governor and his brother Gilbert[27] were members

[27] Gilbert died of a fever, June 20th, 1726, leaving "an excellent set of ser-

of the Astronomical Society, and the former made Astronomy one of his studies in America. In the transactions of the Society for 1724, is a paper communicated by him on the Eclipses of Jupiter's Satellites.

Governor Burnet was averse to leaving the middle colonies. His marriage with a daughter of Cornelius Van Horne, of New York, had greatly multiplied the social and friendly ties which united him to that province, but, as the time approached for his departure, these probably exercised a less binding influence in consequence of the death of Mrs. Burnet, which occurred towards the close of 1727, and the death of a son, which followed in the spring of 1728. But independent of all private considerations, the habits and customs, as well as the theological and political systems of the people of Massachusetts Bay, were not so consonant with his own as those with which he had been familiar for eight years; but the mandate had gone forth; interest or obligation required provision to be made for John Montgomerie,[28] and Burnet gracefully retired.

The Governor reached Boston the 12th July, 1728. The reputation he had earned for popular manners, scholastic attainments and business qualifications, had prepared the way for an agreeable reception. Expectation was on tip-toe in Boston, and more than an ordinary parade marked his entrance into town. A committee of citizens, besides a delegation from the General Court, waited upon him at the confines of Rhode Island, to escort him thither, additions were made to the cavalcade as it proceeded, and at a short distance from the city such a multitude of people on horses and in carriages was congregated, that the display was long remembered as one unprecedented in the history of the country, and for many years unequalled.

A change of government effected no change in the character or disposition of Governor Burnet. He was the same

mons, which we all think," writes his brother-in-law, "will well deserve to be printed."

Thomas, another brother, was Consul at Lisbon for some years, but in 1726 was recalled, in consequence of some difficulty with the Envoy, and in 1729 commenced the practice of the law.

[28] Montgomerie had been Colonel of the Guards and Groom of the Bedchamber to George II. while Prince of Wales.

pleasant companion, the same lover of books, and the same frank and honest gentleman he had been elsewhere, but these characteristics do not always seem to have been well understood and appreciated, by the more staid portion of the New Englanders. It is chronicled, rather as a disparagement of the Governor, that, on one occasion, when dining with a sober member of the General Court, he was asked very deferentially by his host, how he would prefer having the divine blessing invoked, he replied: "Standing or sitting, any way, or no way, just as you please." An answer which cannot fairly be construed into disrespect for the custom, but rather as indicating an aversion to such an adherence to it as tended to render it irksome. For his abhorrence of ostentation and mere formality in religion was well understood, although, as Hutchinson remarks, his avoidance of it led some of the grave people about him to think "he approached too near the other extreme."[29] Such a construction, too, is warranted by the anecdote related by Belknap.[30] On his way through the Province from Rhode Island, the Governor had been annoyed by the length of the graces said by the different clergymen who honored him with their presence at meal times, and asked Colonel Tyler, of Boston, when they would shorten? The Colonel humorously replied, "The graces will increase in length, your excellency, till you come to Boston, after that they will shorten till you come to your government of New Hampshire, where you will find no grace at all." There is a pleasing intimation, however, that his finer points were duly appreciated by men of discernment, in the remark made by one of his biographers, that a coat he sometimes wore, made of cloth and lined with velvet, "was expressive of his character." It would be far better for the world were there were more people whose usefulness and worth, like the governor's coat, could bear an exploration below the surface. His cotemporaries, however, coincide in ascribing to him the possession of a firm belief in the truth of revealed religion, and as has been already remarked, his life appears to have been consistent with that belief, however liberal may have been his views as regarded modes and forms.

[29] Hutchinson II. p. 32.

[30] III. p. 75.

Although the governor still retained his personal attractions, and continued entirely free from any imputations of seeking his own pecuniary aggrandizement—loving money only for the pleasure its disbursement afforded, living generously and to the full extent of his income—and shutting the door of office without scruple to all of an immoral or unfair character—yet his intercourse with his Assembly was not harmonious. His instructions were positive as to the manner in which the government should be supported, and he was inflexible in requiring conformity to them. It was the policy of the mother country to render the representatives of the royal authority in the colonies more independent of the people, by securing to them their stipends by virtue of permanent acts, rather than by yearly appropriations which were so liable to be granted or withheld, according to the degree of favor with which the governor chanced to be regarded at the time, and on this subject Governor Burnet and his Assembly found themselves at variance. The difficulty lay less in the amount of his salary, than in the manner in which it should be raised, but the principle of independence[31] was thought to be involved, and the governor, therefore, intrenched himself under the protection of his instructions, and the Assembly were willing to abide the result of time and opportunity. This was the main cause of dissension between the two, but the frankness and freedom from all disguise which marked the governor, led him to disregard policy, and by the too general proscription of his opponents, and rewarding of his adherents, he contributed to the causes of difference.

'His adminstration, however, was of short duration. On the 31st August, 1729, he was taken ill after exposure on a fishing excursion to Watertown pond, and not adopting proper remedial measures, fever succeeded, which terminated his life September 7th, 1729.[32]

[31] Writing to a friend in New Jersey under date of May 31st, 1729,—when the Assembly of that Province was agitating the question of a government independent of New York—he says: "I am not sorry the Jersey people have shown themselves. This general humour of independency in all colonies will awake the government the sooner."

[32] His funeral sermon was preached by the Rev. Mr. Price from Ecclesiastes ii. 17.

"The world,"—wrote James Alexander,—"loses one of the best of men, and I in particular, a most sincere friend, and one to whom I lay under the greatest obligations. He was a man who, bating warmth, was almost without a fault, and that by degrees he became nearer and nearer master of, and in time, had he lived, would probably have been entirely so."

Governor Burnet was large in stature, combining with his frank manners a dignified demeanor, and possessing a countenance in which intelligence, amiability and good humor were conjoined. A portrait of him hangs in the senate chamber, at Boston, and the likeness which faces this imperfect biography is from one of two miniature sketches in my possession, by John Watson. He left four children. His eldest son, Gilbert, by his first wife, a lively youth of fifteen, at the time of his father's death, went to England, being well provided for through his maternal grandfather. His daughter (Mary) and two sons (William and Thomas), the children of his second wife, were brought to New York, [33] but I know nothing of their subsequent career, excepting that Mary became the wife of Colonel William Browne, of Boston, and left two infant daughters.

Colonel John Montgomerie, who succeeded Mr. Burnet, died in 1731, and William Cosby, his successor, also died, in 1736, but neither of them, so far as I can learn, had any thing like a fixed residence in Amboy. On the death of the latter, the government of New Jersey devolved upon John Anderson, then President of Council, but he too died, in less than three weeks after his assumption of the chief authority,[34] and was succeeded by the next oldest Councillor.

JOHN HAMILTON.

This gentleman was the son of Andrew Hamilton, Governor under the proprietaries, and is the only descendant of whom any knowledge has been obtained. Whether born in America or Scotland, is uncertain.

[33] Letter of James Alexander in Rutherfurd Collection.

[34] The following obituary is from a newspaper of the time:—"Perth Amboy, March 30th, 1736. On Sunday last (March 27th) died here in the 71st year of his age, after a short indisposition, the Honorable John Anderson Esq., President of his Majesty's Council, and Commander in Chief of this Province of New Jersey, which station he held but 18 days. He was a gentleman of the strictest honor and integrity, justly valued and lamented by all his acquaintances."

WILLIAM BURNET.

Governor of New York and New Jersey.. 1720 — 1728.

LITH. OF SARONY & Co. N.Y.

He appears first in public life as one of Gov. Hunter's Council, in 1713, and continued to hold a seat at the board during the succeeding administrations of Burnet, Montgomerie and Cosby, so that he was in some measure prepared by his experience as a Councillor, to enter upon the more extended sphere of duty so unexpectedly opened to him. He was appointed in 1735 an associate Judge of the Provincial Supreme Court, but it is doubtful if he ever served in that capacity, for Mr. Anderson died on the 27th March, 1736, and on the 31st, the proclamation of Mr. Hamilton was issued, confirming in office the incumbents of all civil and military posts in the province; and he continued to administer the government—acceptably to the people, we may believe, in the absence of any testimony to the contrary—until the summer of 1738, when he was relieved by the arrival of a commission appointing Lewis Morris Governor of New Jersey, apart from New York. Governor Morris resided most of his time near Trenton. He died in 1746, and again did Mr. Hamilton become invested with the chief authority; but he had for a long time been very infirm, and before the year closed, he also died:—being succeeded by the next oldest Councillor, JOHN READING.

To. Mr., or, as he was most generally designated, Colonel Hamilton, the colonies were indebted for the first scheme for the establishment of Post Offices in America, for which he obtained a patent from the Crown about the year 1694; but subsequently, for an adequate remuneration, reconveyed it to the government.

He resided in, and it is thought, built the house now known at Amboy as the "Lewis Place," the residence of Mrs. A. Woodruff, beautifully situated, overlooking the broad bay formed by the junction of the Raritan and the sound with Sandy Hook inlet. Tradition represents him as possessing a high and overbearing temper, which, in connection with domestic trials, rendered his declining years, invalid as he was, a period of great distress and unhappiness.

Colonel Hamilton's remains were interred in the burial-ground, then used, lying north of the present Brighton House, but time has long since obliterated every indication of the spot. A memorial of him, however, existed until recently in an old fashioned eight-day clock, once his, which continued to mark with accuracy the passage of the hours in the old Parker mansion at Amboy.

JONATHAN BELCHER arrived as Governor in 1747, landing at Amboy early in the morning of August 8th, having come in his barge from Sandy Hook; the voyage across the Atlantic having been made in the Scarborough Man-of-War. Although apparently well pleased with Amboy, yet Elizabethtown offered greater attractions, and he made that place his residence, and died there in 1757.

FRANCIS BERNARD.

This gentleman succeeded Governor Belcher in the administration of the affairs of New Jersey. He was descended from a respectable family, had been educated at Oxford, and was engaged in the profession of the law at the time of his appointment, being a proctor or solicitor at Doctors Commons in London. He landed at Perth Amboy on Wednesday, June 14th, 1758, from "His Majesty's ship the Terrible"—on board of which he had come as passenger, having with him his wife and family; and as the papers of the day furnish a more particular account of his reception in the province than is given of that of any of his predecessors, it may be well to portray the form and ceremony that in those days "did hedge about a *Governor*."

On the second day after his arrival, attended by the members of his Council, the Mayor, and other authorities of the city, the Governor proceeded to the town hall and published his commission in the usual mode, by causing it to be read aloud in the presence and hearing of the assembled multitude. He then received the compliments of a great number of persons of distinction who had come thither to witness the august ceremony which placed once more over them a representative of Majesty, and the day closed with various suitable demonstrations of joy.

The ensuing day the Corporation of the City waited upon him, and, by Samuel Nevill, Esq., the Mayor, presented him with the usual complimentary address, and the example was followed on the same day by the Corporation of Elizabethtown;—the Governor returning satisfactory replies to both, and assuring Mr. Nevill, that he should "embrace every opportunity to show his regard for the city of Perth Amboy."

A few days were allowed the Governor to recruit after his voyage, but Burlington sharing with Amboy the honors of government, it was necessary that his commission should there be proclaimed in the same manner. He started therefore from Amboy on the 21st June, escorted by most of the inhabitants of note, and on his arrival at New Brunswick was received by the city authorities, James Hude, the Mayor, presenting their written address—a verbal reception in those days being equivalent to none at all. Here he staid the night, proceeding the next morning to Princeton. Notice of his coming had sufficiently preceded him to allow of some preparation by the Trustees for his introduction into Nassau Hall. He was conducted through the building, shown the curiosities, and was then honored by an oration from one of the students in Latin, to which, we are told, "his Excellency returned an elegant and polite Latin answer extempore:" an undertaking which few, if any, of his predecessors or successors would have ventured upon. It speaks well for the ready abilities of the Governor, although, as the effort has not come down to us, we must trust to the record for the faithfulness of the encomiums bestowed upon it. After receiving and replying to an address from the Trustees, the Governor proceeded on to Burlington, arriving there the same day, and again experienced the gratification of having "his knowledge in the law, justice, and candor," eulogized by the Corporation. The minister and vestry of the Church added their congratulations: [35]— the procession was formed, and on its arrival at the court house the commission was again published.

Such were some of the attentions received by Gov. Ber-

[35] The ministers of the Church of England, as a body, presented an address to him on the 30th, after his return to Amboy.

nard during this his first "progress" through the Province, and if the impression made upon him was favorable, he had the satisfaction to know that it was reciprocated on the part of those he was sent to govern. They had the unusual sight presented them of a Governor meeting his Legislature without saying a word about his own compensation, and the sentiments he did express in his opening speech to the Assembly, were calculated to increase the prepossessions in his favor already entertained.

"The excellency of the English constitution," said he "consists in a due balance of its several powers. For my part I cannot more certainly recommend myself to my Royal Master, than by preserving the rights and privileges of his people, nor can you more effectually serve the people than by supporting the power and authority of the crown." * * * * "I came among you with a heart entirely devoted to the service of the country, the care of which must now become my sole business, and I trust that my assiduity and integrity will most properly recommend me to your good opinion." * * * * "And may the great God, on whom we must all depend for success in our undertakings, so direct our counsels that they may be most conducive to that supreme of all laws, the public safety."

He had already given an earnest of the active interest he was disposed to take in the welfare of the Province, by going to Philadelphia to confer with General Forbes and Governor Denny in relation to measures for the prevention of Indian aggressions, which for some time previous had been seriously felt upon the frontiers of New Jersey and Pennsylvania.

His exertions led to the general council held with the different tribes at Easton in October of the same year (the record of which is preserved at length in Smith's History of the Province), which resulted in quieting all claims and causes of complaint on the part of the Indians, to the great advantage of New Jersey. In all these negotiations Governor Bernard bore a prominent part, exhibiting a knowledge of the Indian character, and of the mode of conducting business with them, rather remarkable, when the short time he had been in the country is considered. For the tact and energy he displayed in these matters alone, he merits a conspicuous niche in the gallery of New Jersey Governors, and greater consideration than he has heretofore received at the hands of our historians.

With the political events of Governor Bernard's administration this sketch has nothing to do. He continued to exercise the chief authority until the beginning of the year 1760, when he was transferred by the royal command to the province of Massachusetts Bay. Addressing the Assembly for the last time in March of that year, he said :—

"I do assure you that I shall leave this province with regret. Your good disposition towards his Majesty's government, and your kind acceptance of my services, had given me the fairest prospect of an easy and creditable administration. I had flattered myself that I might have done lasting service to this province, in assisting to compose the differences that still prevail in it, to remove the few fears and jealousies, if any, that now remain, to rectify the little errors in policy which have inadvertently crept into the administration, and above all, to establish a perfect harmony in the general government, upon the surest foundation, an exact balance of the several political powers which compose it."

There can be no doubt of the advantage New Jersey would have derived from a longer continuance of Mr. Bernard as Governor, and the Assembly in their answer appear to have been aware of his merits :—

"Your Excellency's leaving this government (say they), we esteem as a public loss, having in our minds anticipated the happiness we had the greatest probability of enjoying under your administration. Your knowledge in the profession you exercised antecedent to his Majesty's appointment of you to preside here, flattered us with hopes of a speedy and equitable decision in the only litigation of consequence which exists in the colony [an allusion to the land question, involving the titles and rights of the Proprietors], and your general conduct, will remain gratefully impressed on the minds of the people, who will ever consider themselves in a manner interested in your future ease and happiness." [36]

His whole course had certainly met the warm approbation of the people of New Jersey. He had exhibited a talent for business, an activity in the performance of his duties, and a desire to conform himself to the interests of those over whom he had been placed, which exalted him greatly in the estimation of all who had the good of the province at heart. His official connection with it, however, was now closed, and so soon as his new commission arrived (about the 1st of July), he started for his government of Massachusetts Bay ; destined to be far less agreeable to him than the one he was leaving. To form a clearer conception of his character, let us follow him to Massachusetts.

[36] New American Magazine

Two parties had long divided that colony, one endeavoring to curtail the authority of the crown officers, the other to strengthen it, and Governor Bernard was very soon classed with the latter, as might naturally have been expected. Two or three years, however, passed away without the occurrence of any great matter of difference between him and the representatives of the people, but on the passage of the stamp act all the crown officers became doubly obnoxious, and constant collisions ensued. The Governor is accused of having exhibited an arbitrary disposition, hostile to the freedom which was enjoyed in New England, and it is very certain that he supported the measures of the British Ministry with all his ability. He enjoyed, in consequence, the favor of the King, who evinced his regard by conferring on him the baronetcy of Nettleham, in Lincolnshire, and by refusing to act upon a petition for his removal, forwarded by the people of the colony. The opposition, however, becoming so great that a longer continuance in office could only cause him anxiety and distress, he applied for and obtained leave of absence, and bid farewell to America in August, 1769.[37]

Elliott, in his Biographical Dictionary, says of Governor Bernard, "such men never have those friendships which give a charm to social life," and that "he was not calculated to gain the affections of the people;" but we have seen that a different result attended his residence in New Jersey, where high and low regretted his departure, and where his successor had him held out as a pattern for his imitation. He also states that "members of his own household" afforded amusement by most ridiculous representations of his parsimony and domestic meanness; but the character of this testimony, coming, as it very probably did, from those who had expected honors or emoluments from their connection with the Gover-

[37] Elliot mentions some doggerel poetry which was current during his administration in Massachusetts, ending with the lines,

"And if such men are by God appointed,
The devil might be the Lord's anointed,"

which were very properly condemned by his Council as scandalous and blasphemous. The following chorus to an ode sung at *Princeton* College, in 1759, affords a marked contrast:

"We sing great George upon the throne,
And Amherst great in arms:
While *Bernard*, in their milder forms,
Makes the royal virtues known."

nor's family, should lead us to adopt it with caution. From traditions current in the old provincial capital there is reason to believe that the Governor was not particularly attentive to the happiness of individuals in his family, but he certainly exhibited far less anxiety about his pecuniary affairs, his salary and perquisites, while in New Jersey, than most of his predecessors had done; and his liberality to Harvard College, mentioned by Elliott, is also at variance with this reported penurious disposition. To those faults, however, if he had them, were found many counterbalancing good qualities. The only serious charge that can be brought against him is his having too strenuously upheld the presumed prerogatives of the sovereign from whom his own authority was derived, and in that it may be doubted if he did aught that was not sanctioned by sincere convictions of duty on his part.

His character is thus summed up by Elliott :—

"He was sober and temperate, and had fine talents for conversation if the subject pleased him. He had an extensive knowledge of books, and memory so strong as to be able to refer to particular passages with greater facility than most men of erudition. He would sometimes boast that he could repeat the whole of the plays of Shakspeare. He was a friend of literature and interested himself greatly in favor of Harvard College, when Harvard Hall with the library and philosophic apparatus were destroyed by fire; after which he presented to it a considerable part of his own private library. The building which now bears the name of Harvard is a specimen of his taste in architecture.[38] * * * He was a believer in the principles of Christianity, the effect of study as well as of education, and was regular in his attendance upon public worship; attached to the Church of England, but no bigot," * * * when in the country attending service at the nearest Congregational Church."

After he had been in Massachusetts a short time, the Assembly gave him—either as a testimonial of regard or as a bribe to secure his influence—a grant of the Island of Mount Desert. This, however, was subsequently claimed by a French family; and in consequence, or from the confiscation of Bernard's estate in 1778, became lost to his family; but his eldest son, who remained in America and adopted the colonial cause, becoming much reduced in his circumstances, the legislature

[38] The Trustees of Princeton College, in their address to Governor Boone, spoke of Bernard as having shown himself a friend of that institution, but in what way is not stated.

granted to him two townships on the Kennebec in lieu of the island, and he held them as late as 1805.[39] This son, known subsequently as Sir John Bernard, was rated as Adjutant in the New Jersey Regiment raised in 1759, and placed under the orders of the gallant Colonel Schuyler for service on the northern frontier. He was an eccentric character, and, by some, thought to be deranged by the misfortunes to which he and his family were subjected by the revolution. After the war he took up his abode a few miles from Eastport, in a hut built by himself, where, with an unbroken wilderness around him, he lived a solitary life with no companion but his dog. He subsequently changed his quarters, and was much about Boston. Later in life he appears to have been more settled in his mind, and held offices under the British Crown at Barbadoes and St. Vincent, and died somewhere in the West Indies in 1809. He was succeeded in his title by his brother Thomas, who went to England with his father—married a lady of fortune—became identified with many benevolent institutions—and died an LL.D. in 1818.[40]

Governor Bernard wrote several Greek and Latin elegies, which were printed in 1761, and after his return to England he published several pamphlets on American law and policy.

While in New Jersey his residence was the old Johnstone mansion at Amboy, which stood about half way between the "Long Ferry" and "Sandy Point," but which has entirely disappeared from view.

THOMAS BOONE.

Thomas Boone, appointed to succeed Governor Bernard,[41] reached Amboy by land from New York on Thursday, July 3d, 1760. He had been detained some time in the latter city waiting for his commission, which had been issued the November previous, having arrived there from Charleston, S. C. What office he had held at the south, if any, is not known.

[39] Mrs. Warren's American War.

[40] Sabine's Royalists.

[41] He was appointed, Nov. 27th, 1759. Bernard succeeding Thomas Pownal in Massachusetts, who took the place of Wm. H Middleton in South Carolina. Mr. Middleton was transferred to the government of Jamaica

He had been previously a resident of New Jersey, but of his parentage no certain information has been obtained ; it seems probable, however, that he was the son of Thomas Boone, Esq., of the county of Kent, who died in the year 1749 ; and related in some way to two or three of the name who held important trusts under the Crown—one of them, George Boone, being Gentleman of the Bedchamber to the Prince of Wales in 1740.

The Governor was escorted on his way through the county of Essex by a troop of horse commanded by Captain Terrill of Elizabethtown, and through the county of Middlesex by a troop under the command of Captain Parker of Woodbridge. On his approach to Amboy he was met by the Mayor and officers of the Corporation, and conducted by them into the city.

The ensuing day the oath of office was administered, and then, preceded by the Corporation, and attended by his Majesty's Council, he walked in procession to the City Hall, where his commission was published with the usual formalities. An elegant entertainment was subsequently spread for the assembled company, at the expense of the Governor, and the day closed with illuminations and other demonstrations of joy—"usual upon such occasions," says the record,—now no longer occurring within the precincts of the old capital.[42]

As advancement and prosperity were thought in those days, to follow the presence of such a functionary, some anxiety appears to have been felt by the good people of Amboy,

[42] N. Y. Mercury, 1760. The presentation of addresses, &c., systematically followed of course. The Corporation of Elizabethtown appeared on the 7th (J. Woodruff, Mayor), recommending to his favorable regards "the free borough and town of Elizabeth." The Governor, fond of eating and drinking, gave them a public entertainment. On the 8th he left Amboy for Burlington. At New Brunswick he received the Corporation of that place (James Hude, Mayor), and on his arrival at Princeton, attended by Chief Justice Morris and several other gentlemen of distinction, he was introduced into Nassau Hall, by the President and Tutors. Addresses were made, consigning the institution to his care and patronage, having been founded by one and countenanced by another of his predecessors, and he was invited to attend the next examination. It is stated that he was "complimented" by the two youngest of the Senior Class in Latin and English orations—but nothing is said of any response by him. After his return to Amboy he received (15th) official visits from the Judges and other judicial functionaries of Middlesex County, with the ever attendant addresses, and (26th) from S. Cooke, T. B. Chandler, and Robert McKean, on behalf of the Clergymen of the Church of England.

that the Governor should select the metropolis of East Jersey as the place of his permanent abode. Consequently, when the city authorities waited upon him with their "humble address" two days after his arrival, they promised, should he choose Amboy for his residence, to do all in their power to make it agreeable. To this he answered, that "after so obliging an invitation, he knew of nothing to deter him, having the recollection of many happy moments passed there in a private station to induce him." The time of this previous visit has not been ascertained.

Governor Boone met the Assembly of the Province for the first time on the 30th October, having, as he expressed himself in a letter at the time to Horatio Gates (afterwards General), "been married a good while without consummation." "So much the worse for me," he adds, "one should with a woman or an Assembly take advantage of the first impressions."[43]

His opening address was well expressed, but he seems to have had nothing of special interest to communicate, save—what to him was probably an important fact—that the Support Bill had expired some time before. He informed the Assembly—indicating certainly no skill as a seer when the events of following years are remembered—that "there never was a reign when the hands of government might be strengthened with more security to the people, nor ever times more auspicious for reposing confidence and banishing jealousy from their bosoms.' At this and at two succeeding short sessions (March and June following)—the business of which related, almost exclusively, to the raising and equipping the Provincial troops—the Governor and the Representatives of the people were on the most harmonious terms; but again, whatever of a beneficial tendency this concert of action might have produced, was thwarted by a change in the administration.

On the 18th June it was announced in New York that Governor Boone had been, on the 14th April preceding, appointed to the chief authority in South Carolina, and that he was to be succeeded in New Jersey by Josiah Hardy.

[43] Gates' Papers, N. Y. Hist. Soc. Library.

Nothing has been discovered in the matters of legislation during Governor Boone's brief term, upon which to base an enlightened estimate of his qualifications, or from which to gather information respecting his political sentiments;[44] we must, therefore, take the addresses presented to him on leaving the province as proof, in the absence of something more definite, that his capacity for business, character and disposition, were such as to attach the people to him.

The Assembly's last address, presented July 7th, 1761, thus concludes:—

> "If common report may be credited, this is likely to be our last address to your Excellency. Unsolicited by any applications, it may be unexpected, yet permit us to remark, that as we have asked nothing of you unbecoming his Majesty's Representatives to grant, you have refused us nothing we have asked. If it is honorable to distinguish an administration, not only unsullied but publicly kind and benevolent, such an administration as yours demands our grateful acknowledgments. The shortness of the time you have been among us is an objection not in our power to remedy. On your successor, therefore, must remain our hopes; whom we shall be happy to find equally succeeding to our wishes."

The Corporation of Amboy, the day before the arrival of his successor, thus addressed him:

> "It has ever been the custom to address Governors on their first arrival, to enumerate their virtues and good qualities, and to extol their abilities for government, and oftentimes upon no better foundation than the authority of common fame; hence it too often happens, that, upon a better acquaintance, they are ready to unsay all they said and to show the greater joy upon a change or removal. But with respect to you, sir, every day has given us fresh proofs of your Excellency's abilities and upright intentions, and demands our sincerest acknowledgments. No selfish or lucrative schemes have appeared in your conduct, or sullied your administration; on the contrary, all your measures have been dictated by generous and benevolent principles, and your Excellency, in public life,

[44] There is a proclamation of his which may be noticed, being his second official act made public in the newspapers of the day—the first being a proclamation of a day of thanksgiving on 24th October, for successes in Canada. It forbids any person filling the office of schoolmaster in the province after that year without first obtaining a license from him, to be issued only upon a certificate of approbation from two magistrates, and the magistrates are enjoined to be fully satisfied that the applicants for such certificates were of good character, loyal principles, and professed protestants. No law has been discovered under which the Governor could have acted in issuing this proclamation, but it does not appear to have excited any particular notice. In the time of Charles II. instructions were given the Provincial Governors that no one was to be permitted to teach without license from the Bishop of London [Humphries' Hist. Acc't, p. 8], but I am not aware that any similar instructions were given subsequently.

has maintained that good character you so justly and universally acquired in private."[45]

Such language from the authorities of the place where he resided—his personal associates and neighbors—must be considered indicative of more than common feelings of satisfaction.

Governer Boone was present on the arrival and installation of his successor, and did not sail from New York for his new government until December 3d. He arrived and entered upon his duties in South Carolina early in January, 1762, and remained there as governor until May, 1764, when he left for England, being recalled in consequence of differences with his Assembly.[46] As early as November, 1763, William Smith, subsequently the historian of New York, writing to Gates, says :—

"Boone continues still to be, what he is to all whom he favors with his friendship, a faithful correspondent. *The same steadiness is maintained, though the government have hitherto declined a determination of the controversy between him and his Assembly. I fear the cowardly expedient of removing the Governor disliked by his people, whether for good or bad reasons.*" Again, on the 9th March, 1764, he writes: "I hear the Trade [the Board of Trade and Plantations] intend to disavow Boone's contest with a proud and licentious Assembly.[47] I prophesied early that he would

---

[45] N. Y. Gazette. The Council also presented an address on the 29th, the day Gov. Hardy arrived.

[46] The N. Y. Mercury of June 18th, 1764, has the following notice of the departure under the Charleston head: "May 16th. On Friday last (11th), his Excellency Thomas Boone, Esq., Governor in Chief of this Province, went on board the barge belonging to His Majesty's ship Escorte, commanded by Thomas Foley, Esq., which carried him over the bar, where he embarked on board the ship Dorset, Christopher Chisman master, and sailed the same evening for England. His Excellency was attended to the water side by His Honor the Lieutenant-governor, the members of His Majesty's Honorable Council, &c., and at his setting off was saluted by the guns in the forts, bastions and ramparts of Charleston. His Excellency was likewise saluted on his passing the garrison of Fort Johnson."

It is announced under the Charleston head of February 27th, 1762, that the Governor "made a very handsome present for the use of St. Philip's Church, at the same time that he gave the service of St. Michaels.'" The service consisted of two large tankards, one chalice, one paten, and one large alms plate. See *Dalcho's Church of S. C.*, p. 188.

[47] Gates' Papers, N. Y. Hist. Soc. Library. Dunlap in his History of New York refers to this letter in a note to page 41, Vol. II., and on page 412, Vol. I.; but overlooking the fact that Boone had been transferred to South Carolina, thinks the Assembly referred to was that of New Jersey.

In this same letter Smith, who was a stanch and bitter royalist, thus alludes to changes which had recently occurred in New Jersey: "Unhappy Jersey has lost her best ornament" [referring to the death of Chief Justice Morris]. "Franklin has put Charles Read in his place upon the bench, and filled up Read's with one John Berrian, a babbling country surveyor, not fit to be a deputy to any sheriff in England. Oh! how far is Astræa fled! See the mischief of de-be removed. 'Tis rare that a minister cares for more than the maintenance of peace on his own terms. But if the provinces are to have a change of Governors when they please, why not name the man they like at once." * * * "Presuming upon the cowardice of the Ministry, the Carolinians persist in their obstinate refusal to act with Mr. Boone. I had a letter from him of February 1st, in which he says they refuse to make any defence against the incursions of the Creeks, though their borders are a field of blood."

It is remarkable that two successive Governors—Bernard and Boone—should have gone from New Jersey, where they were apparently entirely acceptable to all classes, to other governments where their administrations were condemned, and whence they were both obliged to depart in disfavor with the people.

Mr. Boone, after his return to England, received an appointment as Commissioner of the Customs, which he held for several years. When in New Jersey he was unmarried, but afterward, at the South, selected a lady for his companion who, it is presumed, was a native of South Carolina. In one of his letters to Gates, dated in 1767, he facetiously remarks: "I hope to have an opportunity of presenting my *Yamasee Squaw* to Mrs. Gates, and the papooses when a little more civilized." And in a previous letter, when thanking Mr. and Mrs. Gates for kind invitations, he says: "It is impossible that a poor woman who has been cooped up like a chicken for many

spising Cromwell's maxim 'pay well and hang well.' For want of salary no man asks for the second post in the province and it falls into the hands of a ———. Where is the spirit of dignity that seeks to support the weight and honor of government? Cesar's wife was to be not only innocent but free from suspicion. The Pro-consul of New Jersey differs from the Roman Emperor. Forgive me this severity. I confess myself so much influenced by vulgar prejudice that I do not think any man ought to be employed in the great offices whom the people deride, even though it be without reason. I pity but would not promote the sufferers. I would give him alms rather than high preferment. And with these thoughts I am a little angry at the Jersey successions. Franklin after Boone. After Morris, Read. Patience, kind heavens! You see how broad my slander is. The first error is on your side of the water." * * [Then follows the passage given in the text relative to Boone, and he adds,] "* * We are a great garden, constant cultivation will keep down the weeds; remember they were planted by Liberty and Religion near a hundred years ago. *There are strong roots that will soon despise the gardener's utmost strength.* When Great Britain loses the power to regulate these dependencies, I think 'tis clear she will have no other left. And among the means to preserve all, give us Governors and Judges of spirit and abilities, and support them with courage and steadiness." *That* "power" was lost sooner than the writer of the letter anticipated—and he closed his eyes in Canada long after "these dependencies" were *independent.*

years should at once plunge into an ocean of company. On this account we have declined invitations from our friends and relations."[48]

Mr. Boone's letters are not remarkable as literary productions ; they are written in a lively, free manner, and contain very distinct intimations of a life conformed to the fashionable follies and dissipations of the day ; and the fact that his associates appear to have been officers of the British Army, and others, whose careers were of that character, fully confirm the presumption that there was nothing in his course of life at variance with their tastes and sentiments. Of his talents we have little on which to base an opinion. They are alluded to in some of the addresses made to him while in New Jersey, as being of a high order, but with what precise truth history states not. It is probable, however, that his attractive qualities were more of the heart than the head, and his affability and agreeable manners appear to have closely attached to him many both in New York and New Jersey, whose letters to him, after his removal, evince a warm interest in his happiness and welfare.

In September, 1805, he resigned his office of Commissioner of the Customs, and retired to Lee Place, Kent.

In 1771, his first wife having died or been divorced,[49] he married a Mrs. Ponnereau of South Carolina, who died at his residence in Kent in April, 1812. The time of his own death has not been ascertained.

The New Jersey Historical Society possess a memento of the Governor in four bound volumes, of valuable pamphlets on American affairs, collected by him, and which have his name

[48] He says also in one of his letters that he was about making a considerable purchase in Georgia, where Mrs. Boone's brother resided.

[49] I say "or divorced," for one of his letters, written in 1775—in which he refers to "a separation" which would probably take place, in which a friend "M." [*Monkton?*] was concerned—contains the following otherwise unexplainable passage: "To separate for the sake of forming a new connection is like escaping from the Marshalsea to throw one's self into Newgate. This from you? I think I hear you say. Yes. Honor and inclination determined me to a plan of life which I disapproved and knew the inconvenience of, and the same reasons have not lost their force, but in all probability may never come in question again. It is one thing to contract a new habit—another to persist in an old."

in each written by his own hand. They show that his interest in America continued long after his permanent establishment in England.

JOSIAH HARDY.

Of Governor Hardy very little information has been obtained. The first intimation we have of his existence, is the announcement in the public papers of his appointment on the 14th April, 1761, to succeed Governor Boone, and it does not appear, that he had had any connection previously with the colonies.

The N. Y. Gazette of October 22d, 1761, announces the arrival of His Majesty's Ship Alcide, of 64 guns, having among her passengers "His Excellency, Josiah Hardy, Governor of New Jersey, with his wife and family;" and on the 29th, about 12 o'clock, he landed at Elizabethtown Point on his way to Amboy. He was received on his landing by Governor Boone, Lord Stirling,[50] the members of the Council and some of the chief gentlemen and magistrates of the Borough of Elizabethtown, and the troops of Capt's Terrill and Parker were put in requisition, as they had been for his predecessor, to escort him to the seat of government.

At Amboy, in addition to the authorities of the city, they were met by "Capt. Johnston's Company of Militia, under arms,"—a feature which had not entered into the programme of previous receptions,—and he proceeded at once to the court-house and proclaimed his commission. The ensuing day the Corporation presented their address, after which the Governor left for Burlington.[51] The celerity of his movements indicates no small measure of promptness in the Governor's character, and the answers to the various addresses

[50] Lord Stirling was a fellow passenger with him in the "Alcide."

[51] The N. Y. Gazette of Nov. 5th, contains the addresses and answers at length—others followed of course. On the 13th Nov. the Clergy of the Church of England presented theirs, signed by T. B. Chandler, Robt. McKean, Andrew Morton, Isaac Brown, Colin Campbell and Samuel Cooke. The answer, like all the others, was very brief and almost identical with one returned to the delegates from the Dutch Reformed Assembly which adopted an address at New Brunswick, October 8th, but which was not presented until Dec. 1st, at Amboy.

presented to him show him to have been a man of few words; all of them being very brief, and directly to the point. As a fair specimen the following is given, being his answer to the Trustees of the College of New Jersey, who presented their address Sept. 29th, 1762.

"Gentlemen, I heartily thank you for your address. It will be at all times a particular satisfaction to me to give you every assistance in my power in promoting the prosperity of this useful seminary of learning.
"JOSIAH HARDY."

The Governor met the Assembly on the 30th November, 1761, and in March, April, and September, 1762; but there is nothing in the legislation that ensued, or in the public documents of the time indicative of his character or acquirements; and in February following (1763) he gave place to William Franklin—the last of the Colonial Governors.

The brief duration of Gov. Hardy's administration was apparently owing to some difference which grew up between him and his superiors in England, relative to the appointment of Judges which led to his recall, but he seems to have won the regard of the people of the province.

The corporation of New Brunswick, when addressing Governor Franklin, state that in the course of his short administration, his predecessor had "acquired universal esteem," and the authorities of Amboy, it is said, respectfully bade him farewell, expressing their estimation of the just regard he had displayed for the interests of New Jersey. He did not sail from New York until the 20th September, 1763, and Smith, the Provincial historian, says he was afterward appointed Consul at Cadiz.

Excepting the announcement that his wife and family were with him on his arrival, I have discovered no notice of them.

WILLIAM FRANKLIN.

Dr. Franklin, identified with so much that is interesting in the history of America, had one son. That son, William Franklin, was Governor of New Jersey at the period when, through the blessing of Providence upon earnest self-devoting efforts, our country was happily enabled to throw off the oppressive burdens which the short-sighted policy of England's rulers would have fastened upon her, and assumed 'among the nations of the earth the separate and equal station to which the laws of nature and of nature's God entitled her.'

William Franklin was born in the Province of Pennsylvania, in 1731—but of his youth little is known. He early showed a marked predilection for books, which his father of course encouraged ; but with advancing years the quiet walks of an academic life appear to have lost their charms in some measure, and a disposition was manifested by him to seek employment in the stirring pursuits of a military career. Disappointed in an attempt made to connect himself clandestinely with a privateer fitting out at Philadelphia,[52] he was subsequently gratified by the receipt of a commission in the Pennsylvania forces, and served in one or more campaigns on the northern frontier before he was of age, rising from a subordinate station to the rank of Captain. This expedition is alluded to by his father as being, in one respect, of no service to him. "Will"—says the Doctor, writing in 1750—"is now nineteen years of age, a tall proper youth, and much of a beau. He acquired a habit of idleness in the expedition, but begins of late to apply himself to business, and I hope will become an industrious man. He imagined his father had got enough for him, but I have assured him that I intend to spend what little I have myself, if it please God that I live long enough ; and as he by no means wants acuteness, he can see by my going on, that I mean to be as good as my word."[53]

On his return to Philadelphia young Franklin seems to have become, in a great degree, the companion and assistant of his father in his various scientific and professional pursuits, and subsequently himself entered into official life. From

[52] Franklin's Writings, Vol. VII. p. 12. [53] Franklin's Writings Vol. VII. p. 42.

1754 to 1756 he acted as Comptroller of the General Post-office, then under the management of Dr. Franklin, and in January, 1755—then holding in addition the Clerkship of the Provincial Assembly—he accompanied the troops that were sent under the command of the Doctor to build forts on the frontiers of Pennsylvania; and in June, 1757, his father having been appointed Colonial Agent at London, he sailed with him for Europe.

William Strahan, his father's friend, a man of talents and discrimination, thus alludes to him in a letter written shortly after his arrival in England:

"Your son"—he is writing to Mrs. Franklin—"I really think one of the prettiest young gentlemen I ever knew from America. He seems to me to have a solidity of judgment, not very often to be met with in one of his years. This, with the daily opportunity he has of improving himself in the company of his father, who is at the same time his friend, his brother, his intimate and easy companion, affords an agreeable prospect, that your husband's virtues and usefulness to his country may be prolonged beyond the date of his own life." [54]

Young Franklin entered upon the study of the law in the middle Temple, and was called to the bar in 1758.[55] He travelled with his father through England, Scotland, Flanders and Holland, and appears to have profited, as regards both mental and personal attainments, by the advantages which a visit to those countries under such favorable circumstances naturally afforded. Courted as was the society of his father by men of the highest literary and scientific acquirements, he could not but imbibe in such a circle a taste for similar pursuits, and we consequently find that when the University of Oxford in 1762 conferred upon the father, for his great proficiency in the natural sciences, the honorary degree of Doctor of Laws, the son was thought worthy of that of Master of Arts for having distinguished himself in the same branches of knowledge.[56]

[54] Franklin's Writings, Vol. VII. p. 158.

[55] Ibid p. 170.

[56] The New York Mercury of July 12th, 1762, thus announces this occurrence:—"Oxford, April 30th. Dr. Franklin, eminent for his many extraordinary improvements in electrical experiments, was presented by this University to the honorary degree of Doctor in Civil Law. At the same time his son, who has also dis-

It was in this year (August 1762) he was appointed through the influence of Lord Bute, and without any solicitation on the part of his father,[57] Governor of New Jersey ; previously undergoing, it is said, a close examination by Lord Halifax, Minister of American Affairs ; [58] deemed advisable perhaps on account of his colonial birth and youth, he at that time being only thirty years of age.

There were some persons who regarded this promotion of Mr. Franklin as an event deeply to be deprecated, and intimations are met with to the effect that it was only through the secrecy observed by those concerned in obtaining the commission that remonstrance was not made and steps taken to counteract what was pronounced a dishonor and disgrace to the country.[59] But I have failed to discover any deficiency in the abilities of Governor Franklin when compared with his predecessors, or any peculiarity in his political or private character that justifies the severity of these strictures. On the contrary the circumstances, above narrated, under which the appointment was made, are highly creditable to him—evincing as they do a confidence in his capacity for the office, and in his fidelity to the government, which was not wont to be reposed in those of colonial birth, unless some cogent reasons of policy prompted thereto, or strong claims to the preferment were presented ;—and it is certain that the endeavors made to prejudice the people of New Jersey against their new Governor did not prevent his gathering around him, as members of his Council, gentlemen of the highest respectability and standing in the Province. It is not probable that such would have been the case had his talents and character been calculated only to entail misfortune on the people over whom he was placed.[60]

tinguished himself in the same branch of natural knowledge, was presented to the honorary degree of Master of Arts."—See Sparks' Franklin, and Princeton Review, July, 1847.

[57] Life of Franklin by his Grandson. Vol. I. p. 309. (Edit. 1833.)

[58] Public Characters of Great Britain, Vol. IV.

[59] See a Letter of John Penn's in Duer's Life of Lord Stirling—pp. 70, 71, and one from Wm. Smith quoted on a previous page of this volume.

[60] Dr. Franklin in a letter to a friend dated Dec. 7th, 1762, says : "I thank you for your kind congratulations on my son's promotion and marriage. If he makes a good governor and husband (as I hope he will, for I know he has good principles and a good disposition) these events will, both of them, give me continual pleasure." — Sparks' Franklin, VII. p. 242. There can be but little doubt that the feeling manifested on the appointment of Governor

About the time of his appointment Governor Franklin married Miss Elizabeth Downs—of whom recollections are, or were, cherished by aged persons who knew her, as an exceedingly amiable woman, possessing many virtues, and of very engaging manners. With her he arrived in the Delaware River in February, 1763, and, after some detention from the ice, reached Philadelphia on the 19th, whence he started for New Jersey on the 23d. He slept at New Brunswick on the 24th, and arrived at Perth Amboy the following day.

He was escorted to the seat of government by numbers of the gentry, in sleighs, and by the Middlesex troop of horse; and was there received by Governor Hardy and the members of his Council. The weather was intensely cold, but that prevented not the administration of the oath of office and the proclamation of his commission in public, according to the usual forms; a contemporary chronicler asserting that all was conducted "with as much decency and good decorum as the severity of the season could possibly admit of."[61]

A day or two afterward the Governor proceeded to Burlington to publish his commission there, according to the custom of the province.[62]

Philadelphia having been the place of his previous residence it was natural that the Governor should find stronger attractions in West than in East Jersey, from the contiguity of former friends in the Province of Pennsylvania; he consequently, after some hesitation, secured lodgings at Burlington, and finally took up his permanent residence there until October, 1774, when he removed to Perth Amboy, and became the occupant of the Proprietors' House, of late years, enlarged and improved, the residence of Mr. Matthias Bruen.

The Corporation of Burlington gave him a public entertainment before his removal to Amboy, and the following day

Franklin was owing principally to the illegitimacy of his birth.

[61] New York Gazette.

[62] The usual addresses were presented. Those particularly noticed were from the Corporations of New Brunswick and Perth Amboy—the President and Trustees of the College, and a deputation of Presbyterian Ministers. The Governor, of course, "would omit no opportunity of promoting the general interests of religion or of countenancing those of the particular profession of the gentlemen"—or, at least, said so. The Corporation of Elizabethtown gave a public entertainment to him and his lady at the Point, in June.—Sparks' Franklin, VII. 254.

presented their farewell address, expressing their regard for him, thanking him for his kind deportment and courtesy shown during his stay, and regretting his departure. Neither the address nor the Governor's reply state why he left Burlington.

Almost immediately after his entrance upon his duties in New Jersey, the vexatious measures of the British ministry began to excite throughout the Colonies that abhorrence which eventually led to their separation from the mother country; and Governor Franklin—although favorably disposed towards the Colonies so long as no direct opposition to the authority of Parliament was manifested—advocated and enforced the views of the ministry with a devotion and energy worthy a better cause.

It is well known that Dr. Franklin, however strongly impressed he may have been with the incorrectness of the doctrines advanced by the British Parliament in relation to the Colonies, was far from advocating immediate independence. In his views he was not singular. There were few, if any, prior to 1775, who regarded such a remedy as necessary; and Franklin presumed that the yearly increasing importance of America to the various mercantile and manufacturing interests of Great Britain would at last work out for her that relief which was so earnestly desired. But, when convinced that nothing was to be hoped for from the delay, he became an ardent and uncompromising supporter of the Colonial cause.

Under date of October 6th, 1773, he thus states his own position and that of his son. Referring to some letters of his which Governor Hutchinson of Massachusetts had represented to be advisatory of immediate independence, he says:—

"I shall be able at any time to justify every thing I have written, the purport being uniformly this, that they should carefully avoid all tumults and every violent measure, and content themselves with verbally keeping up their claim and holding forth their rights whenever occasion requires. * * * * From a long and thorough consideration of the subject I am, indeed, of opinion that the Parliament has no right to make any law whatever binding on the Colonies. That the King, and not the King, Lords and Commons collectively, is their sovereign; and that the King, with their respective parliaments, is their only legislator. I know your sentiments [he was writing to the Governor] differ from mine on these subjects. You are a thorough government man, which I do not wonder at, nor do I aim at converting you; I only wish you to act uprightly and steadily, avoiding that duplicity which in Hutchinson adds contempt to indignation. If you can promote the prosperity of your people, and leave them happier than you found them, whatever your political principles are, your memory will be honored."

Upon this letter the Doctor's grandson bases a refutation of the belief generally entertained, that he endeavored to persuade the Governor to withdraw from the royal cause,[63] but I have been assured by one who was cognizant of the fact that, when confirmed in his own course, and after his return to America in 1775, the Doctor visited his son at Perth Amboy, and strove zealously to draw him over to the side of the colonies;—that their conversations were sometimes attended with exhibitions of warmth not very favorable to continued harmonious intercourse, but each failed to convince the other of the impropriety of the course he was pursuing; and it is not probable the Doctor would have expressed his displeasure subsequently in such decided terms had not the Governor slighted his counsel. His son certainly followed his advice in "avoiding duplicity," for he did not hesitate to give manifest tokens of his determination to rise or fall with the royal cause.

One cannot help contrasting this visit of Doctor Franklin to Amboy, and its attending circumstances, with the one he had made half a century before. Then a poor and unknown lad, seeking a place where he might earn his daily bread by laborious exertion, he had passed within the limits of the ancient city a night of feverishness and unrest, after a day of abstinence and exposure; and left it to prosecute on foot his journey of fifty miles to Burlington—drenched in rain and subjected to injurious suspicions.[64] Now, the man of science and the statesman, whose fame had extended to both hemispheres, came from a sojourn in foreign lands and from intercourse with the wise and great of the earth, to confer with his son—become a representative of royalty—in the very place from which he had made so miserable an exit.

Although the conspicuous part performed in the revolutionary drama by Governor Franklin constitutes the most important feature of his administration, yet he was too long in the executive chair not to contract a greater attachment to the Province than his flitting predecessors had done, and to be-

[63] Life of Franklin, Vol. I. p. 310. [64] Franklin's Writings, Vol. I. p. 231.

come acquainted with the wants and aware of the evils under which its population labored. He appears, in consequence, to have exerted himself in a laudable manner to promote its prosperity. At different times he brought to the notice of the Assembly, and encouraged legislation relating to the improvement of roads, the fostering of agriculture by the bestowment of bounties, the melioration of the laws prescribing imprisonment for debt; and, it is thought, proved himself an active and efficient Governor; although in other respects than in approving the course of the British ministry he failed to secure the approbation of the people; yet his known adherence to principles which were deemed inimical to popular rights was probably the foundation of most, if not all, the opposition shown to him.

It would, however, trench too much upon the province of history to narrate here the circumstances which called forth this opposition; it will suffice to remark, as illustrative of the character of the man apart from his public station—the principal aim of this sketch—that at these periods Governor Franklin, while he evinced a determination to persevere in the course dictated by his sense of duty, does not seem to have acted in a way to attach any discredit to himself, other than that which accrues to the politician from acting contrary to the views of his opponents. At times, indeed, he sacrificed his own official popularity to the claims of personal friendship, and when assured of the correctness of his opinions, allowed no apprehensions of personal safety, or of prejudice to his interests, to interfere with their adaptation in practice to the promotion of the public welfare as understood by him.

During the entire period from the passage of the Stamp Act in 1765, until the receipt of Lord North's Declaratory project, the Governor, so far as his communications have come under my notice, observed a commendable prudence in his intercourse with the representatives of the people, and with the people themselves; saying nothing which, considering his relations to the Crown, they could not excuse or extenuate; and we find consequently that a due degree of respect continued to be shown to him and his authority. Even at as late a period as February, 1775, the representatives of the people were warm in their expression of attachment to the government of Great Britain. "We do solemnly and with great truth assure your Majesty, that we have no thoughts injurious to the allegiance which, as subjects, we owe to you as our sovereign; that we abhor the idea of setting ourselves up in a state of independency, and that we know of no such design in others." And again in November of that year the Assembly passed resolutions adverse to independence, and directing the delegates of the Province in the Continental Congress to oppose any proposition of the kind. But they were called to act upon the measure proposed by Lord North, at a time when they had too recently seen the blood of friends and countrymen shed at Lexington, for them to regard it with the forbearance they had previously exhibited, and from this point the intercourse with the Governor became less cordial.

It was at this period that dissension also, for the first time, appears to have entered the Council. Previously, so far as the sentiments of the members of that body have become public, they had, in the main, coincided with the Governor in his views. But in September of this year he felt called upon to suspend Lord Stirling, who was one of the members, in consequence of his acceptance of a military commission under the Provincial Congress, and shortly after, the communications which passed between the Council and the Governor began to evince in no small degree the growing estrangement which soon put an end to all harmonious action, and left the Governor, unsupported, to stem the adverse tide of popular prejudice. Writing about this period to the Earl of Dartmouth, the Governor feelingly remarks, "My situation is indeed somewhat particular and not a little difficult, having no more than one or two among the principal officers of government to whom I, even now, speak confidentially on public affairs." [65]

The despatch containing this passage was intercepted on the 6th of January, 1776, by Lord Stirling, and led to the adoption of measures by that officer to prevent the escape of Governor Franklin, although there is no evidence that he had formed any such intention. He had declared to the Assembly that, unless compelled by violence, he should not leave the Province, and he stated in a letter addressed to the officer

[65] Princeton Review, July, 1847.

having command of the guard placed at his gate, that "such an assurance on his part was certainly equal to any promise he could make." At the solicitation of the Chief Justice of the Province, however, he was induced to give his parole; and for some months continued, amid all the excitement and increasing difficulties of the time, to occupy his house in Amboy, and to exercise nominally the duties of his station.[66] But having received despatches from the Ministry which he was anxious to lay before the Assembly, he issued a proclamation convening that body on the 20th of June. This the Provincial Convention or Congress, on the 14th of June, pronounced a direct contempt of the order of the Continental Congress which abrogated all foreign jurisdiction, and, in a series of resolutions which they adopted, expressed an opinion that the proclamation ought not to be obeyed, and that thereafter no payments should be made to Gov. Franklin on account of salary. Three days thereafter he was arrested at Amboy by a detachment of militia under Colonel (afterwards General) Heard, of Woodbridge,[67] accompanied by Major Deare of Amboy, whose authority for so doing was as follows:—

[66] Duer's Life of Lord Stirling, pp. 119, 121. Force's Doc. Hist. U. S. Vol. IV. Princeton Review, July, 1847.

[67] The name of General Nathaniel Heard is frequently found connected with the revolutionary events in this section of the State. He resided in Woodbridge on the south-east corner of the junction of the old post-road and the road from Amboy, and some marks of his house were visible not long since in the grove of locust trees which now occupies the spot. He had three sons and four daughters. *John* was an officer during the revolution, and served as a Captain in "Sheldon's Dragoons." The author saw him, as General Heard, in his continental uniform of blue and buff, at Woodbridge in 1824, when General La Fayette passed through on his way to Philadelphia from New York. He married a daughter of Samuel Sargant of Amboy, and had several children, but of one only has any information been obtained—their only daughter, *Margaret D.*, who died March 4th, 1839, at Mount Carmel, Illinois—the wife of H. Slack, leaving four children. General Heard after the revolution held several offices under the General and State Governments—among them being the Marshalship of New Jersey and the Collectorship of Amboy (from 1802 to 1806) under the United States, and Surrogate under the State.

James, another son of old General Heard, was also an officer in the revolution, and married a daughter of the renowned General Daniel Morgan.

William, the third son, was never married, and after the death of his father lived with his sisters, and for some cause unknown to the author, committed suicide,

The daughters of old General Heard were much respected. One of them became the wife of Jacob Van Horne; the other three, it is thought, were never married.

"To Colonel NATHANIEL HEARD—

"The Provincial Congress of New Jersey, reposing great confidence in your zeal and prudence, have thought fit to entrust to your care the execution of the enclosed Resolves. It is the desire of Congress that this necessary business be conducted with all the delicacy and tenderness which the nature of the service can possibly admit of.

"For this end, you will find among the papers the form of a written parole, in which there is left a blank space for you to fill up, at the house of Mr. Franklin, with the name of Princeton, Bordentown, or his own farm at Rancocus. When he shall have signed the parole, the Congress will rely upon his honor for the faithful performance of his engagements; but should he refuse to sign it, you are desired to put him under strong guard, and keep him in close custody until farther orders. Whatever expense may be necessary will be cheerfully defrayed by the Congress. We refer to your discretion what means to use for that purpose, and you have full power and authority to take to your aid whatever force you may require."

"By order of Congress,

SAMUEL TUCKER, President.

"In Provincial Congress, New Jersey, Burlington, June 15th, 1776."

The Parole was as follows:—

"I, William Franklin, being apprehended by an order of the Provincial Congress of New Jersey, do promise and engage on my word and honor, and on the faith of a gentleman, to depart within two days from hence to ————————, in the Province of New Jersey, being the place of my destination and residence; and there, or within six miles thereof, to remain during the present war between Great Britain and the said United Colonies, or until the Congress of the said United Colonies, or the Assembly, Convention, or Committee, or Council of Safety of the said Colony, shall order otherwise, and that I will not directly or indirectly give any intelligence whatsoever to the enemies of the United Colonies, or do or say any thing in opposition to or in prejudice of the measures and proceedings of any Congress for the said Colonies, during the present troubles, or until I am duly discharged. Given under my hand this day of A.D. 1776."

Governor Franklin indignantly refused to sign the parole, and he was therefore placed under guard. A report of their proceedings being made by the Provincial Convention to the Continental Congress, that body on the 19th June passed the following resolution:—

"A letter from the Convention of New Jersey of the 18th, enclosing sundry papers, together with their proceedings in apprehending William Franklin, Esq., Governor of that Colony, was laid before Congress. Whereupon Resolved, that it be recommended to the Convention of New Jersey to proceed on the examination of Mr. Franklin, and if, upon such examination, they shall be of opinion that he should be confined, to report such opinion to Congress, and then the Congress will direct the place of his confinement: they concurring in sentiment with the Convention of New Jersey that it would be improper to confine him in that Colony."[68]

[68] Proceedings of Congress.

A guard of sixty men had remained around the Governor's residence until communication could be had with the Convention. That body ordered him to be taken to Burlington, where, on the receipt of the above resolution, he was examined touching such points of his conduct as were deemed prejudicial to the interests of America. His loyalty, firmness and self-possession remained unshaken under the ordeal. Conceiving that the Convention had usurped the authority it exercised, he denied the right of that body to interrogate him, and refused to answer any questions propounded. He was therefore declared an enemy to the country, and Lieutenant-colonel Bowes Reed was directed to keep him safely guarded until the pleasure of the Continental Congress should be known.[69]

As has been stated, the arrest of Governor Franklin was based upon an alleged infraction or implied contempt of the resolution of the Continental Congress, adopted 15th May preceding; but it is probable the proclamation referred to was only adopted as an *available* excuse for doing what had doubtless been for some time determined on.

It has been advanced as a reason for the interference at that precise time, that the object of the Governor was to create confusion in the administration of the public affairs by arraying the Assembly against the Convention. But it must be remembered that for more than a year, during which these two bodies had existed, there had been no conflicting action between them. More than one third of the members of the Convention in 1775 were also members of the Assembly, and there were many others of the latter body equally as well affected to the colonial cause; and, although, in the Convention of 1776, the number of the members of the Assembly in the Convention was reduced to seven, yet the political character of the Assembly remained unchanged, and I have failed to discover any documents that indicate a probability that the Governor could have moulded that body to any sinister views he may have entertained.

The Governor, however, in a long communication addressed

[69] The original minutes, in my possession, have the words "in safe custody" erased and "*under safe guard*" substituted.

to the Council and Assembly, which was written on the day of his arrest, reviews the plea of his opponents in the following warm and emphatic language :—

* * * * "The fact alleged is false, and must appear glaringly so to every man who has read the resolve alluded to, and is capable of understanding it. The Continental Congress, after a preamble declaring their opinion "that the exercise of every kind of authority under the Crown should be totally suppressed," do then resolve that it be recommended to the respective *Assemblies* and Conventions of the United Colonies *where no governments sufficient to the exigencies of their affairs have been hitherto established*, to adopt such government as shall, in the opinion of the *representatives of the people*, best conduce to the happiness and safety of their constituents in particular, and America in general." How any persons can construe and represent my calling a meeting of the *Assembly* at the very time when such an important matter was *recommended* by the Continental Congress to the consideration of *the representatives of the people*, to be a "direct contempt and violation" of the above Resolve, is difficult to conceive, supposing them possessed of common sense and common honesty. The Assembly of Pennsylvania have met since that resolve, and I believe are still sitting, under an authority derived from the Crown. They, no doubt, have had the resolve under their consideration, nor can any good reason be given why the Assembly of New Jersey should not likewise be permitted the opportunity of giving their sentiments (if they should think it necessary or expedient) on a matter of such infinite importance to them and their constituents. If when you met, you had thought it proper to adopt or comply with the resolve, either in whole or in part, it is well known that I could not have prevented it, whatever my inclination might have been. In other colonies where a change of government has been made, one of the reasons assigned in excuse for such measure has been, that the Governor has either abdicated his government, appeared in arms against the people, or neglected to call a meeting of their representatives. But I do not recollect an instance where neither of these circumstances existed, and government could be carried on in the usual way, in such essential points as meetings of the Legislature, passing of Laws and holding Courts of Justice, that any material alteration has been made in such government by a convention; nor that any convention has before presumed to attempt a business of that importance where an assembly existed and were not hindered from meeting. Most probably had I not called the Assembly I should have been much blamed by those very men for the omission (especially as matters of such consequence were in agitation) and accused of not exercising the prerogative vested in me for the good of the people, as I ought to have done. But however that may be, sure I am, that it is the evident meaning of the resolve of the Continental Congress that when assemblies can meet they are to consider the propriety of the measure recommended, and *not* Conventions."

* * * * * * *

In a postscript, added after his arrival at Burlington, June 22d, 1776, he fortifies his position with further references to the course of the Delaware Assembly and Maryland Convention. He says.

"Since writing the above I have seen a Pennsylvania newspaper of June 19th, in which it appears Mr. McKean laid before the Assembly of the three lower counties a certified copy of the resolution of Congress of the 15th May last, which being taken in consideration by that house on the 15th instant, they resolved, among other things, that "*the representatives of the people in* THIS ASSEMBLY met, ALONE *can and ought* AT THIS TIME to establish such temporary authority—meaning the authority they had before determined to be expedient in the present exigency of affairs—"*until a new government can be formed.*" This Assembly met, as well as that of Pennsylvania, under an authority derived from the Crown, and so far from considering such a meeting as a contempt or violation of the resolve of the Continental Congress, they resolved they were the only proper persons to take that resolve into consideration, and to *establish such authority* as was deemed adequate to the occasion. The Assembly of New Jersey might certainly with equal propriety have done the same, had they been allowed to meet.

"It likewise appears by the newspapers that the Governor of Maryland on the 12th instant, had "issued a *proclamation* for dissolving the General Assembly of that Province, and to order writs of election to be issued to *call a new Assembly* returnable the 25th day of July next." But there is not the least surmise that the Provincial Convention of that Province have taken any offence at such proclamation, or so much as pretended to think the Governor had thereby acted in direct contempt and violation of the resolve of the Continental Congress, and was therefore such an enemy to the liberties of this country as that he ought to be tried and imprisoned. Yet the Maryland Convention have shown as much spirit and regard for the liberties of America as any body of men on the continent. But they, it seems, are for peace, reconciliation and union with Great Britain on constitutional terms, and have too much sense and virtue to declare a Governor an enemy to the liberties of this country merely because he is an enemy to the liberties which such designing men are disposed to take with the old constitutional government.

* * * * * * * * * * * *

The Governor commented also at considerable length upon what he was pleased to term the evils of "independent republican tyranny" which he considered impending over the province, as well as upon the injustice with which he had personally been treated. For whatever of an offensive character this communication my contain, due allowance can now be made.[70] To one of his impetuous disposition and high ideas of prerogative, it must have been exceedingly galling to be placed thus at the mercy of a self-constituted tribunal, disposed to exercise the authority it had assumed without regard to any other power or jurisdiction whatever. May we not sympathize with the man, and regret the necessity which called for the rigor manifested towards him, without weakening our abhorrence of the principles which as an officer of the Crown he felt bound to support! He had discernment

[70] For the whole letter see Gaines's Paper, Feb'y 3d, 1777.

enough to perceive that the "independency" which the people's representatives had not hesitated so recently to deny to be the end and aim of their struggle with the mother country, was, in fact, the point to which they were fast tending; had it been less apparent to his mind his course would probably have been more in consonance with the popular will, for so far as his opinions are known upon the matters of difference between the colonies and the parliament, they appear to have been such as to exonerate him—as he asserts in the communication just noticed—from any imputation of cherishing a disposition inimical to the interests of America; entertaining the conviction that by negotiation all the desired relief and redress could be secured. Doubtless the rapid development of the independent movement hastened his seizure.

On the 22d June the Governor addressed a second letter to the Council and Assembly, narrating the treatment received from his escort on his way to Burlington, and the circumstances connected with his examination. From his account of the transactions it would seem that unnecessary strictness was observed in excluding him from the society of friends, and in the restraints placed upon his personal movements. He concludes the letter thus:—

"Why they could not, if they were determined to usurp the powers of government, suffer me to remain quietly in my own home, as they do other Crown officers in the province, I have not heard. They well know I have not either levied or attempted to levy any troops against them, that I could not, had I been so inclined, have given any hinderance to their measures, and that I might have been of service to the couutry in case of a negotiation taking place. I can account for this conduct no otherwise than that they mean to show, by tearing one in my station from his wife and family, how all-sufficient their present power is, and thereby to intimidate every man in the province from giving any opposition to their iniquitous course. But be the event what it may, I have, thank God, spirit enough to face the danger. *Pro Rege and Patria* was the motto I assumed when I first commenced my political life, and I am resolved to retain it till death shall put an end to my mortal existence."

The following extracts from the proceedings of the Continental Congress, mark the course of that body towards the Governor:

"Monday, June 24th, 1776.—A letter of the 21st from the Convention of New Jersey was laid before Congress and read, together with sundry papers enclosed therein, containing the questions proposed to William Franklin, Esq.,—an account of his behavior on the occasion, and the resolution of the Convention, "declaring him a virulent enemy to this country, and a person that may prove dangerous, and that the said William Franklin be confined in such place and manner as the Continental Congress shall direct." Whereupon

"*Resolved*, That William Franklin be sent under guard to Governor Trumbull, who is desired to admit him to his parole; but if Mr. Franklin refuse to give his parole, that Governor Trumbull be desired to treat him agreeably to the resolutions of Congress respecting prisoners."

Governor Trumbull accepting the charge, he was taken to Connecticut forthwith,[71] and quartered in the house of Capt. Ebenezer Grant at East Windsor; his lady being left in the city of New York.

On the 23d November Congress "Resolved, that General Washington be directed to propose to General Howe an exchange of Wm. Franklin, Esq., late Governor of New Jersey, for Brig. Gen. Thompson;" but on the 3d December, he was requested to suspend the execution of the order, should the negotiation with General Howe not have been commenced; and no further mention of Governor Franklin is made until Tuesday, April 22d, 1777; it was then

"*Resolved*, That Governor Trumbull be informed that Congress has received undoubted information that William Franklin, late Governor of the State of New Jersey, and now a prisoner in Connecticut, has since his removal to that State sedulously employed himself in dispersing among the inhabitants the protections of Lord Howe and General Howe, styled the King's Commissoners for granting pardons, and otherwise aided and abetted the enemies of the United States; and that he be requested forthwith to order the said William Franklin, Esq., into close confinement, prohibiting to him the use of pen, ink and paper, or the access of any person or persons but such as are properly licensed for that purpose by Governor Trumbull."

Lord Howe had specially invoked the aid of all the governors who had been expelled from their provinces, in spreading his "protections" among the people; and the foregoing resolution is indicative of the zeal with which Governor Franklin had obeyed the behest. It is probable that he remembered, among others, his neighbors at Amboy, one of the first of these documents that fell into the hands of General Washington having been directed to the inhabitants of that place.[72]

On the 22d July following the order of Congress for his

[71] Capt. Kinney, who escorted him, was cited before the Provincial Congress on the 17th July to exonerate himself from a charge of "loitering on the way,"—which he did, the delay being attributed to accidental causes. —*Original Minutes.*

[72] Botta, I. p. 36.

close confinement, Governor Franklin applied to General Washington for a release on parole. His letter the General forwarded to Congress, accompanied by one from himself, which seems to convey a desire on his part that the request might be granted on account of the low state of Mrs. Franklin's health, which had sunk under the anxieties and sufferings which the state of the country and separation from her husband had entailed upon her. Congress however refused to grant the favor solicited ; assigning as a reason that the intercepted letters of Governor Franklin had been such as to make it evident it would be inconsistent with the safety of the States to allow him any liberty whatever that would afford him opportunities for conferring with the enemy.[73]

Husband and wife consequently met no more in life. Mrs. Franklin died on the 28th of July, 1778, and the next evening, attended by a number of the most respectable inhabitants of the city, her remains were deposited within the chancel of St. Paul's Church. Her obituary notice in the Mercury of August 4th, proclaims her "a loving wife, an indulgent mistress, a steady friend, and affable to all" — characteristics which, from all that has come down to us, would seem by no means to embrace all of her estimable qualities. Ten years subsequently the Governor caused a tablet to be erected to her memory, which still occupies a place in the wall of the church bearing the following inscription beneath the Franklin arms :

"Beneath the Altar of this Church are deposited the remains of
Mrs. ELIZABETH FRANKLIN, wife of His Excellency,
WILLIAM FRANKLIN, Esq., late Governor under
His Britannick Majesty, of the *Province of New Jersey.*
Compelled by the adverse circumstances of the times to
part from the husband she loved, and, at length
deprived of the soothing hope of his speedy return,
she sank under accumulated distresses, and departed this
life on the 28th day of July, 1778, in the 49th year of her age.
SINCERITY and SENSIBILITY,
POLITENESS and AFFABILITY,
GODLINESS and CHARITY,
were
with SENSE refined and PERSON elegant, in her UNITED.
From a grateful remembrance of her affectionate tenderness
and constant performance of all the duties of a GOOD WIFE
This monument is erected, in the year 1787,
By him who knew her worth, and still laments her loss."

[73] Washington's Writings, Vol. V. pp. 6, 7,

The firmness, energy and indomitable perseverance with which Governor Franklin, under all circumstances, held fast to his loyalty, were calculated to make his imprisonment longer than would otherwise have been the case, and we find Congress on the 20th August, 1778, by a deliberate vote, determining that it was inconsistent with the interests of the United States to consent to his exchange.[74] This was in consequence of an application from J. McKinley, Esq., late President of Delaware, to be exchanged for him, presented to Congress ten days previous. Mr. McKinley renewed his application on the 14th September, and after several amendments had been offered and rejected—one of them being a proposition to substitute Brig. Gen. Thompson for Mr. McKinley—the exchange was agreed to, and Governor Franklin returned to New York November 1st, 1778, having been a prisoner two years and four months.

Governor Franklin remained in New York for nearly four years, the companion of Rivington and other noted adherents of the royal cause, and was at one time—how long is not known—the President of the "Honorable Board of Associated Royalists;"[75] in that capacity authorizing or sanctioning, it is said, much cruelty and oppression towards the Americans who were prisoners, but no specific acts have come to my

[74] The question was on granting consent to the exchange, and as was usual, was taken by States, and lost by a tie vote, as follows:

Ayes.—N. H.; R. I.; Conn.; N. Y.; Md.; Va. - - - - - 6
Noes.—N. C.; S. C. - - 2
Divided.—Mass.; N. J.; Penn.; Geo. - - - - - - 4
— 6

The votes of the individual members were: ayes 19; noes 10.

[75] This association of Loyalists consisted of those who were unwilling, or from circumstances prevented from taking up arms in the royal cause. They acted under a commission from Sir Henry Clinton, were put in charge of the small fort at Lloyd's Neck, and were furnished with suitable armed vessels, provisions, arms and ammunition, not only to defend the post, but also to carry on an aggressive warfare against the rebels. They directed expeditions, and commanders made report to them. All captures made were to be their own property, and prisoners taken were to be exchanged for such loyalists as the Board might name. While they professed to be especially desirous of putting a stop to the cruelties the loyalists were subjected to when in the hands of the rebels, they announced their determination to omit nothing to make the enemy feel their just vengeance for such enormities—(See Gaines & Rivington's Papers of the time, and Onderdonk's Incidents of Queens County, pp. 219, 220, 223.)

Sabine (Sabine's Royalists, p. 232) suggests that this Board of Associated Royalists originated principally with another Jerseyman, Daniel Coxe, who was one of Governor Franklin's Council, but Coxe was connected with, and President of an Association of Refugees:—this consisted of deputies se-

knowledge affording grounds either for doubting or believing the charge.

Governor Franklin finally sailed for England in August, 1782. In consideration of the losses he had been subjected to, £1,800 were granted to him by the English Government, and he was allowed in addition a pension of £800 per annum; placing him, so far as his annual income was affected, in a better condition probably than he would have enjoyed had he remained in his government, although a contemporary writer states that both indemnity and pension were considered inadequate to remunerate him for all he had sacrificed.[76] After leaving America he married again; the lady being a native of Ireland. He died November 17, 1813, aged 82.

Benjamin West, in his picture representing the "Reception of the American Loyalists by Great Britain, in the year 1783," introduces him as one of the prominent personages at the head of the group of figures; and in the description of the picture he is mentioned as having "preserved his fidelity and loyalty to his sovereign from the commencement to the conclusion of the contest, notwithstanding powerful incitements to the contrary."

During the whole of the revolutionary struggle, there was no intercourse between Dr. Franklin and his son; and the mutual estrangement continued, in a great degree, even after the cause was removed by the restoration of peace and the acknowledgment of the independence of America. The first advances towards a reconciliation appear to have been made by the Governor, in a letter dated July 22d, 1784; which the Doctor answered from Passy on 16th August following. In his letter he says: "Nothing has ever hurt me so much, and affected me with such keen sensations, as to find myself deserted in my old age by my only son, and not only deserted,

lected from the refugees of the different colonies, and was first organized in 1779. Its objects were the examina- of captured Americans or suspected persons, and the planning of measures for procuring intelligence or otherwise aiding the royal cause. Coxe was appointed President,—so one of his fellow refugees has stated—"to deprive him of the opportunity of speaking, as he had the gift of saying little with many words."

[76] Public characters of Great Britain. Commission on Claims of Amer. Loyalists.

but to find him taking up arms against me in a cause wherein my good fame, fortune, and life were all at stake." He intimates to him that neutrality at least should have been observed on his part, but, as he desired it, is willing to forget the past as much as possible.

The treatment of his son, however, ever continued to afflict him. In a letter written on January 1st, 1788, to the Rev. Dr. Byles, of Boston, he thus feelingly alludes to it, after adverting to the comfort derived from the presence of his daughter: "My son is estranged from me by the part he took in the late war, and keeps aloof, residing in England, whose cause he *espoused*, whereby the old proverb is exemplified:

> 'My son is my son till he gets him a wife,
> But my daughter is my daughter all the days of her life.'"

In his will he left the Governor his Nova Scotia lands with such books and papers as were in his possession, and released him from the payment of all debts that his executors might find to be due from him. The devise to him concluding with: "The part he acted against me in the late war, which is of public notoriety, will account for my leaving him no more of an estate he endeavored to deprive me of." [77]

This estrangement of Doctor Franklin from his son is an instance of the inevitable separation of families and friends which is one among the many evils ever attendant on a civil war. Various as are the characters, dispositions, tastes and habits of mankind, it can never be reasonably anticipated that in those conflicts of opinion which precede the disruption of empires or communities, the ties of consanguinity or association are to prove sufficient for every emergency and withstand the corroding influence of selfishness, prejudice or error.

In the war to which we owe our independence as a nation this evil in every degree of magnitude was painfully manifested; and probably not one of the colonies, in proportion to its population and extent, suffered more from it than New Jersey. Having less of foreign commerce and of inland traffic than many of her sister colonies in which to employ the industry

[77] Franklin's Writings, I. pp. 398; X. pp. 121, 330.

and enterprise of her youth, numbers of the higher classes were accustomed to look for preferment in the administration of the Provincial Government, or to seek for honor and profit in the naval and military service of the mother country; and many were sent to England by anxious parents to secure those advantages of education which were not afforded by the literary institutions of America. These circumstances necessarily involved associations which led in many instances to marriages into families abroad, or into such as were temporarily located in the Province, while the introduction of the royal regiments, which took place some years before the Revolution, caused similar unions between their officers and the daughters of New Jersey.

Independent, therefore, of all pecuniary or other interested reasons for hesitation, both young and old among the inhabitants of the Province became thus, in various ways, involved in the important and solemn inquiry how to reconcile their love of country or allegiance to their king with considerations of personal or domestic happiness. Happy were they whose situation admitted of a decision which did not jeopardize either: but this in a large number of instances was impossible. Mothers were doomed to see their children at open variance, upon whose heads their blessings had with equal fondness descended. Fathers found themselves arrayed in opposition to their sons, and that too, in a contest in which the lives of one and all were at stake. Wives beheld in agony their husbands armed with weapons that were to be used against their friends and countrymen, or perchance against their own brethren; and friends, between whom no personal dissensions had ever existed, ranged themselves under different banners to seal with their blood their adherence to political principles which were made to ingulf every tender emotion of their hearts.

These are no random assertions. Family histories would bring to light many cases of this painful characteristic of our revolutionary struggle, and the case of Governor Franklin is but one of many that are similar.

Governor Franklin's love of books in early life, at a later period naturally led him to collect them, and before the revolution he had amassed a large library, which, on his leaving Amboy, was packed in cases and deposited by Mrs. Franklin within the British lines. The warehouse in which they were placed happened to contain a quantity of military stores that were subsequently burned, and the books shared the same fate.[78] His writings that are met with, although they exhibit no particular superiority of mind or elegance of composition—and are, perhaps, less remarkable than we might expect from the advantages of education and association he had enjoyed—yet give evidence of literary attainments which compare favorably with those of most of the prominent men of that day in the colonies. He was of a cheerful, facetious disposition; could narrate well entertaining stories to please his friends; was engaging in his manners, and possessed good conversational powers. He lived in the recollection of those who saw him in New Jersey as a man of strong passions, fond of convivial pleasures, well versed in the ways of the world, and, at one period of his life, not a stranger to the gallantries which so frequently marred the character of the men of that age. He was above the common size, remarkably handsome, strong and athletic, though subject to gout toward the close of his life. The likeness facing the title-page of this volume is thought to preserve his features faithfully.

He had only one child, William Temple Franklin, who resided in France, became the biographer of his grandfather, and died at Paris, May 25th, 1823.

Such, imperfectly sketched, was the career of the last of our colonial governors, but the materials for a full and satisfactory biography of William Franklin are yet wanting. It is much to be regretted that his papers, which were carried to France by his son, cannot be regained.

It is remarkable how imperfectly known have been all those who, during the provincial existence of New Jersey, wielded the chief executive authority. Of a few, from their ruling over New York and other colonies, some information has been current, but of them as Governors of New Jersey, we have had very little to be relied upon respecting their characters,

[78] Public Characters, Vol. IV.

habits, attainments or adventures. Doubts rest even upon the identity of some of them, and Governor Franklin himself is frequently confounded with his son William Temple Franklin. With the brevity almost of the Scripture annunciation—"So Tibni died and Omri reigned," our historians Smith and Gordon present and withdraw their local potentates like the passing figures of a magic lantern, leaving it to the imagination in many cases to determine whence they came or whither went, and enveloping in dim uncertainty the brief exhibition afforded of their respective careers. It has been, therefore, something of a matter of duty thus to portray some of the characteristics of these functionaries as I have done in the foregoing pages. I trust that others will prosecute the subject to a more successful result.

"A kingdom is a nest of families," and the constituent parts of the history of every community are the acts of the individuals who compose it. In that fact lies the value—the charm—of all private history: not only the private history of public men, but also of those whom their fellows may term humble individuals; for it is not always in the power of contemporaries to discern the bearing, or the historical value of many an event that occurs—of, so-called, trifling circumstances—

> "But trifles, lighter than straws, are levers in the building up of character"—

developing traits and qualities which make their possessor known and felt in the community. The most prominent actors are not always the best judges of the merit which attaches to their own performance, and in the great drama of Life, as in the mimic representations of the stage, much may depend upon him who plays a humble part. Each has his duties,—each must share the responsibility.

In one of the legislative halls at Washington is a timepiece whose device impresses forcibly upon all their obligations to the age in which they live. In the car of Time, on the periphery of whose wheels the hours are marked, stands the Muse of History, recording in a book the events which transpire before her as the wheels of her chariot tell the revolving hours:—by her attitude and expression reminding the assembled representatives of the nation that the history of each passing moment receives from them its impress, is stamped indelibly, by their proceedings, with characteristics which must redound to the welfare or the dishonor of the republic.

We may all, in our respective spheres, heed the lesson. As citizens of the State—as portions of the several communities in which we reside—let us ponder the responsibilities and duties which rest upon us, and in proportion to our faithfulness shall be our reward.[79]

[79] Most of the foregoing sketch was read before the New Jersey Historical Society, Sept. 27th, 1848, and in accordance with the request of the members it was allowed to be printed, as read, in the Proceedings of the Society.

Chapter VI.—Religious Denominations.

> "Each ray that shone, in early time, to light
> The faltering footstep in the path of right,
> Each gleam of clearer brightness shed to aid
> In man's maturer days his bolder sight,
> All blended, like the rainbow's radiant braid,
> Pour yet, and still shall pour, the blaze that cannot fade."

THOSE towns in East Jersey that were settled exclusively by immigrants from New England, possessed advantages over those consisting of more heterogeneous assemblages, in their facilities for securing religious services. Each community formed but one congregation, and the support of a minister, where one could be procured, was rendered easy by including his salary among the annual expenses of the town, for which provision was made by a general rate assessed upon all the inhabitants. We find that Newark and Elizabethtown were supplied with clergymen at an early period, and so continued to be with occasional intermissions; and Woodbridge, although unfortunate in obtaining a permanent pastor, found no difficulty in supporting whoever for the time officiated in the town.[1]

In Perth Amboy a large number of the inhabitants were Quakers and Anabaptists, and many belonged to the Scotch Kirk, while in the adjacent county, Congregationalists or Independents were numerous. This diversity of sects necessarily rendered it difficult to procure a clergyman who would be generally acceptable, and although the want of one was felt and deplored, yet fifteen years elapsed after the settlement without any regular religious services.

[1] See subsequent chapter, and East Jersey, &c., pp. 299, 301.

PROTESTANT EPISCOPALIANS.

About 1695 several of the East Jersey Proprietors applied to Bishop Compton of London for a minister of the established church, and in compliance with their request the Reverend Edward Perthuck was sent to the Province towards the close of 1698. Upon his arrival at Perth Amboy the Board of Proprietors ordered (Feb'y 21st, 1698–9) one of the houses which had been built at the charge of the general proprietaries to be given for a church for the use of the town, and being soon fitted up by a number of the inhabitants, Mr. Perthuck commenced the performance of religious services within it.[2]

This house stood near the Ferry over the Raritan, and tradition designates a small hollow, a short distance south of the avenue leading to the residence of Mr. Paterson, as its location, and that such was the site is rendered certain from its being within the limits of the ground marked on an early map as the "Church lot." It is presumed that the stone bearing the date "1685" inserted in the rear wall of the church recently taken down, was from this building. This was the foundation in Amboy of the congregation of Protestant Episcopalians.

How long Mr. Perthuck remained in Amboy is not known. Humphries, in his "Historical Account of the Society for the

[2] Proprietary Minutes. Humphries' Hist. Acc. The Proprietors ever evinced a desire to foster good principles in the Province in accordance with the device on their seal.

THE SEAL OF THE EASTERN PROPRIETORS.

Propagation of the Gospel," states that prior to the incorporation of that society in 1701, clergymen occasionally visited the place, performing divine service and administering the sacraments; from which it is judged Mr. Perthuck did not continue permanently in charge of the congregation.

The increase of religion in the colonies and the moral culture of the inhabitants, had been the subjects of many private schemes and individual exertions which resulted in little benefit; and it was found necessary, to make the endeavors effectual, to obtain a charter for a society calculated especially to subserve the purposes in view. In consequence of a representation made by Doctor Thomas Tenison (then Archbishop of Canterbury) to King William III., a charter was obtained bearing date June 16th, 1701, incorporating several persons distinguished for their stations and virtues, by the title above given. The proper officers of the society were chosen on the 27th June, and measures were immediately adopted for the obtainment of funds and perfecting other necessary arrangements. The provinces of New York and New Jersey profited at once by the labors of their missionaries.

The instructions of Queen Anne to Lord Cornbury in 1702, relative to religious observances, were full and precise:—

"You shall take especial care"—so runs the document—"that God Almighty be devoutly and duly served throughout your government, the book of Common Prayer, as by law established, read each Sunday and holy day, and the blessed sacrament administered according to the rites of the Church of England. You shall take care that the churches already built there be well and orderly kept, and that more be built as the colony shall, by God's blessing, be improved, and that, besides a competent maintenance to be assigned to the minister of each orthodox church, a convenient house be built, at the common charge, for each minister, and a competent proportion of land assigned to him for a glebe and exercise of his industry.

"And you are to take care, that the parishes be so limited and settled, as you shall find most convenient for the accomplishing this good work. You are not to prefer any minister to any ecclesiastical benefice in that our province, without a certificate from the Right Reverend Father in God the lord bishop of London, of his being conformable to the doctrine and discipline of the Church of England, and of a good life and conversation; and if any person already preferred to a benefice shall appear to you to give scandal either by his doctrine or manners you are to use the best means for the removal of him, and to supply the vacancy in such manner as we have directed.

"You are to give order, that every orthodox minister within your government be one of the vestry in his respective parish, and that no vestry be held without him, except in case of sickness, or that after the notice of a vestry summoned he omit to come.

"You are to inquire whether there be any minister within your government who preaches and administers the sacrament in any orthodox church or chapel without being in due orders, and to give account thereof to the said lord bishop of London. * * * * * And you are to take especial care that a table of marriages established by the canons of the Church of England, be hung up in every orthodox church and duly observed, and you are to endeavor to get a law passed by the Assembly of our said Province (if not already done) for the strict observation of the said table."[3]

In the hands of a discreet and worthy man these regulations would have assuredly contributed essentially to the well being of the Church of England in America, and to the interests of religion generally, but to make Lord Cornbury a censor of morals and manners appeared to most of the good people of New York and New Jersey a ridiculous procedure, if its serious effects did not prevent their regarding it so lightly. The history of that period shows conclusively how much of evil may result from the mal-administration of the best-devised schemes, and is calculated to prompt many regrets that these powers should have been intrusted to such profligate hands.[4]

In 1702 the Rev. George Keith was sent out by the Society as a missionary to the Colonies, having the Rev. Mr. Talbot associated with him. They preached repeatedly in New Jersey, and special mention is made of their officiating at Perth Amboy.[5] Their visits there caused the old church to

[3] Smith's N. J., p. 252.

[4] The following is a copy of one of Lord Cornbury's Licenses:

"By his Excellency Edward Viscount Cornbury, Captain-General, &c. To A. B., greeting: I do hereby license and tolerate you to be minister of the ———— congregation at B, in C county, in the Province of New Jersey, and to have and exercise the liberty and use of your religion pursuant to her Majesty's pleasure therein signified to me, in her royal instructions, for and during so long a time as to me shall seem meet. And all ministers and others are hereby required to take notice thereof. Given under my hand, &c."

For want of these licenses ministers of the Church of England were imprisoned, and several non-conformists prosecuted. See Smith's N.J., p. 333; Smith's N. Y., Vol. I., pp. 148, 149; and other works.

[5] See page 16 for a notice of Keith. In his Journal I find the following notices of his services:—"Sunday, Oct. 3, 1702, I preached at Amboy in East Jersey; the auditory was small; my text was Titus 2: 11, 12; but such as were there well affected; some of them of my former acquaintance, and others who had been formerly Quakers but were come over to the Church, particularly Miles Forster [see page 46] and John Barclay [see page 42]. The place has very few inhabitants. We were several days kindly entertained by Miles Forster at his house there."

"December 12th, 1703, Sunday, I preached at Amboy, at my Lord Corn-

be to some extent refitted in 1702–3, and the erection of a new one to be taken into consideration.[6]

Through the efficient labors of Messrs. Keith and Talbot a congregation was gathered at Burlington, and on the 25th March, 1703, the corner stone of the first church (the present St. Mary's) was laid at that place, and the following year a church was erected by the people of Hopewell.

The Rev. Mr. Brook was sent in 1704 as missionary to Elizabethtown,[7] and by Lord Cornbury's directions he officiated sometimes at Amboy. The irregular services of the sanctuary, with which alone they had been favored, had not been calculated to strengthen or advance the religious character of the people, and at this period the inhabitants both of Elizabethtown and Amboy are represented as being very deficient, many of them professing no religion at all; but under the assiduous care and earnest labors of Mr. Brook they were brought to approve, to a considerable extent, of the doctrines and services of the Church of England. In Elizabethtown a church edifice was erected and covered in 1706, and the people of Amboy commenced a year previous the collection of materials for a similar building.[8]

bury's lodgings, where he was present and many with him. My text was John 12: 35, 36." He preached there again on Christmas day, from 1 Tim. 3: 16; and on January 2d from Heb. 8: 10, 11. On 30th Dec. previous, he preached at both Woodbridge and Piscataway. John Barclay appears to have formed so strong an attachment to Keith, that he travelled with him all the way to James River, Virginia, remaining with him until he saw him on board his vessel, June 8th, 1703, "when," says Keith, "we took our farewell."

[6] On Dec. 1st, 1702, six pounds were appropriated by the Proprietors for "repairing the present church until the new church be built;" and Messrs. Willocks and Forster, on condition of paying all of it themselves, had their lots released from quit-rents. For similar releases, William Frost was obliged to give one month's work, and John Reid to pay ten "hard-pieces-of-eight" towards repairing the old, or building a new church.—*Proprietary Minutes.*

[7] As has been stated in the text, Elizabethtown from an early period had Congregationalist or Presbyterian ministers, but the names have not all been preserved. John Fletcher died August, 1682 (there is a contract of marriage between him and Mrs. Mary Pierson of Long Island on record, Liber 4, p. 20); and from about 1690 to 1699 John Harriman was settled there. On the 20th November, 1692, he applied to the Proprietors for land "at an easie acknowledgement in respect of his numerous family" (seven sons, &c.), and one hundred acres were granted to him, Feb'y 28th, 1692–3.

[8] For an interesting account of the progress of the Elizabethtown congregation the reader is referred to a Historical Discourse by Rev. John C. Rudd, D.D., Rector of the Church, preached Nov. 21st, 1824—part of which is reprinted as an appendix to

There is abundant evidence that Mr. Brook was an active, energetic and efficient servant of the Cross, performing divine service at seven different places, covering ground fifty miles in extent—"at Elizabethtown, Rahway, Perth Amboy, Cheesequakes, Piscataway, Rocky Hill, and in a congregation at Freehold, near Page's." This duty was necessarily difficult and laborious. "Besides preaching he used to catechise and expound fourteen times a month, which obliged him to be on horseback almost every day, which was expensive as well as toilsome to him. However, this diligence raised a very zealous spirit in many of the people."[9] His services, most unfortunately for the province, were brought to a melancholy termination in the autumn of 1707, by his being lost at sea on his way to England.

The circumstances which led to his departure, were as follows.[10] The Reverend Thorowgood Moore, who had been a missionary at Albany and among the Indians, had been induced by the want of ministers in New Jersey to remove into the

Bishop Doane's sermon, "The Bush that burned with Fire," preached in the Church, Dec. 31st, 1840. The following interesting extract from one of Mr. Brook's reports to the Secretary of the Society for the Propagation of the Gospel exhibits the zeal and tact with which he discharged his duties:

He had preached first in Col. Townley's house, but that in half a year's time had grown too small. The congregation then occupied a barn, which, when harvest-time came, they had to relinquish. "Upon which," says Mr. Brook, "the Dissenters who, presently after I came, were destitute of their old Teachers (one of them being struck with death in their meeting-house as he was railing against the church, and the other being at Boston), would not suffer me, upon my request, to officiate in their meeting-house unless I would promise *not to read any of the prayers* of the Church, which I complied with, upon condition I might read the psalms, lessons, epistles and gospel appointed for the day, which I did, and *said all the rest of the service by heart;* the doing of which brought a great many to hear me who otherwise, probably, would never have heard the service of the Church and (through God's blessing) hath taken away their prejudice to such a degree as that they have invited me now to preach in their meeting-house 'till our church be built. Their Teacher begins at 8 in the morning and ends at 10, and then our service begins, and in the afternoon we begin at 2. The greatest part of the Dissenters generally stay to hear all our service."—*Letter of October 11th*, 1706. I must acknowledge the great obligations I am under to Rev. Francis L. Hawks, D.D., for the privilege of examining the manuscript copies of the Records of the Society which are in his possession; obtained by him in England for the General Convention of the Protestant Episcopal Church.

[9] Humphries' Hist. Acc. The widow of Mr. Brook, who was a sister of Christopher Billop of Staten Island, became the wife of Rev. Wm. Skinner. See a preceding page.

[10] From the Society's Records. Mr. Moore's letter, Aug. 27, 1707—Lord Cornbury's, Nov 20, 1707—Mr. Talbot's, Aug. 20, 1708—M. Neau's, Feb. 27, 1708-9.

province in the year 1705, and officiated chiefly at Burlington. Lord Cornbury had an "unfortunate custom"—as it was called by M. Neau the Catechist of the Society in New York—of dressing himself in women's clothes, and in such garb exposing himself on the ramparts of the fort to public view, honoring the great holidays, especially, by his exhibitions, sometimes immediately after partaking of the Holy Communion; and of course, numbers of the populace were drawn thither to witness the spectacle. Mr. Moore, who appears to have been a truly zealous and sincere clergyman of the Church, not allowing his fear of man to influence his duty as a Christian minister, not only condemned the practices of the Governor, but said publicly that his Lordship ought to be excommunicated. On account of some debauchery and profaneness of Lieutenant-governor Ingoldsby, he also refused to administer the Communion to that officer.

For this upright conduct and for some minor offences of a similar character, Cornbury, in August, 1707, summoned the missionary to appear before him in New York; but acting under good advice, Mr. Moore gave no heed to the mandate. New York and New Jersey were distinct governments, and in the absence of the Governor from either, the chief authority devolved upon the Lieutenant-governor; Cornbury consequently, while in New York, could have no authority to compel the attendance of an individual there, charged with misdemeanors committed in New Jersey. Mr. Moore was alike regardless of a sentence of suspension from the ministry attempted to be enforced against him by the Lieutenant-governor; and exasperated by his independence, Cornbury issued a warrant directed to the Sheriff of Burlington County to bring the offender before him at Perth Amboy. To this legal process no resistance was opposed, and the officer and his prisoner presented themselves before the Governor,[11] and after an audience was given to him in the presence only of Ingoldsby, Mr. Moore was remanded to the custody of the Sheriff for several days. On being commanded again to attend his Excellency,[12] he thus graphically describes what followed:

[11] Saturday, August 16th, 1707. [12] Saturday, Aug. 23d.

"I found him at a house about a bow-shot from the water's edge. The Sheriff, having spoke to my Lord, told me he was commanded to attend me into the barge. I told him I could not understand that, however, I would not go unless I was forced; but the Sheriff going again to my Lord into the house (for I was at the door) and returning with fresh commands, I went a little way with him to the other side of the house, where I found my Lord, and told his Excellency what I had told the Sheriff. His Excellency then asked me whether I wanted to be carried, and commanded the Sheriff again to do his office; but he being unwilling to do that which his Lordship called so, his Lordship commanded the Amboy Sheriff who stood by to take me, and force me to go, and the Lieutenant-governor commanding him likewise, he took me by the sleeve; so we went with the rest of the company towards the water side, but as we were walking, I told the Sheriff the danger of what he was doing and bade him have a care how he forced me.

"When I was come pretty near the barge, I told his Excellency I wished him a good voyage and that I designed to go no farther, unless I was forced to it (for the Sheriff had not then hold of me). My Lord in great anger bid the Sheriff again to do his office, and the Lieutenant-governor commanding the same, but the Sheriff refusing to obey them, my Lord comes himself to me, and takes me by my gown and sleeve, and leads me about ten paces, but being persuaded by the Lieutenant-governor, or, rather more probably, by other reasons, he leaves me again to the Sheriff, who, encouraged by my Lord's example and the earnestness of the Lieutenant-governor, took hold of my gown and went before me into my Lord's barge in which my Lord brought me to York."

Arrived there he was committed, a prisoner, to the custody of a guard at the fort.

Mr. Brook, although not subjected to the same rigorous treatment, was looked upon with a sinister eye by the Governor, as it was known he "said Amen to all that Mr. Moore did." He was allowed, however, to visit his friend, and the Governor leaving the city for Albany about three weeks after Mr. Moore's arrival, advantage was taken of the relaxed discipline consequent thereupon to get the prisoner past the sentry; and being joined by Mr, Brook, the two proceeded to Boston whence they sailed for England; "having been so dragooned"—says their fellow-laborer Talbot—"that they had rather be taken into France than into the Fort at New York." They were never heard of more.

The disadvantages under which the clergymen of the Church of England labored in both New York and New Jersey, may be in some measure realized when we find them thus subjected to the tyranny of a dissolute governor, and having to combat not only the prejudices which education and association excited in the minds of the majority of the settlers, but the evil example of one claiming to be their spiritual head.[13]

Mr. Brook was succeeded by the Rev. Edward Vaughan, in 1709, and his mantle, it would seem, could not have fallen upon more worthy shoulders. Mr. Vaughan executed the duties of his holy calling with the utmost application and diligence, rendering himself exceedingly acceptable to the people throughout the country, for he, too, officiated in many different places, Amboy among the number.[14]

The growth of the Elizabethtown congregation requiring more and more of Mr. Vaughan's attention, the inhabitants of Amboy were obliged to procure a separate minister, and the Rev. Thomas Halliday commenced his labors there in the summer of 1711 :—the congregation of Piscataway being also under his charge.

Mr. Halliday had not been long in the Province before he became involved with the political factions which at that time, and subsequently, caused such unhappy dissensions in New Jersey; harmonizing with the party which included those who had supported Cornbury, and who were then engaged in an endeavor to repress the growing power of the Quakers and strengthen the influence of the Church of England with the government. As the leader of this party, Peter Sonmans was

[13] "I am assured"—says M. Neau, writing after the Governor had been arrested for debt, and his household goods sold—"I am assured that he continues to dress himself in women's clothes, but now 'tis after the Dutch manner."

[14] Humphries. Dr. Rudd's Hist. Discourse. Mr. Henderson's Centen. Sermon. To great sprightliness of manner and engaging conversational powers, Mr. Vaughan united a readiness of repartee that made him—although he never lost sight of the dignity of the ministerial office—a most amusing companion. The following anecdote is narrated of him :—Mr. Belcher arrived in the province as Governor a few months before Mr. Vaughan's death, and the Presbyterians were, very naturally, much exhilarated thereby: "our congregations are insulted," wrote a worthy missionary, "for the Independents stick not to say *they* are the established church in this province now, and all others are only tolerated." Among other measures calculated to advance the interests of his denomination was the making of many of the Presbyterian Divines Justices of the Peace; and on one occasion, when Mr. Vaughan was riding on a fine horse, handsomely caparisoned (being fond of such equipments), he was met by two of them, who, relying upon his presumed ignorance of their names, accosted him rudely with, "Why Parson, you are not like your Lord and Master, for he was content to ride upon an Ass"!—"So would I be, brethren," was the quick reply, "but our Governor has made them all Justices of the Peace." The accompanying likeness is from an original drawing by John Watson in my possession.

REVD. EDWARD VAUGHAN.

Missionary to New Jersey from the Society for the Propagation of the Gospel,
1709.

LITH. OF SARONY & CO. N.Y.

almost as objectionable, both in public and in private life, as Cornbury had been. The course of Mr. Halliday was very obnoxious to his congregation at Amboy, most of whom were of the opposition, and one of them, George Willocks, one of its prominent leaders—a state of things which his irascibility of temper, and, probably, some irregularity of life, tended to aggravate.[15] He seems, however, to have been borne with and treated respectfully by his parishioners, until he shocked their sense of propriety by selecting Sonmans for his Church Warden, and denouncing Willocks openly from his desk for a presumed misappropriation of some funds collected for the erection of a church edifice. They then refused him access to the church. This was in the summer of 1713.[16] For some time he continued as missionary at Piscataway, and thereafter, until 1718, remained in the province or in New York, officiating occasionally in different places, much to the annoyance of many of the people.[17]

In 1714, Mr. Vaughan took up his residence in Amboy for the benefit of his health, and at the request of the people, officiated there one Sunday in every four, going to Elizabethtown and Woodbridge the other three ; and this arrangement continued with little intermission for several years.

On the 30th July, 1718,[18] a charter was granted to the congregation by Governor Robert Hunter, acting in behalf of his sovereign, George I., in which William Eier[19] and John

[15] The kind-hearted Vaughan, before Halliday had been two months at his post, wrote: "Mr. H. is not so happy as to gain their affections in this country; every failure in him or in us is improved to the contempt of our ministry. I cannot say he has been so circumspect and prudent in his conduct as became his character." Sept. 12, 1711.

[16] Halliday himself says under date of April 14, 1714:—"They most contemptuously carried away all the goods of the Church, and at the same time told me to be gone; that I was a knave and a villain."

[17] Gov. Hunter writing to George Willocks, Sept. 22d, 1718, says: "As to that wretch Dr. Halliday, I wish the countrey could get ridd of him at any rate. I shall transmitt to the society what the vestry sent, but if the same faction prevails there (of which your good friends —— and Nicholson, are the heads) he'll be in no danger from them, or the B[ishop] of L[ondon] either, on that account."—*Rutherfurd* MSS.

[18] Proprietary Records, Vol. 9, C. 2, p. 16.

[19] This gentleman's "houses and lands near the middle of the town of Woodbridge" were advertised for sale 1732. He was then dead.

Barclay were appointed Wardens; Thomas Gordon, John Rudyard, Robert King and John Stevens, Vestrymen.

To Mr. Gordon, George Willocks, and John Barclay is the church indebted for the ground on which the present edifice stands, and for other lands in the vicinity of the town. Mr. Willocks, also, at the particular request of his wife on her death-bed, shortly afterward conveyed to the church the house in which they lived, and two acres of land adjoining, in the most desirable part of the town, for the use for ever of the clergyman officiating in the parish; and at his death bequeathed to the congregation the ferry over the Raritan, with the adjoining lots. The parsonage and grounds were valued at £400 sterling, and the gift was highly prized.[20] The building, somewhat changed in its appearance, stood, although in a dilapidated condition, until 1844, having for many years served as the residence of the several incumbents; its use, however, as a parsonage having been superseded by the erection of a new one in 1815. In addition to these benefactions, in June, 1719, John Harrison and Mr. Willocks gave twelve acres of land contiguous to the city for the use of the church for ever.

To the memory of these liberal benefactors[21] the congregation, in 1825, erected a tablet in the church, bearing this inscription:—

[20] Records—Mr. Vaughan's letters.

[21] See pp. 42, 60, 80, for notices of these gentlemen. The minutes of the Vestry and the reports of Mr. Vaughan mention John Barclay as one who had contributed generously to build and support the church, but his name was not included in the tablet because it could not be ascertained in what way he had aided in the enterprise—rather an insufficient excuse, and to me the omission seems unfortunate. From Mr. Vaughan's letters it is evident he contributed land, and the probability is that he also furnished ready money, an article of which there is reason to believe Mr. Barclay was himself much in want before his death. From the minutes of the Vestry it appears that on April 4th, 1727, John Parker, Esq., and Mr. Heron Putland were appointed a committee to estimate the old church and lot of land belonging to it; which they did at twenty pounds, money at eight shillings per ounce, and reported accordingly on the 30th May. It was then ordered "that the same be made over and conveyed to John Barclay, Esq., for the consideration of the said sum of twenty pounds *as part payment of a greater sum heretofore by him laid out and expended, in erecting the new church.*" There is no evidence in the Church records of any further payment.

THIS TABLET
is designed to express the gratitude of the
Congregation of St. Peter's Church in this city
to the benefactors of the said church,
whose names follow:
GEORGE WILLOCKS
who died in 1729;
MARGARET WILLOCKS
his wife
who died in 1722;
THOMAS GORDON
who died April 28, 1722
and
JOHN HARRISON.

They loved the habitation of God's house and
the place where his honour dwelleth.

Erected A.D. 1825.

The congregation by the receipt of their charter having become regularly established, commenced the erection of their church—an event to which they had been looking forward with great anxiety for several years. It was begun in the spring of 1719,[22] and was completely inclosed early in 1722, when it was dedicated to the service of Almighty God, by the name of "St. Peters." It was, at first, merely an oblong building of the most simple architecture, forty-eight feet long and thirty broad—crowning the beautiful knoll that overlooks the waters of the bay, which still, after the lapse of one hundred and thirty years, possesses so much that is appropriate in its character to the sacred purpose for which it was selected. Save in the additions made to the number of the silent tenants of the graves around, but few changes had been wrought in its appearance by the passage of time until in 1852, when the old building was removed to give place to a more commodious modern structure. Many in long succession had received upon their brows within its ancient walls the sacred symbol of "Christ's faithful servants,"—before its chancel pledged their marriage vows,—participated in the privileges and blessings of Christian worship, and been borne from the inner congregation

[22] In June, 1719, it was alluded to as "now erecting."

to swell the one without;—the living and the dead of one communion all. Holy men of God and patriarchs, the legislator and the jurist, the artist and the soldier, the matron and the maid,[23] are there again gathered; and there, too, are the babes—who were "carried to their little cells of felicity" (as they are termed by Jeremy Taylor) after wearing "an uneasy garment" for a brief period—entering first upon that secure possession towards which parents and kindred are yet toiling:

"Far better they should sleep awhile
Within the church's shade,
Nor wake, until new heav'n and new earth
Meet for their new immortal birth
For their abiding place be made;
Than wander back to life, and lean
On our frail love once more."

It cannot be that the silent monitions, which speak to the eyes of a worshipper from every side of such a field of the dead, can fall powerless upon the soul. Few can do otherwise than adopt the language of a recent writer[24] and say:—"With old Sir Thomas Browne I love to see a church in a graveyard, for 'even as we pass through the place of graves to the temple of God on earth, so we must pass through the grave to the temple of God on high.'"

Previous to the revolution, an avenue of locusts led to the church from the street in front of it, and others stood around the building, but with the exception of one or two old and decaying trees they have all disappeared.

The completion of the church rendered the congregation more anxious for regular and frequent services; and on 27th March, 1723, at a meeting of communicants, an address was adopted to the Bishop of London and the Society for the Propagation of the Gospel, praying the appointment of a missionary (should they not approve of the removal of the Rev. Mr. Vaughan from Elizabethtown to Amboy, which they requested might be permitted); that he might "settle among them in the character and relation of a pastor and guide to

[23] In Amboy was retained, until a few years since, the old affecting custom of having young females attended to the grave by pall-bearers of their own sex and age, clothed in white and wearing white veils.

[24] Wm. C. Prime in "Owl Creek Letters."

them in things appertaining to God."[25] The Society, however, had previously, unknown to the congregation, appointed the Rev. William Skinner to be their missionary, and he commenced his labors at Amboy in the autumn of 1722, being received by the people with much kindness and civility.[26]

Although the church had been walled in a year previous, yet it was not until the arrival of Mr. Skinner that measures were taken to fit up the interior. On the 10th September, 1723, the wardens were directed forthwith to employ workmen to level and lay the floor of the church, and build a pulpit, reading-desk and altar. These directions were carried out, but pews were not ordered to be built until three years afterward (September 23d, 1728).[27] It was directed that they should all be uniform in size and appearance, and that the different families should construct their respective pews at their own expense, under the superintendence of the wardens, and when completed to hold the same as their property for ever. This provision operated of course to retard their erection, and we consequently do not find any steps taken to carry out these improvements until 1731. In the meanwhile (April 7th, 1724), Mr. Skinner received a call from the congregation to become the regular incumbent of the rectorship of the church, and a petition for his induction was addressed to the Governor.

It was at first intended to occupy part of the body of the church with a vestry room and staircase to the gallery, but this plan in April, 1731, was abandoned—a greater demand for pews existing, probably, than was expected—and it was "agreed that the whole body of the church, after allowance made for the aisle, be pewed."[28] On the 28th June, half the pews were completed, but it was not until December 10th that

[25] Minutes of Vestry.

[26] Mr. Chapman's Discourse gives the date as 1723, but Mr. Skinner states in a letter to the Secretary, of March, 1722–3, that he arrived at Amboy on the 22d November previous. He was not, however, regularly inducted into his living before September 11th, 1724.

[27] At this meeting resolutions of thanks were passed to the widow of Rev. John Talbot for the present of a silver chalice and ewer, and a silver paten, which are still used in the services of the church.

[28] Andrew Sharp did the work for seventy-five pounds, New Jersey currency.

they were all finished and ready to be alloted to the members of the congregation.

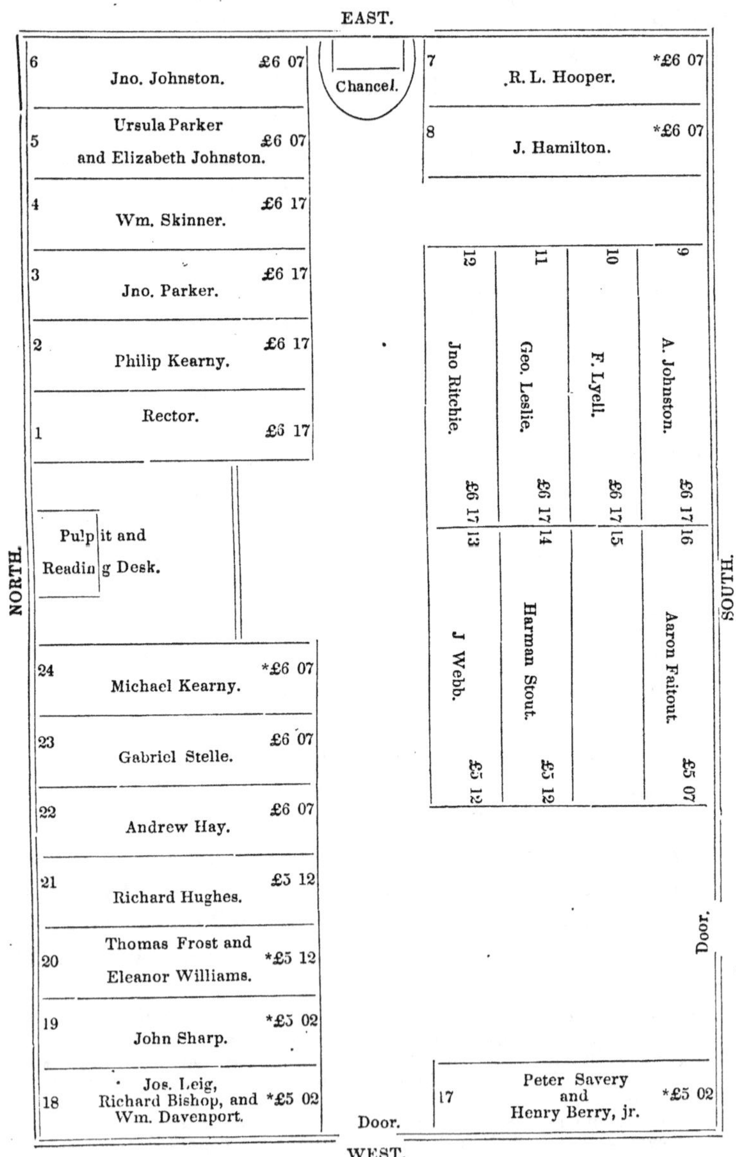

The Vestry taking into consideration "the ruinous condition of several other parts of the church," proceeded to fix the rate at which the several pews were to be taxed over and above their actual cost, in order to raise a fund for making the necessary repairs. It is to be hoped that, though their temporalities were in so sad a condition, the congregation may have been rich in their spiritual concerns.

The preceding plan shows the probable arrangement[29] of the floor of the church as divided at this time, with the name of the occupant and rate of each pew.

Those pews marked with an asterisk were declared forfeited August 6th, 1751, in consequence of non-payment of their cost, and they were bought, No. 7, by Philip Kearny; No. 8, by John Johnston; No. 17, by Thomas Fox; No. 18, by Griffin Desbrow; No. 19, by Elias Marsh; No. 20, by Thomas Skinner, jr.; No. 24, by John Barberrie.

At the same meeting which decided the construction of pews throughout the body of the church, the minutes of the Vestry state the gratifying fact that the pews thus planned would not be sufficient for the congregation, and it was consequently determined that the money raised by the rates laid upon them should be expended in "pewing the gallery and doing such other things as may be necessary to complete the same;" from which it appears the gallery had not yet been finished although nine years had elapsed since the erection of the church.[30] But alas! the generation that wanted

[29] "The *probable* arrangement"—as no plan exists in the Church records. On Easter Tuesday, 1737, "It was agreed that Col. Robert Lettice Hooper and Mr. Lawrence Smyth have liberty to render the pews to them in said church belonging [the pews on each side of the chancel, it is presumed] more convenient by boarding the walls and raising a canopy over said pews as shall to them seem most fit, provided that uniformity and exact likeness be maintained."

[30] From a fragment of a subscription list in my possession it appears that the ground was enclosed and the church plastered in 1737. The names and amounts on the paper are: "John Hamilton £7; R. L. Hooper £3 10s.; Andrew Johnston £3 10s.; Fenwick Lyell £3 10s.; Lewis Johnston £5; Lawrence Smyth £3 10s.; Adam Hay £3 10s.; James Hooper £2 10s. On June 4th, 1736, the Congregation of St. Peter's Freehold received their charter. In this year (1736) the Society for the Propagation of the Gospel had sixty-two missionaries in the Colonies:—In New England 8; Newfoundland 1; New York 16; New Jersey 6; Pennsylvania 8; N. Carolina 1; S. Carolina 9; Georgia 1; Bahamas 1. Their salaries amounted to £3,015. They had each ten pounds worth of books and five pounds worth of tracts annually for distribution.

seats might have passed away, and probably did, before the pews in the gallery were ready for them. They were not commenced till May, 1753, and it was not till September 17th that they were in a condition to be rented.

On the 23d August, 1742, a measure was adopted which, followed subsequently by others, gave to the church the appearance it wore at the time of its demolition. Dr. Lewis Johnston and "Capt. Samuel Nevill" were appointed a Committee to make such repairs to the building and premises as "they in their judgment should for decency's sake think fit to be done," and they were directed to "use their utmost and speedy endeavors to erect a steeple of brick and lime at the west end of and adjoining to said church;"—but so far as the steeple was concerned several years elapsed before any thing was done.

When Mr. Skinner entered upon his duties at Amboy in 1722, the number of communicants reported by him was about 20; and although there were but few capable of contributing to his support, he gratefully acknowledges the receipt of £18 13s. 4d.: one third of which, however, was from the Provincial government. He "might have expected more," he says in his report, "were it not for the expenses they had incurred." The number of families belonging to the congregation he estimated in 1724 to be above 70; he ordinarily had 150 auditors in summer, and from 60 to 90 in winter. His custom was to preach in the morning and catechise the children in the afternoon. Every third Sunday he officiated at Piscataway, and occasionally visited Woodbridge in the afternoon. He also took under his charge the people of Monmouth County, and in 1726 commenced officiating regularly for them once a month; and through his exertions the congregation there rapidly increased. In an appeal for a resident missionary which he made in their behalf in 1732, he states that when he last visited them he baptized 26 children, and his auditors were thought to be 600 in number. He expected to go to them again before Christmas, to administer the communion to 40 or 50, and baptize 30 children, "work enough," he adds, "for a winter's day."

In 1741, although his congregation had not enlarged, the

number of his communicants had increased to 53, and his services at Piscataway were appreciated by large assemblages. About 1745, the Monmouth congregations having been for some time supplied with regular services from resident missionaries, Mr. Skinner took under his care the South River settlement, which appears to have profited by his occasional services for several years.

In 1747, in consequence of Governor Morris having fixed his residence at Trenton, Amboy had lost many of its population, and the winter of 1746–7 proving fatal to many from the prevalence of the smallpox, St. Peter's congregation fell off materially—Mr. Skinner's auditors numbering one hundred or less;—but he subsequently reports that the church was again prospering, and the minutes of the vestry give evidence of a larger attendance in succeeding years.[31]

In 1758 the congregation was deprived by death of the labors of their pastor and friend. After thirty-six years of faithful service he went to his reward, having attained the allotted span of "threescore years and ten."[32]

In 1759 the Rev. Philip Hughes was appointed Missionary to Amboy, but declined the situation, and the congregation remained in consequence without any stated services for that and part of the next year; during which the Rev. Mr. Palmer entered the station and continued to officiate as Missionary until about 1762, when he resigned and removed to New Haven, Connecticut.[33]

In February, 1763, the Rev. Robert McKean arrived with a notification of his appointment as Missionary, and entered at once upon his duties at Perth Amboy exclusively, to which his services were restricted at the request of the vestry; it having been the society's intention that he should also officiate at Woodbridge. The previous year he had officiated at Piscataway. In April, 1764, he reports the number of families

[31] Such was the want of room in the church at Amboy in 1751, that Mrs. Stelle, widow of Gabriel Stelle, who with two daughters occupied a pew, was specially directed by the Vestry "to take in two such creditable persons as the Vestry should nominate, such persons paying their proportion of the fees, three persons not being sufficient to fill a pew."

[32] Records of Soc. for Prop. Gos. Mr. Chapman's Discourses.

[33] Rev. Mr. Chapman's Hist. Discourses.

professing to belong to the Church of England as between 40 and 50; and there were 12 or 15 more that attended upon his services in preference to any other—"these together," he states, "include near two thirds of the inhabitants; the rest are Presbyterians chiefly, and a few Quakers." His communicants numbered 34.

It is not stated in the records when the tower or steeple, directed to be built in 1742, was undertaken; but in April, 1764, a committee were authorized "to carry on the outside walls of the church as far as the end of the steeple and enclose it, and to build a plain spire on the top of the steeple, and do any other matter the vestry shall think necessary towards completing the same." This added about twelve feet to the length of the church and made space for a small robing-room, and stairway to the gallery. The cost of these additions was defrayed by means of a Lottery, authorized in 1762 for the benefit of the church, and which was drawn in 1764 under the direction of Messrs. Sargant and Smyth.[34] It was not then considered contrary to good morals to encourage lotteries, and schemes for every kind of object were yearly set on foot.[35]

[34] Their accounts were closed in 1767, and they reported they had expended—

For the Church - -	£581	8	6
" Parsonage, Glebe, &c.	305	3	3
" Long Ferry Property -	3	0	2
" Payment of Prizes -	1772	14	8
" Expenses of Lottery -	7	7	1
	£2669	13	8

The particulars of the lottery are not given.

During Mr. McKean's incumbency (1765) the lady of Governor Franklin presented a new surplice to the church, thanks for which were specially returned by a delegation of the Vestry. The church plate in 1767 comprised 1 Flagon, 2 Chalices, and 1 Salver.

[35] For a notice of some of these lotteries see a subsequent chapter.

Smith in his History of the Province published in 1765, gives information respecting the number of the various congregations in the province, from which the following table is compiled:

Middlesex Co. Episcopalians 5; Presbyterians 7; Quakers 4; Baptists 2; Seventh-day Baptists 1; Low Dutch Calvinists 1.

Monmouth Co. Episcopalians 4; Presbyterians 6; Quakers 3; Baptists 4.

Essex Co. Episcopalians 3; Presbyterians 7; Baptists 1; Dutch Calvinists 2.

Somerset Co. Presbyterians 3; Low Dutch Reformed 5; Dutch Lutheran 1; Baptist 1.

Bergen Co. Dutch Calvinists 7; Dutch Lutherans 2.

Burlington Co. Episcopalians 2; Presbyterians 1; Quakers 15; Baptists 1.

Gloucester Co. Episcopalians 1; Presbyterians 5; Swedish Lutherans 1; Baptists 1; Moravians 1: Quakers 7.

Salem Co. Episcopalians 2; Quakers 4; Dutch Lutherans 1; Presbyterians 3; Baptists 2.

Cumberland Co. Episcopalians 1; Presbyterians 4; Baptists 2; Seventh-day Baptists 1, Quakers 1.

Cape May Co. Presbyterians 1; Quakers 1; Baptists 1.

Hunterdon Co. Episcopalians 3; Presbyterians 9; Low Dutch Calvinists 1; German Presbyterians 1; Quakers 2; Baptists 2.

Morris Co. Presbyterians 9; Lutherans 1

The sketch here introduced is a faithful representation of the church as it appeared before its demolition, while yet the numerous poplars surrounding it were unaffected by age.

OLD ST. PETER'S CHURCH, 1832.

Mr. McKean died October 17th, 1767. He had officiated as missionary for more than four years, and left an excellent character both as a clergyman and physician, having practised in the latter capacity during his residence in Amboy.[36] He was a brother of Governor McKean of Pennsylvania, who

Anabaptists 1; Quakers 1; Separatists 1; Rogerians 1.

Sussex Co. Low Dutch Calvinists 5; Baptists 2; German Lutherans 1; Quakers 1.

Summary.

Episcopalians	21
Presbyterians	55
Quakers	39
Baptists	20
Seventh-day Baptists	2
Low Dutch Calvinists or Reformed	21
Dutch Lutheran	4
Swedish Lutheran	1
Moravians	1
German Lutheran	2
Separatists	1
Rogerians	1
Lutherans	1
Total	169

[36] He married the daughter of Hon. Edward Antill, of Raritan Landing—a young lady of very gay and independent spirit, not calculated, it is said, to enhance the domestic happiness of the reverend missionary. Her mother, who was a Morris, inherited some of the eccentricities of the males of that family. On one occasion Mr. Antill, who was himself an oddity, lamented to his wife the degeneracy of the women of that day, spending their time in idleness or profitless pursuits, instead of "abiding in the fields with their maidens," assisting in gathering the wheat or the rye, the flax or the barley. It chanced to be at a time when the farmers were pulling their flax, and the following morning, on coming down from his chamber, Mr Antill found himself the sole occupant of the house, Mrs. A. had gone out with her servants. Finding that no meal was to be procured, he sallied forth in search of his household, and at last discovered his wife according to his wishes, she said, "abiding in the field with her maidens" pulling flax. He was invited to partake of the refreshment they had provided for themselves, but it was impossible for her to return home before the evening

reared a tombstone above his remains, which were deposited in rear of the church. It bears the following inscription :—

In memory of
The Rev. Robert McKean, M.A.,
Practitioner in Physic, &c.,
And Missionary from the Society for the Propagation of
the Gospel in Foreign parts,
to the City of Perth Amboy :—
Who was born
July 13th, 1732, N.S.,
and died October 17th, 1767,
An unshaken friend,
An agreeable companion,
A rational divine,
A skilful physician,
And in every relation of life
a truly benevolent and
honest man,
Fraternal love hath erected
this monument.

Immediately after the death of Mr. McKean measures were taken to secure a successor, and in the meanwhile the Rev. Mr. Preston, Chaplain to the 26th Regiment, then quartered at Amboy, was requested to officiate—the necessary funds for his remuneration to be raised by subscription. Mr. Preston acceded to their request, but refused all compensation save the occupancy of the parsonage. So well satisfied were the congregation with this arrangement, that no further steps towards procuring a missionary seem to have been taken until December, 1758. At that time the Rev. Mr. Brown, Missionary at Newark,[37] informed the Vestry that he had the Society's permission to remove to Amboy, and wished to know if it would be agreeable to the congregation for him to do so. A meeting was held, and some dissent to the arrangement being expressed, Mr. Brown immediately relinquished the mission.[38]

[37] For a highly interesting account of this mission see "Days of Old," a Centennial Discourse by the Rev. Matthew H. Henderson, preached in Trinity Church, Newark, February 22d, 1847—one of the best productions of the kind.

[38] This application of Mr. Brown for the parish was the cause of some unpleasant feelings on his part. He visited the congregation in September or October, 1768, but the Vestry then declined receiving him, on the ground of his not always enjoying good health and their preference for a clergyman from England. Probably doubting the truth of these objections, he addressed to them the formal proposition mentioned in the text, which they again declined ; and in letters subsequently written to the Secretary, for the purpose of exculpating themselves from a

The Vestry then tendered it to Mr. Preston, who accepted it on condition that he should be allowed to retain his chaplaincy, which being granted by his General, he was nominated, and in due time appointed by the Society their Missionary to Perth Amboy and Woodbridge, with a salary of fifty pounds per annum.[39]

Mr. Preston remained at Amboy until 1774, when the "tide of war" caused his removal. He was a Scotchman, tall of stature, and with an athletic frame, surmounted by a bushy wig; he was a bachelor and had accumulated considerable property, the loss of which, by the failure of his banker, caused his death—bringing him to the grave old and brokenhearted. The character he bore in the recollection of aged citizens, who have certified it to the present generation, was that of a truly amiable and pious man, performing his duties in sincerity and truth. Under his administration the congregation steadily improved.

In September 1768—there having been for several years applicants for pews, who could not be supplied—on its being determined that no new arrangement of the pews could be made that would afford additional accommodation, a proposition was accepted from several persons to erect a gallery on the south side of the church at their own expense, they to hold their pews under the same rules and regulations that were in force towards those in other parts of the church. Seven pews were consequently constructed in the course of the ensuing year, which were to revert to the vestry should the occupants remove, and they were made subject to assessments for the Clerk and Sexton.[40]

charge of unkindness to Mr. Brown, they state that "the peace and harmony of the church made it necessary to refuse him." They add that Mr. B.'s practising as a physician had been the fruitful source of contention with his Newark parishioners through the bills rendered by him in that capacity; and as they had experienced some bad effects from Mr. McKean's practising, they thought it advisable to avoid the possibility of dissension by procuring some other clergyman.—*Records of Soc. for Prop. Gos.*

[39] Minutes of Vestry.

[40] These rates were laid Dec. 26th, 1769. One pew paid 4s. 4d. and the other 3s. 6d. each to the sexton and double these sums to the clerk—these rates were increased in 1771. The pay of the sexton in 1733 was about 5*l.* 5s. raised by a tax on the pews, and the same amount was paid to the clerk. The list of these worthies is not

Although the congregation had thus increased, the communicants had not. Mr. Preston reports them in 1770 as only thirty in number. He says: " We are in this town very little intermixed with dissenters of any denomination. There are only two Quaker families, and some few Presbyterians, but these last frequently come to church. They have a meeting house here, but the doors of it have not been opened for these two years past." He estimates the population of the town at that time to be 500.

From January 3d, 1774, to November 11th, 1782, there are no records of the Vestry's proceedings, and it is doubtful if any meetings were held. The dire consequences of the civil war raging throughout the colonies fell upon the small congregation of St. Peter's and scattered them abroad,—many of them to seek in foreign lands a home they might no longer claim within sight of the church in which they had so long worshipped—and others, who would have watched over its welfare and protected its altar from insult, obliged to attend elsewhere the calls of their own or their country's interests. " The sacred edifice was soon laid open to the injuries of the weather; the works in the inside were torn to pieces; the floor, cleared of the pews, was occupied as a stable for horses, and the graves and monuments were exposed to injury by the destruction of the fences:—Against the headstones fires were lighted by the soldiers to prepare their food, and the tombstones they occupied as tables for the meals which they thus pre-

complete. Previous to 1764, *John Stockton* was sexton, and dying that year, *Henry Richards* succeeded him. No others are mentioned by name previous to the revolution, at which time *Edward Aswell* was clerk. January, 1785, *Hugh Brady* was appointed sexton, and in August, 1791, *Thomas Griggs*, with a salary of 3*l*. In 1764 *John Griggs* was clerk, and in October he informed the vestry, the fees of the office were so small as not to be worth his acceptance, and therefore desired leave to resign the situation. But Mr. Griggs was too valuable an officer to lose, and a farther tax was laid upon the pews in order to increase his salary a pound. In Dec. 1769, by the addition of the south gallery the fees were farther increased to 8*l*. 5*s*. and the sexton's to about 7*l*. 10*s*., and in 1771, another graduation took place, by which the fees of the sexton were fixed at 7*l*. 2*s*. 6*d*., and the clerk's at 10*l*. 2*s*. 6*d*. In 1805 *Baltus Leonard* was appointed sexton, and held the office thirty-two years, digging in that time it is said *four hundred graves* with his own hands. He died in 1837, and was succeded by *George Fothergill*, whose salary was $20 and fees; and in 1846 *John Foster* was put in the responsible and valuable post, which he held until his death, in 1854, being succeeded by his son, *George Foster*, the present incumbent.

pared." [41] Had not the church been built of durable materials, the trial to which it was subjected would have proved fatal ; and to those who subsequently for so many years gathered together beneath its roof it was ever a matter for congratulation, that in the providence of God it escaped the fiery ordeal. In this connection the following letter from Mr. Preston is interesting :

Mr. Preston to the Secretary. (Extract.)

PERTH AMBOY, NEW JERSEY, Jan'y 2d, 1777.

Reverend Sir :

My correspondence with the Society has been interrupted for some considerable time, owing to this place having been made a garrison-town of the Rebels, and their endeavoring to intercept all letters that were writ from hence; which was attended with bad consequences to the writers of them. Whilst they were here they never interrupted me in the discharge of my duty, they threaten'd, indeed, to compell me to observe the Fast Day that was appointed by Congress in May last, which I not choosing to do, I left town for two days, and on my return had service in church as usual without any molestation, which I continued till the end of June, when Independence was declared. After that it would not have been prudent in me, nor, indeed, would they have have suffered me to officiate, unless I would have conformed to the alterations which they made in the Liturgy. Upon the King's troops taking possession of Staten Island, which is separated from this place by a narrow channel, they crowded in 6,000 or 7,000 men into this little town, filled all the houses with soldiers, and took the church and made a Barrack of it; they at last gave out an order that any person that had any connections or acquaintances upon Staten Island should quit the place. Upon this the greater number of the Inhabitants were obliged to leave Town. I retired 40 miles back into the country, where I remained till one of the King's Regiments passed along, which had been made prisoners and were going to be exchanged, and I Join'd them and got to this Town the 20 of December. I had service in the church the Sunday before Christmas and had that day 20 communicants. Few of the inhabitants have as yet been able to return here, the Roads are all beset by the Rebels and their houses are now filled with the King's Troops. I found the Parsonage House so demolished that it was not habitable: the windows broke to pieces, the Partitions torn down, the Outhouses and Fences all burnt and destroyed:—£300 will not repair the damage and how that is to be done I know not; for every body here have been such sufferers that it cannot be expected that they should contribute much towards it. Many of them will find it a hard matter to repair their own losses. My own private losses I do not bring into the account, tho' I have been a considerable sufferer; part of my Household Furniture is gone, and some of my books, amongst which was the Register of Baptisms, &c., so that I can make no return to the Society of the occasional duties for these two years last past.

I am, Reverend Sir, Yours.

JOHN PRESTON.

During the years 1782, '83 and '84 the Rev. Abraham

[41] Mr Chapman's Hist. Discourses.

Beach occasionally officiated in the parish, being appointed in 1783 by the Society for Propagating the Gospel, at the request of the Vestry, their temporary missionary. The revolution over, and all civil and ecclesiastical connection with Great Britain severed, Mr. Beach continued to serve as missionary by the invitation of the congregation until succeeded by the Rev. John Hamilton Rowland, in 1784, who was at that time settled as Rector of St. Andrew's Church, Staten Island. He officiated for the congregation at stated periods for two or three years and then removed to Nova Scotia. As yet nothing had been done towards repairing the church. It was in such a dilapidated state, that, saving the expense of walls, the cost of repairs promised to be equal to that of its first construction; but in Ootober, 1784, the vestry commenced devising plans for fitting it up for the services of Mr. Rowland, but they matured very slowly. Subscriptions to a trifling extent were obtained at once, and the first repairs effected show in how ruinous a state the church then was. The Committee were directed to glaze the two south windows, and half the end window, to board up all the others, and put a lock on the door: but it is doubtful if the building was made use of in this condition.

The following March (1785) resolutions were passed having in view the complete reparation of the church, commencing with the windows and floors, by effecting a loan to the amount of £150, secured by a lien upon the rents of the church lands, and subsequent donations. On the 16th April the vestry petitioned the Board of Proprietors of the Eastern Division for aid, and received from them a grant for one hundred acres of land, which were sold and the proceeds made available, forming, with the above-mentioned sum and private contributions of the inhabitants, a sufficient fund to warrant the completion of the interior. The arrangement of the pews was changed by placing the pulpit at the east end, instead of leaving it as before between the two north windows, and leaving one aisle to run the length of the building.

The pews were completed in October, and they were subsequently sold to the following persons: the war having worked a great change in the list of attendants on the services of the church.

No.	Name	No.	Name
No 1, 2, 3, 4	Unsold.	32, 31, 30, 29	Unsold.
5	Capt. John Moore.	28	George Buchanan.
6	Margaret Campbell.	27	James Dobbin.
7	John Clark. [42]	26	James Parker.
8	Jacob Weiser.	25	John L. Johnston.
9	Norris Thorp.	24	James Parker.
10	John Griggs. [43]	23	John Halsted.
11	Matthias Halsted.	22	John Johnston.
12	John Rattoone.	21	Thomas Farmar.
13	Joseph Taylor.	20	Andrew Bell.
14	Jane Lyell. [44]	19	Lambert Barberrie.
15	Sophia Terrill.	18	Henry Farley.
16	Poole England.	17	Joseph Marsh.

It is presumed that Mr. Rowland's labors in Amboy ceased about August, 1786, for in that month Mr. Joseph I. Bend, a candidate for orders, who then resided in the town and taught a school, was engaged by the congregation as lay reader. On being ordained, Mr. Bend removed to the South,[45]

[42] In 1791, John Hampton.

[43] In 1791, Ravand Kearny.

[44] In 1791, Anthony Butler.

[45] He was thought to be something of a poet, and a MS. copy of a poem entitled "The Pennsylvaniad," with some other pieces, has been seen by the author in a good state of preservation. He was of an irascible, querulous disposition, and before leaving Amboy, from a supposition that many of the inhabitants were inimical to him, he invoked the Muses in a "Prophetic Vision inscribed to Miss Eliza Parker,"—in which he kindly condemned the place and its people to numerous ills. It may satisfy the curiosity of some, to give some specimens of this vision. The reader must first be informed that Mr. B.'s Guardian Angel

"Induced by pity to unhacknied youth,
A foe to base deceit, a friend to truth,"

wings his flight to his protegé's "retired abode," to bring him "wise instruction from on high." After upbraiding him for his restlessness under the dispensations of Providence, he takes the poet first to the Church and thus addresses him:

"Here view effects of war's destructive rage,
And borrow wisdom from its bloody page.
When Britain's King possessed this wide domain,
And lovely peace maintained its gentle reign;
Here did a decent, modest train repair,
To join in praise, to join in ardent prayer.
They prais'd, they pray'd, they felt their hearts rejoice,
With silence heard the reverend preacher's voice; *
He from the treasure of his sacred lore
Dispens'd, with liberal heart instructions pure,
Improv'd each transient moment as it flew,
And 'bove this world he rais'd their wond'ring view."

* * * * *

But

"Snatched from this corrupt world, his labors o'er,
Where oft his towering soul was wont to soar
He dwells in bliss, and from his blest abode
Complacent views the servants of his God.
By his example fired, another rose †
And taught the way to bliss, to sweet repose;
Short was his reign: he yielded to his doom,
And tears sincere bedewed his early tomb."

* * * * * *

The prophetic vision so far as the Church was concerned showed,

"Religion gasping in the gloomy shade;
Her priests far hence by worthless scandal driven,

* Rev. Mr. Skinner.

† Rev. Mr. McKean.

and was succeeded in his school, and probably in his clerical duties also, by George Hartwell Spieren. In June, 1788, this gentleman was called by the congregation to be their minister as soon so he should be ordained, which took place on the 9th July following, at Amboy, — the Right Rev. Dr. Provost, Bishop of New York, officiating,— and on the 18th July he was admitted to Priest's orders in New York.[46] Thus the first ordination in New Jersey according to the forms of the Protestant Episcopal Church, took place within the walls of old St. Peter's at Amboy.[47] Mr. Spieren was an Irishman, who had received a good education, and is described by an English traveller as "a man profoundly versed in the languages of Greece and Rome, and not unconversant with the delicacies of the English; and a powerful preacher.[48]

On first entering the ministry he was exceedingly diffident, so much so as to be obliged to prepare himself for his public ministrations by first reading to small assemblies in private houses, and to associate others with him when making his pastoral visitations. He had enjoyed the advantages of good society, wrote poetry, and *danced elegantly.* He was married, but his lady does not appear to have moved in the same circle with himself.

While Mr. Spieren was in charge of the congregation, measures were taken to procure a new bell. In April, 1773, it was recommended to lessen the clapper of the bell they

Her votaries few, who raise their thoughts to heaven,
Her temple ruined, tottering to its fall,
Her friends depress'd lament the hanging wall."

He is next directed to the "Government House," now "Brighton," which had been burnt during the revolution.

"Yon ruined mansion view; observe it well,
There wit and mirthful glee were wont to dwell,
Prudence and courage, manly sense refined,
With every great endowment of the mind.
There by his proxy Britain's Monarch reigned,
Unshaken loyalty its court maintained.
The sad reverse, the mournful prospect see,
And yield submission to the stern decree,—
Defac'd the glory of the neighboring plain,
Its naked, ruin'd walls alone remain
A sad memento they shall ever stand,
And find no friendly, no assisting hand.
Remorseless foes shall on its ruins jest,
And screech-owls, toads and snakes the walls infest."

* * * * * *

But we cannot follow the poet in his wanderings. Enough has been extracted to show that Mr. Bend's Guardian Angel was no *seer.* The moral of the vision appears to be, that for the injustice of its inhabitants to Mr. Bend, the ancient city would in due time be delivered up to destruction.

[46] Minutes of Vestry.

[47] Mr. Chapmans's Hist. Discourses.

[48] Travels of John Davis in the U. States, from 1798–1802, p. 140.

then had, but nothing more is entered in regard to it, until January, 1787, when, anticipating the receipt of the funds from the sale of the lands given to the church by the proprietors, the Vestry ordered a committee to "consult Mr. David Ross, of Elizabethtown, to know his price for a bell about 3 *cwt.*, and report his terms," the great necessity for one having been considered and the old one being unfit for use; but the negotiation seems to have been unsuccessful.

In 1788 a ship commanded by Capt. Philip Lytheby, a Scotchman, arrived at Amboy from the Bahama Islands, and learning that the place had been settled principally by his countrymen, and grateful for the civilities shown to him while there, he offered to procure the casting of a bell of the size required, and by resolution of the vestry on the 9th November, the old bell was placed in his possession towards payment therefor. A vote of thanks to "Capt. Lytheby also passed, not only for his kind offer, but also for "the use of his ship's bell to be hung in the State House until the vestry are supplied with a proper one for the church." The bell was procured, and in due time made its appearance as a present from Capt. Lytheby, and took its station in the tower of the church.[49] Many have heard it ring forth its summons to the worship of God, without knowing that around it is this quaint inscription:

"IN PERTH AMBOY MY SOUND ENJOY, 1789."

In June, 1790, as the previous lottery had resulted so advantageously for the church, an application was presented to the Legislature, then in session at Amboy, for another, and an act was passed authorizing a scheme to raise the sum of £350. It was put under the management of John Rattoone, Michael Kearny and Andrew Bell, and the lottery was drawn in October, and an additional sum was secured by private subscription.[50]

[49] Capt. Lytheby became afterward a regular trader out of Amboy. His store or warehouse was under the hill adjoining, on the south, the precincts of the old Parker mansion. Some remains of its foundation were visible until with a few years.

[50] It was drawn at the Court House—the Hon. James Parker, still living, being one of the boys employed. The

Mr. Spieren did not long remain in charge of the congregation. He removed into the diocese of New York, and subsequently into that of South Carolina, where he assumed the charge of the Georgetown Seminary,[51] and where he died.[52] The precise time of his leaving is not known, but in 1791, the Vestry, in conjunction with that of Christ Church, New Brunswick, invited the Rev. Henry Van Dyke of Poughkeepsie to become the Rector of the two churches. Having accepted the invitation he arrived at Amboy with his family on the 19th April, and officiated alternately between Perth Amboy and New Brunswick, until June or July, 1793, when he removed to Burlington.[53]

The church being thus left vacant, the Vestry thought it advisable, until they could offer greater inducements to a permanently settled minister, to get one of the neighboring clergymen to supply the pulpit occasionally, or for a stipulated time, and complied with the unanimous wish of the congregation in engaging, on the 25th November, 1793, the Rev. Richard. C. Moore, of Staten Island, to officiate for them once a fortnight.[55] The services of Mr. Moore, afterward Bishop of Virginia, endeared him to the small flock over which he thus became the overseer, and after his removal to other fields of labor, his occasional visits were full of interest; the surviving members of the congregation welcoming him with all the warmth of personal friendship and regard; and the descend-

high prize of $1,000 fell to General Frelinghuysen. It is probable this lottery led the people of New Brunswick to think of a similar plan for the benefit of their church. In 1791, 750*l.* was raised by lottery there. It was drawn in July under the inspection of Col. John Bayard, *President of New Brunswick;* James Parker, Esq. *Mayor of Amboy*, and Archibald Mercer, *Deputy Governor of the Manufacturing Society of New Jersey.*

[51] Davis's Travels, p. 140. It was at Georgetown that Davis met with Mr. Spieren. He was there when the news of the death of Gen. Washington was received, and Mr. Spieren preached a funeral sermon. "Never was there a discourse'—he says—"more moving. Tears flowed from every eye, and lamentations burst from every lip," p. 514. Davis alludes also to Mr. S.'s dancing, and gives a humorous piece of poetry written to commemorate the participation of "the Parson and the Doctor," his friend, in a dance at Waccamaw, and their interference with the enjoyment of the party by their ignorance of its mysteries. On his leaving South Carolina, Davis took letters of introduction from Mr. Spieren to Bishop Moore of New York, which seem to have secured him a favorable reception.

[52] Rev. Mr. Chapman's Discourses.

[53] His salary was 100*l.*·N. Y. currency.

[54] Minutes of Vestry. His salary was to be 50*l.* per annum.

ants of all estimating as they should the privilege of receiving the administration of the holy ordinances of the church from the same hands, and listening to the words of truth from the same lips, to which their parents had looked for similar benefits.

Mr. Moore for several years performed his duties in the parish with great punctuality and fidelity, notwithstanding the difficulty and danger attendant upon crossing the Sound at all seasons; but the growth and welfare of the congregation requiring the services of a permanently settled pastor, the Vestry after some considerable delay—arising from the scarcity of unengaged clergymen at that time—finally called, in 1804, the Rev. Jasper D. Jones to the rectorship; who continued in charge of the congregation until the spring of 1809, when he resigned, and removed to Connecticut, where he died in 1823.[55] On the 9th September, 1809, the Rev. James Chapman was chosen Rector, and continued to be the incumbent for the long period of thirty-five years. He resigned in 1844, but still resides in Amboy, performing missionary services in the neighborhood.

At the time of Mr. Jones's resignation the church was much embarrassed with heavy debts, but in 1813 arrangements were made by which these obligations were discharged. The erection of a new parsonage, however, in 1815, again unfavorably affected the finances of the congregation, but under prudent management, St. Peter's has since been placed on as firm a foundation as it at any former time possessed.

In 1794 a new pulpit and reading-desk were erected, and in 1811 a new chancel constructed, and in 1825 the church was thoroughly refitted and numbers of forest trees set out, that will cast their shade upon the graves around, and add to the beauty of the already delightful site. To afford room for the growth of these and others subsequently set out, most of the tall poplars that are represented in the sketch on a preceding page were cut down, many of them having become decayed. A new fence was also placed around the churchyard in 1824, which, after the lapse of sixteen years, gave place to a better in 1841.

[55] Rev. Mr. Chapman's Discourses.

After the rectorship of Mr. Chapman closed, the church was supplied by various clergymen for some months, but the next year (1845) the Rev. Hamble J. Leacock, then officiating as Missionary at Woodbridge and Piscataway, was called to the charge of the congregation—and continued its rector till 1848, when he resigned; his private affairs having called him to the West Indies the year previous. Mr. Leacock's services were highly regarded, and the congregation relinquished them with regret. The vacancy was not filled until the summer of 1849, by the calling of the Rev. H. E. E. Pratt; the church in the intermediate time being supplied by occasional services from different clergymen. The new church was first used for public service, while yet not entirely finished, on Sunday, June 19th, 1853. It is to be regretted that the old edifice, hallowed by so many pleasing associations, could not have been preserved for all time; but its limited dimensions, and, in some respects, dilapidated condition, rendered its destruction unavoidable. Mr. Pratt removing to California, in 1854, the Rev. Alexander Jones, D. D. was called to the Rectorship, January 1st, 1855, and is the present incumbent.

Such is the history of St. Peter's Church, Perth Amboy, drawn from authentic sources, and I cannot better close the sketch than by appealing to those who like myself feel an interest in its prosperity, in the words of a former rector:—"To make it—now venerable for the length of time it has maintained its standing, and respected for the many pious and distinguished individuals whom in a long succession it has numbered among its members and supporters—still an honor and a blessing to the city;—to make it still more respected in the eyes of all abroad, and a standard here for the defence and maintenance of the precious doctrines of the gospel, and an example of the power of godliness over the hearts and lives of those who cherish the faith that was once delivered to the saints, and who profess their love for the habitation of God's house, and the place where his honor dwelleth."[56]

[56] Rev. Mr. Chapman's Discourses.

In 1809 there were connected with the parish 20 Families, the Communicants numbering 22.

In 1841 there were 28 Families and 38 Communicants.

In 1855 there are 47 Families and 59 Communicants.

From September, 1809, to August 1, 1855, there were 566 Baptisms.

Since 1812, when the first Confirmation was held by Bishop Hobart, 151 have renewed their baptismal vows in that apostolic rite.

The following is a complete list of the officers of the congregation to the present time, with the years of their election :[57]

WARDENS.

William Eier,	1718	John Smyth,	1763–74
John Barclay,	1718–22	Stephen Skinner,	1772–74
Robert King,	1719	[Revolution.]	
John Rudyard,	1720	Norris Thorpe,	1782–84
Wm. Burnet, "Governor,"	1721	John Johnston,	1782–89
John Stevens,	1722–25	John Halsted,	1785–96, 1800–01
John Parker,	1723–26	John Rattoone,	1790–1801, 1809–10
Robert L. Hooper,	·1726	James Parker,	1797
John Hamilton,	1727–29, 1737–41	Ravaud Kearny,	1798–99
Michael Kearny,	1727–29	Andrew Bell,	1809–42
Andrew Johnston,	1730–41	Joseph Marsh,	1811–41
Fenwick Lyell,	1730–36	Abner Woodruff,	1841
Lewis Johnston,	1742–62	John R. Watson,	1842–55
Samuel Nevill,	1742–62	Edward Brinley,	1843–51
Samuel Sargant,	1763–71	James Parker,	1852–55

VESTRYMEN.

Thomas Gordon,	1718–22	John Barclay,	1730–32
John Rudyard,	1718–19, 21	Laurence Smyth,	1734–45
Robert King,	1718, 20–35, 44–45	William Cosby, "Governor,"	1734
John Stevens,	1718, 26–30, 49–52	Robert L. Hooper,	1734–38
William Nicholls,	1719, 21	John Webb,	1735–40
Alexander Farquerson,	1719–20	Gabriel Stelle,	1737–38
John Sharp,	1720	Lewis Johnston,	1739–41, 63–73
John Johnston,	1722–28, 30–31	Adam Hay,	1739
George Leslie,	1722–29	Samuel Nevill,	1741
Michael Kearny,	1723–26, 30–33	Philip Kearny,	1742–74
Andrew Johnston,	1726–29, 42–62	John Deare,	1742–62
Heron Putland,	1726–28	Francis Brazier,	1744–45
John Parker,	1727–32	John Dodsworth,	1745
Fenwick Lyell,	1727–29, 37–41	Gerard Sayrs,	1749
Andrew Hay,	1729–39	John Smyth,	1749–62
John Hamilton,	1730–36, 42–45	George Leslie,	1750–52

[57] A dash between years indicates a continuance in office during the inter vening time.

John Barberrie,	1753–62
John Johnston,	1753–74
Cortlandt Skinner,	1755–74
Samuel Sargant,	1757–62, 72
Stephen Skinner,	1763–71
James Parker,	1763, 74, 85–96
Alexander Watson,	1763–74
Jonathan Deare,	1770–74
Ravaud Kearny,	1770–74, 82–83, 86, 91–93, 1797, 1800–01
Elijah Dunham,	1770–74
Frederick Smyth,	1774
John Rattoone,	1782–89
Thomas Lyell,	1782–84
John Halsted,	1782–84, 99
Elias Marsh,	1782–86, 95, 98
Stephen Deare,	1782–83
John Griggs,	1784–85
Poole England,	1784–85, 88–90
Norris Thorp,	1785
Samuel Farmar,	1785–86
Thomas Farmar,	1785–88
Matthias Halsted,	1785–86, 88–94, 97
Richard Stevens,	1786–88
John L. Johnston,	1786–87
Andrew Bell,	1787, 1789, 1808
Michael Kearny,	1790
John Johnston,	1791–93, 95–96
Joseph Taylor,	1794–1801
Joseph Marsh,	1794–97, 1810
Robert Palmer,	1798
James Parker,	1799–1837, 1843
Jas. H. Kearny,	1809–11
Abraham Webb,	1809–36
Philip Ten Eyck,	1809
David Thorp,	1810–29
B. H. Tomlinson,	1811
C. A. Forbes,	1812, 1816–17
Abraham Thompson,	1812–19
George Buchanan,	1813–21
William Hamilton,	1814–15, 30–31
Robert Arnold,	1816–17, 22–29
Jeremiah Martin,	1818–30
Richard Griggs,	1818–19
Archer Gifford,	1820–21
Abner Woodruff,	1822–25, 28–37
F. W. Brinley,	1822–23
Wm. Whitehead,	1824–34
Thomas G. Marsh,	1826–51
Lewis Gelding,	1827–54
Robert A. Thorp,	1830–35
Samuel Angus,	1830
Benoni Mandeville,	1834–37
Charles C. Lawrence,	1836–37
Jedediah Paine,	1837
James A. Nicholls,	1838–50
John Arnold,	1838–55
John R. Watson,	1839–41
Charles Hamilton,	1842
Charles McK. Smith,	1843–55
Lawrence Kearny,	1851–55
Lawrence Boggs,	1852–55
William King,	1852–55
Joseph D. Forbes,	1852–55
Eber H. Hall,	1855
S. V. R. Paterson,	1855

PRESBYTERIANS.

Very little information has been obtained of the formation of the Presbyterian congregation. The first notice of its existence is found in the Minutes of the Eastern Proprietors, at a meeting held July 22d, 1731, when the following petition was presented, and acted on as is stated in the subjoined extract :—

" The humble petition of some of the inhabitants of some of the City of Perth Amboy humbly petitioneth—

To the Hon. Council of Proprietors now sitting in Perth Amboy:

Whereas several of your petitioners have in the old Burial place so called, our parents, wives and children interred, we your petitioners humbly beg that your honorable house would take it into consideration and grant us a right of that piece of ground, that we may have a right to erect a meeting-house for the worship of God, and likewise for a Burial place; and that it may be your Honorable Council's order that the said piece of ground may be dedicated to the said use and no other, and your humble petitioners will for ever pray.

John Matthie,	John Gaschrie,
William Thompson,	Thomas Inglis,
Thomas Loggans,	James Leigh,
John Moore,	John Herriott,
John Thompson,	Samuel Moores,

Alexander Carnes."

"Which petition being taken into consideration by this Board, they are of opinion that the said piece of land do remain as formerly intended for a public Burial place for the inhabitants of this city. But that the petitioners have liberty to erect and build a meeting-house on the south-east corner of the same, and this Board do hereby lease, as far as in them lies, unto the said Petitioners, so much of the said piece of land, in the said south-east corner, as shall be necessary for that purpose not exceeding one chain square, for the term of one thousand years."

The land here referred to is situated on State formerly Back street, and from long occupancy is now known as the "Presbyterian Burying Ground," although set apart on the settlement of the town as a public cemetery, and no special or exclusive right having ever been granted to that congregation other than appears in the foregoing proceedings of the Board of Proprietors.

It is not probable that a congregation, regularly organized, existed at this time; but between 1731 and 1735, the privilege accorded by the Proprietors was secured by the erection of a small building which long continued to be occupied by the Presbyterians as their house of worship. There is no evidence to be found of any settled minister, and the information obtainable of those who, from time to time, administered to the spiritual necessities of the small flock that was here gathered into a fold, from the time their edifice was built until its destruction during the Revolution, is very limited. I am indebted to the Rev. Richard Webster of Mauch Chunk for the following items:—

"On the Synod Records, Sept. 17th, 1724, a supplication from some of the inhabitants of Perth Amboy, desiring sermon sometimes, being referred to the Presbytery of Philadelphia [which then included both East and West Jersey] was ap-

16

proved by the Synod, and Mr. Anderson was appointed to write a letter to them."[58]

"June 29th, 1735. Gilbert Tennent preached at Amboy on the 'Necessity of Religious Violence to Durable Happiness,' which was afterward published."

"From various circumstances I suppose that the Rev. John Cross of Baskenridge served Perth Amboy and Staten Island, then constituting one congregation. August 2d, 1742, Amboy asked New Brunswick Presbytery to send to them the Rev. Charles McKnight, then just licensed; a few months afterwards Baskenridge and Staten Island presented a call for him."

"In 1761 the South Ward of Amboy (South Amboy) appears as supplicant for sermons. The Rev. Elihu Spencer, then residing at Eatontown in Monmouth, supplied that place, Shrewsbury, and Middletown Point, for years."

Previous to the revolution the meeting-house had become much dilapidated, and in 1764 an attempt was made to get a lottery authorized for its benefit, but without success. The late William Dunlap was the only individual known to the author who had worshipped within its walls or recollected its appearance. Subsequent to the revolution, and until the commencement of the present century, the meetings of the congregation were held either in the old Court-house or in private dwellings, but they had no settled minister.

In 1801 Captain John Angus, who had been a resident of Amboy for a few years, commenced a course of persevering efforts towards the erection of a new meeting-house; and, proving the sincerity of his views by the personal donation of an eligible site, excited sufficient interest in the object both at home and in various parts of the country to induce liberal subscriptions and donations, and in May, 1802, the foundation was laid. The prosecution of the work was intrusted to Mr. Angus, Mr. David Wait, and Captain James Harriot.[59]

[58] Mr. Anderson was the pastor in New York, and belonged to the Long Island Presbytery. His daughter was married and resided at Amboy. She was the ancestress of the Breese family.

[59] Among the donations was a handsome folio Bible from the press of Isaiah Thomas, bearing this inscription: "The gift of General Ebenezer Stevens of New York to the Presbyterian Church, Perth Amboy, 21st September, 1802."

To the energy and perseverance of Captain Angus is the congregation mainly indebted for the neat edifice it yet occupies, standing on the public square, of which a representation is here given.

THE PRESBYTERIAN CHURCH.

For the following items of information the author is indebted to the Rev. Benjamin Cory, at present (1855) the pastor of the congregation:—

"The new edifice was opened for divine service on Thursday the 9th day of June, 1803, with a sermon by Dr. Samuel Stanhope Smith, President of the College of New Jersey, from the text "Remember that Jesus Christ of the seed of David was raised from the dead."—(2d Tim., 2, 8.)

"In January, 1802, after measures had been entered upon for the building of this house, the people invited Mr. Elias Riggs, a licentiate of the Presbytery of New York, to settle among them in the double capacity of minister of their embryo Church and teacher of a school in the Academy. He accepted of their invitation, and began his stated ministerial labors among them on the 7th of March, and on the following Monday opened his school. Public worship was held in the Academy till the Church was finished.

"On the 2d day of August, 1803, Mr. Riggs was ordained with a special reference to this field of labor. The ordination took place in the new meeting-house. Mr. Riggs remained about four years with the congregation, but was never installed as pastor.

"On the 28th of August, 1803, the Sacrament of the Lord's Supper was celebrated for the first time in Amboy, so far as we know, after the Presbyterian form—the number of communicants being seven.[60]

"In October, 1807, a Mr. Keys appears on the records as the officiating minister, but he was not the settled pastor of the congregation, and continued only about a year.

"It next appears on the Session Book that the Rev. Peter Stryker received a call to the pastorate. Mr. Stryker was then minister of the Dutch Reformed Congregation at Belleville, New Jersey. He accepted the call and was installed Pastor Nov. 28th, 1809. The Installation Committee, appointed by the Presbytery, were the Rev. Doctor Roe and Rev. Messrs. Picton and Carll. Mr. Picton preached the sermon from 1 Cor. 2 : 2, "For I determined not to know any thing among you, save Jesus Christ, and him crucified." Dr. Roe presided, and gave the charge to the Pastor, and Mr. Carll gave the charge to the people. Mr. Stryker remained only about nine months, when he notified the congregation of his intention to leave them. The following is the minute in the case :—In a meeting of the Session held Aug. 28th, 1810, Mr. Stryker informed the Session that he had received a call from the congregations of Belleville and Stone House Plains in the Reformed Dutch connection, and said that for several reasons founded on a special call in Divine Providence, and the peculiar circumstances of his present situation, he would accept of the call made upon him from these united congregations, and resign his present charge—not, however, without expressing much regret at leaving a people whose affectionate regards and marked attentions have laid him under great obligations ever to esteem and love them." [It is presumed Mr. Stryker immediately left Amboy, and for four years or more the congregation was dependent upon occasional supplies, but whose services were obtained is not now known.]

"In Dec. 17th, 1814, the Rev. Joshua Young commenced preaching to the congregation; he continued but for a very short time. From some traditions respecting him it would seem that his ministerial character soon became suspicious,

[60] John Angus, Margaretta Angus, Margaret Clark, Elizabeth Coddington, Phebe Harriot, Rachel Friend, and John Lewis.

occasioning uneasiness among the people, and he ceased to be their minister.

"After this, about June 6th, 1816, the Rev. Josiah B. Andrews began his ministerial labors here. The particulars respecting his settlement I am not able to furnish. He was pastor of the church between seven and eight years, when a very serious disturbance arose between him and the congregation, which resulted finally in his removal.

"The congregation was then without a stated minister till 1828, when Mr. Nicholas A. Wilson, a licentiate under the care of the Elizabethtown Presbytery, became their preacher as a stated supply. He was shortly afterwards, by the request of the session, ordained with reference to Amboy as the field of his labors. Mr. Wilson was a most excellent and devoted man, and much beloved by the people. After remaining here between two and three years he removed to Philadelphia, where he shortly afterwards died, greatly lamented.

"The next after Mr. Wilson was the Rev. Peter H. Shaw. He came in 1831. His continuance was only about 16 or 18 months. He was succeeded by the Rev. David R. Gillmer. Mr. Gillmer came in 1834, and left after a brief term of about 11 months. The cause of his leaving was a change of views in regard to Church polity. He had an impression that the Episcopal form was more apostolical, and accordingly went out from among us. But whether he is still an Episcopalian I am not able to say. My impression is, however, that he is not. I think I heard of his coming back to the Presbyterian Church, and that he has settled somewhere in Pennsylvania."[61]

The Rev. Benjamin Cory succeeded Mr. Gillmer, and entered upon his duties November 9th, 1834. He preached six months as a stated supply, and on 6th May, 1835, was ordained and installed pastor of the congregation. During his ministrations both the temporal and spiritual condition of the congregation have much improved, and at no time during his

[61] Mr. Gillmer was very young when he left Amboy. He subsequently applied to be admitted as a Candidate for Orders in the Episcopal Church, but failed to pass the preparatory examination, and his disappointment, it is thought, prevented any further attempts to connect himself with that denomination.

long pastorate of twenty-one years has it been more prosperous; there are at the present time 59 pewholders and 144 communicants.

OFFICERS OF THE CONGREGATION.

Ruling Elders and Deacons.

(The offices are united in the same person.)

John Angus, January 22d, 1804—died June 10th, 1817.
David Wait, do died November, 1810.
John Lewis, do died April, 1815.
Alexander Semple, 1810—removed to Pittsburgh, Sept., 1826.
John V. Crawford, Oct. 14th, 1822—removed to N. Brunswick, May, 1824.
John D. See, April 2d, 1836—removed August, 1840.
Zadoc Mundy, April 2d, 1836—removed August, 1837.
James Harriot, 1814—died Nov. 13th, 1848.
Samuel R. Ford, Oct. 14th, 1822—died August 1st, 1855.
Charles Ford, Feby. 22d, 1824—died June 15th, 1847.
*Samuel E. Woodbridge, April 2d, 1836.
*John D. See, August 5th, 1848.
David Crowell, Oct. 21st, 1849—died May 30th, 1853.
*Daniel Selover, do.
Stephen G. Woodbridge, do —died January 30th, 1853.
*Cornelius D. Selover, January 21st, 1855.
*Caleb C. Pierson, do.

TRUSTEES.

The names of the Trustees prior to 1838 cannot be given, the Trustees' Book having been destroyed by fire in 1840.

Benjamin Maurice,	appointed	1838.
David Crowell,	"	1838.
Charles F. Maurice,	"	1838.
Edwin Ford,	"	1838.
Wm. J. Ford,	"	1838.
*John Wait,	"	1838.
Stephen G. Woodbridge,	"	1846.
Alexander M. Bruen,	"	1847.
*William Paterson,	"	1847.
Cornelius H. Schapps,	"	1847.
David T. Wait,	"	1847.
*Charles Keene,	"	1855.
*Edward J. Hall.	"	1855.
*Henry D. Tyrrell,	"	1855.
*William Hall,	"	1855.

BAPTISTS.

The first organization of a Baptist Congregation took place on the 26th August, 1818, clergymen of that denomination

* Present Officers.

having officiated in the place during the preceding year. Elder T. Winter was called to the charge of the congregation, and continued its pastor until 1823, when he was succeeded by Elder Jabez C. Goble. Religious services up to this period were held in the old Court-house or at the residences of individuals, but their numbers increasing, measures were adopted for the erection of a meeting-house, and in 1824 the building was commenced :—it was not completed, however, for two or three years, and wore for several years the appearance it has in the subjoined sketch. This year (1855) it has undergone extensive alterations, consequent upon changes in the grade of the street on which it stands.

THE BAPTIST CHURCH—AS FIRST BUILT.

The successors of Mr. Goble have been :—

Elder J. Booth,	called in	1826,
Elder — Bloomer,	"	1829,
Elder J. Sloper,	"	1832,
Elder T. Reekea,	"	1835,
Elder J. Blain,	"	1837,
Elder John B. Case,	"	1839,
Elder John Rodgers,	"	1842,
Elder G. F. Hendrickson	"	1845,
Elder J. M. Carpenter,	"	1849–50,
Elder John E. Reynolds,	"	1852–53,
Elder B. S. Rogers,	"	1854.

On the organization of the congregation in 1818 there were 15 members. In 1854 the number of communicants was 69.

OFFICERS.

George Compton,	elected Deacon,	1818.
Thomas Freeman,	"	1818.
Uriah Burdge,	"	1825.
James Compton,	"	1829.*
John Hart,	"	1832.
William Hart,	"	1845.*
John P. Woglum,	"	1848.*
George F. Tryner,	"	1848.*

* Now in office.

METHODISTS.

THE METHODIST CHURCH.

The services of Methodist preachers commenced in Perth Amboy about 1813 or 1814,[62] but a regular congregation was not formed until 1818, and not until 1837 was permanence given to it by the erection of a small, neat edifice for its accommodation. The success of this undertaking was principally owing to the exertions of the Rev. Isaac Cross, who had officiated occasionally in the town, and who became in 1838 the first settled minister of the congregation. According to the rules of the Methodist Church Mr. Cross remained but two years, and his successors were as follows:—

1840—Benjamin Day,
1842—Josiah F. Canfield,
1843—Curtis Tully,
1844—Robert Lutton,
1846—Alexander Gilmore,
1848—John N. Crane,
1850—Jacob B. Fort,
1852—John W. Barrett,
1854—James H. Dandy.

When organized in 1818 there were only 12 or 15 members; in 1839 they had increased to 70; in 1840 they numbered 87; in 1841, 98; in 1842, 106; in 1843, 107; in 1844, 102; in 1845, 105; in 1846, 103; in 1847, 108; in 1848,

[62] Occasionally in earlier years a transient preacher would visit the place, and Bishop Francis Asbury, as early as 1772, says in his Journal (p. 20), under date of Thursday, Feb'y. 27th: "After having preached in a large upper room at Mr. T.'s in Amboy, where many came to hear, and I was much favored in my own soul; an innkeeper invited me to his house and was kind enough to desire that I would call on him when I came again."

102; in 1850, 79; in 1852, 100; in 1854, 115; in 1855, 90.

TRUSTEES.

Joseph Palmer,	1836–43.	Abraham Sleight,	1846–55.
Medad Munson,	1836–38.	Abm. Thompson,	1846–52.
Digby Odlum,	1836–43.	Benj. D. Kinsey,	1846.
Samuel Harriott,	1838.	David Noe,	1846–55.
Wm. Thomas,	1838–52.	Thomas M. Hull,	1846–47.
Franklin R. Street,	1838–43.	Wm. R. Freeman,	1847–55.
Willis Larkins,	1843–46.	Gilman Harned,	1852–55.
Cornelius Sleight,	1843–52.	Joseph L. Crowell,	1852–55.
Joel Smith,	1843–55.		

ROMAN CATHOLICS.

The first services according to the rites of the Roman Catholic religion were held about the year 1842, in the house of Mr. James Tuite, on every alternate Sunday. In 1844 a neat brick church was erected on Centre street, and the congregation is now under the charge of the Rev. Thomas Quin.

Chapter VII.—Public Buildings and Places.

THE TOWN OR COURT HOUSE.

THE first intimation we have of a structure of this kind is in the Proprietary Minutes, under date of May, 14th, 1685, as follows :—

"It is agreed and ordered that the Town House be built on that piece of land fenced in by Thomas Warne, next Thomas Hart's and Clement Plumstead's lots, and in case any damage be done thereby to Thomas Warne's corn, now sowed, before reaping, that he be paid for the same."

It is uncertain where this lot was situated, but it was, probably, one running through from High street to Water street, about the location of what has of late years been termed "the Lewis Place."

In April, 1696, twenty pounds were voted to Mr. Warne on condition that he released the lot again to the Proprietors, from which it would seem that the building was still standing upon it. They had however, previously, on the 5th May, 1695, directed Thomas Gordon to fit up one of the old houses belonging to them as a Court-house, under the advice of Governor Hamilton. Whether this continued to be occupied under the royal provincial government is not known.

In 1713 an act was passed for building and repairing Jails and Court-houses in the Province, and Amboy is particularly named as the site for the jail and court-house of Middlesex County. The building erected in conformity with this act stood on the north-east corner of High street and the Public Square, and served for both the triers and the tried, the prison being under the same roof with the court rooms. It is mentioned as existing previous to 1718, and continued to be used not only for courts but also for legislative purposes, the sittings of the General Assembly being held within it.[1] Each Governor on his arrival—from Governor Hunter to Governor Franklin inclusive—proceeded to it in stately pomp to proclaim to the assembled throng the good pleasure of the Sovereign of England, to the effect that they should respect and obey his representative; and beneath its roof did Whitefield preach some of his spirit-stirring sermons to attentive congregations. There is no memorial to bring to our view the aspect of the venerable structure that such associations might incline us to revere. In 1765 or '66 it was destroyed by fire—accidentally it is said, in the act providing for the erection of another—but there is a tradition that it was purposely set on fire by a man named Martin incarcerated in it for debt.[2]

On the destruction of this Court-house the General Assembly passed an Act, June 28th, 1766, authorizing the erection of another, and also of a jail, upon two lots of ground which had been allotted by the inhabitants for the purpose. The act provided for its erection "where the market-house stands so as to leave room for the market underneath," should the plan be approved of by Thomas Bartow, John Smyth, and Stephen Skinner; the first two being named as commissioners to superintend the erection of the buildings.[3] The approba-

[1] During a part or the whole of Governor Morris's administration, however, the legislature did not meet within it. The Assembly occupied a room in the old Parker mansion, and the Council was accommodated elsewhere in private houses. Thus in the Bill for the support of the government, 1738, we read of an appropriation "To Mrs. Jannet Parker, for the Use of a Room, Fire Wood, &c., for the House of Representatives, the Sum of *Thirty Shillings per Week*, during this present Session.

"To Mr. Andrew Hay the Sum of *Twenty Shillings per Week* for the Use of a Room, &c., for the Gentlemen of the Council during this present Session."

In October, 1741, and December, 1743, the executors of John Parker received twenty shillings per week from the Assembly, and Mrs. Sargant (in 1793 Col. Hamilton), fifteen shillings per week from the Council.

[2] Coupled with this tradition is a romantic story of his having fired the building out of chagrin at having assisted in erecting it—he being a mason—but as it had stood about fifty years we may reasonably doubt that part of the statement. Indeed, from a letter in my possession, dated September, 1769, it is doubtful if the story applied at all to the building referred to. Philip Kearny writes, "It is thought by some that Martin has set the jail on fire, but I cannot hear of any positive proof—there are some circumstances on his side which look bad." This date refers of course to the jail subsequently built.

[3] John Johnston became, subsequently, one of the managers, and his account, as such, is in my possession.

tion required was not given, it is presumed, for the building erected is the one now standing, and of which a representation is here given as it appeared in 1832. Some change has since

THE OLD COURT-HOUSE.

been made in the shape of the cupola or belfry. The act particularly described the kind of building to be erected, but the directions were not followed. It was to have "one large room in the middle or centre, for holding the courts of the said county and province in general; also two sufficient and fit rooms, one in each end of the said court-house, for the jury or juries of said county and province;" instructions which, if carried out, would have resulted in an edifice of only one story erected on stilts.

As it now stands was the Court-house finished in 1767, and from that time till 1775 it was occupied by the courts and provincial assembly; from beneath its roof came forth some of the patriotic resolutions and addresses by which that body warmed the hearts of Jerseymen and prepared them for the struggle to which events were impelling them; and there too did the Thespians of the Ante-revolutionary period delight select but appreciating auditories.[4]

[4] Dunlap's American Theatre, p. 22.

Since the War of Independence and the transfer of the county seat to New Brunswick, the court-house has been used as a school-house and for public meetings. It was thoroughly repaired in 1826 and at different periods since, and will probably remain a monument of the days of "good King George III." until another generation shall have looked upon it. It has recently, however, ceased to be a public building, having passed into private hands.

JAILS.

It is probable that Jails did not commonly exist in the different counties before 1684, although laws requiring their erection had been enacted previously. The first one built at Amboy, of which any information has been obtained, was erected in conformity with an Act passed in 1713, and stood until 1765 or 1766, when it was destroyed by fire, together with the court-house which was under the same roof, as stated on a preceding page.

The erection of another was authorized by Act of Assembly June 28th, 1766, and it was finished in 1767 at an expense of more than two hundred pounds.[5] It contained rooms for the keeper's family in addition to those for prisoners, and its general appearance may be realized from the above sketch, representing it as it stood at the time of being torn down. It

THE OLD JAIL.

All the bills for its erection are in my possession.

was located in Back now State street, adjoining the old burial ground, and at one time an alley-way led to it from High street, to facilitate the passage of criminals and officers between it and the Court-house.

In consequence of having no attention paid to its preservation, from the little need of such a building after the transfer of the county seat to New Brunswick, it had been for some years prior to its destruction in a most dilapidated condition, a receptacle for the most wretched and depraved class of inhabitants, in common with what was usually termed "the yellow house" in its vicinity, which continued a depository of misery and want for several years after its companion had disappeared; but which at a later period was repaired and rescued from its desecration, to become comparatively a respectable residence.

A quarrel having arisen within the precincts of the jail on New Year's Eve, 1825–6, which resulted in the receipt of some very severe wounds by two individuals engaged in the affray, the city authorities in the course of the year sold it with the condition that it should be destroyed; which was done.[6]

This was the jail in which Richard Stockton was confined in December, 1776, when on his way to New York a prisoner to the refugee royalists, in company with his friend John Covenhoven, at whose house in Monmouth he was residing at the time of his capture. The severe weather to which Mr. Stockton was exposed while in the jail, and the subsequent harsh treatment of the English in New York, laid the foundation of disease that terminated his existence in 1781.

Some remains of the old jail's foundation yet mark the spot where it stood.

[6] The nett proceeds of the jail were $252.92. The head of the family that then were the miserable inmates of the place was nearly related to one occupying a station in society in West Jersey as high as his was low. An instance of the wide difference that vice and intemperance can work in the destinies of men starting from the same point.

THE STOCKS.

* * * * * * * "An ancient castle,
* * * all of wood ; by powerful spell
Of magic, made impregnable,
There's neither iron bar nor gate,
Portcullis, chain, nor bolt nor grate,
And yet men durance there abide
In dungeons scarce three inches wide."—*Hudibras.*

It is only a few years since the remains of this formidable instrument of the law's vengeance,

"Such as basest and contemnedst wretches
For pilferings and most common trespasses
Were punished with—"

vanished from the ancient capital. The lower piece and the uprights, serving in some measure as a warning to the ill-behaved, stood in the square a few feet south of the Market until 1827, when on making some reparation to that building they were removed as "encumbering the ground." The author remembers gazing, when a boy, with wonder and doubt at the semi-circular receptacles to be seen in the portion that remained. No one with whom he has conversed recollects their being used.

THE OLD MARKET.

This memorial of the days when the good citizens of Perth Amboy called themselves "the most dutiful and loyal subjects" of the King of Great Britain, was taken down in 1842, having for a long while been untenanted, and for many years only used on special occasions.

It was several times repaired within the memory of the writer, but the corporation conceiving it to be useless, or undeserving the expense of repairs called for in the year above mentioned, sold it to the highest bidder. The subjoined sketch gives a correct idea of its appearance at the time of its demolition.

When it was erected is not known, but it is mentioned as in existence as early as 1766. It was then double or twice the length of the building represented in the sketch, a passage being left across the square from east to west through, or between the two lengths of, the building. When the southern half was taken down is not known ; each half was about fifty feet long by twenty broad.

During the revolution this Market-house was closely boarded up and transformed into a barrack for the troops.

THE BARRACKS.

The erection of these buildings was authorized in 1758, at the same time with others at Trenton, New Brunswick and Elizabethtown. They were intended to accommodate three hundred men, but, as planned, probably received a greater number.

Twenty-six hundred pounds were appropriated by the Province for their construction, and they were erected and furnished under the superintendence of Samuel Nevill, Thomas Bartow and John Smyth. Andrew Johnston, James Hude and John Johnston were appointed trustees for the province, to receive the title deeds for the land, which was not to exceed one acre in quantity,[7] and on the completion of the buildings, in 1759, they were placed in charge of Samuel Sargant and Thomas Skinner, who received each £20 per annum for their services.

The barracks were first occupied by the troops returning from the capture of Havana, in 1762, and from that time until the evacuation of New Jersey by the British, they were seldom unoccupied for any length of time,—a regiment being generally quartered at the different posts in East Jersey. The "47th foot" was the last that occupied them previous to the Revolution, and left New Jersey to participate in the perils of Bunker Hill and Saratoga.

A high close fence surrounded the grounds, from a line forty or fifty feet in the rear of the buildings, to the road, leaving a considerable space on each side. A portion of the area on the west side was occupied as a wood-yard, and the remainder used for the morning and evening parades. The regular reviews, and drillings for inspection, took place on what are now the lands of Mr. John R. Watson, towards Sandy Point.

On the breaking out of the Revolution, the Barracks were taken possession of by Captain Conway's company of militia, who marched down and paraded on the old race-course with the air of an invading army; this, too, while all the British colonial officers were yet nominally in possession of their respective offices. Captain Conway's official report is among the Stirling Papers in the New York Historical Society Library, as well as an inventory of the furniture, &c., he found in the buildings. The minuteness with which he details the various articles, when the worthlessness of some of them is considered, is somewhat amusing. From the quantity of bedding found, it would seem that provision only existed then for about eighty men.

[7] More must subsequently have been obtained.

Being public property, these buildings were confiscated to the United States; and by a resolution of Assembly, June 19th, 1783, they were placed in the charge of John Griggs, who was authorized to put them in "tenantable repair." They were subsequently sold to a Mr. Lloyd, who, in expectation of realizing considerable profit from the sale of the bricks—at the time commanding a high price—commenced tearing them down, but finding the expense greater than he had anticipated he desisted after demolishing part of the centre. The property afterward went into the possession of the Parker family, and some years since it was purchased for a Manufacturing Company. For several years prior to 1832, a large number of poplar trees stood about the premises,—planted after the Revolution, when a rage for that species of tree prevailed very extensively—but they were then cut down.

It is not probable that the "pomp and circumstance of glorious war" will ever again enliven these buildings, or withdraw them from private uses. Within a few years they have become occupied for various purposes by Mr. Solomon Andrews, previous to which time they were in a ruinous state; the habitation of the poor and destitute.

THE OFFICE OF PROVINCIAL RECORDS.

THE OFFICE OF PROVINCIAL RECORDS

The building, of which a representation is annexed, standing on the south-east corner of Gordon (formerly Gully) street and High street (at present the property of the Sunday School Society of St. Peter's Church), was erected by order of the Provincial Assembly in the year 1761, as a place of deposit for the records of the Eastern division of the province, a fire-proof apartment occupying one end o the building.

The act under which it was built was passed December 5th, 1760, and appropriated six hundred pounds for the erection of two edifices, one at Amboy and one at Burlington ; Messrs. Thomas Bartow, John Smyth and Andrew Smyth, being the commissioners appointed to superintend the erection of the one at Amboy.

How long it was occupied for the purposes for which it was built, and why vacated, I have not learned.

BRIGHTON HOUSE.

The first government house was erected on ground near the public square, in pursuance of orders from the proprietaries in England, in 1684. What its appearance and dimensions were, are not known. It was occupied by Governor Andrew Hamilton, but probably ceased to be the residence of the officials of the province when the government was transferred to the crown. The royal governors who preceded Governor Franklin, took up their abode wherever their convenience prompted.

The Board of Proprietors in March, 1762, adopted a plan, and gave the necessary directions for building a proprietary house where the present Brighton stands. It was completed about the year 1764–5, and comprised only a part of what is now the main edifice. From May 1766 to May 1771, it was occupied by Chief Justice Smyth, at an annual rent of twenty-five pounds New York currency, and in October, 1774, it became the residence of Governor Franklin.

While Amboy was in the possession of the British troops, their commanders' head-quarters were at this house; but some time after the Revolution its interior was destroyed by fire, and in 1785, it was sold by the Board of Proprietors It was subsequently rebuilt and enlarged by Mr. John Rattoone.

The appearance and dimensions of the building as it is at present, were given to it while in the possession of a firm who, in the year 1809, established it as a public house by the name it now bears. It was kept in the style of the best houses at the watering places; servants abounded, bands of music were in constant attendance, and every arrangement made about the premises to accommodate the public on the most extensive and agreeable scale. For a year or two it was much frequented, and the proprietors had collected all the materials for constructing another wing, similar to that on the south of the main building, to enable them to entertain a still greater number of visitors, but the progress of the war with Great Britain put a stop to all their proceedings;—their prospects were blighted, they became insolvent, gave up the business, and the property was sold.

Soon afterwards it was purchased by the late Matthias Bruen, Esq., and was for several years, until his death, his residence, but is now a place of summer resort.

INNS AND TAVERNS.

In connection with the ferry across the Raritan, established by Deputy-Governor Lawrie in 1684, was erected what has been long known as the "*Long Ferry Tavern*"—and the author has ofter heard it spoken of by his seniors as the customary resort of the gentlemen of the town previous to the Revolution:—the spot

"Where grey-beard mirth and smiling toil retired,
And village statesmen talked with looks profound."

It was the first public house opened in Amboy. One hundred and seventy years and more have much altered the appearance of the grounds around it. There was a beautiful grove of locusts on the bank of the river westward of the house, which, in addition to the advantages of a delightful situation, commanding an extensive and agreeable prospect, possessed another attraction in its name;—it was called "Love-Grove," and was a favorite and much frequented walk, the resort of the population generally on a summer's afternoon; the sea breeze invigorating the failing limbs of age, and bringing on its wings additional life and energy to youth.

Although it is probable that the house sustained a good name—generally the consequence of good qualities in the host—but little information can be gathered of its occupants. Previous to the Revolution it was kept for a long period by a man of large stature named Carnes,[8] but of his predecessors nothing is known. Probably "mine host" of Lawrie's time was James Emott.

There was an opposition establishment on the other side of the street, which, for several years previous to 1765, was kept by Isaac Iseltine, but in that year it was sold, and appears to have been bought by Elias Bland, and occupied as a private residence.

The buildings on the north side of Smith Street at its junction with High Street, were kept as taverns for some years previous to 1776. One of them for some years has been closed, and it is not probable that the wants of the place will require it to be re-opened. The present City Hotel was occupied at the time of the Revolution by Whitehead Hicks—a connection of the New York family of that name, who had seen better

[8] "When I asked my earliest friend and instructor (after my parents), Thomas Bartow, for the meaning of 'Giant,' his answer, was 'such a man as Carnes;' and I remember when looking over the pictures in Milton's Paradise Lost before I could read, I remarked to the old gentleman, pointing to the *head* of the figure of Sin—'*that* is like Tom Carnes.'" Wm. Dunlap—in a letter to the author. A son of Carnes was Steward and Quartermaster to the General Hospital in New York, in 1776.

days. Rivington's paper was "to be had at Hicks' tavern in Amboy." Among the names of inn-keepers we find Andrew Hay, in 1730, Elijah Dunham, John Thompson and Robert Rattoone about the period of the Revolution, and John Hooks, in 1692. The public houses under the hill, on the Sound, were in the olden time mere ferry houses.

THE LONG FERRY TAVERN.

The Long Ferry tavern as it now stands, bears evident marks of having received additions since first erected. It is supposed that the portion with the high stoop and dormer windows was all that was built in the time of Lawrie. The sketch annexed was taken in 1832, and the single tree introduced, may assist the imagination in forming an idea of the appearance of the place previous to the destruction of the locust grove which extended westward.

The encroachments upon the bank, which caused the destruction of the grove, do not seem to have been serious until after the Revolution, but they had commenced in 1761. In November of that year the vestry of St. Peter's Church, to whom the property belonged, being of opinion that a wharf was necessary for the preservation of the bank as well as for the advantage of the ferry, appropriated funds for its construction. Nothing, however, was done until July, 1765, when a Committee was appointed "to inspect the building of a low wharf to be immediately constructed, and if the sums appropropriated be sufficient, a block at the end to protect the boats."

This block and wharf do not appear to have been very substantially built, for in May, 1770, it was considered necessary to raise the wharf, and "the remains" of the block at the end were to be made use of in the work. It was completed in August.[9] For many years the wharf has ceased to exist.

THE SPA.

This Mineral Spring in the road which divides the townships of Woodbridge and Perth Amboy, though of less strength, is similar in character to the water of Schooley's Mountain. It does not appear to have attracted any special attention at an early period, and is not alluded to in any papers or documents which have come under my notice prior to 1772. In the New York Journal of July 9th, in that year, it is referred to in connection with the advertisement of a "new and convenient Bath lately erected at Amboy." The bath is said to be highly beneficial "from being about two miles distant from mineral water similar to the German *Spaw*," which had been of great efficacy in many disorders; its distance, it is said, "procuring moderate exercise after bathing, has proved in many instances very assistant to the medicinal quality of the waters, which with great success have been directed after bathing in sea water. The qualities of this Spaw have been well examined by several physicians of ability, and frequently recommended by them, particularly by the present Doctor Johnston and his father." Whether a walk of four miles, which a visit to the spring rendered necessary, could be termed "moderate exercise," some may be allowed to doubt. No name is affixed to

[9] The contractor was James Morgan; the contract price 35*l*.

the advertisement, so that the originator of this public improvement [10]—such as the city even at the present day cannot boast of—remains unknown.

The spring, within the recollection of the writer, has several times been fitted up with seats, a roof, and other appliances, at the cost of such inhabitants of the two towns as have been accustomed to visiting it, but the waters have never been of sufficient repute to attract attention from abroad.

THE COVE.

A considerable inlet existed at the time of the settlement, at the foot of Tower Hill. Gawen Lawrie, in one of his letters, describes the spot as resembling the keys in London; and supposing it to be particularly applicable to commercial purposes, he laid out the adjoining lots accordingly, as will be seen on reference to the map at page nine. The high ground around was to be occupied by stores and warehouses, while a canal dug around the low ground in the centre would permit small vessels to come up to their doors; and it was from the great protection from the winds and waves which it was supposed they would thus secure, that it had its name. The alterations of late years have so changed the topography of this part of the city, that the spot will no longer be recognized as the one set apart by Lawrie for the use of shipping. We can hardly realize the fact that such plans were formed with reference to its peculiar capabilities, but one hundred and seventy years have done much towards filling up and rendering firm ground what was once a marsh. Within the recollection of old inhabitants, boats large enough to carry several cords of wood, deposited their freight some distance inside the bridge which crosses the basin of what a few years since was the coal-yard of the Lehigh Company, and the miniature ships of even the present residents—"when life with them was new"—were here set afloat

[10] This Bath was "near the wharf opposite the bay." It had a dressing-room with a staircase leading into the bathing apartment, whence egress could be had by a door, by those who wished to swim out into deep water.

on quite an extensive surface of water, and their canvas trimmed to the breeze.

Previous to the commencement of the filling up, which preceded the occupation of the Coal Company, a considerable portion of this low ground was overflowed at high water.

TOWER HILL.

This elevation of ground, west of the Cove and in front of the Baptist and Methodist Churches, was so designated many years before the Revolution. The name was conferred in consequence of its having been the place where on some few occasions criminals were executed.

THE WRECK OF THE CALEDONIA.

Lying in shoal water, nearly in front of the brick-yard of Mr. Hall, are the remains of a vessel which used to be much resorted to, and may be still, in consequence of their harboring numbers of fine fish.

The vessel was the "Caledonia," and her name has become very generally known, and—it may be said—reverentially spoken of, from her having borne to New Jersey many Scotch families, immigrating from Scotland during the troubles that agitated that country in 1715. She was commanded by Robert Drummond, and, for some cause not now known, the captain and crew deserted her while lying at the wharf at Amboy, and, a storm arising, she broke from her moorings and drifted to the spot above mentioned. It is probable that she was an old vessel and unseaworthy, which will account for no measures being adopted for her preservation.

This view of the case is confirmed by the fact that in a despatch of Lord Bellamont to the Board of Trade, in the New York Colonial Papers, dated October 20th, 1699, a ship named Caledonia is mentioned as having made voyages between Scotland and America;[11] and if she was the same vessel, of

[11] He says, "When the two Scotch ships, called the Caledonia and the Unicorn, came to New York, they were in a miserable condition, having lost great number of people on their voyage from Caledonia by famine and sickness;

which there is every probability, it is not surprising the lapse of sixteen years should have rendered her no longer serviceable. There are several relics of the old vessel in different parts of the State, in the possession of those who claim descent from those she brought to our shores.[12]

[12] There are many fabulous stories current relative to the vessel and her passengers, possessing as much foundation in truth as the assertion of an old negro woman in Amboy; who was wont to date the advent of a certain old citizen as corresponding with the arrival of "Ham and Columbo (Columbus) in the old Caledonia."

Chapter VIII.—Travelling Facilities.

"* * * * * * Some do rise so fast
They do forget what climates they have past."

In these days of travelling facilities, when steam on water and on land renders distance a matter of little or no consideration, it is difficult to realize the state of things which pervaded the land a century or a century and a half ago. Some reflection has to be exercised ere the mind can grasp the fact, that the same difficulty or infrequency of communication between distant points which at present exists in the yet unsettled West, once prevailed throughout the section of country we inhabit.

Even since the general introduction of steam upon our streams, the improvements in speed and comfort have been so great, that the present facilities afford almost as remarkable a contrast to what existed at that epoch, as was then presented in comparison with the early years of the country. As late as 1816, travellers left New Brunswick for New York at six o'clock in the morning, at nine were off Amboy, at eleven reached Elizabethtown Point, and at one o'clock in the afternoon arrived at the end of their voyage, having been seven hours, and in a *steamboat*, going the distance which is now performed by similar vessels in little more than one third the time. And the recollection of any person at all advanced in life, can revive many instances of improvement equally, if not more noticeable, within the same period.

It is intended in this chapter briefly to notice the various routes through New Jersey, and the modes adopted for the transportation of freight, passengers, and the mails previous to the establishment of the Federal government: it being no unimportant question to ask ourselves—do we, with all our advantages, as faithfully discharge the obligations resting upon us as good citizens, as did our ancestors, who so materially advanced the welfare of the country and the happiness of their fellow men, under restrictions upon intercourse and the means of diffusing knowledge, which, to us, seem to have been almost positive prohibitions?

The principal path or track of the Indians in the northern and eastern portion of New Jersey, was one which ran from Shrewsbury River, near the Navesink hills, to Minisink Island in the Delaware River, near the north-west point of the province. It ran along the southern shore of Raritan Bay, past the present site of Middletown, till it came to the river about three miles above Perth Amboy. Here it crossed and ran in a northerly direction, until in the latitude of Elizabethtown—being about five miles west of where that place now is—and then took a sweep north-westerly to Minisink.

The first settlements by the English being upon water-courses, or in their immediate vicinity, the want of roads was not immediately felt, so that until 1675 and 1676—when the Legislature adopted some general regulations for the opening of roads, which were enlarged and systematized in March, 1682–3, the only thoroughfare of importance within the limits of New Jersey appears to have been that by which the Dutch had communicated with their settlements on the Delaware. It ran from Elizabethtown Point, or its neighborhood, to where New Brunswick now stands, and was probably the same as that now—widened and improved—known as the "old road," which follows the highest ridges between those places. At New Brunswick the river was forded at low water, and the road thence ran almost in a straight line to the Delaware (above where Trenton is now situated), which was also forded. This was called the "upper road" to distinguish it from the "lower road," which branched off about 5 or 6 miles from the Raritan, took a sweep towards the east, and arrived at the Delaware at the site of the present Burlington. These roads, however, were very little more than footpaths, and so continued for many years, affording facilities principally to horsemen and pedestrians. Even as late as 1716, when a ferry had been established at New Brunswick for 20 years, provision was only made in the rates allowed by the Assembly for "horse and man" and "single person." Previous to that time, however, the road had been improved, and was considered the main thoroughfare to Pennsylvania; for in 1695, the *Innkeepers* at Piscataway, Woodbridge and Elizabethtown were made subject to taxation for five years, to prevent its "falling into decay." The sum required annually to keep this road in repair at that time, was only *ten pounds.* Three pounds were to be paid by the Innholders at Piscataway; fifty shillings by those at Woodbridge; and four pounds ten shillings by those in Elizabethtown. The road was placed under the superintendence of George Drake, of Piscataway, who was made accountable for the proper disbursement of the money, and the execution of the repairs.[1]

The proprietaries, ever solicitous for the growth of their Capital, in July, 1683, expressed their wish to Deputy-governor Lawrie, that "it might be discovered whether there may not a convenient road be found betwixt Perth Town and Burlington, for the entertaining of a land conveyance that way." This was done by Lawrie the ensuing year, and he connected with the road a ferry boat to run between Amboy and New York "to entertain travellers"—but notwithstanding strenuous exertions were made to draw to this road the principal travelling through the province, the old Dutch road continued to be preferred; and Governor Basse in 1698 was directed to bring the matter before the Assembly, and have an act passed that would "cause the public road to pass through the Port town of Perth Amboy from New York and New England to West Jersey and Pennsylvania"—but this indorsement of the Assembly was not obtained, owing probably, in part, to the fact that only three years before they had virtually taken the other road under their care.

Such were the two routes travelled between New York and Philadelphia under the Proprietary government, but no public

[1] East Jersey under the Proprietors, p. 95, 160, 161. Bill in Chancery, p. 5. Grants and Concessions, pp. 118, 256, 294, 221.

conveyance for the transportation of either goods or passengers existed on either. One Dellaman was permitted by Governor Hamilton to drive a wagon on the Amboy road, but had no regular prices, or set times, for his trips.

In April, 1707, the Assembly, enumerating their grievances to Lord Cornbury, complained that patents had been granted to individuals to transport goods on the road from Burlington to Amboy for a certain number of years, to the exclusion of others, which was deemed not only contrary to the statute respecting monopolies, but also "destructive to that freedom which trade and commerce ought to have." The Governor, in his reply, gives us an insight into the facilities afforded by this wagon. After stating the difficulties which had previously attended the carriage of goods upon the road, he says, "at present, every body is sure, *once a fortnight*, to have an opportunity of sending any quantity of goods, great or small, at reasonable rates, without being in danger of imposition, and the settling of this wagon is so far from being a grievance or a monopoly, *that by this means and no other* a trade has been carried on between Philadelphia, Burlington, Amboy and New York, which was never known before: and *in all probability, never would have been.*" As none of the grievances suffered under Lord Cornbury's administration were removed until his recall in 1710, it is probable this wagon continued to perform its journey "once a fortnight" till then, if no longer. Soon after, however, the road seems to have been more open to competition.

The "ferry boat" which Lawrie "set up" in 1684, to run between Amboy and New York, takes precedence in the records of all but one, established under the Proprietary government. That one was established in 1669 at Communipau, under the charge of Pieter Hetfelsen, for the accommodation of the people of Bergen and Communipau, exclusively, in communicating with New Amsterdam. By his commission Hetfelsen was obliged to keep his boat in readiness at all times, but more particularly on three days in the week, "unless some other extraordinary occasions does hinder him, *viz.*, Mondays, Wednesdays and Fridays, or upon such other days as they (the people of Bergen and Communipau) shall *unanimously* agree upon" when they were required to attend.[2] Some idea may be formed of the nature of the traffic between the provinces at that time from the schedule of rates established, which was as follows :—

	In wampum.
"Every scheppel of Corn	2 stivers.
Half-barrel or half-fat of Beer	10 do.
Barrels of Beer, and other goods and liquors in casks in proportion, each	20 do.
Horses, Mares, and Oxen, per head	4 guilders.
Cows, each	3 do.
Hogs, Sows, Sheep, per head	15 stivers.
For every Passenger	6 do.
For his freight extra, if but one man	4 guilders."

If by night or in unseasonable weather, the rates were to be as the parties might agree.

In 1697 the ferry across the Raritan was granted to John Inians and his wife, or the longest liver of the two, during their lives, for the yearly rent of five shillings sterling ; and for many years, the present location of New Brunswick was known as Inian's ferry.

These, with one from Amboy to Navesink, granted to Arthur Simson in December 1700, for fifteen years, are all the lawfully established ferries that are mentioned in the proprietary records. Others may probably have existed, both on the Passaic and Hackensack, and between Elizabethtown and New York, but of a more private and irregular character.

In 1716 more attention seems to have been attached to the condition of the public roads. An Act was passed confirming all highways that were six and four rods wide, which had been laid out in pursuance of previous laws, and annulling all others. The system of laying them out was remodelled, and provisions adopted to which those of our own day have a resemblance. Rates of ferriage were established at different places by a public ordinance, and about this time we find in existence a ferry from Amboy to Staten Island ("Captain Billop's"), and one from Perth to South Amboy called "Redford's Ferry,"[3] and passengers and produce were transported

[2] E. J. Records, Lib. 3, p. 27.

[3] So called from Andrew Redford, then owner of the lands at South Amboy. In February, 1717, Governor Hunter, writing to George Willocks, says: "I shall not grant the ferry over both sides to Redford—I promised, indeed, to hear what Rudyard has to say."

also directly from South Amboy to Staten Island. There was a ferry likewise about this time from "Weehawk" to New York, and a law was passed, obliging all ferrymen to obtain licenses, and to comply with other regulations calculated to advance the interests of the traveller. Thereafter ferries multiplied considerably. One between Staten Island and Blazing Star was established in January, 1725; in January, 1734, Archibald Kennedy received a grant for one between Bergen county and New York, and in May of the same year Stephanus Van Cortlandt was authorized to have a ferry or passage boat to go between the counties of Essex and Bergen.

A "transporting place" on the Passaic is mentioned as early as 1718, and in 1765 it was erected into a regular ferry in connection with one over the Hackensack, forming the direct route to New York from Newark. At this latter period ferries existed across the Hudson both from Paulus Hook and Bergen Point.

The ferries from Perth Amboy across the Raritan and the Sound, were in 1719 granted to George Willocks and wife; and a house for the accommodation of travellers by the latter ferry, was about being built in the vicinity of the present Hay-press at the time of Willock's death in 1729.

In 1728 Gabriel Stelle received a patent for a ferry from South Amboy to Staten Island, touching at Perth; and these ferries continued to be of essential service until travelling and transportation fell into other and more convenient channels. Of late years the steamboats plying between New Brunswick or Amboy and New York, have afforded all needful facilities to those wishing to cross either the Raritan or the Sound; but previously, for many years, skiffs for passengers and a scow for an occasional vehicle, were all the conveniences required. A charter was granted a few years since for a horse-boat ferry, but it is not probable that any use will ever be made of it.

The mode and frequency of transmission of the mails during these early times deserve some notice; for although the full advantage of regularity in their arrival and departure can only be appreciated by those who have been so situated as to be deprived of such means of communication altogether, yet any one of the present day cannot but prize his own privileges, when considering those of his forefathers; the contrast being sufficiently great to excite inward congratulations that he is not so completely shut off, as they were, from "hearing or seeing some new thing." The true condition of things as they existed in by-gone days may be gathered from the following items:—

To Colonel John Hamilton, son of Governor Andrew Hamilton, of New Jersey, (himself at one time acting Governor, as President of Council,) were the Colonies indebted for devising the scheme by which the Post-office was established.[4] This was about the year 1694. He obtained a patent for it, and afterwards sold his right to the Crown. It is presumed that the mails were carried regularly, or an attempt made to have them so carried, soon after this period, but the riders made their trips without much reference to speed. It is probable that the wagon which has been mentioned as running between New York and Philadelphia before the surrender of the proprietary government, was the conveyance by which the mails were sent at this time through New Jersey,[5] Governor Andrew Hamilton, for some years acting as "Postmaster-General" over the infant establishment.

The progress made in the extension of the mails and in the speed of their transmission was very slow. In 1704 Madame Knight, who wrote a journal of her travels, was about a week travelling from Boston to New York, "with the postman generally as her guide."[6] The same year, in the "pleasant month

[4] See page 169.

[5] The Post between East Jersey and Pennsylvania is several times referred to in the Pennsylvania Colonial Records,—Vol. 1, pp. 463, 467, 540.

[6] Watson and others, referring to the jaunt of this lady (who would seem from her book to have travelled on business) state that she was two weeks on the way—but this is an error. She left Boston Oct. 2d, at 3 o'clock P.M., and arrived at New Haven on the 7th

of May," the New York paper says "the last storm put our Pennsylvania post *a week behind, and is not yet* com'd in."

Watson, in his Annals of Philadelphia,[7] gives an extract from a letter written in Dec., 1717, which states that there was at that time a settled post from Williamsburg, in Virginia, to Boston—"whereby advices from Boston to Williamsburg is completed in four weeks from March to December, and in double that time in the other months of the year." He states that a mail from Philadelphia to Annapolis was also established in 1717. Some doubts are entertained whether the mails south of Philadelphia continued to be carried long. The following article appeared in a public journal a few years since as a relic of the olden time, and from it we may judge there was no mail south of Philadelphia at the period to which it refers, which was presumed to be "about the year 1720":—

"An account of ye Posts of ye Continent of North America, as they were regulated by ye Postmasters of ye Posthouse. The western post sets out from Philadelphia every Friday, leaving letters at *Burlington* and *Perth Amboy*, and arrives at New York on Sunday night; the distance between Philadelphia and New York being 106 miles. The post goes out eastward every Monday morning from New York, and arrives at Seabrook every Thursday noon; being 150 miles—where the post from Boston sets out at the same time, the New York post returning with the eastern letters, and the Boston post with the western. Bags are dropt at New London, Stonington, Rhode Island, and Bristol. The post from Boston to Piscataway, being 70 miles, leaves letters at Ipswich, Salem, Marblehead, and Newberry. There are offices kept at *Burlington* and *Perth Amboy*, in New Jersey, New London and Stonington, in Connecticut, at Rhode Island, Bristol, Ipswich, Salem, Marblehead, and Newberry, and the three great offices are at Boston, New York, and Philadelphia."

A writer in the New York Gazette of July 31st, 1732, states that mails were not then established farther south than Philadelphia. In 1722 a Philadelphia paper announces that the New York Post was *three days* behind his time, and not yet arrived. In 1729 the mail between the two cities went once a week in summer, and once a fortnight in winter, and this continued to be the case till 1754. In April of that year,

in the afternoon—5 days. She left there Dec. 6th, at 11 A.M., and arrived at New York on the evening of the 8th—2½ days. So that she was actually travelling little more than a week.

[7] Page 626, 1st Edition.

notice is given at New York that the Boston and Philadelphia posts would both leave weekly on Monday at 3 P. M.

That year (1754) the Post was put under Dr. Franklin's superintendence, and an improvement immediately took place. His son William (afterwards Governor) acted as Comptroller under him, and in October gives notice that, until Christmas, the Post would leave the two cities every Monday, Wednesday, and Friday, at 8 o'clock A. M., and arrive the next days at about 5 o'clock P. M. (33 hours.) After Christmas, it was to leave at 10 o'clock on Tuesday and Saturday, and arrive on the mornings of Thursday and Monday, "being frequently delayed in crossing the New York Bay." Dr. Franklin continued to discharge the duties of Postmaster in person or by deputy until about 1773, when he was dismissed by the British government. The Continental Congress re-appointed him so soon as their attention was drawn to the necessity of keeping up a regular communication between the colonies.

Under Dr. Franklin's superintendence farther improvements were made both in speed and frequency. In January, 1764, James Parker, Comptroller, then residing at Woodbridge, under a heading "For the benefit of Trade and Commerce," gave notice that a post rider with the mail would leave New York that day at one o'clock for Philadelphia, and, until farther orders, would leave each city every alternate day "if weather permits." Letters to pass from city to city in less than twenty-four hours.

For some time the only offices in New Jersey were at Perth Amboy and Burlington: being on the direct route from New York to Philadelphia, they probably partook of the benefits of the first arrangements. Letters for large districts of country were sent to those places for distribution. In December, 1733, a notice is inserted in the Philadelphia Weekly Mercury stating that "there are a number of letters in the Post Office at Amboy for persons living in the counties of Somerset, Monmouth, and Essex"—and directing the inhabitants of those counties to apply for their letters to sundry individuals named in the advertisement.

In December, 1732, it appears from a remark in a communication to the New York Gazette, that the post ran from Amboy to New York at that time only once a fortnight; during the summer it is probable letters were transmitted once a week.[8]

In September, 1734, notice is given that a Post Office is established at "Trent Town," at the house of Joseph Read, Esq., his son Andrew Read being appointed Post Master. When the offices at Newark and other principal towns were established does not appear, but it must have been at a much later period.

The following rates of postage were established in 1765:

Letters between London and any American port in British packet boats, 1 shilling.

Letters by sea from one port to another in any of the British dominions, in such packets, 4 pence.

Letters by land to or from any chief post office in America, from or to any other part thereof, not over 60 miles, 4 pence.

Over 60 and not exceeding 100 miles, 6 pence.

Over 100 and not exceeding 200 miles, 8 pence.

Any farther distance, not exceeding 100 miles, 2*d* additional.

And all farther distance 2*d* additional.

Double, treble, and ounce letters paying in proportion.

What the rates were previously is not known. In December 1753, Parker, the Editor of the Post Boy, complained that he had to pay "twenty pence" for the postage of a communication from New Jersey that could not have filled a sheet; from which we may judge that the rates were then much higher.

The following is the only intimation I have discovered of the mode of communicating with North-western New Jersey. It was circulated in manuscript for the purpose of obtaining subscribers:—

ADVERTIZMENT.

"This is to let all Gentlemen and others know, that by the incouragement I have from Several Gentlemen, That I, Jacob Abel of Philipsburgh, in Sussex County West New Jersey, have resolve to Ride Post for the good of the Public. Intended to begin on the 5th day of February next on Mon-

---

[8] The holders of the honorable office of Postmaster in Amboy, previous to the Revolution, have not been ascertained but in one instance. John Fox was the incumbent in 1751.

day in every Fortnight till the 5 day of April, and from the 5 day of April to the 5 day of December next ensuring every Monday in a week.

Take therefore myself the Liberty to recommand myself in the favour of the Public, Advising them that on my return to Philadelphia shall Ride to Garman Town and then turn off on York Road, cross the River at Darram and purpose to Lieve my Packet at the following Person, as,

George Taylor Esqr	Mr. Jones
Thomas Pots Esqr	Mr. Sprowl
Gast Bairs	Arter Henry
Thomas Peterson	Straw Tavern
Jacob West	James Stewards
Joseph Mocka	William Carr

and Several Packit at East-Town and Palling Skill.

The Garman Papers at Four Shilling & Six Pence a year

The English Papers at Seven Shilling & Six Pence a year

Desiring the prompt Payment each quarter.

Any Parsell or letters What any Gentlemen Person or Persons will be pleased to trust to the Rider Care, may depend they shall be safely delivered, and if it should be required am willing, (as able,) to give security. Any Person or Persons that is willing to give incouragement to the Rider are desire to signe their worthy Names on the Subscription Paper left in several Hands and you will greatly oblige

Gentlemen Your most obedient humble
Servant

JACOB ABEL

Philipsburg the 15th January 1776.

All Gentlemen & Others that are willing to incourage the Post Rider Jacob Abel of Philipsburgh, Sussex County West New Jersey are desire to sett their Worthy Names (according to the advertizment on this

SUPERSCRIPTION PAPER.

ENGLISH NEWS				GARMAN NEWS
Geo Taylor[9]	£1	10	0	
for Hall & Sellers Gazette Bradford Journall Humphrey's Ledger Town Evening Post				
Thomas Long—Dunlap's Paper				
James Gallagher—Hall & Sellers				
Hugh Oriton ditto				
Samuel Heilborn do				

endorsed

"To George Taylor Esq:
at
Durham"

In 1791 there were only six offices in New Jersey—Newark, Elizabethtown, Bridgetown (Rahway), Brunswick, Princeton and Trenton,—Amboy and Burlington the first to enjoy the benefit being cut off, from their not being then on the main route. The total receipts of these offices from October

[9] One of the Signers of the Declaration of Independence, from Pennsylvania.—*National Intelligencer*, 1855.

5th, 1790, to October 5th, 1791, amounted to $530 !—of which the Postmasters received $108 20, leaving $421 80 as the net revenue.

The Post Office at Amboy was established in 1793 ; John Thompson receiving the appointment of Postmaster. The mail was brought from Woodbridge (that town then and until 1807 or 1808 being on the main route between New York and Philadelphia) three times a week, and continued so to arrive until the year 1812 ; when, for some reason not now known (probably through the influence of the proprietors of Brighton House, for the accommodation of their guests), it was brought in daily. This arrangement, however, did not last long, and for some years it was received as before, three times a week. About 1825, it arrived daily (except Sundays) during the summer, and three times a week in winter, which continued to be the case until the present arrangement was established in 1830, under which it is received and departs daily, Sundays excepted.

The following are the names of the various Postmasters since the establishment of the office under the United States government ; with the dates of their respective appointments :—

July 1, 1793—John Thompson,
Nov. 1, 1794—Edward John Ball,
Sept. 1, 1795—Joseph Golding,
Nov. 1, 1796—George Wright,
June 20, 1798—Robert Rattoone,
April 15, 1801—Simeon Drake,
May 29, 1812—Robert Arnold,
March 10, 1827—Lewis Golding,
October 23, 1830—James Harriott,
Lewis Golding,
Benj, F. Arnold,
W. S. Russ,
John Manning.

The following items will show the gradual progress made in providing for the comfort and convenience of the traveller, and for the accommodation of the mercantile community in the transportation of merchandise.

The first public packet, noticed as "set up" by Lawrie in 1684, carried freight as well as passengers, but how frequently her trips were made is not stated.

The rates to be charged on this route were prescribed in the general Act of 1716, which has been mentioned, and were as follows :—

"Passage-boat Hire from Amboy to New York, *Twelve shillings.*
Passengers in Company, Man and Horse, if above two, *Five shillings.*
Common Passenger, *Fourteen pence.*
Flour, per barrel, *Five pence.*
Beer, Cider, and other Liquors, per barrel, *Ten pence.*
Rum, Molasses, &c., per hogshead, *Four shillinys and six pence.*
Wine, per pipe, *Five shillings and six pence.*
Every thing, per bushel, *Two pence.*
Iron, per hundred weight, *Four pence half penny.*
Beef, per quarter, *Nine pence.*
Dry Goods, per ton, *Eight shillings.*
And so in proportion for greater or smaller quantities." [10]

The first advertisement noticed relating to the transportation by this route is in Bradford's Philadelphia Mercury, of March, 1732–3, as follows :—

"This is to give Notice unto Gentlemen, Merchants, Tradesmen, Travellers, and others, that *Solomon Smith* and *James Moore*, of *Burlington ;* keepeth two *stage waggons* intending to go from *Burlington* to *Amboy* and back from *Amboy* to *Burlington* again, Once every Week or offt'er if that Business presents: They have also a very good store house, very Commodious for the Storing of any sort of Merchants Goods free from any Charges, where good Care will be taken of all sorts of Goods."

In April, 1734, Arthur Brown gives notice that he pliės in a boat between New York and South River in New Jersey, and that he will carry goods to *Allen's Town, Burlington* or *Philadelphia* as cheap as other lines *via* Amboy or New Brunswick ; from which it would seem that boats then ran to both those places. At South River, Samuel Rogers would take charge of the goods and transport them for *one farthing per pound* to "Borden's landing [Bordentown] on Delaware

[10] Nevill's Laws, I., p. 59. In 1704 the value of the Spanish dollar in the Colonies was fixed at six shillings.

River"—where his boat would receive them on board for Philadelphia. Arthur Brown would be at New York "once a week, if wind and weather permit, and come to the Old Slip." This was the first line between New York and Philadelphia by way of Bordentown.

In October, 1742, William Atlee and Joseph Yeats petitioned the General Assembly that their stage wagon, which they had been at the expense of running between Trenton and New Brunswick, might be continued under such Legislative enactments as might be thought advisable, desiring, it is presumed, to have it vested with particular privileges; but the application was laid upon the table and not acted on.

No new arrangements appear on record from this time till June, 1744; when William Wilson of New Brunswick notified the public that he had purchased the stage wagon belonging to Atlee, and would run it twice a week, leaving Trenton on Mondays and Thursdays, and New Brunswick on Tuesdays and Fridays. It is uncertain how long Atlee's wagon had run. In the correspondence of Governor Morris, mention is made by him of the receipt of a box *via* New Brunswick in 1742.[11]

In October, 1750, a new line was established, the owner of which, Daniel O'Brien, resided at Perth Amboy. He informed all gentlemen and ladies "who have occasion to transport either themselves, goods, wares, or merchandise from New York to Philadelphia," that he has a "stage boat" well fitted for the purpose, which, "wind and weather permitting" —that never-forgotten proviso—would leave New York every *Wednesday* ("and at other times if occasion") for the ferry at Amboy on *Thursday*, where on *Friday* a "stage wagon" would be ready to proceed "immediately" to Borden's Town, where another stage boat would receive and carry them to Philadelphia—nothing being said (very wisely) of the time when they might expect to arrive there. He states, however,

[11] He complains that the box (containing bottles of beer) had not been sent by way of Philadelphia, "whereas at New York it was first landed, then carted up the Broad-way, then down again to the water side, then put on board a boat to New Brunswick, and then carted 30 miles to this place (Trenton)."

that the passages are made in *forty-eight hours* less time than by any other line. His rates were the same as charged *via* New Brunswick and Trenton—indicating a continuance of that route—and he adds "as the passages are much shorter and easier performed, and the roads generally drier, it is hoped this way will be found the most deserving of encouragement."

The next year, 1751, the route having been found to answer, O'Brien might be "spoke with at the house of Scotch Johnny" in New York, every Monday, proceeding the next day to Amboy, where "at John Cluck's, John Richards' wagon" would receive the passengers, &c. A notification is given that after March, 1752, they purposed going twice a week, on Thursdays and Sundays, and that arrangement seems to have been carried into effect. The proprietors promised they would "endeavor to use people in the best manner they are capable of"—keeping them, be it observed, *from five to eight days on the way!*

The success of this line seems to have led to an opposition in 1751, originating in Philadelphia. A boat left "Crooked billet wharf" once a week for *Burlington,* whence "a stage wagon with a good awning"—kept by Fretwell Wright, at the "Blue Anchor in Burlington,"—John Predmore at Cranberry, and James Wilson at Amboy Ferry—ran to the latter place, where "good entertainment for man and horse would be found" at the house of Obadiah Ayres. Great dependence seems to have been placed upon the attractions of their passage-boat between Amboy and New York, which was commanded by Matthew Iseltine. She is described as having "a fine commodious cabin, *fitted up with a tea table,* and sundry other conveniences." It was believed that by this route passengers could go through in twenty-four or thirty hours less time than by any other, but nevertheless they seem to have required the same number of days as O'Brien's line.

In June 1753 Abraham Webb makes his appearance with a boat "exceedingly well fitted with a handsome cabin and all necessary accommodations."[12] He probably merely took

[12] As indicative of the speed attained esewhere, it may be noticed that Governor De Lancy of New York in June 1754, attended a conference with the Indians at Albany—His departure is announced in the paper of the 10th as

the place of O'Brien on the line; for the next year (July 1754) the latter had two boats leaving New York for Amboy on Mondays and Thurdays unconnected with the route through, as he offers to forward goods either *via* Burlington or Bordentown, as parties might choose; both lines meeting at Amboy.[13]

The New York stage *via* Perth Amboy and Trenton was instituted in November, 1756, by John Butler, at the sign of the "Death of the Fox" in Strawberry Alley, Philadelphia, to arrive at New York in three days.

In October, 1762, Mary Lott advertises in the Philadelphia papers, that "the magistrates having forbid the Bordentown boats sailing on Sunday as usual," she is obliged to change her stage days, and the boat would thereafter leave on Tuesdays and Fridays.

In May, 1763, a would-be wit, who styles himself "Lord Thomas Story," announces his return from a six months' cruise against his Majesty's enemies, and "desires it may be made known to all, that he attends his old employ of Amboy stage, and that all ladies and gentlemen desirous of freight or passage in his *ship*, lying at Whitehall, will please to inquire for him on board, or at the "Fighting Cocks," at "Whitehall slip."

In 1765 a second line of stages was "set up" at Philadelphia for New York, to start twice a week, and to go through in three days at two pence per mile. The vehicle used was a covered Jersey wagon without springs;—but the lapse of nine years seems not to have worked any increase of speed. The following year a third line of "good stage wagons, and the seats set on springs," was established to go through in two days in summer and three in winter, at three pence per mile, or twenty shillings for the whole route. These lines it is thought

having taken place "*on Friday last.*" On the 17th it is announced that he was spoken on the *Wednesday after his departure* about 104 miles up the river; and the next week his arrival at Albany *on Thursday* is made known. He had thus been six days on the way, but his safe arrival was not announced *through the newspapers* at New York until three weeks after his departure.

[13] Shortly after this, O'Brien makes his last appearance in the public papers as Captain of the Sloop Thomas and Elizabeth. He had made a voyage to Philadelphia, and on his arrival there reported having experienced a most severe gale, in which he had expected to founder—his vessel having been on her beam ends for half an hour—lost his boat, &c. He may not have been out of his reckoning, but this storm is said to have been felt "off the Capes of Virginia"—He subsequently was lost at sea, never having been heard of.

ran to the Blazing Star ferry, on the sound below Elizabethtown. The wagons used were modestly called "Flying Machines"—and the title soon became a favorite.

Mr. Watson in his interesting Annals of Philadelphia, gives to that city the credit of originating the enterprise which prompted the establishment of the several travelling conveyances to New York. So far as the lines of stages are referred to, the praise is certainly due to Philadelphia, but the majority of previous schemes and improvements evidently originated with individuals in New Jersey—not a few of them residents of Amboy or its vicinity.

From 1765 to 1768, attempts were made by the Legislature to raise funds by lottery for shortening and improving the great thoroughfares, but without success.[14] Governor Franklin, alluding to them in a speech to the Assembly in 1768, states that "even those which lie between the two principal trading cities in North America, are seldom passable without danger or difficulty."

Such being the condition of the roads, it was a great improvement to have John Mersereau's "flying machine," in 1772, leave Paulus Hook three times a week, with a reasonable expectation that passengers would arrive in Philadelphia in *one day and a half.* This time, however, was probably found too short, for two days were required by him in 1773–4. From November till May the machine left only twice a week. The advertisement conveying this information to the public is ornamented with a representation of a covered country wagon,

[14] In 1765, Commissioners were appointed to survey the roads (for the purpose of shortening and straightening) from Burlington to Amboy, through Bordentown and Cranberry;—from Bordentown to Kingston, New Brunswick, Elizabethtown and Newark, to Second River (Belleville);—from New Brunswick to Perth Amboy, and from the latter place to Elizabethtown. In 1768, many of the Commissioners being members of the Assembly, they notice the remarks of the Governor, in their answer to his speech. They say they had not been able to draw the lottery granted for the purpose of raising the requisite funds,—that straightening the roads in many places had been found impracticable from the nature of the soil, and from the great detriment that would arise therefrom to many individuals; obstacles that could not conveniently be removed.

The amount to be raised by lottery was only 500 pounds, and it does not tell well for the public spirit then prevailing, that the Commissioners should have been unable to realize that sum for so desirable an object:—"the first attempt of the kind on the continent," as it was then considered. The distance between New York and Philadelphia was expected to be shortened twelve or fifteen miles.

with four horses attached, and it is stated, that "as the proprietor has made such improvements upon the machines, *one of which is in imitation of a coach,* he hopes to merit the favor of the public."

In 1773–4, another step in the scale of improvement was taken—a line of "stage coaches" was established by Mersereau, leaving Paulus Hook every Tuesday and Friday morning at or before sunrise, and proceeding as far as Princeton the same day, where passengers were exchanged with the coaches from Philadelphia. Inside passengers paid thirty shillings: those riding outside twenty shillings *proc,* each passenger being allowed fourteen pounds of baggage, and paying two pence per pound for any extra quantity. "The flying machine" still continued to perform its trips in the same time and manner as the coaches, leaving on different days; thus affording opportunities four times a week. The passage by this conveyance was twenty-one shillings. Passengers were requested to cross over to Paulus Hook the night before leaving.

During the Revolution all regular lines of transportation were, of course, broken up, and when re-established a retrograde movement was made in some instances, both as to speed and comfort.

The establishment of the stages in 1765 and 1766, put an end to the travelling from Philadelphia to New York by way of Amboy; the packets continued however to run for the transportation of merchandise and for the accommodation of way passengers, but became less numerous, until about 1775, when there was but one sailing between Amboy and New York, commanded by Captain John Thompson.

In 1785–6, the "Sloop Eliza" performed the service. The following account of the number of trips and the passengers carried by her for several months, is derived from memorandum books in my possession.

1786.	*To New York.*		*From New York.*	
January,	5 trips,	36 passengers.	6 trips,	57 passengers.
February,	5 "	35 "	6 "	30 "
March,	6 "	29 "	5 "	17 "
April,	7 "	36 "	7 "	27 "
May,	5 "	35 "	6 "	25 "
June,	7 "	34 "	6 "	22 "

In November and December, 1785, there were received from Bordentown by the stages, and forwarded to New York by the boat, 240 packages, weighing 284 cwt. and 60 packages sent on to Bordentown from New York. This line was *via* New Brunswick, Princeton, Maidenhead and Trenton.

In this connection it may not be uninteresting to give some idea of the facilities for intercourse between Newark the chief town of the colony, and New York, prior to the revolution.

It is probable that, for some time subsequent to the settlement of Newark, the principal, if not the only, means of communicating with the city of "Manhadoes" was by water; at least, no account of the road between the two places at an earlier period can be found.

The first ferry established across the North River, as has been stated already, was at "Communipaw," a commission being granted to P. Hetfelsen to be ferryman in June, 1669; but this seems to have been merely for the accommodation of the inhabitants of Bergen. No others appears to have been legally established until 1716, when the one to "Weehawk" was authorized; but that at Communipaw seems to have been the one used so soon as a land communication westward was opened.

Two roads about this time were travelled from Newark towards Bergen; one following the bend of the river, running along the south bank, and the other pursuing a more direct route, to the "transporting place," afterwards known as "the ferry," and as such remembered by our old inhabitants. From this point it is presumed the two united, and ran eastwardly to the Hackensack. In 1718, the Assembly proposed to settle "several controversies and disputes" concerning the two roads from Newark, and decided that the most direct should thenceforth be considered "the public road," and it continued to form part of the main route to New York till the construction of the present causeway. The principal intercourse must still have been by water, from the great difficulty attendant upon crossing the great swamps and low meadows which intervened: but the licenses to Stephanus Van Cortlandt and

Archibald Kennedy, which have been mentioned, indicate a growing want of other and more direct routes.[15]

The first attempt to form a continuous route from Newark to New York was made in 1765. In June of that year, the Assembly passed an Act, directing a road to be laid out, four rods wide, to connect with one already existing between Bergen Point and Paulus Hook, several of the most distinguished men of Newark being among the trustees; they and their successors being erected into a body corporate, with authority to receive donations, construct the necessary causeways, establish the two ferries required over the Passaic and Hackensack, &c. This was what is now recollected as "the old road," leaving Newark from the south end of the town, and following a course corresponding in whole or in part with the road prescribed by the law of 1718. After crossing the Passaic, a straight causeway led to the road from Bergen Point, which it joined about three fourths of a mile south of the town of Bergen,—the Hackensack being crossed some distance below, where the bridge is at present, which is at a point then known as "Dow's ferry." At some subsequent period previous to the Revolution, two other roads left Newark from points opposite "Hedden's dock" (the site of the present bridge), and "Camp's dock" (now the Stone dock); these avoided the ferry over the Passaic, and crossed the Hackensack at Dow's.[16]

In 1772, an Act was passed authorizing the sum of 1050 pounds to be raised by lottery, for covering with gravel the causeways forming part of the main road, but it did not receive the sanction of the King (which was made necessary) until April 1774.[17] Allison, in his edition of the laws, published in 1776, gives Col. John Schuyler, of Belleville, the credit of constructing this causeway.

It was a work of considerable magnitude, and Brissot de

[15] In 1754 a regular packet sailed between the two places commanded by Isaac Ogden.

[16] In May 1769, Ezekiel Ball, of Newark, advertises an "ingenious machine," invented by himself, "for levelling roads; in the form of a triangle drawn by horses, cutting off and filling up the ridges to admiration."

[17] Mr. Sayres Crane, of Newark, drew the highest prize in the lottery ($5000).

Warville, the French traveller, speaks of it as exciting his astonishment: "Built wholly of wood," he says, "with much labor and perseverance, in the midst of water, on a soil that trembles under your feet, it proves to what point may be carried the patience of man, who is determined to conquer nature." Another traveller thus describes the delights of the road: "All the way to Newark (nine miles) is a very flat marshy country, intersected with rivers: many cedar swamps abounding with mosquitoes, which bit our legs, and hands, exceedingly; where they fix they will continue sucking our blood, if not disturbed, till they swell four times their ordinary size, when they absolutely fall off and burst from their fulness." "At two miles we cross a large cedar swamp: at three miles we intersect the road leading to Bergen, a Dutch town, half a mile distant on our right: at five miles we cross Hackensack River: at six we cross the Passaic River (coachee and all), in a *scoul*, by means of pulling a rope fastened on the opposite side."

The traveller now, can form but a slight conception of the inconvenience that then attended a *journey* to New York. In 1791, an act was passed authorizing the construction of a new and more direct route, the Revolution having prevented an earlier attention to the subject. Commissioners were appointed for erecting bridges over the two rivers—selecting the proper route, &c. The different courses covered by the preparatory survey are exhibited in a map appended to the N. Y. Magazine for July, 1791 (from the original in the possession of John Pintard, Esq., who was one of the commissioners), the route selected was that by "Hedden's Dock." The bridges were commenced in 1791, during which year £14,000 were raised by lottery, under the management of John N. Cumming and Jesse Baldwin of Newark, and John Delvey of New Brunswick, for the laying out and improving the road, but two or three years elapsed before the undertaking was sufficiently advanced to admit of travelling on the route. A traveller in June 1794, says, "*I went a mile out of the town* (meaning a mile from the old Gifford House where he stopped) to see the new bridge over the Passaic. It is neatly framed of wood, with a drawbridge, &c." The Duke De Rochefoucault travelled over the road a year or two later, and speaks of it as very disagreable to the traveller and difficult for carriages, being so narrow in some places as not to admit of passing, and exceedingly rough: "it consists," he says, "of trees having their branches cut away, disposed longitudinally, one beside another, and slightly covered with earth." It is this road, however, improved, which has continued to the present time as the great thoroughfare between Newark and New York.

It is not so easy to trace the progress of the public means of transportation of passengers and merchandise. Newark not being on the main route to Philadelphia, until some time after the Revolution, did not profit as much as Elizabethtown and other places, from the improvements made previous to that time in transporting passengers between that place and New York. The first regular conveyance by stage, so far as I have ascertained, were the "flying machines," established in 1772, and the subsequent lines gave of course the means of communication to and from New York. In 1782 a stage ran from Paulus Hook to Elizabethtown via Newark, connecting with the Philadelphia line: and soon after this other facilities existed, and not only the Philadelphia stages, but such as were for the sole accommodation of the inhabitants of Newark, ran to and from New York. Speed, however, was not then so much regarded. In 1794 passengers left New York at 5 o'clock in the morning—were an hour and a half crossing to Paulus Hook—breakfasted at Newark, at the old Gifford House at the corner of Market and Broad streets, which many yet living recollect. Its sign is remembered by the writer as exciting his youthful admiration; the red coats of the hunters, the number of the hounds, the beauty of the horses and the brightness of the landscape, are all vividly impressed upon his memory. Dinner was taken at New Brunswick—they supped and slept at Princeton, after a most fatiguing day's journey, and arrived at Philadelphia about noon of the next day. At that time *one* stage, for the accommodation of those who "lived in Newark and carried on their business at New York," left the former place every morning in summer at 6 o'clock, returning from

New York at three o'clock in the afternoon; putting up in the city on the corner of Cortlandt street and Broadway. "It is very convenient for those who live at Newark, and carry on their business at New York," says the traveller Wansey. The number of individuals *then* travelling daily in that *one* stage between the two places, are now represented by more than thrice as many hundred.

Chapter IX.—Miscellaneous Topics.

EARLY EDUCATION SCHEMES.

PREVIOUS to the war of Independence but little legislative supervision was exercised over the instruction of children in the Province, the different towns being left to form such plans and perfect such measures as might be deemed expedient or best suited to their local circumstances. So far as can be discovered, no law was passed relating to the subject during the entire period of the existence of the royal authority in New Jersey, covering seventy-five years. This may excite less surprise, however, when it is recollected that this period was ushered in by an order that, "Forasmuch as great inconvenience may arise by the liberty of printing in our said Province, you [the Governor] are to provide by all necessary orders that no person keep any press for printing, nor that any book, pamphlet, or other matters whatsoever, be printed without your especial leave and license first obtained." [1]

Schools and schoolmasters were twice made the subjects of legislation under the proprietary governments. In 1693 the inhabitants of any town, by warrant from any Justice of the Peace, might meet and choose three men to make a rate and establish the salary of a schoolmaster for as long a time as they might think proper; a majority of the inhabitants to compel the payments of any rates levied and withheld; the Act setting forth that "the cultivating of learning and good manners tends greatly to the good and benefit of mankind." This act being found inconvenient "by reason of the distance

[1] Lord Cornbury's instructions.

of the neighborhood," in 1695 another one was passed, directing the choice of three men annually in each town, to be authorized to agree with a schoolmaster, and appoint the most convenient place or places where schools should be kept.[2]

There is no information extant concerning the character of the instruction meted out to the young of Amboy and its vicinity, or of the establishment and continuance of schools until, comparatively, a late period; but we are warranted, from the high position in society occupied by many of the inhabitants, and their literary attainments, in believing that they were not unmindful of their responsibilities in that respect.

The first intimation of a school which I have discovered is in the minutes of the Vestry of St. Peter's Church, in July, 1765; when the Rev. Mr. KcKean, the Rector, informed that body that a school-house was immediately necessary, as the Barracks in which the school was then kept could not be longer had without hiring. The Vestry took the subject into consideration, approved of a plan, directed subscriptions to be obtained, and the immediate construction of the building. It was erected somewhere near the intersection of Rector and Gully (now Gordon) streets, but does not appear to have been used long as a school-house; no remains of it are now visible.

From the connection in which the above notice appears, it is probable that Mr. McKean taught this school himself; and this opinion is confirmed by the fact that in 1768 the town was without a teacher, Mr. McKean's death having occurred the October previous.

Most, if not all, of the documents referring to the schools of the place from 1768 to 1775 are in my possession. In April of the former year, a house was hired for the occupancy of a school for seven pounds per annum, by a committee appointed for the purpose, and in August a school was commenced by Mr. McNaughton, and continued until May, 1770. Why discontinued does not appear, but "the master" seems

[2] East Jersey, &c., p. 169.

to have been in the town for some time thereafter and teaching in the school-house in Rector street.[3]

No farther steps appear to have been taken to secure the possession of a good school until August, 1773, when, at a meeting of parents having children, the consideration of the subject was referred to a committee, at the head of which was the Rev. Mr. Preston, who at a subsequent meeting presented a long formal report, in which they express their conviction that a man "proper for a public school in this town should be capable of teaching the Latin, Greek, and English languages grammatically, with the mathematics, ciphering, writing, and other useful branches of literature." A committee was appointed to receive subscriptions at the rate of £4 per annum for every child to be sent, and such additional sums as "the generous might contribute to so laudable a purpose." The sum to be paid the teacher was limited to £100 per annum, and it was deemed advisable to provide a proper house immediately.

It is evident from this report that high anticipations were entertained of the success of the plans proposed. "It is expected," say the Committee, "that upon a proper school being opened many scholars will be sent from other places," and regulations were prescribed by which any excess of income from such pupils should be applied to the reduction of the price of tuition—from which it may be gathered that £4 per annum was an extraordinary price in those days.

At a subsequent meeting, attended by the Chief Justice of the Province, the Rev. Mr. Preston, and the most respectable gentlemen of the place, subscriptions were reported to the amount of £144 10*s.*,[4] and committees appointed to perfect the

[3] This appears from a letter from the late Wm. Dunlap. Mr. D. says, "I was sent to learn my letters while yet in petticoats to Mrs. Randall, who had a swarm of such manikins about her, in a house in the street leading out to the barracks [Smith street]. From this nursery school I was transferred to Master MacNaughton, a black-looking Irishman, who had his school in a wooden building near the gully which divides the church green from the buildings north of it. When the hour for "school going in" arrived, he used to appear at the door and beckon us to leave sport on the church green and come to the dominion of his strap and ferule."

[4] The subscribers were: *James Parker* £12; *Cortlandt Skinner* £12; Stephen Skinner £12 10; Elizabeth Goelet £8; *Elias Bland* £8; Alex.

arrangements and secure the erection of a school-house; but it was never built.[5]

The fiscal arrangements made, the equally important requisite—a teacher—remained to be secured; but nothing appears to have been done towards it until February, 1774. An advertisement of a gentleman who represented himself as particularly qualified, having appeared in Rivington's paper in New York, Dr. Miles Cooper, President of King's College—the personal friend of many of the gentlemen interested—was written to on the subject. This correspondence furnishes additional evidence of the hopes that had been excited in Amboy as to the character and success of the contemplated school.

Dr. Cooper's first letter was not received until March, and its tenor was unsatisfactory, as no proper person could be obtained, for, says the Doctor, "he who advertised himself in Rivington's paper *said* too much, in my opinion, to be worth much. Indeed, according to his own estimation, he was a greater man than either Newton, Boyle or Locke." Puffing, therefore, is not a plant of modern growth. In June, however, the Doctor heard of Mr. Thomas Johnston, an Englishman who had "studied some time at Oxford," and whom he found to be a scholar; he therefore recommended him to the gentlemen of Amboy, for, although nearly a year had elapsed, their school had not yet commenced.

Mr. Johnston entered upon his duties in July, for £60 per annum, New York currency. The school was kept in the court-house, and was open from 6 to 8, from 10 to 12, and from 3 till 6—upon the principle, it is presumed, of getting "a day's work" out of the teacher, and to enable the scholars to

Watson £7; John Johnston £7; Stephen Johnston £7; *John Smyth* £6; *Thomas Skinner* £6; *Samuel Dunlap* £6; *John Preston* £6; Lewis Antill £5; Jonathan Deare £4; Gertrude Barberrie £4; Philip Kearny, jr. £4; Wm. Burnet £4; Thomas Stephens £4; Henry Cuyler £4; *Ravaud Kearny* £4; *Thomas Lyell* £4; Saml. Sargant £4; Michael Kearny £1 10; John Barberrie £1 10; Wm. Terrill £1 10; Frederick Smyth £4. Those in italics, not anticipating the events of coming time, subscribing for five years.

[5] £63 10 were obtained as follows: J. Parker £15; C. Skinner £12; E. Bland £12; S. Skinner £12 10; J. Smyth £6; Thos. Stephens £2; Lewis Antill £2; Wm. Terrill £2.

make up for lost time.[6] The subscription list of the school falling off, Mr. Johnston remained only a few months, and was succeeded by a man with one hand, named Carrick, who had been his assistant. He kept his school on Tower-hill, and it is thought continued to teach until the revolution overturned all customary pursuits and employments.

This narrative of events connected with the schools of Perth Amboy during this period has been given thus particularly, from its exemplifying the imperfections attendant upon the education of those youths whose parents were not in circumstances that would allow of their being sent abroad; and if such was the state of education in the capital of the province, the seat of government and residence of most of the officers, what must it have been in the towns of less note?

The Revolution over, matters remained very much in the same state; several of the missionaries and pastors of St. Peter's Church added to their limited incomes by teaching, but until a few years past every school established existed only for a short time, and the attendants were so constantly subjected to changes in teachers, changes in books, and changes in discipline, that it was almost impossible to acquire any great degree of proficiency.

Under an improved system of State education, and through several private enterprises successfully carried out, a marked change for the better has been wrought in late years.

COMMERCIAL PROJECTS.

The founders of Perth Amboy regarding its situation as highly advantageous for commercial purposes, thought themselves warranted in anticipating a rapid increase in its business and population, from an extension to it of the privileges

[6] The list of the children who attended this school is now before me. Their destinies, how various! the lives of many how checkered! Among them appears the name of Wm. Dunlap, who (the last survivor but one, that one Cortlandt Skinner of Belfast, Ireland) died September, 1839. During his last illness this list was read to him, and as the name of each remembered schoolmate met the old man's ear, his countenance brightened, and the infirmities of age seemed for the time forgotten in the vivid recollections of the scenes and companions of his youth.

and facilities of a Port of Entry. In January, 1683, they reminded the Deputy Governor that "care is to be taken that goods be not exported to New York or other places, but that all goods are to be brought to Perth as the *chief staple* ;" [7] and, notwithstanding the opposition which attended their exertions to make the province independent of New York in this respect,[8] they never remitted them, and, eventually, by order of Council, August 14th, 1687, the Collector of New York was directed to allow vessels bound to New Perth to proceed thither without first entering at his port, which they had previously been obliged to do, provided the Government of East Jersey would allow some persons appointed by the Government or Receiver-General of New York, to receive the customs and imports. [9] This power having been accorded by the government of East Jersey, Miles Forster was appointed by Governor Dongan, "Collector and Receiver at New Perth," on the 26th November, 1687, and was recognized as such by the Council of the Province on the 30th of the same month.

He was directed to levy similar duties upon Imports and Exports to those levied at New York, which were as follows —the table showing what were the principal articles of trade at that time :—

ON IMPORTS.

Rum, Brandy and Distilled Spirits - - - -	4d. per gall.
Madeira, Fayal, St. George, Canary, Malaga, Sherry, and all sweet Wines - - - - - -	£2 per pipe.
Red, White and Rhenish Wines - - - - -	£1 per hhd.
All other goods from Europe - - - -	2 *per cent. ad val.*
All other goods from other ports - - - -	12 *per cent. ad val.*

ON EXPORTS.

Beavers - -	9d.	4 Capps - -	9d.	10 Racoons -	9d.
3 Dullings -	1s. 6d.	4 Fox Skins -	9d.	4 Fishers -	9d.
4 Cats - -	9d.	6 Minks - -	9d.	3 Otters - -	1s. 6d.
2 Bears - -	9d.	4 Wolves -	9d.	24 Muskrats -	9d.
10 Martins -	9d.	24 Moose -	9d.	24 Deers - -	9d.

All other peltry and skins equivalent to Beaver, excepting Ox, Bull and Cow-hides.

On goods sold to the Indians 10 *per cent. ad val.* upon certain valuations. [10]

---

[7] Proprietary Records, A, p. 368.

[8] See East Jersey under the Proprietors, pp. 69, 70, 109–111.

[9] MS. order in my possession.

[10] East Jersey Records, Vol. 4, C. Laws, p. 125.

The intercourse with "New Perth" seems to have been carried on under these regulations for some years, but in 1694 the Assembly of East Jersey, for the better encouragement of its trade, established a custom-house entirely distinct from New York.

The independence thus impliedly asserted, caused the claims of the officers of New York to exercise authority in East Jersey also, to be renewed, and for several years the greatest confusion prevailed from the attempts of the two governments to enforce obedience to their respective mandates. New York, possessing greater means to support its authority, was generally enabled to prevent any benefits accruing to Amboy from the proprietary arrangements, if nothing more. Vessels were seized and other oppressive measures adopted, not even prevented by the appointment, in November, 1696, by the Commissioners of the Revenue in England, of a separate Collector for Amboy, in Thomas Coker, who entered upon his duties in April, 1698.[11]

Coker, however, must have died soon after his arrival, for on the 12th July of the same year, Charles Goodman was appointed Collector, by Edmund Randolph, Surveyor-General of the Customs in America, and he was sworn into office on the 15th. He continued to hold the office until his death in 1701, when (April 21st) John White received the appointment under Queen Anne.

It was not until 1701 that a decision of the Queen's Bench in England, put to rest the dissensions with New York, and fully established the rights of New Jersey. While awaiting this determination, and negotiating for the surrender of the government of the province to the crown, the proprietaries were zealously engaged in upholding their right to have their capital created a Port of Entry.

They stipulated in their first proposition to the Council of Trade in 1699, "That upon the annexation of the government of the province to that of New York, the port of Perth Amboy should be established for entering ships, and importing goods

[11] For the particulars of this controversy the reader is referred to East Jersey under the Proprietors, pp. 141-146, 222.

there and exporting from thence, without being obliged to enter their ships at any other place; paying the same or like customs to his Majesty as are, or shall from time to time, be payable at New York." In answer to this reasonable request the Lords of Trade replied that it would be "very improper for his Majesty to oblige himself to a compliance with it by any clause in the new charter." [12]

In January, 1700, the Proprietaries observe, in reply to this remark of the Lords, that they are "surprised at the dubious answer received," and add among other arguments for the measure, that "the obtaining a port to be continued for ever was their main inducement to consent to a surrender of the government, and therefore they insist that in the new charter to be granted them by his Majesty, there be an express clause inserted, whereby Perth Amboy shall be established a port for ever, * * * * and that such port shall not be forfeited or taken away for any misdemeanor whatsoever, but only the persons guilty of the misdemeanor shall be accountable for it;" [13] and again, in August of the following year, they reiterated their demand, and success attended their efforts, but not to the full extent of their wishes.

Although they thus manifested their conviction of the importance of foreign commerce to the growth and prosperity of their province, and of their principal town in particular, yet they seem to have erred greatly in judgment as to the measures which would most effectually secure it, both before and after the privileges of a Port were obtained.

Smith in his History of the Province [14] speaks of the pleasant situation and commodiousness of the harbor, and attributes the failure to make it a business place to "a fatality" which attended it; but what he thus designates may be regarded more as the result than a cause. Mistaken legislation in all probability was the first obstacle in the way of the

[12] Smith's N. J., pp. 560, 562.

[13] Smith's N. J., p. 564. How similar this reasoning to that used by Josiah Quincy, *seventy-five years later*, in his observations on the Boston Port Bill: "What is it that the *town* of Boston has done?" asked he, "* * * punishments that descend indiscriminately on all ought to have the sanction of unerring wisdom and Almighty Power."

[14] Page 489.

commercial prosperity of the province, and ere it could be overcome the current of business set too strong in the direction of New York to be drawn into new channels. Russell in his History of America says, when treating of New Jersey, "as long as this province stands in need of intermediate agents it must remain in the state of languor into which it is plunged. This it is thoroughly sensible of, and all its efforts have for some time been directed to enable it to act for itself."[15]

The course of trade would naturally cause such markets as the more populous cities of New York and Philadelphia afforded the inhabitants of New Jersey, to be early resorted to in preference to the increased risk and uncertainty which must have attended a traffic with those of foreign lands; but, losing sight of the fact that injurious consequences always result from an interference with the regular course of commercial operations of whatever character, the proprietary Government first, and then the law-makers under that which succeeded, in their attempts to make Amboy "the chief staple" and to dispense with "intermediate agents," so materially interfered with the trade of the province, throwing such obstacles in the way of a free intercourse with such places as the interests of the people prompted them to engage in—that they retarded, instead of advancing its prosperity.

Bounties and other facilities to those who should engage in foreign traffic might have effected what they so anxiously desired, but legislation when brought to bear upon the subject was of a prohibitory character, the produce of the province was made to move in certain directions only, and, as a necessary consequence, production was checked by lessening the number of avenues of demand.

As early as 1678, when the condition of the province was so favorable for grazing that a great number of cattle could have been raised at little or no expense, a law was passed prohibiting the transportation out of the province, or sale to any one not residing within it, of all hides or tanned leather; and the following year the prohibition was extended to Indian

[15] Vol. II., pp. 273, 274.

dressed skins. So in 1694, "for the better encouragement of builders of ships and other vessels, within the province"—as if the whole continent should depend upon the skill of Jerseymen—the exportation of any "timber, planks, boards, oak-bolts, staves, heading, hoops, or hop poles," was expressly forbidden, excepting to some port "over the broad seas (that is to say) into the Kingdom of England, the West Indies, or to any of the Summer or Wine islands directly, and there to unload the same"—and even to these ports the exportation was incumbered by the requisition of bonds and other vexatious restrictions. Inspectors were appointed in all the towns to prevent the infringement of this act, Wm. Frost (November 26th, 1694) being charged with the duty within the bounds of Perth Amboy and Piscataway.[16]

This Act was necessarily hurtful. By confining the consumption of the produce of the forests to the people of the province alone, it took away from the new settlers, one inducement, at least, for clearing their lands, and thus operated to retard their cultivation; and by lessening the demand, the value of timber must have been also affected to the prejudice of the proprietaries' interests; but it was by their approval that it became the law of the land. There is no evidence of its having benefited the class of persons for whom it professed to be framed, for it is doubtful if one vessel was built more than would have been without it. At Amboy,—which, being the chief seat of commerce, should have been benefited by the law if any benefit resulted—we find it probable that no vessel was built until 1702; on the 1st December of that year Miles Forster receiving a town lot "in consideration of his having built the first sloop in Perth Amboy belonging to the province, and to be navigated hence."

The same system was pursued after the surrender of the

[16] E. J. Records, East Jersey, &c., pp. 172, 173. In 1701, East Jersey was thought to have exhausted *Pennsylvania* of coin to pay for cattle imported thence for the supply of Philadelphia; and to prevent its continuance, and to encourage the raising of all kinds of cattle at home, every one having 40 acres of clear land was to keep 10 sheep, no person was to kill more than half their neat cattle, and none at all were to be sold from 10th June to 6th Sept. Penn. Col. Records. I. p. 22.

government to Queen Anne. In 1714 the exportation of pipe and hogshead staves to the neighboring provinces was burdened with a duty of thirty shillings on every thousand; and twenty shillings per thousand were to be paid when shipped to any other part of the continent, the reasons given being the "great discouragement to the trade" of the province such exportation caused, and the destruction of timber which was the result. In 1717, however, this was repealed, being found, as might have been anticipated, "to be prejudicial to the inhabitants," but in 1743, for fear there "might not be enough left for the necessary use of the Eastern Division," these duties together with others upon timber generally were revived, and the law continued in force until the Revolution.

The exportation of grain became also the subject of legislative action. In March, 1714, a duty was laid upon wheat exported from the Eastern Division to any of the British colonies upon the continent of America. This law coming into existence at the same time with the first, imposing a duty on staves, ran its course and was repealed at the same time; showing that they were regarded as of similar character and productive of like results.

Its repeal caused much discussion,—many pamphlets [17] were published pro and con on the subject, and the legislature seems to have been completely at fault as to what measures should be adopted.

Gov. Hunter in 1719 thus plainly addressed the Assembly:

"As for the measures of advancing, or rather for giving a being to trade amongst you, the generality of you have shown such aversion to solid ones, and others such a fondness for imaginary or ruinous ones, that without a virtue and resolution of serving those you represent against their inclination, your endeavors will be to little purpose; but if any thing of that nature fall under deliberation, I cannot think of a better guide, than a just inspection into the trade of other provinces, where it is in a good and flourishing condition. The means by which it became so, can be no mystery; where it is otherwise, or has decayed, you will find the true cause of such decay conspicuous, and it is but a rational conclusion, that what has formed trade, or that on which it depends, credit, in one place, cannot but be the most proper means either to begin it or preserve it in another.[18]

---

[17] Among these see "Proposals for Trade and Commerce in New Jersey, &c," in Philadelphia Library.

[18] Smith's N. J. p. 411 note.

Nothing of any consequence seems to have resulted from this expression of the Governor's views.

The re-establishment of the export duty on wheat was again tried in 1725, for a limited period, and on the expiration of the time no attempt was made to revive it,--and thereafter its transhipment appears to have remained untrammelled with restrictions.

In May, 1740, a Bill was introduced into the Assembly for establishing two Trading Companies or bodies corporate for carrying on a Foreign trade, one of them to be located at Burlington and the other at Amboy. The measure attracted considerable attention, and the Assembly had it printed for the information of their constituents, postponing action upon it until some future period ; but the proper time never arrived. To afford some idea of what the notions of the legislators of those days were in relation to commerce, the following synopsis of the bill is here introduced.

After providing names and location, for the companies, Commissioners from the Counties of Middlesex, Monmouth, Essex, Somerset and Bergen were empowered to record the names of all such persons as were disposed to become associated with the Amboy company : and similar officials from the counties of Hunterdon Burlington, Gloucester, Salem and Cape May, were to perform the same duty for the Burlington Company ;—the persons so subscribing to give security,—if in lands for double, and if in houses for treble the amount of their respective subscriptions.

Such property to be the basis for the issue by the province of £40,000 of paper money—twenty thousand to each company—which was to be the capital upon which they were to trade : and so confident were they of success, that it was provided for in the bill that for twenty days after the books were opened, no person was to be allowed to subscribe for more than one share—and for the second twenty days for not more than two shares—the shares being one hundred pounds each.

It seems to have been expected by the framers of the bill that in ten years the profits of the companies would be sufficient to sink the forty thousand pounds—but should such not prove to be the case, then the property held as security was to become liable for any deficiency. Benjamin Smith of Hunterdon introduced the bill, but with whom it originated is not known.[19]

In March, 1758, Acting Governor Reading brought the languishing state of trade to the notice of the legislature, and recommended an export duty "such as would be felt" upon *all articles* sent to be exported from New York or Pennsylvania, excepting common daily provisions for the markets, and the granting of a bounty upon such as were shipped directly from the province ; but his suggestions were not heeded.

The frequent changes in the laws regulating the disposition of wheat was of course injurious to the planters, and, in all probability, had no restrictions ever been placed upon the intercourse with New York, the ready market there afforded them would have gradually led to a largely increased production. An aged inhabitant of Amboy informed me some years ago that he had heard from the grey beards of his youthful days, of times when forty vessels at once could be seen loading with wheat at that place—at some period probably when the duty upon its exportation was not levied.

The mistaken policy of thus desiring to make the business of Amboy one of a peculiar character must be considered the principal cause of its never arriving at the height of commercial greatness which its founders so confidently expected it to attain. A considerable amount of foreign commerce, nevertheless, continued to be carried on before the War of Independence. The arrival and departure of vessels are found frequently noticed in the New York papers, but the rapid growth of that city had to so great an extent overshadowed and obscured its humble neighbor, that the removal of the officers of the Provincial Government, and its ceasing to be no longer of note in a political point of view, at once destroyed its commercial importance, and it has remained unresuscitated to the present day ; the little intercourse with foreign ports which has existed, being the result almost entirely of enterprises by New York merchants, in the prosecution of which the proximity of the port to their city affords facilities which are occasionally made available.

[19] Votes and State Papers, Vol. I. in State Library.

The materials for estimating the extent of the commerce of Amboy before the Revolution are exceedingly scanty ;—the only particular tabular statement I have seen is the following, relating to the business of the year ending June 24th, 1751.[20]

ARRIVALS.		DEPARTURES.
2 Ships	From and to *Foreign Ports* and *Coastwise ;* not including, however, ordinary coasting vessels not obliged to enter and clear.	2 Ships
2 Snows		3 Snows
7 Brigantines		8 Brigantines
18 Sloops		13 Sloops
10 Schooners		10 Schooners
2 Shallops		2 Shallops
41		38

Imports from Foreign Ports for the same time.
39,670 Galls. Rum.
31,600 " Molasses.
333,968 lbs. Sugar.
437 bbls. Naval Stores.
123 Pipes Wines.
12,759 Bushels Salt.

Exports for Foreign Ports for the same time.
6,424 bbls Flour.
168,500 lbs. Bread.
314 bbls. Beef and Pork.
17,941 Bushels Grain.
14,000 lbs. Hemp.
And small quantities of Butter, Hams, Beer, Flax-seed, Bar-iron and Lumber.

Mr. Russell, in his work on America, printed in 1778, estimated the commerce of the province at the commencement of the Revolution to be twice as great as it was in 1751. The "fee book" of Jonathan Deare, "Naval Officer" at Amboy, is in the possession of the New Jersey Historical Society, showing the number of entrances and clearances from June 8th, 1784, to February 8th, 1788 — three years and eight months—to have been as follows :—

Entrances.		*Clearances.*	
Snows	2	Snows	2
Brigs	6	Brigs	6
Ketch	1	Ketch	1
Schooners	10	Schooners	7
Sloops	33	Sloops	34
	52		50

[20] Douglas Vol. II. p. 294. Correct View of the Colonies, London, 1775, and other works. There are of course full and complete returns in the English Archives. For the sake of comparison it may here be stated that during the year ending September, 1750, the arrivals at *New York* were 232 and departures 286. At Boston in the year ending Christmas, 1748, the arrivals from foreign ports only were 430 and departures 540, and the coasting trade was estimated to employ as many more. From January 1st, 1734, to March, 1736, the entrances at *Philadelphia* were 226, clearances 263. Entrances at *New York* 209, clearances 227. Entrances at *Boston* 892, and clearances 725.

Coastwise Entrances 19.		*Clearances* 21	
From New York	12	For New York	11
" Philadelphia	1	" Nantucket	1
' Boston	1	" Providence	1
" Charleston	3	" Virginia	2
" Savannah	2	" Charleston	3
		" Maryland	1
		" New Haven	1
		" Savannah	1

Entrances from Foreign Ports 34.		*Clearances for Foreign Ports* 29.	
From Nova Scotia	12	For Nova Scotia	8
" St. Eustatia	6	" Antigua	3
" St. Croix	3	" St. Eustatia	3
" Tobago	3	" Tobago	3
" St. Johns, N. B.	2	" St. Johns, N. B.	2
" Barbadoes, Tortola, St. Christopher, St. Martins, St. Domingo, Jamaica, England and Madeira each one.	8	" St. Croix	2
		" Fayal, St. Domingo Gaudaloupe, Bahamas, Trinidad, Madeira, England and Surinam each one.	8

In this statement vessels engaged in the ordinary coasting trade are not included, neither were they in the preceding one, and consequently from a comparison of the two, the difference in the commerce of the place before and after the Revolution is very perceptible.

The following is a list of the Collectors of Perth Amboy since the establishment of the government of the United States to the present time. No complete list of the officers previous to that time can be obtained.[21]

John Halsted—August 2, 1789.
Andrew Bell—March 18, 1800.
Daniel Marsh—June 13, 1801.
John Heard—June 1, 1802.
Phineas Manning—February 25, 1806.
Daniel Perrine—April 15, 1809.
Aaron Hazard—June 12, 1812.
John Brewster—April 1, 1818,
Robert Arnold—January 20, 1821.
James Parker—April 1, 1829.
Joseph W. Reckless—March 11, 1833.
David K. Schenck—June 23, 1838.
Charles McK. Smith—July 10, 1841.
Francis W. Brinley—Aug. 24, 1843.
Solomon Andrews—June 15, 1844.
Jas. A. Nicholls—May 6, 1845.
Charles McK. Smith—July 31, 1849.
Francis W. Brinley—March 26, 1853.

[21] From 1786 to 1789, John Johnston was Collector.

FAIRS AND RACES.

Regular Market days and Fairs being formerly considered essential to the prosperity of all towns and cities, the Proprietors, ever assiduously devising plans for the improvement of their capital, directed, at an early period, their establishment at Amboy. Under date of 2d January, 1683, they say in their instructions to Gawen Lawrie, "It is not to be forgotten that as soon as can be, weekly Markets and Faires at fitt seasons be appointed at Perth Towne." Accordingly, at the first session of the Assembly held at Amboy, April, 1686, Wednesday in every week was made market-day, and semi-annual Fairs authorized to be held on the first Tuesdays in May and October—each continuing three days.

With what spirit this law was carried into effect is not known, but it is presumed from the interest manifested for its passage (as it seems to have been drawn up in accordance with the views of the inhabitants of the province generally), and from the markets and fairs being often adverted to, that its provisions were found to have a beneficial tendency.

Fairs and market-days were stipulated for by the Proprietaries on the surrender of the government to the crown, and authority to establish all that might be necessary was in consequence given to Lord Cornbury in his commission. In the Act of Incorporation granted the city in 1718 was a clause directing *two* market-days weekly throughout the year, on Tuesdays and Saturdays—Christmas day and holydays excepted—in the market place "near the Court-house or City Hall, and nowhere else." Two fairs were also authorized to be held annually on the second Tuesdays in May and November "for all sorts of goods, chattels, wares and merchandises that are usually sold at fairs"—each to continue four days. Subsequently only one fair was held per annum, and that on the first day of May. These continued until the Revolution—William Dunlap remembered one or more in his youth. Circumstances of other places seem not to have warranted the same continuance. Some were abolished by special Acts of the Assembly,[22] others were neglected to be held, and became consequently irregular and unserviceable.

The Fairs at Amboy were held on the hill towards Sandy Point, now the property of Mr. Watson, which, with the surrounding fields, has for many years been distinguished by the title of "the Race Ground." Races took place there at the time Brighton House was open for the reception of the public, but the name was conferred at a much earlier period; those who resorted to the fairs amusing themselves with races, several of which are advertised in the old New York journals.

Gay and animated was the scene then, where now little but the cheerful repose of nature meets the eye; a gayety and an animation that a visitor to the spot may never reasonably expect to witness there again. The booths with their gay streamers—the horses and riders—the gentry and yeomanry—every variety of vehicle, and a heterogeneous collection of articles for sale, will never again cover those pleasant grounds, over which the assembled multitudes, when not engrossed by the spirit-stirring race, or the pursuits of traffic, were wont to scatter in various groups as age or circumstances impelled. A parcel of youngsters in all the light-heartedness of youth performing in one place their gambols on the green sward; in another a knot of greybeards discussing the prospects of the season or the state of crops; while widely wanders many a pair in search of the

> "Hawthorn bush, with seats beneath the shade,
> For whisp'ring lovers made."

To some whose eyes may fall upon these pages how many

> "painful,
> Albeit, most pleasing recollections,"

will the reference to these fields occasion. How many happy

[22] Salem in 1763. Grenwich, Cumberland County, 1765. Burlington, Princeton and Windsor, 1772; and in April, 1750, Governor Belcher issued a proclamation that he had accepted the surrender of the charter of the Borough of Trenton, and gives notice thereof, "to prevent trouble and attendance upon the fairs, which will not be held as usual." In 1797 an Act was passed abolishing all fairs.

moments, dear to memory, have been passed beneath the shades where

> "The velvet grass seems carpet meet
> For the light fairies' lively feet."

But ere the silver cord will be loosed or the golden bowl be broken of many who have of late years wandered in all the gayety of youth about these premises, a change will have come over them. Prosperity or adversity—innovations under the name of improvement, if the first; or impoverishment of soil, through neglected culture, the wash of water, and the fall of trees, if the last—will so work upon

> "These glades so loved in childhood free,"

that one may look in vain for the land-marks of memory.

Already has the hand of Time impaired the beauty of scenes rendered interesting to the writer by associations that can never be forgotten. Trees that chronicled the names of chosen companions in connection with his own no longer exist; vines that furnished him and them their luscious fruit have disappeared, the victims of the axe or of old age; foliage that offered a grateful relief from the noonday sun has vanished, but still, the

> * * * * * * * "Scenes that soothed
> Or charmed him young, no longer young he finds
> Still soothing; and of power to charm him still."

RACES.

Horse-racing seems to have become prevalent in the province at an early period, and to have been followed to such excess as to call for the restraining hand of the legislature in 1748. In that year all horse-racing for "lucre of gain" was declared to be a nuisance, excepting at fairs, and on the first working days after Christmas, Easter and Whitsuntide (making the festivals of the church thus serve as days of preparation), when races were permitted for any sum not exceeding forty shillings, or any article not of greater value; and any one betting more than that sum was liable to a penalty of five pounds. Corporations, however, might raise the stake to twenty-five pounds.

This Act continued in force until 1761, when it was discovered "that many persons of vicious or unguarded conduct, taking advantage of the toleration granted in said law, assemble themselves together, from many parts of the country, at some of the yearly fairs, and game and lay wagers to an immoderate degree, to the great prejudice of some families, and the hinderance of trade and industry, and the corruption of the morals of youth, and against the peace and quiet of many of his Majesty's liege subjects." A law was accordingly passed prohibiting all races both by corporations and individuals, whether for purses or not; but inasmuch as "the improvement of the breed of horses might be a matter of consequence, and by some thought in part to depend on their public exercises," authority was given to any three magistrates to legalize a race at any time by giving written permission, provided they attended in person, to prevent all wagers, drunkenness, and other disorderly conduct; but no race was ever to be allowed within two miles of any place of public worship.

Notwithstanding these restrictions, we find that races were run at Amboy and elsewhere; and continued so to be occasionally at various places in the State until quite recently, under some difficulties, perhaps; but our legislators, now, do not seem to regard the practice as detrimental to society as did their predecessors in the periods referred to.

The following are some of the notices which have been alluded to:—

"April 21st, 1755. Whereas, by the charter of Perth Amboy a fair is to be held yearly in said city, on the 1st day of May; This is to give notice that on the first of next May said fair will be opened, on which day a purse of ten pounds value will be run for by horses in said city."

A similar advertisement appears in 1760—the races to continue two days:—

"The plate or purse to be of twenty pounds value, Jersey money; no horse allowed to enter that has won a purse before; entrance money to be paid to Alexander Watson and William Faudrill—twenty shillings if paid four days before, and thirty-five shillings if paid subsequently. Horses to run three heats of two miles each, and the horse that wins two heats and saves his distance the third, to be entitled to the purse. The entrance money to be run for the second day by any save the winning and distanced horses of the first day—not less than four horses to run."

1763. "The Elizabethtown Free Mason's Plate of twenty pounds value to be run for in the field of John Vanderbilt on the south side of Staten Island on Thursday, 4th day of October next, being the first day of Elizabethtown fair. All disputes to be determined by three master masons to be appointed for that purpose."

May 1st, 1766. "A Purse of twenty pounds is to be run for at Amboy on Thursday, the day appointed for the fair by the charter, open for any horse, mare or gelding not more than half blood, carrying nine stone; the best of three heats two miles each. The horses to be entered with Elijah Dunham or William Wright, on or before 26th April. Entrance $2, or $4 at the post. The entrance money to be run for the next day—not less than four horses to start."

THE PUBLIC BATHING DAY.

In vain has a clue been sought to the certain origin of the custom, so general with the farmers and others of the neighborhood, of visiting Amboy on the first or second Saturday after the full moon in August for the purpose of bathing.

To all inquiries the answer has been returned "it has always been so;" but this long continuance, so that "the memory of man runneth not to the contrary," although it may satisfy a lawyer of the soundness of those legal doctrines that are based on custom, only serves to give a double zest to the researches of an antiquary. But it must be given up—like the object of interest to the renowned Syntax,

"Its history perhaps may be
Far in remote antiquity,
But memory does not now recal
A trace of the original."

It is probably safe to attribute the rise of the custom to the establishment of the fairs before mentioned. They served, doubtless, to make the inhabitants of the surrounding country acquainted with the conveniences for bathing afforded them, and of which they would be led to avail themselves when the labors of harvesting were over and some relaxation and recreation necessary; the custom spreading from one family to another until, as at the present day, hundreds meet without any previous concert.

Of late years the number of visitors generally has not been so great as it was formerly; the author has himself counted more than two thousand persons, of all ages, sexes and colors, returning from the shore in the course of three hours on one of those days, most of whom had probably been in the water at the same time; and he has understood that during some late years the number has been far greater.

FIRES AND ENGINES.

To Amboy the visitations of "the devouring element"—oftentimes so destructive to the labor of years and to the prospects of the most industrious and prosperous—have been comparatively few, when it is considered that the largest proportion of the houses are built of wood, and that the means for the speedy arrest of fires have been wanting during the whole period of the city's existence. Endeavors were made at different times previous to the Revolution to effect the establishment of engines, and on one occasion a machine was actually received from New York.

A letter in my possession from Elias Bland, dated New York, May 15th, 1767, says:—

> "I hope the worthy gentlemen of your Corporation will not suppose I want to impose on them respecting the fire-engine, which comes herewith, with a certificate from the person who has the care of those belonging to this city. I had three; two of 'em wanted something done to 'em, owing to being long out of use. This now sent has wanted nothing done. Stoutenburgh says it is a very good engine, and (unless abused) will last forty years. However, if not approved let it come back per Thompson[23] at my expense." A note at the foot gives as the value of the engine, "20 guineas at Current Exchange, at present 77½ per cent."

This engine must have been returned, or else have been rendered unserviceable soon after its arrival, for in March, 1774, an Act was passed by the General Assembly authorizing the Corporation to raise, by a tax on the inhabitants, a sufficient sum of money "to amend the public roads and streets, to repair the town wharf, *to purchase a fire engine with the*

[23] The only navigator at that time between the two ports.

necessary paraphernalia, and to dig public wells,"[24] but the oldest resident cannot remember that an engine was ever procured at this or at any other time.

The following are the only notices of fires that have been met with or heard of:—

September, 1737. The barn and stacks of corn and hay belonging to Philip Kearny, Esq., were set on fire by a negro boy belonging to him and entirely destroyed.

April 13th, 1768. The houses of Mr. John Skinner and Mr. William Burnet both took fire, but were saved from entire destruction.[25]

December 28th, 1776. The dwelling house of Stephen Skinner, which stood on the bank in the rear of what are now known as the Bruen Stores, was accidentally set on fire and entirely consumed. The New York Mercury says "the warehouse adjacent was filled with military stores which were saved from destruction by the activity of the 32d Regiment quartered there, and the sailors belonging to the ships in the harbor."

Some time after the Revolution the interior of what is now Brighton was destroyed.

In July, 1795, a two story dwelling house and a storehouse belonging to Anthony Butler, Esq., standing "under the hill" was destroyed. Mr. Marsh's old store retained on its roof some marks of the fire up to a very recent period. A ship on the stocks was also destroyed. The loss was supposed to amount to nearly $30,000, the store and cellar of the dwelling house being filled with merchandise. It was presumed

[24] What is now known as the "Town Well" at the junction of Smith and High streets, was probably dug at this time.

[25] A remarkable prevalence of fires on this day is noticed. Besides the two mentioned in the text, there was a large fire at New Brunswick, destroying the dwelling of Widow Deldine, the dwelling and bake-house of John Van Norden, jr., a dwelling, two storehouses, cooper's shop and bolting-house containing a large quantity of produce, belonging to James Nielson, Esq., the dwelling and store of Peter Vredenburg, and the dwelling of Widow Carmers. The fire was not subdued until several buildings were pulled down. Mr. Nielson was out of town about two miles, watching his mills that were in some danger from fire in the woods. Besides these buildings, Mr. Bard's house between Newark and Elizabethtown; Mr. William Nicholl's house and barn in Freehold; Widow Martin's house at Lebanon, and the Durham Iron Works near that place, were also destroyed.

to have been the work of incendiaries, for a day or two afterward several officers arrived from New York in search of a number of men who were suspected of having occasioned a conflagration in Albany a short time before, the description given of them and of their boat corresponding with the appearance of a party seen at Amboy on the night of the fire.

From that time to the present no fire of any consequence has occurred to the knowledge of the writer, with two exceptions. In 1837, two dwelling houses in High street, south of the premises now occupied by Mr. Merritt, were entirely consumed; and in 1850 a house on the north side of "the Cove."

THE PIRATES AND THEIR HIDDEN TREASURES.

"He that had wit, would think that I had none
To bury so much gold * * * *
And never after to inherit it."—*Titus Andronicus.*

"At all hours I have cross'd this place
And ne'er beheld a spirit's face;
Once I remember late at night
I something saw both large and white
Which made me stop and made me stare
But —— 'twas the Parson's grizzle mare."—*Dr. Syntax.*

There is hardly a bay or river in this section of the country that has not been made by tradition the theatre of some exploit of the renowned William Kidd, or his associates. The harbor of Amboy and the Raritan River are included in the number, both of them having been visited, it is said, by Kidd when seeking for proper places for the deposition of his ill-gotten wealth, and it is thought that on one occasion he ascended the river in his vessel as far as was found practicable.

That buccaneers at different periods previous to 1725 infested the shores of New Jersey and the Atlantic provinces generally, there can be no doubt, and that Kidd, after his return in 1699 from his expedition to the East Indies, gave some cause for alarm to the good people of New Jersey is probable. In August, 1699, Governor Basse issued a proclamation authorizing his arrest and the detention of his vessel, "the Adventure Galley."[26]

The pirates along the coast multiplied considerably after Kidd's execution, which occurred in 1701, and in 1717 it was supposed they were "fifteen hundred strong at least," and the shores of New Jersey were much frequented.

On 3d August, 1708, the Council of Pennsylvania was convened with special reference to these privateers and pirates; "the greatest pressure and grievance," the Governor said, this province as yet has felt in having our rivers and capes so beset with the enemy that our navigation has been rendered almost entirely impracticable." On 7th May, 1709, one of these vessels landed about 60 men at Whore-kills, and plundered the inhabitants; and other instances are mentioned in the Colonial Annals of Pennsylvania.

A Captain Harris was captured under the black flag off Sandy Hook, in 1723, by a ship of war, and the crew, consisting of 37 whites and six blacks, were all hung in one day on Long Island. A companion of Harris, one Lowe, in company with him at the time, escaped with his vessel, having, it was thought, £150,000 sterling on board. It is probable they had visited the waters of Amboy previous to this adventure, as it was announced just before that "two piratical vessels had looked in there." After 1725 the buccaneers were not heard of.[27]

There is little doubt that considerable treasure was deposited by Kidd, and perhaps by others, on the shores of Long Island, but that Amboy was ever so favored is scarcely possi-

[26] East Jersey, &c., p. 146.

[27] Watson's Annals of Philadelphia. Mr. Watson gives the "Song of Captain Kidd," current after his execution, which has been frequently printed, commencing:—

"My name was Captain Kidd } Repeat.
When I sailed, when I sailed, }
My name was Captain Kidd,
And so wickedly I did,
God's laws I did forbid, } Repeat.
When I sailed, when I sailed." }

The song is evidently a parody of the "Soul's Knell" by Richard Edwards (1561) the last verse of which is:—

"Toll on the passing bell
Ring out the doleful knell
Let the sound my death tell
For I must die,
There is no remedy
For now I die."

The concluding verse of Kidd's song is:—

"My name, &c.,
Farewell for I must die
Then to eternity
In hideous misery
I must lie, I must lie."

ble. Searches, however, were often made in various places in olden time for the hidden gold, and even as late as fifty or sixty years ago there were credulous persons who believed in the existence of the buried wealth, although no attempt to obtain the least portion of it had ever been successful.

A boulder, lying on the shore in front of the property of late years occupied by Mr. William King, familiarly called "the big rock,"[28] was overturned at one time, with the certain expectation of finding "something" beneath it, and if sand and gravel answered the description, the gold hunters were not disappointed. Numerous pits among "The Cedars" also attested at one period, the industry of these lovers of filthy lucre.

The spot last selected for "a digging" expedition was in the Episcopal church-yard—the undertaking ending rather ludicrously. The circumstances as narrated by a participator in the frolic were as follows :

A female domestic living with Mrs. Oliver, then residing in what in late years has been known as the Raritan House, was selected as the proper recipient of the astounding information, that an immense treasure was buried in the Churchyard, which could be procured only through the intervention of a man named Halsted, possessing enough credulity and none too much intellect, to fit him especially for the enterprise.

This dream effectually turned the girl's head. She immediately communicated it to a male fellow-servant, and to Halsted, and the night was fixed upon for the commencement of their operations. On the afternoon of the day preceding, the fellow-servant of the girl presented himself at the store of Mr. M., the gentleman from whom the story was received, to purchase a spade, a Bible, and some flour ; this last article to be burnt and sprinkled as the digging progressed. The man was indebted to this gentleman a considerable sum already, and he therefore felt no inclination to increase the amount by furnish-

[28] The *progressive improvement of the age*, which too often demolishes what cannot be reconstructed, has recently shattered into fragments this remnant of other days—"the big rock" is no more.

ing the articles desired. Assurances were given that in a very few days the whole amount should be paid—that money would be plenty, and other hints dropped of a nature to lead to the suspicion for what service the articles were required. After some time Mr. M. obtained possession of the secret, and to amuse himself at their expense asked, and, after some consultation, obtained leave to make one of the party.

The hour having been made known to him at which they were to set out upon their undertaking, Mr. M. had sufficient time to inform several young friends of what was going forward, and to give them instructions for the part he intended them to play in this farce of the "Night Walkers." Dressed in white, and furnished with powder and spirits which they were to ignite at the proper time, they preceded the digging party and stationed themselves behind the tomb stones to await their arrival.

Towards midnight the adventurers made their appearance, five in number, another auxiliary having been pressed into the service in addition to Mr. M. The Bible was deposited on the ground, a circle made, and an incantation, in a language incomprehensible and untranslatable, uttered for the benefit of the guardian spirits:

"For mighty words and signs have power
O'er sprites in planetary hour."

Some burnt flour was then sprinkled, and the digging commenced in profound silence.

Already was there a considerable excavation made and the hearts of the miners began to beat with an inexplicable sensation, when suddenly a light was observed, and then a flash, which notwithstanding the darkness of the night, made every object plainly perceptible. Their tools were at once dropped and some symptoms of desertion became apparent. Endeavors were made by Mr. M. to detain them, but in doing so he unfortunately spoke, which was thought to have inevitably destroyed the charm, at least for that night.

As it was evident, however, from the luminous appearance they had witnessed, that the money was there and guarded by unseen spirits, it was concluded to return the ensuing night; but before any thing very definite could be fixed upon, the young men in ambush, no longer able to control themselves, set fire to their liquor, and from the midst of the sulphurous flames with a terrific yell made their appearance on the ground. It is almost needless to say what effect their white drapery had upon the already terrified gold-hunters. They separated, each one taking his own road, and, moving off with incredible velocity, left Mr. M. and his friends in possession of the ground.

The joke was too good a one to be lost. The next day it was known throughout the town, and as a fitting climax to the mortification of those concerned, they had to fill up the cavity they had made.

SLAVERY.

Whether any slaves were brought to New Jersey directly from the old world, under the Concessions of Berkley and Carteret, is uncertain. If there were, the number must have been small, for as late as 1680—fifteen years after the Concessions were issued—the number of negroes at the different settlements appears to have been only about one hundred and twenty, and many of these undoubtedly were brought into the province from other parts of the country.[29] After the provinces passed into the hands of subsequent proprietors none probably were introduced.

The East Jersey records throughout do not designate any of the "servants" brought over as "slaves," and in all documents referring to the distribution of land the word is no longer made use of, which would not have been the case had there been slaves to receive a less quantity per head than other servants. It is evident, therefore, that the proprietors cannot be charged with encouraging, particularly, the importation of slaves at the period of settlement, although the existence of slavery in the province before it was transferred to the royal Governors, is undeniable. As early as 1696 the Quakers of

[29] East Jersey, p. 34, *note* 271, &c.

New Jersey united with those of Pennsylvania to recommend to their own sect the propriety of no longer employing slaves, or at least to cease from further importation of them; but it does not appear that the example was followed by other classes or denominations of Christians.

The instructions to Lord Cornbury from her Majesty Queen Anne were of such a character that any disposition felt to put a stop to the traffic in slaves must have been effectually checked. The Royal African Company was particularly brought to the notice of the Governor as deserving his encouragement, and the instructions then proceed: "And whereas we are willing to recommend unto the said company that the said province may have a constant and sufficient supply of merchantable negroes, at moderate rates, in money or commodities; so you are to take especial care that payment be duly made, and within a competent time, according to agreement." "And you are to take care that there be no trading from our said province to any place in Africa within the charter of the Royal African Company, otherwise than prescribed by an act of Parliament, entitled an act to settle the trade of Africa. And you are yearly to give unto us an account of what number of negroes our said province is yearly supplied with, and at what rates."[30] The returns, here directed to be made, if they are yet preserved in the archives of England, can alone determine to what extent the traffic was engaged in by the people of New Jersey.

Barracks of considerable size once stood in Perth Amboy, near the junction of Smith and Water streets, in which the slaves were immured as imported; and there, as in almost every place, the labor of families, with very few exceptions, was exclusively performed by blacks for many years previous to the Revolution. In 1776, Thomas Bartow's house is said to have been the only one in the place the inmates of which were served by hired free white domestics.[31]

In 1757, a young gentleman in England, writing to his father in Amboy, begs that he may be favored with a young negro boy to present to a brother of the then Duke of Grafton, to whom he

[30] Smith's New Jersey, p. 254.

[31] MS. Letter of Wm. Dunlap.

was under obligations, as "a present of that kind" would be very acceptable.[32]

There are notices to be found of two or three "risings" that disturbed the peace of the Province. One occurred in the eastern division in the vicinity of the Raritan early in the year 1734,[33] in consequence of which one negro (if not more) was hung. The design of the insurrection was to obtain their freedom (kept from them, they believed, contrary to the express directions of the King) by a general massacre, and then join the Indians in the interests of the French. That they were at that time numerous in the province is pretty evident, as is also the fact that, although generally treated with kindness and humanity, there was a severity of discipline and rigor of law exercised towards them which must ever exist to a greater or less degree wherever slavery is found. The newspapers contain frequent allusions to crimes and punishments in which the offence and its consequence are brought into astonishing proximity, *burning alive* being a punishment frequently resorted to.[34] Perth Amboy was the scene of one of those judicial murders on the 5th July, 1750, the victims, two in number, suffering in two weeks after the commission of their offence. The circumstances were these:—The wife of Mr. Obadiah Ayres was shot through the window while seated in her own house, and her murderer was soon discovered to be one of her own negroes, actuated by revenge for some trifling censure of his mistress. He prevailed upon "a new negro"—as those recently imported were called—who also belonged to Mr. Ayres, to procure for him his master's gun, and with it committed the fatal deed. He then induced the new negro, who was a mere boy, pining for his home and willing to do any thing that would be likely to bring about his return to it, to run into the woods and shoot the first man he encountered, assuring him that the shedding of blood in that way would certainly bring

[32] MS. Letter of Capt. Wm. Skinner.

[33] N. Y. Gazette, March 25, 1733-4.

[34] An instance of this is recorded in the New York Gazette of 28th January 1733. A negro *attempted* an assault upon a white woman on Friday, 20th; he was tried, convicted by summary process, and was burnt alive on Thursday, 26th. In 1741 the "negro plot," *which had its existence only in the panic-stricken minds of the people* of New York, caused many executions both by hanging and burning.

about the result he so ardently wished. The boy followed his directions, but, from his unskilfulness or through a providential interference, his gun missed fire, and he was safely secured before a second attempt could be made.

The object of the wily negro, it was presumed, was to ensure the execution of the boy for the crime urged upon him, or as the suspected murderer of his mistress, before an explanation could be obtained that would designate him as the criminal. Nothwithstanding the boy's imperfect acquaintance with the language, means were found to make his confession available, and in connection with other facts elicited at the trial, sufficient proof was obtained fully to convict the elder negro of the murder; and, notwithstanding his evident ignorance of consequences, or indeed of the nature of the offence in which he had acted the part of an accessory, it was deemed proper that the boy also should suffer. They were both condemned to be burnt alive.

The site of this barbarous execution was the ravine on the north side of the town, which, from that circumstance, has been known as "Negro Gully." The negroes were all summoned from their homes, and obliged to be present, in order that they might be deterred from the commission of like offences, and the day was long remembered with awe.

At a later period a negro was hung at the junction of the New Brunswick and Woodbridge roads—a short distance out of town—for theft.[35]

The act under which these and other negroes were tried and condemned was passed in March, 1714, which provided for trials for murder and other capital offences before three or more justices and five principal freeholders of the county, the

[35] A negro was hung for murder on the 6th May, 1791, in front of the old Court House and Jail in Newark. According to custom, he was taken to the first Presbyterian Church, to hear his funeral sermon, and, much to the discomfiture of the younger members of the family, was seated in the pew of one of the author's ancestors. The preacher was Dr. Uzal Ogden; the church was crowded, and in allusion to the fact of the criminal's sincere repentance, the Doctor thoughtlessly ended his sermon by hoping the 'latter end of his numerous hearers might be like his,' which naturally enough excited much comment at the time.

Subsequently, early in the present century, another negro was hung in Newark, on the Common, for poisoning his wife, who lived with the family of Caleb Sayrs.

pains of death to be suffered "in such manner as the aggravation or enormity of their crimes (in the judgment of the said justices and freeholders) shall merit and require;" [36] and although the mode of trial was changed in 1768, even then the manner in which death should be inflicted was not specified.

In 1772 an insurrection was anticipated, but was prevented by due precautionary measures. In connection with this "rising," a sort of *colonizationist* made his appearance in the public prints, urging the passage of a law by parliament, obliging the owners of slaves to send them all back to Africa at their own expense.

In 1713 an act was passed, for a limited period, levying a duty upon every negro imported, which was permitted to expire, and no attempt was made to renew the duty until September, 1762. An act was then passed, but, having a suspending clause, was for certain reasons never laid before the King by the Lords of Trade. The duty it imposed was forty shillings in the eastern, and six pounds in the western division —an inequality obviated in subsequent laws passed in June, 1767, and November, 1769:—the former was limited to two years, the latter to ten, and it consequently remained in force until the Revolution severed the connection with Great Britain. The amount of duty laid by these acts was *fifteen pounds* proclamation money to be paid by the purchaser of every slave.

On the 24th February, 1820, the act was passed which gave freedom to every child born of slave parents subsequent to 4th July, 1804, the males on arriving at twenty-five years, and the females at twenty-one years of age; and under the operation of this act slavery has almost disappeared from the State of New Jersey. Previous to its passage the number of slaves had materially diminished. There were in the State in

1790	11,423	1830	2,254
1800	12,422	1840	674
1810	10,851	1850	236
1820	7,557		

[36] Nevill's Laws, I., p. 19.

LOTTERIES.

"No debts, no cares, no party ties,
An honest heart, a head that's wise,
A good estate, a prudent wife;
All these are prizes in this life.
If blessed with these, give Fortune thanks,
Tho' all your tickets come up blanks."

Lines "On the many Lotteries now on foot;" in Nevill's "New American Magazine." 1759.

Lotteries, though for several years comparatively few, have become subject to notice by grand juries, and public opinion is every where arrayed against them. Their day is over, and much of the revolution which has worked their destruction has taken place in late years; yet, without recurring to a period, 90 or 100 years ago, the full magnitude of the change can hardly be realized. They were early resorted to in most of the colonies to raise funds for particular objects, which were frequently of great public utility. Such, in the infancy of enterprise and wealth, were calculated to receive the favor of the several governments, and the practice, fostering as it did the love of gain, and furnishing excitement to the multitude, became soon the most popular system for "raising the wind," as well for individual benefit as for public enterprises.

Watson, in his Annals of Philadelphia, states that the earliest mention of a lottery there occurs in 1720, and soon afterwards schemes appear to have been introduced into New Jersey; for in the year 1730, an act was passed prohibiting both lotteries and raffling, their frequency having "given opportunity to ill-minded persons to cheat and defraud divers of the honest inhabitants" of the province. As this act referred more particularly to lotteries for the disposal of "goods, wares and merchandise," those who were inimical to its provisions, or who were blind to their deleterious influences, appear to have thought lotteries for money not affected by it, so that by 1748 there was hardly a town that had not some scheme on foot. The following are some of them, noticed in the New York papers of the time, having in most instances the names of the most respectable citizens annexed as managers:

Elizabethtown Lottery, for building a parsonage—£1,050 to be raised, 1500 tickets at 14 shillings; 304 prizes only, the highest being £60.

One in New Brunswick to relieve Peter Cochran from imprisonment for debt; and another at the same place for completing the church and building a parsonage—£337 10s. to be raised, the highest prize being £100. The managers of this were Peter Kemble, James Lyne, John Beman and John Broughton.

One at Raritan Landing in Piscataway township, advertised by Johannes Ten Brook, the prizes being real estate; and another of the same kind advertised by Peter Bodine, the prizes being 195 lots, "some of them in the heart of that growing place known by the name of Raritan Landing, which is a market for the most plentiful wheat country of its bigness in America." This is something like a real-estate scheme of 1836 or '37, Raritan Landing being now about as much improved as some of the embryo cities of those years will be one hundred years hence!

One at Turkey (now New Providence), for a parsonage, the sum to be raised £152 5s.

One at Hanover to buy a parsonage house and land, the sum to be raised £200.

One at Amwell for finishing the Presbyterian meeting house—the sum required £630.

One at Newark for completing the church—the sum to be raised £337 10s. The managers of this were Col. Peter Schuyler, Col. Wiliam Ricketts, Col. Jacob Ford, Messrs. Frind, Lucas, and Uzal Ogden.

The foregoing are all found advertised the same year; but, in the estimation of the Legislature, "the ends did not sanctify the means," and towards the close of 1748, and act was passed deprecating the increase of lotteries and their attendant vices "playing of cards and dice, and other gaming for lucre of gain," and prohibiting the erection of any lottery within the province under heavy penalties. As this, however, did not affect those already advertised, James Parker, the printer, advised the proprietors to take up their schemes in rotation, for while the public attention was drawn to "so many at once they were like cabbages too thickly planted, which never suffer one another to come to a head!" This act was evaded by having the lotteries drawn out of the province, and the first infringement noticed appears to have been in the very next year in a lottery for the benefit of the "New Jersey College" (now Nassau Hall, Princeton), one for £1,500 being "set up" at Philadelphia. Another for finishing the church at Trenton was drawn the same year on the other side of the Delaware River, and in 1753, another for the benefit of the college was drawn in Connecticut.

In 1758, the provincial government authorized a public lottery to raise money to purchase certain lands from the Indians, and this bad example was immediately seized upon as giving a license to the practice again to an unlimited extent. The year 1759 gave birth to the following schemes:—

One for making an addition to, and repairing St. John's Church, Elizabethtown. "Tickets to be had of Rev. Mr. Chandler."

One for building Trinity Church, Newark, the highest prize $1,000: the managers of which were John Schuyler, Josiah Hornblower, Josiah Ogden, Daniel Pierson and Gabriel Ogden.

One to raise £1,500 for the benefit of the Church in New Brunswick. The managers made the following appeal to the *benevolent*—"The people of the Church of England in and near the city of New Brunswick, having long uneffectually endeavored to finish and complete their church, find themselves reduced to the necessity of thus soliciting the charitable assistance of well-disposed persons, in emulation of many of their pious neighbors in this and the adjacent provinces. They hope, therefore, their attempt will not be thought singular, but as it is wholly for the promotion and honor of religion that it will meet with such encouragement as will enable them to effect their purpose." This lottery was to be drawn on "Biles' Island," and the highest prize was £1,000. It was under the superintendence of Edward Antill, Peter Kemble, Bernardus Legrange, Wm. Mercer, Francis Brazier, John Berrien, Sam'l Kemble and Wm. Harrison.

In 1760, there was a Parsippany lottery for purchasing ground and building a parsonage, and another at Bound Brook for finishing the Presbyterian church :—the sum to be raised, $750. The legislature again interposed this year by an "Act to prevent the sale of tickets in lotteries erected out of this province and more effectully to prevent gaming ;" but with great inconsistency by the same act revived three public lotteries for the same object as that of 1758. Schemes appear to have decreased in some measure for a few years, but notwithstanding legislative enactments means were found to evade the designs of the law-makers, and lotteries continued to exist more or less numerous until the Revolution.

In 1773, the College of Princeton again adopted this mode to raise 5,626 pounds, in connection with the Presbyterian congregation of Princeton and the united Presbyterian congregations at New Castle and Christiana Bridge.

Among others immediately after the Revolution are noticed one granted by the Legislature to the Borough of Elizabeth "to raise a sum of money for building the Court House and Jail, and finishing the Academy in Elizabethtown, which during the late war were occupied by the United States, and burnt by the enemy." "Tickets sold at the Printing Office, and by the Post Rider." Managers Jona. H. Lawrence, and Elias B. Dayton. Highest prize $500. Tickets $1 ;—and another "to raise £750 for repairing the Episcopal Church in New Brunswick :" the drawing to take place "under the inspection of James Parker, Esq., Mayor of the city of Amboy, and Archibald Mercer, Esq., Deputy Governor of the Manufacturing Society of N. Jersey." Tickets $3. Highest prize $2,000.

Amboy did not escape the contagion, as has already been noticed in the account given in a previous chapter of the Episcopal and Presbyterian churches, and doubtless in many places the system was productive of most beneficial results, however much we may deprecate it now, means being realized through the agency of lotteries which in no other way could have been obtained.

Chapter X.—Events during the Revolution.

"* * * * * Importing change of times and states."

As the seat of government of the Province, and the residence of the principal royal officers, Perth Amboy at the commencement of the War of Independence became a place of some interest to both of the conflicting parties. Its commanding position also gave to it in a military point of view an importance which neither were disposed to overlook.

Previous to November, 1771, the 29th Regiment of Foot had been garrisoned at Amboy, New Brunswick and other towns, for a considerable period.[1] In that month, however, it was withdrawn, and the next regular garrison was composed of a part of the 60th Regiment, under Colonel Prevost, which sailed in November, 1772, for Jamaica, and was succeeded in a few months by the 47th Regiment. These troops were called to New York in July, 1774, and remained there until the May following, when they proceeded to the eastward and partook of the dangers of Bunker Hill and Saratoga.[2] As

[1] There were some troops came into the province from Albany, in October, 1758, and in December, 1759, the Battalion of Royal Scotch took up their quarters at New Brunswick for the winter, whence 400 of them left, the May following, for Quebec. But the first regular garrison, as noticed on a preceding page, was probably composed of the troops returning from Havana in 1762. The 29th Regiment appears to have made itself very popular in the Province. On its withdrawal, James Parker, the Mayor of Amboy, returned the thanks of the Corporation, to Lieutenant Maurice Carr for the peace, good order and harmony which had characterized the intercourse of the regiment with the inhabitants, and tells him it was the first time the compliment had ever been paid. Capt. French, who commanded the three companies stationed at New Brunswick, received the thanks of that Corporation, and, subsequently, with the other officers, was invited by the gentlemen of the place to a public dinner at the Whitehall tavern.

[2] On the 25th July the Corporation of Elizabethtown published a card of thanks to Capt. Richard England for the good behavior of his command

after this no garrison was established at Amboy, on the organization of the two Jersey Provincial Regiments in 1775 Captain Conway's Company marched down from New Brunswick, and took possession of the Barracks.[3] This was about the 12th of December. Captain Longstreet's regiment soon followed, and on the 19th, Colonel Lord Stirling ordered Capt. Howell, at Elizabethtown, to march his company the next morning also to Amboy, there to quarter them with such other troops as he might find there, or that might be sent ; and being the senior officer he was to assume the chief command. The troops were to be kept at the Barracks, to be exercised frequently, and kept ready for duty.[4]

The Governor and other Colonial officers still continued nominally in the possession of their respective posts, and for some months no act of open hostility occurred to mar the general harmony which outwardly prevailed.

As was the case in almost all the towns of note in the province, the inhabitants held a meeting to discuss the measures in contemplation for the relief of the country. It was held on Friday, April 28th, and it was then

"Resolved, unanimously, that James Parker, Stephen Skinner and Jonathan Deare, Esqrs., or any two of them be a standing Committee of Correspondence for the north ward[5] of this city."

"A copy of a letter from the Committee of Correspondence of Princeton, signed by Jonathan Sergeant, Esqr., Clerk to said Committee of Cor-

---

stationed there. On the 19th May preceding, the whole regiment was reviewed at Amboy.

Among the officers of this regiment were Colonel Nesbit—afterwards notorious at Boston for tarring and feathering a country lad who had asked a soldier the price of his musket—Major *Smelt*, Captains Mar—afterwards knighted—*Craig*, of Light Infantry—afterward Sir James Craig and Governor of Canada—*Alcock*, Irving and *Richard England*—afterwards General; Lieutenants *Hilliard*, *Gould*, Story, and Poole England, who married subsequently and lived in Amboy : those in italics were wounded at Bunker Hill, and Hilliard and Gould died in consequence.

[3] Lord Stirling ordered Capt. Conway to retain a picket-guard at Amboy, and send the remainder of his company back to New Brunswick ; but before these orders were received, on the 17th, Capt. C.'s men had applied for leave to return thither, until their services were more imperatively required ; expressing their opinion that the Barracks were unsafe without arms and ammunition, the market for provisions high, and as many of their homes were in New Brunswick they could be better accommodated there.

[4] Stirling papers in the N. Y. Hist. Soc. Library.

[5] South Amboy was the *South* ward.

respondence, transmitted to the Committee of Woodbridge, and by them directed to the inhabitants of this city, was read; wherein, after mentioning the very alarming intelligence lately received, a Provincial Congress for this Province is proposed to be held on the 5th day of May next; and a meeting of the inhabitants being now called, that their sense might be taken in the necessity and propriety of choosing deputies to attend the said Congress. The question was therefore put whether deputies shall be sent or not, and carried in the affirmative unanimously."

"James Parker, Stephen Skinner and Jonathan Deare, Esqrs., were then nominated as deputies to attend the said Congress to represent this city, and were unanimously chosen; and it is requested that they or any one or more of them do attend the said Congress accordingly."

"It is also agreed by the inhabitants now assembled, that the expenses of the deputies who shall attend the said Congress be defrayed by this city."

"It is also requested that Mr. Deare acquaint the committee of Princeton and Woodbridge of the proceedings of this meeting."

"By order of the Committee,

JOHN THOMPSON, Clerk."

Mr. Deare attended the Congress accordingly, but took his seat as a member from Middlesex County, and not especially from Amboy.

From a paper in my possession it appears that some idea was entertained of obtaining a pledge from those liable to militia duty, to arm and equip themselves for service under the royal banner "to maintain and support their just rights, and the constitution of the Province against any power and all persons who shall attempt to alter or infringe the same, * * * and use their best endeavors to restore peace and harmony between the colonies and the parent state upon principles of equity and justice." No signatures are appended, and it is doubted if the plan succeeded.

As a set-off, probably, to this scheme, the officers of a militia company, attached to the first Regiment of the County, which had been formed some years, signed the following pledge in February, 1776.

"We the subscribers, officers in the 1st Regiment of Militia in the County of Middlesex, and colony of New Jersey, do hereby promise and engage, under all the ties of religion, honor and regard to our country, that we respectively will duly observe and carry into execution to the utmost of our power all and every the orders, resolves and recommendations made, or to be made, by the Provincial Congress of this Colony for defending our constitution, and preserving the same inviolate; and that we will

* N. J. Journal, May 8th, 1775.

also render due obedience to such officers, who either by rank or superiority are regularly placed above us.

JONA. DEARE, 1st Major,
HEATHCOTE JOHNSTON, Capt.[7]
THOS. BRUEN, 1st Lieut.
JOHN THOMSON, 2d. Lieut.

Perth Amboy, Feb'y 24th, 1776.

During the early part of 1776 the boys of the ancient city seem to have imbibed—but certainly not generally from their parents—many of the liberal sentiments becoming prevalent in the Province, and from hearing of, and seeing, the warlike demonstrations which the spirit of resistance had produced, they endeavored to copy the example set them by their elders, formed themselves into a company for military parades, and with their wooden guns and other similar paraphernalia, they became of prominent interest to the citizens generally.

It is rather singular that although most of the youngsters were the sons of those directly or indirectly connected in sustaining the royal domination, they were permitted to assume the character of young rebels by placing on their caps the motto: "Liberty or death." They called their corps, however, "the Governor's Guards," and not long before Governor Franklin was taken prisoner they went through their evolutions before him, and were entertained in the government house with a collation specially prepared for them. The Captain of this redoubtable company was Lambert Barberrie, the Lieutenant, John Skinner, and the Ensign, Andrew Smyth, who are elsewhere mentioned in these pages.[8]

At a later period many of these boys proved serviceable auxiliaries to the American officers, by watching the sentinels and guards, and reporting any observed failure in duty or discipline.

On the 2d April, Capt. Bloomfield's company of the 3d Regiment of Jersey troops arrived, crossing the Raritan from

[7] This document is from the original in my possession. Captain Johnston (as mentioned on a preceding page) soon after left the "rebellious" company with which he was here associated.

[8] Messrs. Joseph Marsh and William Dunlap were members of this corps, and retained many vivid recollections of their performances. From both of these gentlemen I received much interesting information relating to this period.

South Amboy in the afternoon, but the barracks being already occupied by Colonel Heard's Militia, they were obliged to proceed to Woodbridge and thence the next day to Elizabethtown. On the 10th the company returned, and from that time to the 28th—when they again marched to Elizabethtown—they were engaged in throwing up intrenchments under the direction of Major F. Barber of the First Battalion.[9]

The circumstances connected with the arrest of Governor Franklin and his removal from the place, have been already narrated.[10] Abut the time of his departure several others of the adherents to the royal cause sought refuge in New York, and thereafter so long as Amboy was in the possession of the Colonial forces there was a more active display of organized resistance to British rule and influences.

Towards the close of June, soon after the departure of the Governor, Sir William Howe arrived at Staten Island, with a large body of troops from Massachusetts,[11] for the purpose of preventing the intercourse between the Eastern and Middle States, thinking thereby to frustrate any common plan of operations. The Island was taken possession of between the 2d and 4th of July, and it became expedient, therefore, to form a camp immediately in this region, and from the peculiar feelings of the people, Amboy was selected for its location and General Hugh Mercer placed in command.

General Washington thus communicated the fact to Congress under date of July 4th, 1776, from New York :

> "The camp will be in the neighborhood of Amboy. * * * * The disaffection of the people of that place and others not far distant, is exceedingly great, and unless it be checked and overawed it may become more general and very alarming. The arrival of the enemy will encourage it. They, or at least a part of them, are already landed on Staten Island, which is quite contiguous; and about 4,000 were marching about it yesterday, as I have been advised, and are leaving no arts unassayed to gain the inhabitants to their side, who seem but too favorably disposed. It is not unlikely that in a little time they may attempt to cross to the Jersey side, and induce many to join them, either from motives of interest or fear, unless there is a force to oppose them.

---

[9] Elwers' Journal N. J. Hist. Soc. Proceedings, Vol. II. pp. 100–101.

[10] See page 193, &c.

[11] Colonel Taylor informed the Provincial Congress on 29th June that 19 sail of the Enemy's fleet were at the Hook and 45 in sight.—*Original Mi'utes of Congress.*

Troops were in consequence immediately marched towards Amboy, about a thousand men being brought together there and at Blazing Star, in a few days, to aid in these preventive measures. Among the first were 450 of the Middlesex Militia, under command of Major Duyckink, who arrived on the 5th July, [12] and two armed vessels and several armed whale-boats were stationed there during the month.[13] One of these lay at anchor for some time immediately in front of the town.

It was about this period that a British brig of war, mounting 12 guns, entered the harbor and anchored off St. Peter's Church, about midway between the two shores. The Americans at night procured from Woodbridge an eighteen-pound gun, placed it behind the breastwork by the church, and, when morning dawned, opened a fire upon the

[12] Major Duyckink and his troops were somewhat alarmed by rumors the same day, that they were to be attacked by an overwhelming force from Staten Island, that night, and in pursuance of orders from General Heard, sought a safe retreat outside of the town; but their fears were groundless. They returned to their quarters the next day, and the Major reports to Gen. Livingston the arrest of John Smyth, Philip Kearny, Michael Kearny, William Hicks, Thomas Skinner, Dr. John Lawrence, Captain Turnbull, Johnston Fairholme and Isaac Bunnell, whom he sent to Elizabethtown. The General did not know exactly what to do with the prisoners, and applied to Gen. Washington for directions, vouching for the great integrity of Mr. Smyth. They were subsequently sent to the Convention with the exception of Mr. S. who was released on his parole. The persons named were on the 13th July allowed by a vote of the Convention to return home for a limited time upon their parole, and were then assigned various places of residence and certain limits beyond which they were not to go. On the question of their being allowed the privilege of returning home for a limited period, the Convention stood Ayes 12, Noes 10. The ladies of Amboy petitioned that Dr. Lawrence might be permitted to remain there, "apprehending fatal and melancholy consequences to themselves, their families and the inhabitants in general if they should be deprived of the assistance of Dr. L."—and the following courteous reply was ordered to be sent to Mrs. Franklin, one of the petitioners, signed by the President.

"Madam,—I am ordered by Congress to acquaint you, and through you the other ladies of Amboy, that their petition in favor of Dr. John Lawrence has been received and considered.

"Could any application have procured a greater indulgence to Dr. Lawrence, you may be assured yours could not have failed of success. But unhappily, Madam, we are placed in such a situation that motives of commiseration to individuals must give place to the safety of the public.

"As Dr. Lawrence has fallen under the suspicion of our generals we are under the necessity of abiding by the steps which are taken,—and are

"Madam, yours, &c."

Original Minutes.

[13] The Committee of Newark on 17th July requested Congress to order four gondolas or row galleys to be built and mounted with cannon to ply between the mouth of the Passaic and Perth Amboy.—*Original Minutes.*

vessel. It was returned, but being so near the shore she was obliged to consult her safety by retiring; she would otherwise have been sunk. Probably it was at this time that the tombstone of Captain William Bryant, in the rear of the church, was broken off by a ball; which was the case, so says tradition, some time during the Revolution.

The ball, which left its mark in the east end of the old church, was fired from a vessel lying the other side of Billop's Point. The English kept a vessel almost constantly there for the convenience of traders; and it is said some of the ancestors of the present population derived considerable profit by trafficking with this vessel in a neutral character.

The resolutions of Independence by the Continental Congress were received by the New Jersey Convention on 17th July. The letter containing them was referred to Messrs. Mehelm, Ellis and Paterson, who subsequently brought in the following preamble and resolution, which were adopted :—

"Whereas, the Honorable Continental Congress have declared the United Colonies free and independent States, we, deputies of New Jersey in Provincial Congress assembled, reresolve and declare, that we will support the freedom and independence of said States, with our lives and fortunes, and with the whole force of New Jersey." Nobly did they and their successors redeem the pledge thus given.

The Virginia Gazette of August 10th, 1776, contains the following extract from a letter wrtiten by an officer in the 2d Battalion of Philadelphia, dated Amboy, July 22d.

"We arrived here on Saturday morning from Woodbridge with our Battalion, except Captain Wilcox's company, who are stationed at Smith's farm on Woodbridge neck. We are now in full view of the enemy only separated by the sound; our men are in high spirits and longing for an opportunity to have a skirmish."

"Yesterday Col. Atlee's battalion came in and marched along the beach, they made a good appearance, and I think alarmed the enemy not a little. We could distinctly see a number of officers observing with spy-glasses, and their men drawn up in line, appeared greatly surprised.[14] We have

---

[14] Our officer must have been possessed of peculiar vision, unless their "surprise" showed itself in an extraordinary manner, to have observed this with an intervening space of a quarter of a mile.

in all about 1,500 men. It is supposed the enemy have about 1,000 men opposite us.

"When our numbers are a little more augmented it is expected we shall do something.

"To-day our encampment will be marked out and to-morrow the battalion will pitch their tents." [15]

It was the intention of General Washington to have done "something" as the officer expected. In a letter to Congress of August, '76, he says :—

"In my letter of the 27th July, I informed Congress of my views and wishes to attempt something against Staten Island. I am now to acquaint them that by the advice of General Mercer and other officers at Amboy, it will be impracticable to do any thing upon a large scale for want of craft, and the enemy have the entire command of the army all round the island."

"The Pennsylvania Gazette of July 29 contains an extract from a New York paper, stating that "on Thursday preceding (24th), several cannon were fired from our battery at Amboy at a number of boats from Staten Island bound to Sandy Hook, supposed to join part of the ministerial fleet lying there. This brought on a cannonade from the encampment near Billop's Point, on the Island. Firing on both sides was very hot for near an hour. The boats got clear, but many of the Regulars were seen to fall, and several were carried off, supposed wounded. On our side a soldier in the Philadelphia line was killed, one wounded, a horse in a carriage had his head shot off in the street, and some damage done to the houses."

"Our battery," referred to in this article was on the hill over what is now the steamboat wharf and in front of Mr. Parker's residence. It was merely a breastwork with 4 guns. The firing from the opposite side was from two guns brought down for the occasion and posted under some trees near "Billop's House."

Mr. Marsh, who recollected the day perfectly, did not think that any of the British were killed. The boats were two sloops that left the Island at the Mill Creek, opposite Grass or Ploughshare Point, and although the firing was first commenced at them almost immediately, and continued while

[15] The tents of the Pennsylvania troops were pitched in the fields on the east side of what have been termed of late years, "Harriott's woods." The 1st and 3d divisions of Philadelphia Associators "having served with cheerfulness and alacrity" their six weeks, Col. Matlack's rifle battalion and Col. Ross' battalion of Lancaster, were all honorably discharged during the latter part of August and first of September, and returned home.

[16] Allen's Rev'n, 1, 423. General Mercer not long before had digested a plan for a simultaneous descent upon Staten Island from different quarters It may be found in the American Archives, Vol. 1, 5th Series. Col. 433.

they passed the town with a very light breeze, yet from want of skill in gunnery, no damage was sustained by them, excepting a hole in one of their mainsails made by a passing ball. As they proceeded down the Bay our guns were removed to another small battery near St. Peter's Church, whence the firing was recommenced, but still ineffectually. The horse was killed in High street a short distance south of the Town-well. Mr. Marsh remembered that a man was killed while confined in the Court-house, by a shot from the Island entering the upper part of it, which was then used as a guard-room ; and probably it was the one alluded to in the foregoing account.

Appearances at this time indicated an intended attack upon Amboy or an attempt to cross the Sound, and, as most of the troops there had been sent to New York early in August, when the city was menaced by the British fleet, the following notice was published :—

"WAR OFFICE, Philadelphia, August 28, 1776.

"As there is the most pressing necessity for all the troops, without exception, who are now in Philadelphia, or on their way to the camp, to march to Amboy in the State of New Jersey, it is hereby most earnestly requested that they do immediately proceed without waiting for further supplies of arms or any other matter or thing, as care will be taken to furnish them when they arrive at the camp."

"RICHARD PETERS, Secretary."

Fifteen hundred were to be stationed at Amboy, four hundred at Woodbridge, and five hundred at Elizabethtown.

It was just after the issuing of this order that the attention of the colonies was directed to the fruitless conference between the English Commissioners with the Committee of Congress, which was held in the Billop House opposite Amboy.

It was doubtless deemed by Lord Howe a most fitting time to open a correspondence with Congress, just after the disastrous result of the battle of Long Island, and a fortunate circumstance that a captured general could be sent as his envoy. Their future, in whatever way viewed, seemed shrouded in gloom, and he could scarcely have anticipated other than a favorable consideration of his message, however unsatisfactory may have been the reception given to his previous advances.

It was on the 2d September, 1776, that General Sullivan, under parole, presented himself before Congress with a verbal message, which he was desired to reduce to writing, to the effect that Lord Howe, although he could not recognize Congress as a legally constituted body, was desirous of conferring with some of its members in their private capacity, having in conjunction with his brother, General Howe, full powers to compromise the dispute between Great Britain and America upon terms advantageous to both;—that many things which the colonies had not yet asked for might and ought to be granted, were Congress disposed to treat,—and, should the conference find any probable ground of accommodation, the authority of Congress would be afterwards acknowledged, or the compact would not be complete. Congress two months previously had approved of Washington's course in refusing to receive from Lord Howe, a letter addressed simply to "George Washington, Esq.," and had directed all commanders to observe the same propriety by declining to receive any communication from the enemy not addressed to them in their respective official capacities;—they were therefore not disposed to accede to the Admiral's proposition as to the character of the Committee to be raised, and General Sullivan was on the 5th September made the bearer to him of the following resolution:—

"*Resolved*, That General Sullivan be requested to inform Lord Howe, that this Congress, being the representatives of the free and independent States of America, cannot with propriety send any of its members to confer with his lordship in their private characters, but that, ever desirous of establishing peace on reasonable terms, they will send a committee of their body to know whether he has any authority to treat with persons authorized by Congress for that purpose in behalf of America, and what that authority is, and to hear such propositions as he shall think fit to make respecting the same."

The Committee was chosen the next day. It consisted of the sage and experienced Franklin, John Adams, and the youthful Rutledge of South Carolina. There was a manifest propriety in the selection of Franklin as Chairman. Lord Howe had sought his acquaintance when in England as Agent for several of the colonies, with a view to ascertain his sentiments in relation to the practicability of effecting a reconciliation; succeeding through the agency of his sister, who obtained an introduction to Franklin under the plausible pretence of desiring to play chess with him—of which the Doctor himself has given us a very graphic account. But neither then, nor subsequently, after his arrival in America, when he opened a correspondence with Franklin, could Howe secure the co-operation of that patriot in furthering any plan of reunion based upon further subjection to the British crown; yet each for the other seems to have contracted a sincere regard, such as could have existed only between men of honor and intelligence; a regard with which their political relations had not been allowed to interfere.

Having been notified of the appointment of the committee, Lord Howe, under date of the 10th, informed Dr. Franklin that he would meet him and the other gentlemen the next morning "at the house on Staten Island opposite to Amboy, as early as the few conveniences for travelling by land on Staten Island will admit"—he being then on board of his vessel in the harbor of New York. A boat would be sent with a flag of truce over to Amboy for the committee, who were requested to wait for it at that place.

This arrangement was carried out, and was attended by a mark of consideration on the part of the Admiral, and of confidence on the part of the Committee, which is worthy of record. On the arrival of Lord Howe's barge at the dock, foot of Smith street, one of his principal officers was found to be on board, who had been directed to remain with the Americans as a hostage until the return of the Committee; but as this had not been desired, the officer was taken back to the island. Lord Howe himself received the Committee on landing, and conducted them through his guards to a room in Colonel Billop's house, where, for three or four hours, they consulted upon the momentous measure which had brought them together; but, as is well known, with no beneficial result. The report of the Committee, made at first verbally, and afterward in writing, will be found entered in the Journals of Congress, under date of September 17th; and Doctor Franklin has given in his "Account of Negotiations in London" a full recital of his previous intercourse with Lord Howe. It is well said by Botta, that "it seems in this revolution to have been the destiny of things, that the remedies should always arrive after the evils were become incurable; and that the government refusing, out of pride at the favorable moment, to acquiesce in useful concessions, should afterwards have to submit to the rejection of its useless propositions." [17]

The parting between Franklin and Howe is said to have been marked by an exhibition of feeling which did honor to their hearts without detracting from their credit as negotiators, and which must give to the spot that interest which ever attaches to those consecrated by acts of self-denial or of sacrifice. Who can estimate the mental trials which our Revolutionary struggle brought upon those to whom the ties of kindred or of friendship were as naught compared with the claims of their country?

During the night of 16th October, 1776, General Mercer passed over to Staten Island with a portion of the troops stationed at Amboy, hoping to capture a force said to be in the vicinity of Richmond, composed of one company of regulars, one of Hessians and one of Skinner's militia.

A detachment, under the command of Colonel Griffin, consisting of Colonel Patterson's battalion and Major Clarke's riflemen, was sent to fall upon the east end of the town, while the remainder of the force enclosed it in on the other sides. Both divisions reached their positions by the break of day, but the enemy having been warned were on the alert, and after discharging a few volleys retreated in disorder, leaving two of their number mortally wounded and 17 prisoners in the hands of the Americans. Two of the attacking party were killed, and Colonel Griffin and Lieutenant-colonel Smith were slightly wounded. Forty five muskets and other arms were brought off, together with a standard of the British Light Horse.

From the vicinity of the two armies desertions were frequent. On one occasion an Irishman, who had enlisted in the Pennsylvania line, swam the Sound notwithstanding the firing

[17] See John Adams' Works (Diary), Vol. II. p. 73, &c.

of the American riflemen, and was seen going into the bushes on the other side in safety. It was customary for considerable numbers of the men to bathe at the same time beneath the hill north of the town, just above the Cove, under the eye of sentinels stationed on the top of the bank. This fellow was observed making his way at a rapid rate towards Staten Island, and a ball was immediately sent whizzing at his head, the only part of his body visible. This of course brought out an increased number of men, and although it was supposed two hundred men made him the object of their aims, he nevertheless escaped unhurt. Single shots were oftentimes fired from rifles and muskets from one side to the other; and on one occasion when a number of English officers were regaling themselves under the trees on the Island, Richard Griggs, the father of the late Thomas Griggs, so well aimed his piece that the ball shivered a bowl filled with some refreshing beverage which an officer was in the act of putting to his mouth—the company soon dispersed. The musket (or rifle) which aided in the execution of this feat was in the possession of the family a few years since, and may be so yet.

The breastwork, of which some remains may here and there be seen along the top of the bank towards Staten Island, was not thrown up until after a soldier had been seriously wounded while on parade in the street, in front of the residence of the Hon. James Parker. It was made to guard the men from similar accidents, and to serve as some protection in case of an attack from that side. The more regular works or small earth redoubts (with the exception of one called the "lower entrenchment," capable of holding 200 men, which was constructed by Capt. Bloomfield's company in 1776), were thrown up by the British when they obtained possession of the place. There are some remains of these yet visible, in State street, in the Presbyterian graveyard, at the parting roads, and on the farm of Mr. Parker.

In November, 1776, Washington's retreat through New Jersey commenced. His head-quarters were at Hackensack from the 19th to the 21st of November; at Aquackanonck on the 21st; at Newark from the 23d to the 27th; at New Brunswick from the 30th to the 1st December; and at Trenton from the 3d to the 12th; the army crossing the Delaware about the 7th.[18] "Thus to suffer the shattered remains of the rebel troops," writes a British officer,[19] "a set of naked, dispirited fugitives, encumbered with baggage, to run a race of ninety miles, and outstrip the flower of the British army three times their number, appears to be an omission, not to give it another name, without example." The English took possession of Amboy about the 1st December, the Americans there under General Greene, joining Washington's retreating forces.

By this retreat New Jersey was left in the undisputed possession of the enemy; but Washington, having been reinforced by a detachment which had remained in the State of New York, again crossed the Delaware on the night of the 25th December, and by the brilliant affairs of Trenton and Princeton, re-established the supremacy of the American arms south and west of New Brunswick, and enabled his harassed and suffering army to go into comfortable winter quarters at Morristown.

The British concentrated all their forces upon Brunswick and Amboy, relinquishing all the advantages they had gained during the preceding month, excepting the retention of these two places. Sufficient time, however, had elapsed while they remained in possession of New Jersey, to make people fully aware of the true character of the enemy that was deluging their soil with the blood of their friends and kindred, and every day the English cause lost ground. "Sufferers of all parties rose as one man to revenge their personal injuries and particular oppression," and whenever attempts were made by the Brit-

[18] It was during this retreat that General Charles Lee negligently, as some thought, or purposely, as others were uncharitable enough to suggest, remained so far in the rear, that on the 12th December he was taken prisoner, by a detachment under Colonel Harcourt, and, it is thought, taken first to Amboy; and I have been told of the excitement which attended the arrival of the squadron having him in charge, as they rode into the Market Square. He was subsequently removed to New Brunswick, and arrived in New York from there January 22d, 1777. See Allen I., p. 561; Botta I., p. 396; Marshall I., p. 124; Lossing's Field Book of the Revolution, Vol. II., p. 222. Mr. L. says "he was conveyed to New York" at once; but the papers of the day will be found announcing his arrival there on the day I have named.

[19] Captain Hall's Civil War in America, p. 216.

ish to forage in the surrounding country, they were obliged to go in large parties, and generally sustained some loss. Mr. Dunlap thus describes their conduct, of which he was an eye-witness at Piscataway, when they advanced upon the retreating footsteps of Washington:—

"I saw the soldiers plundering the houses, the women of the village trembling and weeping, or flying with their children—the men had retired to await the day of retribution. In many houses helpless old men or widowed females anxiously awaited the soldiers of monarchy. A scene of promiscuous pillage was in full operation. Here a soldier was seen issuing from a house armed with a frying-pan and gridiron, and hastening to deposit them with the store over which his helpmate kept watch. The women who had followed the army assisted their husbands in bringing the furniture from the houses, or stood sentinels to guard the pile of kitchen utensils, or other articles already secured and claimed by right of war. Here was seen a woman bearing a looking-glass, and here a soldier with a feather bed—but as this was rather an inconvenient article to carry on a march, the ticking was soon ripped open, and a shower of goose feathers were seen taking higher flight than their original owners ever attained to."[20]

And Governor Livingston draws a still more revolting picture of their excesses. In a speech to the Council and Assembly, February 25th, 1777, he says:—

"They have plundered friends and foes. Effects capable of division they have divided; such as were not they have destroyed. They have warred upon decrepit age; warred upon defenceless youth! They have committed hostilities against the professors of literature and the ministers of religion; against public records and private monuments; against books of improvement and papers of curiosity; and against the arts and sciences. They have butchered the wounded asking for quarter; mangled the dying weltering in their blood; refused the dead the rites of sepulture; suffered prisoners to perish for want of sustenance; violated the chastity of women; disfigured private dwellings of taste and elegance; and in the rage of impiety and barbarism profaned edifices dedicated to Almighty God!"

The New Year opened with quite active hostilities north of the Raritan, the skirmishes being frequent with varied results.

A party of Jersey Militia on Sunday, 5th January, 1777, attacked a regiment of British troops in the neighborhood of Spanktown (now Rahway), and notwithstanding great disparity of numbers, the skirmishing continued for two hours—a sufficient time to enable the enemy to bring up reinforcements from Woodbridge and Amboy. The object of the attack was

[20] History Amer. Theatre, p. 236.

to obtain possession of a thousand bushels of salt which the enemy had secured.

It was about this time that Elizabethtown was evacuated on the approach of General Maxwell with a considerable body of continental and provincial troops, between 70 and 100 prisoners falling into his hands; and General Heath, a few days after, is reported to have destroyed more than one hundred flat-bottomed boats at the Point.

On Monday, January 20th, there was an engagement took place at a bridge over the Millstone River, about two miles from Somerset Court House, between 450 militia men of Pennsylvania and New Jersey, under General Dickinson, and about 600 of the enemy in charge of a quantity of cattle and forage, in which the former were very successful. Finding that they could not cross the bridge in consequence of its being defended by the British with three field-pieces, they sought a ford below, and breaking the ice, waded through the river, flanked the enemy, and routing them, captured 43 baggage wagons, 104 horses, 118 cattle, 60 or 70 sheep, and made 12 prisoners. Their loss was only 4 or 5, while the enemy's killed amounted to five or six times that number. General Washington alluded to this engagement in the following terms: "General Dickinson's behavior reflects the highest honor upon him, for though his troops were all raw, he led them through the river middle deep, and gave the enemy so severe a charge, that although supported by three field-pieces they gave way and left their convoy."

Three days after, a similar detachment of the enemy under Colonel Preston, with two pieces of cannon, was attacked on its way to Amboy from New Brunswick by an advanced party from the 6th Virginia Regiment; but Lieut.-colonel Parker in command of it, not having been supported by his superior Col. Buckner, was obliged to retreat, after keeping up a short contest, for twenty minutes, but without loss. The British lost, however, 65 in killed and wounded; Col. Preston being among the killed, and his second in command being dangerously wounded.

About the 1st February there was a skirmish at Piscataway

between 700 Americans and about 1,000 British, the latter having 3 field-pieces. They were obliged to retreat, however, leaving 36 men dead on the field; but, subsequently, having obtained reinforcements, with 3 additional guns, they returned and renewed the attack, obliging the Americans to retire. The latter lost in both affairs 9 killed and 14 wounded.

The foraging and scouting parties of the Americans which kept ranging through the country between Amboy and New Brunswick, effectually cut off all communication with the latter place during the month of February, excepting by the river Raritan. Lord Cornwallis had his head-quarters at New Brunswick, and his detachment became quite short of provisions. It was no very pleasing sound, therefore, just as their expectant eyes had descried, on the 26th February, a fleet of boats coming up the river from Amboy with the needed supplies, to hear the reverberations of a battery of six 32-pounders, which the vigilant provincials had put in position the night before on a high bluff below the town, overlooking the river, and to see the dire effects upon the boats. Four or five were sunk, and the remainder returned to Amboy and thence to New York. General Howe himself subsequently attempted to open the communication, but failed, narrowly escaping capture, and New Brunswick continued shut up until late in March.

This risk was incurred by General Howe in the neighborhood of Bonhamtown. He was at that place on the 8th March, and with the view of facilitating his return to Amboy, about 3,000 of the enemy, which was presumed to be the entire force then stationed there, marched out with artillery and posted themselves in an advantageous position, on what the contemporaneous account designates "Punk Hill." To disguise their real object they had wagons with them, as if to forage, but there was none of any consequence then obtainable in that neighborhood. The enemy were too strongly posted to be attacked by General Maxwell's troops in that quarter, but advanced parties having been sent out, skirmishes ensued between them and detachments under Colonels Potter and Cook of Pennsylvania, and Colonel Thatcher of New England, which brought reinforcements to both sides, and led to a more general engagement, in which it was thought the British lost 60 in killed and wounded, and they left three field-pieces and a baggage wagon in the hands of the Americans.

General Washington having wintered in Morristown, towards the end of May, 1777, made advances upon New Brunswick, from which place General Howe marched on the 14th June, to take the field against him.[21] He had received some reinforcements, but not so many as had been looked for. Mr. Oliver De Lancey of New York and Attorney-general Skinner of New Jersey,[22] who were considered to be particularly influential, were made Brigadier-generals, and authorized, the former, to raise three battalions, and the latter five; but their joint endeavors could only get together 1,114 men: a convincing proof of the increasing unpopularity of the royal cause, arising from the sufferings and insults the people had experienced. General Washington thus alludes to them in a letter to the President of Congress, under date of Jan. 1st, 1777:—

> "I have sent into different parts of New Jersey men of influence to spirit up the militia, and I flatter myself that the many injuries they have received will induce some to give their aid. If what they have suffered does not rouse their resentment, they must not possess the common feelings of humanity. To oppression, ravage, and a deprivation of property, they have had the more mortifying circumstance of insult added; after being stripped of all they had without the least compensation, protections have been granted for the full enjoyment of their effects."[23]

Among reinforcements received by General Howe were some troops from Rhode Island, intended to strengthen Amboy and New Brunswick should his Lordship deem it advisable to attack the troops at Morristown, and to open the communication with New Brunswick,[24] then closely surrounded, as we have seen, by the watchful Americans. They arrived in February, and the following graphic account of their debut on the

[21] On 6th June, 1777, one of those melancholy spectacles, a military execution, took place in New Brunswick. Abraham Patten was executed as an American spy, having bribed a grenadier to carry four letters to Generals Washington and Putnam, giving information respecting the town, engaging to set fire to it, &c. He would not accuse any as his accomplices, but it is said acknowledged at the gallows that he was a principal in setting fire to New York.

[22] See notice of him on a preceding page.

[23] Washington's Writings, Vol. IV., p. 255.

[24] General Howe's Despatch, February 30th, 1777.

scene of action in New Jersey, is extracted from Mr. Dunlap's vivid recollections of that period:[25]

"They were landed on a fine, clear winter's day, and with all the 'pride, pomp, and circumstance of glorious war.' I saw them march into the rebellious country adjacent, attended by a long train of wagons to procure forage. I walked out of the village (Amboy), to see the last of the brilliant show, and tried to keep up with a tall grenadier of the 42d, whose height and beauty particularly attracted my attention. I returned and placed myself at a garret window, which commanded a view of the roads leading on the left to Brunswick, on the right to Woodbridge, that I might catch another view of the long procession, which I saw passing over the hill, and vanishing as it moved on towards the nearest village.

"I have a confused recollection that my thoughts that day were occupied altogether by the proud display I had witnessed, and the events which might be passing in the interior; and the sound of distant musketry gave activity to these thoughts—my mind was on the stretch. I took my way up the road by which the army had passed, and I met a wounded man returning, assisted by a less injured comrade. A little further on stragglers were met returning, more or less hurt, and evincing pain. I next met the gigantic grenadier of the 42d, his musket on his left shoulder, his right hand bound up; he walked fast, but he no longer looked like the hero I had admired. I turned about and followed him. It was soon known that the militia had assembled, and were skirmishing with the *regulars*. In the evening it was known that this gallant military array were returning, their baggage wagons loaded with the wounded instead of the booty they went in search of. By the fireside I heard the heavy rumbling of the wagons over the frozen earth, and the groans of those who were borne to the hospitals. I had now seen something of war."

This was on Sunday, the 23d February. The detachment consisted of the 3d Brigade, with the battalions of light infantry and grenadiers, and was destined for what is now Rahway. Capt. Hall, who refers to the expedition, says:—

"As the body proceeded, the enemy, discovering its force, withdrew their advanced parties, but when we had completed our forage and were returning, having collected, they attacked us in our retreat, and behaving much better upon this occasion than they had been accustomed to do, they pressed hard upon the rear of the detachment, notwithstanding the fire of our field-pieces, which occasionally played upon them whenever they showed themselves in numbers. It was dark before the detachment reached the garrison, having been marching through deep snows for ten hours, losing in the action four officers and near one hundred killed and wounded."

That this skirmish was very severe is evident from the number of killed and wounded, and one circumstance which he states shows the precision with which the Americans used their guns. "Lieutenant Peebles," he says, "out of twenty grena-

[25] Hist. American Theatre, p. 236.

diers that flanked with him that day, alone escaped, keeping his ground in the action till the whole of his party was either killed or wounded, and then joining the grenadiers unhurt." [26] A letter-writer of the day states that the officer in command was placed under arrest, for not having at once proceeded towards New Brunswick, instead of marching out of his way in the hope of capturing General Maxwell and his troops at Rahway, to grace his entrance into the beleaguered town.

The occasional visits to the surrounding country made by the British troops, were sometimes returned in a way to excite considerable alarm. On the night of the 23d of April, 1777, a detachment of 60 men and three subalterns, commanded by Capt. Lacy, marched from the neighborhood of Rahway to surprise the picket in the suburbs of Amboy, but they failed in their object in consequence of its removal. They killed, however, one sentinel and wounded another,[27] and caused much apprehension. Numbers of the Hessian soldiers came running into town from the barracks, exclaiming "the rebel in the bush;" and expecting a general attack, all the troops were ordered out, and formed a semicircle extending from the water to the "parting roads." [28] This placed them on their guard, and the following night a similar expedition of 20 or 30 men, bewildered by the darkness, got within the lines, and not one escaped to tell the fate of the rest.[29]

On the 10th May there was a skirmish at Piscataway between portions of the regiments of Colonels Cook and Hendrick, and 71st Regiment of Scotch Regulars. The latter were forced to retire, and the Americans got possession of some part of their quarters, but a reinforcement arriving from Bonhamtown, the Highlanders were reinstated, although with considerable loss. The provincials behaved well, losing 26 or 27 in

[26] Hall's Civil War in America, p. 262. The American account made the British force 2000 strong, with 6 field-pieces, and it was stated that the action lasted all day from 9½ o'clock, A. M. The Americans had to retreat 5 or 6 miles, but being reinforced by 1,400 men of General Maxwell's Brigade, they eventually gained the day, with a loss of only 3 killed and 12 wounded, while the British loss is put down at 500!!

[27] Elmer's Journal, N. J. Hist. Socy. Proceedings, Vol. III., p. 90.

[28] Verbal information from Mr. Joseph Marsh.

[29] Elmer's Journal. The Captain and 25 of his men were sent to New York on the 25th as prisoners.

killed, wounded and prisoners. The firing drew out a number of the enemy from Amboy, but they retired again on finding their movements were observed. General Maxwell was present at the affair.[30]

The following day a detachment of English went as far as Woodbridge, but effected nothing.

We return to the events of June, 1777. The British army did nothing against Washington. They retreated again to New Brunswick, and, on the 22d June, after committing many outrages, left there for Amboy, and on the road, houses were burnt and other damage done to the property of individuals. A few of the British troops and the heavy baggage were passed over to Staten Island, to lead General Washington to believe they intended to evacuate the State forthwith, but the real object of General Howe was to draw the Americans from the strong position they occupied. So soon, therefore, as General Washington advanced his forces to Quibbletown, General Howe, having recalled the troops from Staten Island, directed his march towards him on the 25th in two columns, with a determination to bring on a general engagement. The Americans, however, withdrew from the low ground which they had occupied on advancing, and after engaging a division under Lord Stirling, subjecting it to some trifling loss, General Howe continued the pursuit to Westfield. He remained there until the next day at 3 o'clock, when he retired to Rahway, the day after reached Amboy, and on the 30th the whole British Army embarked, leaving all New Jersey in the quiet possession of General Washington.[31] The harbor of Amboy was filled with their vessels, and many troops embarked at once from our shores on board the transports that conveyed them to the Chesapeake,[32] and shortly

[30] Elmer.

[31] Washington's Writings, Vol. IV., p. 497.

[32] Washington's Writings, Vol. IV., p. 481. As this expedition was one undertaken with much preparation by Lord Howe, and with high expectations of success, I give here such portions of Lord Howe's official despatch of July 5th, 1777, as refer to it.

"The necessary preparations being finished for crossing the troops to Staten Island, intelligence was received that the enemy had moved down from the mountain and taken post at Quibbletown, intending, as it was given out, to attack the rear of the army removing from Amboy; that two corps had also advanced to their left—one of 3,000 men and 8 pieces of cannon,

afterwards the battle of Brandywine took place.[33] The Americans remained in undisturbed possession of Amboy the remainder of the war; the English never making their appearance

under Lord Stirling, Generals Maxwell and Conway: the last said to be a Captain in the French service; the other corps consisting of about 700 men, with only one piece of cannon. In this situation of the enemy, it was judged advisable to make a movement that might lead on to an attack, which was done the 26th, in the morning, in two columns: the right, under the command of Lord Cornwallis, with Major-general Grant, Brigadiers Matthew and Lesslie, and Colonel Donop, took the route of Woodbridge towards Scotch Plains—the left column where I was, with Major-generals Sterne, Vaughan and Grey, Brigadiers Cleaveland and Agnew, marched by Metuchin Meeting-house to join the rear of the right column in the road from thence to Scotch Plains, intending to have taken separate routes about two miles after the junction, in order to have attacked the enemy's left flank at Quibbletown. Four battalions were detached in the morning, with six pieces of cannon, to take post at Bonhamtown.

"The right column, having fallen in with the aforementioned corps of 700 men soon after passing Woodbridge, gave the alarm, by the firing that ensued, to the main army at Quibbletown, which retired to the mountain with the utmost precipitation. The small corps was closely pursued by the light troops, and with difficulty got off their pieces of cannon.

"Lord Cornwallis, soon after he was upon the road leading to Scotch Plains from Metuchin Meeting-house, came up with the corps commanded by Lord Stirling, who he found advantageously posted in a country much covered with wood, and his artillery well disposed. The King's troops, vying with each other upon this occasion, pressed forward to such close action, that the enemy, though inclined to resist, could not long maintain their ground against so great impetuosity, but were dispersed on all sides, leaving behind them three pieces of brass ordnance, 3 captains and 60 men killed and upwards of 200 officers and men wounded and taken. His Lordship had 5 men killed and 30 wounded, and 13 prisoners; [see Gen. W.'s letter to Congress, June 29, 1777. He says, Lord Stirling assured him his loss was light except in the 3 field pieces.] Capt. Finch, of the light company of the Guards, was the only officer who suffered, and, to my great concern, the wound he received proving mortal, he died the 29th June at Amboy. The troops engaged in this action were—1st Light Infantry, 1st British Grenadiers, 1st, 2d and 3d Hessian Grenadiers, 1st Battalion Guards, Hessian Chasseurs, and the Queen's Rangers. I take the Liberty of particularizing these corps, as Lord Cornwallis in his report to me so highly extols their merit and ardor upon this attack. One piece of cannon was taken by the Guards, the other two by Col. Mingerode's battalion of Hessian Grenadiers.

"The enemy were pursued as far as Westfield, with little effect; the day proving so intensely hot, that the soldiers could with difficulty continue their march thither; in the mean time it gave opportunity for those flying to escape by skulking in the thick woods, until night favored their retreat to the mountain.

"The army lay that night at Westfield, returned the next day to Rahway, and the day following to Amboy. On the 30th, at 10 o'clock in the forenoon, the troops began to cross over to Staten Island, and the rearguard, under the command of Lord Cornwallis, passed at two in the afternoon. The embarkation of the troops is proceeding with the utmost despatch, and I shall have the honor of sending your Lordship further information as soon as the troops are landed at the place of their destination.

"With the most perfect respect, &c.,

"W. HOWE."

[33] The bridge of boats which was intended by the British for the Delaware, answered a very good purpose at Amboy in facilitating the crossing of a portion of the army to Staten Island.—*Marshal Botta.*

in its vicinity in any numbers after the evacuation of the place, although predatory excursions to Woodbridge, Rahway, Elizabethtown, and up the Raritan were frequently undertaken, and attended with more or less annoyance to the inhabitants.

General Vaughan commanded the garrison while the place was in possession of the enemy. His head-quarters were in the Government-house, which then occupied the site of the present Brighton. The troops were a mixed assemblage of Germans, Hessians, Highlanders and English. The Highlanders were an object of considerable curiosity and wonder from their dress, wearing a low checkered bonnet, a tartan or plaid, a short red coat or with a kilt, leaving their knees exposed to view and to the winds, and their legs only partly covered by the many-colored hose of their country.

The musket, bayonet, broadsword, dirk and pistols showed a formal array for the strife of blood, and the ornamental portion of the dress was completed by a pouch hanging in front of the kilt decorated with tassels. This costume was changed after the first or second campaign, the temperature of the country and species of warfare being both unsuited to it.

The dress of a Hessian soldier as described by Dunlap [34] was as follows: "A towering brass-fronted cap; moustaches colored with the same material that colored his shoes, his hair plastered with tallow and flour, and tightly drawn into a long appendage reaching from the back of the head to his waist; his blue uniform almost covered by the broad belts sustaining his cartouch box, his brass-hilted sword, and his bayonet; a yellow waistcoat with flaps, and yellow breeches were met at the knee by black gaiters; and thus heavily equipped he stood an automaton, and received the command or cane of the officer who inspected him."

The following are notices of some of the expeditions referred to above, as having been set on foot by the British after their evacuation of Amboy and the vicinity, and of some other events of interest from contemporary accounts:—

[34] American Theatre, pp. 45, 47.

On 19th August, 1777, a detachment of 60 men of the Battalion of New Jersey Royal Volunteers, came over from Staten Island and, it is said, marched 27 miles into the interior, taking off 14 prisoners, 62 head of cattle, 9 horses, and a quantity of arms and ammunition, destroying much they could not remove. On returning they posted their pickets and sentinels so well, that, although the American Light-horse, under the command of Captain Barnet of Elizabethtown, made their appearance on the heights north-west of the town; they did not venture to attack them, and all their booty was transported in safety to the island.

On the 12th April, 1779, Commissioners appointed by General Washington and Sir Henry Clinton, met at Amboy, to make arrangements for a general exchange of prisoners.

On October 12th, 1779, about 50 of "the Greens" crossed over from Staten Island early in the morning, and had secured upwards of a hundred cattle and horses before any American troops could be collected; but about 10 o'clock a detachment from Elizabethtown, under Captain Davis, came upon them unexpectedly, and obliged them to retreat, leaving most of their booty behind them.

Soon after this, occurred, what the gallant Henry Lee says "was considered by both armies among the handsomest exploits of the war," and from the interest attaching to it, from the ground traversed, and other circumstances, no apology is offered for giving an account of it, principally in the words of the chief actor in the affair—Lieut. Col. Simcoe of the Queen's Rangers—whose corps was characterized throughout the war by its gallantry and success.

"There was a general rumor of an intended attack on New York. Lt. Col. Simcoe had information that fifty flat-boats, upon carriages, capable of holding seventy men each, were on the road from the Delaware to Washington's army, and that they had been assembled to Van Vechten's bridge, upon the Raritan. He proposed to the Commander-in-Chief to burn them. Sir Henry Clinton approved of his plan, as did Earl Cornwallis, and directed it to be put into execution. Colonel Lee, with his cavalry, had been at Monmouth: Sir Henry Clinton, upon Lieut. Col. Simcoe's application to him for intelligence of this corps, told him, that by the best information he had, Lee was gone from that part of the country. There were no other troops in the vicinity: the Jersey militia only, and those tumultuously assembled at the moment of the execution of the enterprise could, possibly, impede it.

"Lieut. Col. Simcoe's plan was, to burn the boats with as much expedition as possible; to return, with silence, to the heights beyond the town of Brunswick, before day; there to show himself, to entice all who might follow him into an ambuscade; and if he found that his remaining in the Jersies could effect any valuable purpose, the Commander-in-Chief proposed to reinforce him.

"On the 25th of October, by eight o'clock at night, the detachment, which had been detailed, marched to Billop's Point, where they were to embark. That the enterprise might be effectually concealed, Lieut. Col. Simcoe described a man, as a rebel spy, to be on the island, and endeavoring to escape to New Jersey; a great reward was offered for taking him, and the militia of the island were watching all the places where it was possible for any man to go from, in order to apprehend him. The bateaux, and boats, which were appointed to be at Billop's Point, so as to pass the whole over by *twelve o'clock* at night, did not arrive till *three o'clock* in the morning. No time was lost; the infantry of the Queen's Rangers were landed: they ambuscaded every avenue to the town; the cavalry followed as fast as possible. As soon as it was formed, Lieut. Col. Simcoe called together the officers; he told them of his plan, 'that he meant to burn the boats at Van Vechten's bridge, and crossing the Raritan, at Hillsborough, to return by the road to Brunswick, and, making a circuit to avoid that place as soon as he came near it, to discover himself when beyond it, on the heights where the Grenadier Redoubt stood while the British troops were cantoned there, and where the Queen's Rangers afterwards had been encamped; and to entice the militia, if possible, to follow him into an ambuscade which the infantry would lay for them at South-river bridge.' Major Armstrong was instructed to re-embark, as soon as the cavalry marched, and to land on the opposite side of the Raritan, at South Amboy: he was then, with the utmost despatch and silence, to proceed to South-river bridge, six miles from South Amboy, where he was to ambuscade himself, without passing the bridge or taking it up. A smaller creek falls into this river on the South Amboy side: into the peninsula formed by these streams, Lieut. Col. Simcoe hoped to allure the Jersey militia. In case of accident, Major Armstrong was desired to give credit to any messenger who should give him the patrole of 'Clinton and Montrose.' It was daybreak before the cavalry left Amboy. The procuring of guides had been by Sir Henry Clinton entrusted to Brigadier Skinner: he either did not or could not obtain them, for but one was found who knew perfectly the cross-road he meant to take, to avoid the main road from Somerset court-house, or Hillsborough, to Brunswick. Captain Sandford formed the advance-guard, the Huzzars followed, and Stuart's men were in the rear; making in the whole about eighty. A Justice Crow was soon overtaken; Lieut. Col. Simcoe accosted him roughly, called him 'Tory,' nor seemed to believe his excuses, when in the American idiom for courtship, he said 'he had only been sparking,' but sent him to the rear-guard, who, being Americans, easily comprehended their instructions, and kept up the justice's belief that the party was a detachment from Washington's army. Many plantations were now passed by, the inhabitants of which were up, and whom the party accosted with friendly salutations. At Quibbletown, Lieut. Col. Simcoe had just quitted the advance guard to speak to Lieut. Stuart, when, from a public house on the turn of the road, some people came out with knapsacks on their shoulders, bearing the appearance of a rebel guard: Captain Sandford did not see them till he had passed by, when, checking his horse to give notice, the Huzzars were reduced to a momentary halt opposite the house; perceiving the supposed guard, they threw themselves off their horses, sword in hand, and entered the house. Lieut. Col. Simcoe instantly made them remount: but they were afraid to discover some thousand pounds of paper-money which had been taken from a passenger, the master of a privateer, nor could he stay to search for it. He told the man, 'that he would be answerable to give him his money that night at Brunswick, where he should quarter;' exclaimed aloud to his party, 'that these were not the Tories they were in search of, although they had knapsacks,' and told the country people who were assembling around, 'that a party of Tories had made their escape from Sullivan's army, and were trying to get into Staten Island, as Iliff (who had been defeated near this very spot, taken, and executed) had formerly done, and that he was sent to intercept them.' The sight of Justice Crow would, probably, have aided in deceiving the inhabitants, but, unfortunately, a man personally knew Lieut. Col. Simcoe, and an express was sent to Governor Livingston, then at Brunswick, as soon as the party marched. It was now conducted by a country lad whom they fell in with, and to whom Captain Sandford, being dressed in red, and without his cloak, had been introduced as a French officer: he gave information, that the greater part of the boats had been sent on to Washington's camp, but that eighteen were at Van Vechten's bridge, and that their horses were at a farm about a mile from it: he led the party to an old camp of Washington's above Bound brook. Lieut. Col. Simcoe's instructions were to burn these huts, if possible, in order to give as wide an alarm to the Jersies as he could. He found it impracticable to do so, they not being joined in ranges, nor built of very combustible materials. He proceeded without delay to Bound brook, from whence he intended to carry off Col. Moyland, but he was not at Mr. Vanhorn's: two officers who had been ill were there; their paroles were taken; and they were ordered to mark 'sick quarters' over the room door they inhabited, which was done; and Mr. Vanhorn was informed, that the party was the advanced guard of the left column of the army, which was commanded by General Birch, who meant to quarter that night at his house; and that Sir Henry H. Clinton was in full march for Morristown, with the army. The party proceeded to Van Vechten's bridge: Lieut. Col. Simcoe found eighteen new flat-boats, upon carriages; they were full of water. He was determined effectually to destroy them. Combustibles had been applied for, and he received, in consequence, a few port-fires; every Huzzar had a hand-grenade, and several hatchets were brought with the party. The timbers of the boats were cut through; they were filled with straw and railing, and some grenades being fastened in them, they were set on fire: forty minutes were employed in this business. The country began to assemble in their rear; and as Lieut. Col. Simcoe went to the Dutch-meeting, where the harness, and some stores, were reported to be, a rifle-shot was fired at him from the opposite bank of the river: this house, with a magazine of forage, was now consumed, the commissary, and his people, being made prisoners. The party proceeded to Somerset court-house, or Hillsborough. Lieut. Col. Simcoe told the prisoners not to be alarmed, that he would give them their paroles before he left the Jersies; but he could not help heavily lamenting to the officers with him, the sinister events which prevented him from being at Van Vechten's bridge some hours sooner, as it would have been very feasible to have drawn off the flat-boats to the South river, instead of destroying them. He proceeded to Somerset court-house; three Loyalists, who were prisoners there, were liberated; one of them was a dreadful spectacle; he appeared to have been almost starved, and was chained to the floor; the soldiers wished, and it was permitted, to burn the court-house: it was unconnected with any other building, and, by its flames, showed on which side of the Raritan he was, and would, most probably operate to assemble the neighborhood of Brunswick at its bridge, to prevent him from returning by that road: the party proceeded towards Brunswick. Alarm guns were now heard, and some shots were fired at the rear, particularly by one person, who, as it afterwards appeared, being out a shooting, and hearing of the incursion, had sent word to Governor Livingston, who was at Brunswick, that he would follow the party at a distance, and every now and then give a shot, that he might know which way they directed their march. Passing by some houses, Lieut. Col. Simcoe told the women to inform four or five people who were pursuing the rear, 'that if they fired another shot, he would burn every house which he passed.' A man or two were now slightly wounded. As the party approached Brunswick, Lieut. Col. Simcoe began to be anxious for the cross-road, diverging from it into the Prince-town road, which he meant to pursue, and which having once arrived at, he himself knew the bye ways to the heights he wished to attain, where having frequently done duty, he was minutely acquainted with every advantage and circumstance of the ground: his guide was perfectly confident that he was not yet arrived at it; and Lieut. Col. Simcoe was in earnest conversation with him, and making the necessary inquiries, when a shot, at some little distance, discovered there was a party in the front. He immediately galloped thither; and he sent back Wright, his orderly serjeant, to acquaint Captain Sandford 'that the shot had not been fired at the party,' when, on the right at some distance, he saw the rail fence (which was very high on both sides of the narrow road between two woods) somewhat broken down, and a man or two near it, when putting his horse on the canter, he joined the advance men of the Huzzars, determining to pass through this opening, so as to avoid every ambuscade that might be laid for him, or attack, upon more equal terms, Colonel Lee, (whom he understood to be in the neighborhood, and apprehended might be opposed to him,) or any other party; when he saw some men concealed behind logs and bushes, between him and the opening he meant to pass through, and he heard the words, 'now, now,' and found himself, when he recovered his senses, prisoner with the enemy, his horse being killed with five bullets, and himself stunned by the violence of his fall. His imprisonment, the circumstances which attended it, and the indelible impressions which it has made on his memory, cannot, even at this distance, be repeated without the strongest emotions.

"Lieut. Col. Simcoe had no opportunity of communicating his determination to any of his officers, they being all with their respective divisions ready for what might follow upon the signal shot of the enemy, and his resolution being one of those where thought must go hand in hand with execution, it is no wonder, therefore, that the party, who did not perceive the opening he was aiming at, followed with the accelerated pace which the front, being upon the canter, too generally brings upon the rear; they passed the ambuscade in great confusion: three horses were wounded, and the men made prisoners, two of them being also wounded. The enemy who fired were not five yards off: they consisted of thirty men, commanded by Mariner, a refugee from New York, and well known for his enterprises with whale-boats. They were posted on the very spot which Lieut. Col. Simcoe had always aimed at avoiding. His guide misled him: nor was the reason of his error the least uncommon of the sinister events which attended this incursion. When the British troops quitted the camp at Hillsborough, and marched to Brunswick, among other houses which were unwarrantably burnt was the one which the guard relied upon, as marking out the private road the party was to take: he knew not of its being burnt, and that every vestige had been destroyed, so that he led them unintentionally into the ambuscade; which when the party had passed by on the full gallop, they found themselves on the high grounds beyond the barracks at Brunswick. Here they rallied; there was little doubt but Lieut. Col. Simcoe was killed: the surgeon, (Mr. Kellock,) with a white handkerchief, held out as a flag of truce, at the manifest risk of his life, returned to inquire for him. The militia assembling, Captain Sandford drew up, and charged them, of course, they fled: a Captain Voorhees, of the Jersey Continental troops, was overtaken, and the Huzzar, at whom he had fired, killed him. A few prisoners were taken. Captain Sandford proceeded to the South river, the guides having recovered from the consternation. Two militia men only were met with upon the road thither: they fired, and killed Molloy, a brave Huzzar, the advance man of the party, and were themselves instantly put to death. At South river the cavalry joined Major Armstrong; he had perfectly succeeded in arriving at his post undiscovered, and, ambuscading himself, had taken several prisoners. He marched back to South Amboy, and re-embarked without opposition, exchanging some of the bad horses of the corps for better ones which he had taken with the prisoners. The alarm through the country was general; Wayne was detached from Washington's camp in the highlands, with the light troops, and marched fourteen miles that night, and thirty the next day; Colonel Lee, who was in Monmouth county, as it was said, fell back towards the Delaware. The Queen's Rangers returned to Richmond that evening: the cavalry had marched upwards of eighty miles, without halting or refreshment, and the infantry thirty." [35]

It must be remembered that this is a partisan statement, passing over as lightly as possible the outrages committed. There was no necessity for firing the Court-House, nor the dwellings, nor for visiting upon the few prisoners taken the indignities, of which there are many traditionary accounts.

[35] Simcoe's Military Journal, pp. 107–117. Colonel Lee says of this expedition:—"Simcoe executed his object completely, then deemed very important * * * passing through a most hostile region of armed citizens; necessarily skirting Brunswick, a military station; proceeding not more than eight or nine miles from the legion of Lee, his last point of danger, and which became increased from the debilitated condition to which his troops were reduced by previous fatigue. What is very extraordinary, Simcoe, being obliged to feed once in the course of the night, stopped at a depot of forage collected for the continental army, assumed for his corps the character of Lee's cavalry, waked up the commissary about midnight, drew the customary allowance of forage, and gave the usual vouchers, signing the name of the legion-quartermaster, without being discovered by the American forage commissary or his assistants. The dress of both corps was the same, green coatees and leather breeches; yet the success of the stratagem is astonishing."—(Lee's Memoirs of the War, II., p. 9, *note.*) As Simcoe says nothing of all this, the correctness of the story may be doubted. The time, too, is all out of keeping. "It was *daybreak*," says Simcoe. "before the cavalry left Amboy."

Captain Voorhees of the 1st Jersey Regiment, was cruelly wounded by the Rangers, so that he lived but a few hours, although incapacitated, by an accident to his horse, from making any resistance. He was to have been married the next day. Dr. Ryker and Mr. John Polhemus were taken prisoners by Major Armstrong's covering party. The militia made six prisoners and killed three. Colonel Simcoe remained a prisoner until the last of December, having been most of the time in close confinement at Burlington, suffering under rigorous treatment in company with Colonel Billop,[36] in retaliation for the hardships to which Capt. Nathaniel Fitz Randolph of Woodbridge, and others, were subjected to.

British Major-general Phillips, Lieutenant-colonels Gordon and Norton, and American Major-general St. Clair, and Lieutenant-colonels Hamilton and Carrington met at Amboy early in March, 1780, for the purpose of arranging a general exchange of prisoners.

On June 1st, 1780, a party of about 30 refugees from New York landed at Sandy Point on the Raritan, and proceeding thence to Woodbridge, made Justice Freeman, Mr. Edgar, and eight other persons prisoners, whom they carried off.

On the 4th January, 1782, a party of 300 British landed before day in the lower part of New Brunswick, and obtained possession of the town and retained it for some hours, but their object was apparently only to take possession of the whale boats, which having accomplished, they retired doing very little injury, having had four of their party killed. Under date of 11th January, Governor Livingston thus alludes to it in a letter to Lord Stirling.

"The enemy with about 300 men (a motley of British and refugees) have made an irruption into the City of Brunswick by water; have captured Captain Haylies' (*Quere* Hyler's) gun boats (one of the first rates of New Jersey) and three whale boats, plundered two houses, carried off about five or six prisoners (some of them probably volunteers), and wounded five or six men. The extreme darkness of the night and the impossibility of collecting a sufficient force on so short a notice, they could not be repelled nor prevented from executing the object of their enterprise, but the few men collected behaved with the greatest bravery, or in the *charming* language of General Burgoyne, "to a charm." [37]

[36] See page 95.

[37] Stirling Papers in N. Y. Soc. Lib.

Many instances of personal heroism and devotion to the interests of the colonies may be culled from contemporaneous papers, but neither the limits nor the scope of this volume will admit of their being introduced here. There is scarcely a town or village in the State that has not its local traditions or veritable accounts of "valiant doings in the country's cause," waiting for the patient chronicler to gather and preserve them. May this imperfect attempt to revive some of those relating to the district we have had under review, induce others to pursue similar researches in other quarters.

Chapter XI.—Woodbridge.

* * * * * "We but hear
Of the survivors' toil in their new lands,
Their numbers and success; but who can number
The hearts which broke in silence at their parting,
Or after their departure; of that malady
Which calls up green and native fields to view
From the rough deep, with such identity
To the poor exile's fevered eye, that he
Can scarcely be restrained from treading them."

WOODBRIDGE was one of the townships, the creation of which was contemplated in an agreement entered into by Daniel Pierce and his associates, with Carteret, Ogden, and Watson, December 11th, 1666. This agreement was confirmed by a deed dated December 3d, 1667, and on the same day, Pierce was commissioned as Deputy-surveyor to run the boundary lines, and lay out the lands to the different associates. On June 1st, 1669, a charter was granted and "thankfully accepted" which erected the tract, said to contain six miles square, into a township to comprise not less than sixty families, and by a resolution adopted on that day, this number was not to be exceeded unless by special order of the town.[1]

The following persons received patents from the Proprie-

[1] East Jersey under the Proprietors, pp. 41, 183.—Woodbridge Town Records.—I have derived much satisfaction from inspecting the venerable and veritable "town book" which records the public acts of settlers from February, 1668–9 down to 1700. The first years' papers are not on record, Joshua Pierce having, for some reason not stated, retained them in his possession. The existence of these records has been little known or their contents little valued, but they contain much matter calculated to interest any one connected with the township. Among other items of record are the births, marriages and deaths for many years. Would that there were more towns in the State possessing such original materials for their history.

tors, principally in the year 1670, for lands within the bounds of the township; and were all, it is believed, actual settlers. The nine original associates were allowed to retain 240 acres of upland and forty of meadow in addition to the regular allotment to each freeholder, but at what time, or by what method, the first divison was effected has not been ascertained.

	Acres		*Acres*
John Adams	97	STEPHEN KENT,	249
Ephraim Andrews (1673)	98	Stephen Kent, jr.	104
Thomas Auger or Alger	167	Henry Lessenby	88
Obadiah Ayres	171	George Little	100
Samuel Baker or Bacon	170	HUGH MARCH	320
Joshua Bradley	171	David Makany	168
JOHN BISHOP	470	Samuel Moore	[6] 356
John Bishop, jr.	[2] 77	Matthew Moore	177
Matthew Bunn, "Mariner"	165	Benj. Parker "Joiner"	105
Thomas Blomfield	326	Elisha Parker (1675)	182
Thomas Blomfield, jr.	92	JOHN PIKE	308
John Blomfield	90	John Pike, jr.	91
John Conger	170	DANIEL PIERCE	456
John Cromwill	173	JOSHUA PIERCE	[7] 30
William Compton [3]	174	*Daniel Robins*	173
ROBERT DENNIS	448	*Robert Rogers*	91
John Dennis	[4] 107	JOHN SMITH "Wheelwright"	512
Samuel Dennis	94	Samuel Smith (1676)	103
John Dilly (1676)	94	John Smith, "Scotchman"	176
Hugh Dun	92	*Isaac Toppan*	172
Jonathan Dunham (1672)	213	Abraham Toppan	95½
John French "Mason"	15	John Taylor "Blacksmith"	92
Rehoboth Gannit	[5] 448	Israel Thorne [8] 1676)	96
Daniel Grasie	164	Robert Vanquellen, or La Prairie	175
Samuel Hale	167		
Jonathan Haynes (1673)	97	John Watkins	92
Elisha Ilsley	172	Nathan Webster	93
HENRY JAQUES, Henry Jaques, jr.	368	John Whitaker	91
		Richard Worth [9]	172

And in addition to these we find in the list of Freeholders in the Town Register (but without date):

[2] In Town Book this quantity is given as 92.

[3] Mary Compton, daughter of William and Mary Compton, was *the first child born in Woodbridge*, (November, 1668.) She married Caleb Campbell on 1st January, 1695–6, and died February 15th, 1735, aged 67 years and 3 months. Her grave is still marked by a head-stone, recording the fact above stated.

[4] In Town Book 177.

[5] Ibid 126.

[6] Ibid 286.

[7] Ibid 310.

[8] Admitted "instead of his uncle Jedidiah Andrews."

[9] These names are from the East Jersey Records, and see Elizabethtown Bill in Chancery, p.98.

	Acres		Acres
Thomas Adams		*Hopewell Hull*	
John Allen "Minister" -	97	John Ilsley - - -	97
John Averill		John Martin, Sen'r - -	255
William Bingley - -	186	*Thomas Pike*	
Jonathan Bishop		John Trewman - - -	97
Capt. Philip Carteret - -	313	Lords Proprietors - -	1000
James Clawson, or *Clarkson*		For the Ministry - -	200
Jonathan Dennis		Maintenance of School - -	100

The names in small capitals are those of the original associates; those in italics are not found in a "list of each man's land" under date of 1682,—having either disposed of their rights or been admitted as freeholders subsequently—in which list there are, also, some variations in the quantity of land held by some of the individuals.

A second division of land—80 acres to each freeholder—was authorized in February, 1687, the allotments lying west of the highway leading to Elizabethtown;—a third division of 50 acres each, was made in March, 1701; a fourth of sixty acres in 1706, and one of twenty acres the year following.

Most of the foregoing names will be still recognized as those borne by many families in the vicinity, and the following lists will show which of them were coupled with honorable distinctions in the first years of the settlement.

DEPUTIES TO THE GENERAL ASSEMBLY.

1668–9	Robert Dennis.	Samuel Moore.
1669–71	John Smith.	Samuel Moore.
1671–2	John Smith.	Robert Dennis.
1675	Samuel Dennis.	Thomas Blomfield.
1676	Matthew Bunn.	Ephraim Andrews.
1679–82	Samuel Dennis.	John Ilsley.
1682–3	John Ilsley.	Samuel Moore.
1684–5	John Ilsley.	John Bishop.
1685–6	John Ilsley.	Ephraim Andrews.
1686–7	Ephraim Andrews.	Ezekiel Blomfield,
1687–8	Samuel Dennis.	Samuel Moore.
1692	Ephraim Andrews	John Ilsley.
1692–3	Thomas Thorp.	John Pike.
1693–4	Nath'l Fitz Randolph.	John Ilsley.
1696	John Ilsley.	John Pike.
1697–8	Samuel Dennis.	John Pike.
1699	John Worth.	Thomas Pike.
1700–1	Elisha Parker.	Adam Hude.
1701	Jonathan Dunham.	Jonathan Bishop.
1702	Elisha Parker.	John Compton.

Officers of Township Court.

	President.	Assistants.
1671	John Pike.	John Smith, John Bishop, senr., John Martin, Samuel Moore.
1672	Saml. Moore.	John Smith, John Pike, J. Bishop, senr.
1674	John Pike.	J. Bishop, senr., Thos. Blomfield, senr., Stephen Kent, senr., Samuel Dennis.
1679		Ephraim Andrews, John Ilsley.
1681	John Pike.	Ephraim Andrews, Samuel Bacon, John Ilsley, J. Bishop, senr.
1688	John Bishop.	John Ilsley, Nathl. Fitz Randolph.
1693	John Bishop.	Samuel Hale, Samuel Dennis, Ephraim Andrews.

	Marshals or Sergeants.	Clerks.
1672	Samuel Hale.	Jonathan Dunham.
1681	Joshua Bradley.	Samuel Moore.
1687	Thomas Collier.	
1692	Daniel Robbins.	Thomas Pike.
1693	John Bloomfield.	
1695	Isaac Toppan.	
1696	Abraham Toppan.	
	William Stone.	

Town Clerks.

1668–78, Samuel Moore—1688–92, Samuel Dennis—1692–93, Thomas Pike—1694, Samuel Dennis—1695–1707, Thomas Pike. (From 1707 to 1711 it is uncertain who held the office.) 1711–1730, Moses Rolph—1732–1756, Edward Crowell—1757–1768, Nathaniel Fitz Randolph—1769–1774, Daniel Moores—1775–1776, Robert Fitz Randolph. (From 1776 to 1783, there are no entries in the records.) 1783, David Frazee—1784, Charles Jackson. (There is another break in the records from 1784 to 1788.) 1788–1793, James Paton—1794, Robert Ross, jr.—1795–1799, Ichabod Potter.

The post of Constable was not a very desirable one, and a change appears to have been made every year, so that scarcely a prominent settler escaped the honor in the course of time. The offices in the militia were first conferred, in 1675, upon John Pike, Samuel Moore and John Bishop, as Captain, Lieutenant, and Ensign respectively; and thereafter, the Pikes, Bishops and Samuel Hale appear to have monopolized the military honors for several years.

Little novelty is afforded the chronicler in the events which mark the passage of months and years amid the quietness and sobriety of a secluded agricultural people. Coming from New England and most of them of Puritan parentage, the inhabitants of Woodbridge pursued the even tenor of their way with a staidness becoming their origin, undisturbed by the turmoil of the world around, and, it would seem, but little affected by the strife of parties with which the Province was so early afflicted. Secure in the possession of their lands—for the existence at any time of any difference of moment between them and the Proprietaries has not been discovered—they were alike loyal to the Dutch and English Governors, to Proprietary interests or Royal prerogatives, whichever had the ascendency ; and it is somewhat ludicrous to observe with what ease, plain "Samuel Dennis, *Justice*," under the English rule, became "Samuel Dennis, *Skeepen*," when the Hollanders had the supremacy ; and the town with equal facility was transferred from the Province of New Jersey—to the "Schoutship of Achter Kol in the New Netherlands."

But intending only to embody in these pages a few items, exhibiting in some measure the progress of the town in its infancy, I will not attempt a connected narrative, where the observance of system must detract from the interest which the contemporaneous records throw around the matters referred to.

The town was named after the Rev. John Woodbridge of Newbury, Massachusetts ; and its original projectors, withsome of its most prominent residents, deserve notice.

Daniel Pierce, "Blacksmith," and his son, Joshua Pierce, although among the first to move in the enterprise of establishing the town, do not appear to have exerted any special influence in the management of its affairs. The father on his arrival in America, first settled at Watertown, Mass. ; thence, about 1637, he removed to Newbury, where, in 1652, he purchased considerable property of a nephew named John Spencer,[10] and his interests there induced him to return to Massachusetts soon after the settlement of Woodbridge, and he

[10] MS. Letter from Joshua Coffin, Esqr., of Newbury—and see Coffin's History of Newbury.

died in Ipswich, December 26th, 1677, leaving one son, *Daniel*, who was a resident of the same town.

Joshua, the son, born May 15th, 1642, had died in Woodbridge, about the latter part of 1670, and a month subsequent to his death, the birth of a son Joshua is recorded. There is a previous record of the birth of a daughter on March 18th, 1668, on "the fifth of the week, about break of day."

Daniel Pierce left his property in Massachusetts to his son Daniel (born in Watertown, 1636), and his heirs male; with the proviso that it should "never be sold nor any part divided"—a condition, however, which was violated in subsequent years. He had been twice married—to his last wife, Anne Milward, December 26th, 1654. She died, November 29th, 1690.

In the graveyard of Newbury, Mass., the tombstone of Daniel Pierce, the son, is yet to be seen, bearing the following inscription:

"Here lyes interred what was mortal of ye Honorable DANIEL PIERCE, Esq., who, having faithfully served his generation both in church and military station, fell asleep, April ye 22d, 1704, aged 60 years.

"Here lies interred a soul indeed,
Whom few or none excelled;
In grace if any him exceed,
He'll be unparalleled."

JOHN PIKE seems to have become the prominent man of the town immediately after the settlement. He, as well as the Pierces, Bishops, Jaques, and Marches,—was from Newbury in Massachusetts of which he was one of the first settlers, in 1635. He returned thither in April, 1671, for a limited time with the view of disposing of the property belonging to himself and son.[11] He had previously been elected President of Woodbridge, and in that year (1671) was chosen to be one of Governor Carteret's council. After 1675, when he was ap-

[11] He filled several offices, and was an active citizen of Newbury. On one occasion, in May, 1638, it is recorded that "John Pike shall pay two shillings and six pence for departing from the [town] meeting without leave and contemptuously."—*Coffin's History of Newbury*.

pointed "Captain" of the militia, he was uniformly distinguished by that title.

His lands, which are described as lying "west of Strawberry Hill, alias the Sheep Common,[12] were granted to him at a meeting of the associates, December 9th, 1667, and they were confirmed to him by the Governor, in February following.

On the 30th June, 1685, he married Elizabeth Fitz Randolph, of Piscataway, and died in January, 1688-9, leaving the following children; all of them, it is thought, by a previous wife:

John, who filled at different times various offices, and died August 13th, 1714, aged 75. His gravestone is yet standing in the Woodbridge Presbyterian Cemetery. He married Feb. 2d, 1675, Elizabeth Stout, of Middletown, and left several children.

Thomas, who received as a part of his legacy from his father a "half right in my book, writ by David Dickson:"— some indication of a scarcity of literature in those days.[13] He was three times married. His first

[12] A triangular piece of ground set apart for a sheep-common in September, 1669, including a hill on the road to Amboy. Under the influence of progressive improvement the hill, like many other old landmarks, has nearly vanished. The writer remembers it with its naked summit for many years crowned with an old school-house which, like Ichabod Crane's, had numerous posts and sticks against doors and windows impeding egress, but offering no special hindrance to admission.

[13] This is presumed to have been Dickson's "Therapeutica Sacra." On the 25th July, 1661, he applied to the Privy Council of Scotland for their license and privilege to print it, now translated into English by himself. The Council appointed Mr. Andrew Fairford to revise it, and report if it was fit to be reprinted. "Now indeed the world was changed in Scotland," says old Wodrow—"when Mr. Fairford is pitched upon to revise Mr. David Dickson, professor of divinity, his books," (I. p. 244.) This divine was one of the presbytery of Edinburgh, and "outed" for not conforming, but died in 1662. The following year, the application to the Council was renewed by his son, and it being made evident that "that excellent book. is upon a subject the managers needed not be afraid of, and did not in the least concern politics, or their government in church and state, but was entirely calculated for the promoting of real godliness and practical religion, and hath been singularly useful unto thousands,"—it was ordered, on Oct. 13th. 1663, "The Lords of Council do hereby licentiate and give warrant to the printing of a book called Therapeutica Sacra, translated out of Latin into English by Mr. David Dickson." (Wodrow, &c. I. p. 376.) The copy in the possession of the Pikes was probably one brought to Woodbridge by the unfortunate immigrants of 1685. The scarcity of books was not confined to the Pike family: in Joshua Pierce's inventory, (1672,) amounting to 131*l*. 3*s*., "books and other small things," were valued at only 30 shillings; Stephen Kent's, (1679,) contained "one great bible and another book,"—and most others do not mention books at all. The Rev. Seth Fletcher's, of Elizabethtown, (1682,) was a notable exception, his estate was valued at 559*l*. 5*s*. 8*d*., of which his books formed the considerable item of 175*l*. 4*s*. 4*d*.

wife, Elizabeth Parker, he married, Jan. 25th, 1686. She died September 12th, 1688, and on August 14th, 1689, he married Hester Bunn, by whom he had children, and she dying in 1694, he married Mary Philips, June 30th, 1699.

Joseph, who was killed by Indians, at Haverhill, Mass., September 4th, 1694.

Hannah, who married Obadiah Ayres, and died May 31st, 1689.

Ruth, who married Abraham Tappan, Nov. 9th, 1670. There is a document on record dated April 9th, 1678, which warrants a supposition that Tappan was not always sane. He agrees that his wife shall return to her father's house with her children, taking with her such articles as she and her father may deem necessary in consequence of the extremity of her distressed condition in respecto f sicknesses and illnesses, and on the 14th the witnesses appear before the Secretary of the Province and testify that Tappan was then "in his senses." [14] Domestic difficulties led to their separation for some time, but in June, 1687, having agreed again to live together, Captain Pike bestowed upon them a tract of land.[15] They had several children. Tappan returned to Newbury, and died there, in 1704.[16] The name in the Records is, at first, given as Toppan.

There were two other daughters, *Mary* and *Sarah*, and one son, *Samuel;* but it is presumed they did not survive their father.

Captain Pike died with his "fair fame" impaired through calumnious assaults, the effect of which the General Assembly by two solemn acts, at two different times, subsequently endeavored to counteract.

In September, 1684, he and his son John were convicted of felony in consequence of some goods being found secreted in their house, and under this imputation the father died. The good that men do is "oft interred with their bones" 'tis said, and it seems that the remembrance of all that Captain Pike had done for the infant settlement and province availed little towards rescuing his name from the obloquy thus cast upon it. Ten years afterwards, in 1694, the matter was brought to the notice of the Assembly, and it was enacted that "the said John Pike [the son] together with the family aforesaid be restored to their former good name, and to all other immunities, equal with any of their majesties' liege people, as if never any such thing had been,"—and they pronounced it lawful for John Pike or his family to commence an action for

[14] E. J. Records II. Lib. 1, p. 141.

[15] Ibid. V. D. p. 32. The Captain in his will also mentions his son-in-law, Obadiah Ayres, and Richard Worth—the former receiving *six pence* and the latter *one shilling*.

[16] A copy of his will is in my possession. He left all his property to a brother, John Tappan, he having been at great charge and expense in keeping him in his old age, and a small legacy to a son of his wife.

defamation of character against any one "reproaching or scandalizing them." This was still insufficient to bridle the tongues of Rumor, and in 1698, it was enacted that whoever should defame the family "directly or indirectly" or by implication, by words, speeches, reports, libels, revilings, or any other manner or way whatsoever, by reason, cause, or occasion of the said judgment,"—should be liable to a prosecution at the instance of any of the posterity of the said Captain John Pike and his son. These acts, it is stated, were passed only after "diligent search and inquiry by evidence and clear proof" presented to the Assembly.[17] They inculcate a useful lesson—that it is much more easy to inflict a wound on that sensitive portion of man's nature—his character—than it is to cure one.

The graves of John Pike, who died February 1st, 1761, aged 43;—Joseph Pike, who died Feb. 16th, 1730, aged 36; —James Pike, who died, May 15th, 1761, aged 39;—another James, who died February 18th, 1759, aged 33;—great-grandchildren of the first John Pike;—Mary the wife of James, who died February 18th, 1757, aged 32; Zebulon Pike, son of John Pike, junr., who died February, 6th, 1763, aged 70;—and Nathaniel Pike, who died Sept. 22, 1766, aged 42;—are yet designated by stones in the Woodbridge Cemeteries. Major Zebulon Pike, of the revolutionary war, and his son, General Zebulon Montgomery Pike, who distinguished himself during the last war with Great Britain, were of this family.

Robert Dennis, another of the associates, was from Yarmouth, Massachusetts. On the 3d December, 1674, being "by the providence of God disabled from managing and carrying on his outward occasions," he transferred to his children, Jonathan, Joseph and Elizabeth, all his property (the real estate to the sons, and to the daughter "two cows, five yearlings, with all his moveables in the house"), on condition that they should allow himself and wife (Mary) a comfortable maintenance

[17] Grants and Concessions, pp. 339, 375.

"for meat and drink, washing, lodging and apparel" during their lives. [18]

It was probably owing to these infirmities of body that his name ceases to be mentioned in connection with any public office after 1675, or thereabout. For several years he was placed on the Committee for assessing the town rates, an indication that he enjoyed a full share of the confidence of his neighbors. There is no record of his death.

John and Samuel Dennis were probably brothers of Robert.

JOHN SMITH, "Wheelright"—so designated to distinguish him from John Smith, "Scotchman," another of the settlers—was honored, immediately after the organization of the town, with the post of Constable; was thence promoted to be a Deputy to the Assembly, an Assistant Judge, &c. The town meetings were at first held at his house, he acting as Moderator; and, from various other offices conferred upon him, appears to have been an esteemed citizen.[19]

There is no mention made in the records of his family. The Smiths, who subsequently became numerous in that vicinity, were probably descendants of Richard Smith whose name is mentioned not long after the settlement was made; but what connection there was between him and John, if any, is not known.

JOHN BISHOP, SENR., was a carpenter by trade. Like many of his associates, he held several prominent offices in the town, but is not mentioned in the records in a way to throw

[18] Another instance of this transfer of property by parents to their children occurred among the early settlers of Newark. In August, 1675, Jasper Crane transferred some lands to his two sons, *Azaria* and *Jasper*, "on condition," said the grant, "that my said two sons, their heirs and assigns shall keep and maintain us as long as we both or either of us shall live with all things convenient according to our condition and quality." As in neither case does a revocation of the grant appear, we may presume the conditions to have been faithfully fulfilled.

[19] "John Smith, *Scotchman*," had the compliment paid him in July, 1671, of being appointed "to size all half bushels by his own," all those selling or buying by any other measures until other provisions should be made by law, should be "accounted willing to buy or sell by unjust measures."

any light upon his character. He had married in Newbury (October, 1647), Rebecca, widow of Samuel Scullard, daughter of Richard Kent, by whom he had eight children, all born before his arrival at Woodbridge. He died in October, 1684.[20]

His sons, John, Jonathan and Noah, became freeholders and prominent citizens; and the latter left several children. There are no births, deaths or marriages, recorded relating to the others.

Henry Jaques, Senr., was also a carpenter.[21] He married in Newbury (October, 1648), Anna Knight, by whom he had several children, one of whom only (Henry, junior), it is thought, accompanied him to Woodbridge. The father, probably, returned to Newbury. He died in February, 1687.

The son, Henry, was born in July, 1649; he married Hannah ———, and two sons, John and Jonathan, appear to have survived him; the former of whom left children.

Hugh March, also a carpenter, does not appear to have filled any prominent position in the young community, and subsequently returned to Newbury; where in 1676 he commenced keeping an "ordinary," and continued to do so for several years. He died in 1693. His son George March was admitted a freeholder of Woodbridge in August, 1669, but he also returned to Newbury, married and left descendants. It has been generally thought that the Marsh family were descendants of Hugh March, the orthography of the name having become changed in the course of time; but such is not the fact, the two families were of different origin.[22]

[20] Coffin's History of Newbury. To this interesting work, and to the MSS. letters from Mr. Coffin, the author is indebted for many important items referring to the immigrants from Newbury.

[21] As such he in 1661 built a gallery and made for it "three payre of stayres and whatever else is requisite to compleate the said gallery," and also laid a floor "all over the meeting-house" in Newbury.

[22] In 1653, his wife, with two other good women of Newbury, was "prosecuted for wearing a silk hood and scarfe," but was discharged on proof that her husband was worth two hundred pounds.—*Coffin's History of Newbury.*

STEPHEN KENT is presumed to have been an old man on his arrival in the province. He was one of the earliest settlers of Newbury, and came to Woodbridge by way of Haverhill. He was married three times, his third wife being Eleanor Scadlock, widow of Wm. Scadlock, whom he married in May, 1662. He had several children, but only one of them, Stephen, seems to have accompanied him to New Jersey.

In 1674–5 he was chosen one of the Assistants of the Township Court—the only office with which the name of Kent seems to have been associated in the early years of the settlement. His son (born March, 1648) married Jane Scott, Dec. 25th, 1683, and the births of two children are recorded.

A portion of their lands lay on the Raritan, and the location is yet known as Kent's Neck.

SAMUEL MOORE, who for twenty years, from 1668 to 1688, held the office of Town Clerk, seems to have more completely severed his connection with Massachusetts than most of the other immigrants. He and his brother Matthew regarding New Jersey as their permanent abode from the time of their arrival, and leaving several children whose descendants "remain with us to this day."

Samuel's first wife was Hannah Plumer, but she having died in December, 1654, about eighteen months after marriage, he took for his second companion (Sept., 1656) Mary Ilsley, who accompanied him to Woodbridge, and the births of two children by her are recorded. It is probable he was married a third time (Dec., 1678), to Ann Jaques. He died May 27th, 1688.

MATTHEW MOORE married Sara Savory in March, 1662. They brought two children with them to the province, and three others are mentioned. He died in March, 1691.

[23] In 1652, while a resident of Haverhill, he was fined ten pounds for suffering five Indians to be drunk in his house.

John Cromwell, Samuel Hale, Jonathan Haynes, Obadiah Ayres, George Little, Robert Rogers, John Smyth, the Ilsleys and the Tappans were all Newbury men.[2] Haynes and Little did not remain in the province.

George Lockhart, "practitioner of physic," is mentioned in 1679 as residing in Woodbridge; and in 1683, then being in England, the proprietaries mention him as possessing, according to his own statement, "a considerable plantation in the province," and "desirous to have the Marshal's place;" he offering, in case they would grant him the commission and a lot of ten acres in "Perth town," to build them a prison and town house.[25]

It was left to Deputy-governor Lawrie to perfect this arrangement, or not, as he might think proper; and, although it is asserted by one historian[26] that he was appointed Marshal, there appears to be no reason for supposing it to have been done: there is no record of the commission or of the grant of ten acres, and it is certain that neither prison nor town house was built by him. A son, *Gawen*, is mentioned several years thereafter in the Woodbridge books as a resident, and the births of several children are recorded.

Peter Dessigny, another practitioner of physic, or "Chirurgeon," also resided at Woodbridge. He married Ann, widow of Robert Rogers, in August, 1685, and was yet living there in 1692. The birth of a daughter (Mary) is recorded in May, 1690—one of the same name having died previously.

Rev. Archibald Riddell. This zealous and pious preacher was brother to Sir John Riddell,[27] and, as has been before stated, cousin to the wife of George Scot, and a passenger

[24] Coffin's History of Newbury.

[25] Grants and Concessions, p 175.

[26] Wynne's British Empire in Ameca.

[27] Sir John was himself a sufferer from persecution, and a garrison was stationed at his house in 1675 more effectually to guard against the keeping of conventicles in the neighbor hood.—Wodrow II. p. 282, III. 470.

with them in the "Henry and Francis."[28] He and the Rev. Thomas Pattersone—who also intended emigration, but was subsequently induced to remain in Scotland—are described by the proprietaries as "two Persones who have been in Prisone in Scotland for Nonconformity and are greatly esteemed among the People who are of their Perswasions in Matters of Religion;" and, as they were willing to "transport themselves to East Jersey and settle there, which will be the Occasion of Inviting a great number to follow them," the necessary directions were given to have two hundred acres of land allotted to each immediately on their arrival, in such place as might best accommodate them, provided they built houses and continued their own or some other families therein for three years.[29] Although the name of Mr. Riddell appears among those of other preachers who had drawn upon them the attention of government by attending conventicles as early as 1674, yet the first serious proceedings against him seem to have been prompted by his connection in some way with the rising of Bothwell in 1679, the Privy Council ordering, on the 25th June, that he should be sought for, and offering a reward for his arrest. He was arrested in September by the laird of Graden, a relative of his wife, and sent to the tolbooth of Jedburgh, whence he was removed to the prison in Edinburgh.[30]

On the 1st October, and again on the 9th December, Mr. Riddell was called before the Committee for public affairs, and so conducted himself as evidently to secure the respect of his examiners, and to excite in them a disposition to extend towards him more than ordinary clemency. The authority of the civil magistrates—allegiance to the King and submission to the lords of the council, as well as to the Committee before whom he was arranged, were by him duly acknowledged." "My lord," he said to Lord Linlithgow, "I do own authority, as knowing that the same Lord Jesus who commanded us to fear God doth also command to honor the King; and as I judge it my duty to give God what is God's, so to give Cæsar what is Cæsar's"—but he would not clear himself from the

[28] See pages 26 and
[29] E. J. Records, A., p. 385.
[30] Wodrow I., pp. 114, 197; III., p. 196.

accusation of having preached in the fields, by taking an oath to that effect—oaths being "tender things and not rashly to be meddled with, or upon every occasion"—although declaring upon the word of a gentleman that he had not preached out of a house since the prohibition—neither would he engage to refrain from field preaching in future; "there is," said he, "a great difference betwixt the forbearance of an action, when inconvenient, and an engagement never to do such an action, not knowing what necessity there may be for such an action afterwards." On being reminded that the law construed an assemblage, when some of the hearers were out of doors, to be a field conventicle, and asked if such had been the case at any time when he had preached, he acknowledged that it had been; but, with an independence worthy of admiration, he told the committee, "poor people are so dogged and distressed, that preaching can hardly be had in ten miles of way; and when I am called to preach, and scarce a house can be had that will contain thirty or forty persons, and all the rest must be without, shall the people who come ten miles or more to hear sermons be thrust away as they come? Surely, if I be called to preach at all, I may not decline it in any case." * * * "I know not but he who has called me to preach this while bygone in houses, may, before I go out of the world, call me to preach upon tops of mountains, yea, *upon the seas;* and I dare not come under any engagements to disobey his calls."

Although his examiners were convinced of his moderation and loyalty, yet his refusal to enter into the engagements required caused him to be remitted to prison; and not being able, or willing, to give security "not to keep conventicles," he was kept in confinement until released on the application of the laird of Pitlochie, with the view of emigrating to New Jersey.[31]

[31] The whole of his interesting examination, from his own notes, is in Wodrow I., pp. 197–202. During this period, in April, 1681, he was allowed to visit his dying mother; and in the following June he was charged with having broken his confinement, keeping conventicles, and baptizing children, and, in consequence, the place of his imprisonment was changed—he being sent to the Bass.—*Wodrow* III., p. 264.

On board of the ill-fated "Henry and Francis" we are not permitted to follow him, save in imagination. But though there be no account extant of his own trials and sufferings, except that his wife is named among those who died, we cannot greatly err in considering him as the source of comfort and consolation to his afflicted fellow passengers: inspiring hope and confidence, while by precept and example he enforced that faith and patience of which they stood so much in need; and that thus called "to preach upon the seas," he was found the same unswerving disciple of his Master he had ever been upon the land.

It is thought that, besides his wife, four children accompanied him, who were spared to contribute to his happiness in his new home in Woodbridge, where his two hundred acres were allotted to him, and where also he purchased other lands.[32] The inhabitants were not slow to avail themselves of the opportunity afforded by his presence among them to secure the services of a minister of the Gospel so distinguished and well tried; for during the month following his arrival an arrangement was entered into with him,[33] and he probably retained the charge of the congregation until his return to Europe in 1689: for his native land possessed charms for him which New Jersey had not, and political changes having removed the obstacles to the enjoyment of life and liberty by the nonconformists within its borders, he determined to return to Scotland.

He set sail with a son ten years of age in June, 1689,[34] but was doomed to further trials and disappointments before arriving at the end of his voyage. Favorable weather attended him, but on the 2d August, when off the coast of England, the vessel was captured by a French man-of-war, and the passengers sent to the common jail of Rochefort, whence they were subsequently marched to Toulon, chained two and two by their arms, and, at first, each ten pair tied to a rope, but this

[32] E. J. Records, D., p. 57.

[33] Woodbridge Town Book. He also received a call to Long Island, which he declined.—*Wodrow* IV., 335.

[34] Probably on board the same vessel with Governor Andrew Hamilton. See East Jersey, &c., pp. 123, 129.

being found an impediment to their travelling was abandoned after the second day. Mr. Riddell was chained to his son, whose slender frame gave their captors no little trouble, three different chains having to be forged before one was got small enough to confine his wrists.

They were six weeks on the way to Toulon, the hardships of the journey causing the death of many, and on their arrival were consigned to the hold of an old hulk in the harbor ; but after the detention of a month Mr. Riddell and his son, with others, were taken back again to Rochefort, and thence to Denain, near St. Malo, where for more than a year they were kept prisoners in a vault of an old castle. At last, after having been prisoners nearly two years, they were exchanged for two Romish priests, and allowed to return to Scotland.[35] Mr. Riddell settled at Kirkaldie, but of his subsequent career I am ignorant.[36]

A daughter of Mr. Riddell (Janet) was married January 26th, 1686, shortly after their arrival in the province, to JAMES DUNDAS, who may have been a fellow passenger. He was the son of Sir James Dundas, of Armestown, and became a resident of Perth Amboy, his house lot being located on Smith street. He was selected by William Dockwra in 1688 for one of his deputy Receivers-General, but would not accept the office ; however, on being appointed by the Proprietaries in January, 1694, Receiver-General, he consented to serve, and held the office till his death. He was appointed Administrator on Lord Neil Campbell's estate in January, 1693, and was a Commissioner of the Court of Small Causes for Amboy from May 4th, 1696, to the close of 1698, when he died.

Mrs. Dundas survived her husband, and administered on his estate, but what became of her or of their children, if they had any, does not appear. It is probable that she or they returned to Scotland, together with the other children of Mr. Riddell, as Wodrow states that the losses of that worthy man

[35] Wodrow, IV., p. 335.

[36] In 1700 he sold his Woodbridge lands to Thomas Gordon, and in the deed is called "Minister of the Gospel at Kirkaldie, in the county of Fife, Scotland."

"were all made up, and he and his four children were in better circumstances than if he had conformed to prelacy." [37]

Robert McLellan, "of Barmagechan in Kirkcudbrightshire," was a passenger in Scot's vessel. He suffered greatly from sickness on the voyage, and was so reduced that he was brought on shore in the arms of men. His three children who were with him also escaped the pestilence. The son of Presbyterian parents, and brought up in the principles of the church of Scotland, he, with others of his parish, disowned the episcopal clergyman placed there "as neither called of God nor invited by them." Fined heavily for his nonconformity, and burdened with the keeping of parties of soldiers billeted upon him, his property destroyed, and his personal liberty endangered, he engaged in the Pentland rising, and on being defeated fled to England, and resided there quietly for four years. The forfeiture of his estate which ensued was compounded for two thousand merks, and he ventured to return to his own house; but the constant oppression under which he suffered from those in authority induced him to engage in the Bothwell affair, which led to a second flight to England, and a second forfeiture.

He was seized in England in 1684, and sent, with others, a prisoner to Dumfries, thence to Leith and Edinburgh, and finally to Dunottar, and into banishment: during most of this time being in irons.

Mr. McLellan bought a plantation in Woodbridge, and resided there until June, 1689, having for an inmate with his family the Reverend Mr. Riddell. They sailed for Europe together, and Mr. McLellan participated in all the hardships which have been referred to, growing out of their capture by the French. He had one son with him (what became of the other two children I have not learned), and both being sick, they were separated from Mr. Riddell at Toulon, remaining until an exchange of prisoners took place. Having been put on board of a vessel for Genoa, he sailed thence for Cadiz, where they embarked

[37] IV., p. 335.

for Amsterdam, was wrecked on the coast of Ireland, subjected to much ill-treatment from the Irish, and eventually reached his own house in Scotland on the last day of October, 1691. His whole career was one of romantic interest. Much distress would he have avoided had he been contented with his American home, and probably a greater degree of prosperity and happiness secured, for Wodrow, to whose book I am indebted for these items respecting him, closes his narrative with the remark that, "after all, this excellent person had no reparation after the Revolution, only he possessed his own lands again."[38]

The Hude Family. Among the passengers in the "Henry and Francis" who were induced to regard America as their future home, was Adam Hood, or Hude, as the name was spelt by himself. Where he at first established himself does not appear, but in June, 1686, we find him among the others brought before the Court of Common Right at the instance of Captain Hutton, and in 1695 he resided on Staten Island. During that year he purchased some land in Woodbridge, removed thither, and built a farm house for his own residence, which, in an altered condition, is yet standing about a mile north of the church on the road to Rahway.

He is styled in the old records "weaver," but in 1718 he was appointed one of the Judges of the Court of Common Pleas for Middlesex, soon became the Presiding Judge, and still acted in that capacity as late as 1733—the records of the Court exhibiting a marked regularity in his attendance upon its sittings. At one time he was also Master of Chancery and a Member of the Provincial Assembly. Nothing is known of his character, but he seems to have enjoyed in a great degree the confidence of his fellow citizens.

The tombstone of himself and wife are yet to be seen in the Presbyterian cemetery at Woodbridge. The latter bearing the following inscription:—

[38] Wodrow, IV., pp. 334-336.

"Here Lyes ye Body of Mrs Marion Hude, Wife of Adam Hude Esqr For ye Spase of 46 years dearly beloved in Life and lamented in death. She lived a Patern of Piety, Patience, meekness and affability, and after she had served her generation in ye love and fear of God in ye 71 year of her Age fell asleep in Jesus Nov. ye 30, 1732."

Mr. Hude's death occurred on the 17th June, 1746, in his 85th year—having for many years been a communicant in the Presbyterian church. Two sons and one daughter survived the parents: [39]

Of ROBERT little is known. He was born Sept. 5th, 1691; was a member of the Assembly in 1740–42, and in April of the latter year was appointed a Judge of Middlesex Pleas. He resided in New Brunswick, and died January 30th, 1748–9. The other son, JAMES, was a gentleman of considerable note in New Brunswick, much respected and esteemed. He was a merchant there in 1726; was appointed one of the Judges of the Pleas in 1732, and continued in the exercise of his duties as such till 1743. He was elected a member of the Assembly in 1738; on the accession of Governor Morris, in 1745, was taken into the Council, continued his consistent supporter throughout his administration, and was one of his attendants to the grave. He was also a member of subsequent Councils, a Master in Chancery, &c. He had several children:—

James died young.

Robert lived and died in New Brunswick, marrying just before his death.

Ann married Ravaud Kearny, and is noticed elsewhere.

Susan married Mr. Wm. Neilson of New York, who left children.

Mary married a Mr. Livingston of New York.

Catherine married Cornelius Lowe of New Brunswick. A daughter of theirs married Mr. Jacob R. Hardenbergh, and another Mr. Hugh Wallace of New York.

One daughter died young and unmarried.

The following obituary notice of Mr. Hude is from the New York Mercury of Nov. 8th, 1762:—

"On Monday last (Nov. 1st) between the hours of eleven and twelve in the forenoon, departed this life in an advanced age, after a long and tedious indisposition, the Hon. Colonel James Hude, of New Brunswick, Esq., a gentleman who, for his great probity, justice, affability, moral and political virtues, was universally esteemed and beloved by those who knew him. He passed through almost all the honorable offices and employments in the government where he lived, as well as those in the voice of the people. At the time of his death he was one of His Majesty's Council, Mayor of the Corporation of New Brunswick, &c., &c. His death is not only an irreparable loss to the poor, who had at all times free access to his person, and his advice and assistance without fee or reward, but to the public is a subject of great regret. He was a most tender and loving husband, an indulgent father and kind master. He has left a disconsolate and weeping widow and children. 'Blessed are the dead, &c.'"

---

[39] One son, John, died an infant in 1687, and one daughter, Agnes, was born October, 1689.

The daughter of Adam Hude (Mary) was the wife of one of the numerous family of Bloomfield, in Woodbridge, and died July 21, 1773, aged 77.

James Parker was the son of Samuel Parker of Woodbridge, and was born in that town in 1714. In 1725 he was apprenticed to Wm. Bradford, the first printer in New York, who in that year commenced the publication of the "New York Gazette." From some cause not now known, Parker ran away from his employer in May, 1733, and was advertised in the Gazette of the 21st of that month; but we find him again in New York, in good credit, and at the head of an establishment himself in less than nine years thereafter; fostering no ill-will towards Bradford, to whom, at his death in 1752,[40] he gives an excellent character in an editorial article published in his paper.

The New York Gazette having been discontinued by Bradford, it was "revived in the Weekly Post Boy," by Mr. Parker, in 1742–3. Where he had resided previously is not known. This weekly sheet of *large foolscap* "containing the freshest advices, foreign and domestic," advertisements, &c., issued from his press for many years, and is now a most valuable source of original information for the antiquary and historian.

In 1751 Mr. Parker established the first press in New Jersey, at Woodbridge, and from time to time printed the proceedings of the Legislature and other official documents. In January, 1753, he commenced a partnership with William Weyman, which continued until January, 1759, he residing most of the time in Woodbridge, attending to the interests of the press there, which he conducted on his own account: but an extended notice of Mr. Parker's business connections cannot be given here.

In 1752 the "Independent Reflector," edited by William Livingston—afterward Governor of New Jersey—and others,

[40] Bradford's headstone may be seen in Trinity Church-yard, New York. He was 92 years of age, "quite worn out with old age and labor when he left this mortal state."

was printed by Parker and Weyman, but the fear of men in authority, whose ire might be excited by its independent character, led the former to decline the responsibility of its continued publication. Although he remained connected with the presses in New York he resided principally at Woodbridge, where, in 1758, he printed the New American Magazine, edited by Samuel Nevill, elsewhere mentioned. In 1755 a partnership with John Holt (who subsequently removed to New York and attended to the business there), led to the establishment of a press at New Haven, from which the "Connecticut Gazette," the *first* newspaper in that province, was issued.

In 1761 he printed the 2d volume of Nevill's compilation of the Laws of New Jersey,[41] the imprint being "Woodbridge in New Jersey. Printed by James Parker, Printer to the King's most Excellent Majesty, for the Province." In 1762 the press in New York was leased to Holt, but Mr. Parker resumed it in 1766, in connection with his son (Samuel F.), and it was carried on by them until a few months before the death of the father, in 1770. In 1764 Mr. Parker compiled and printed a "Conductor Generalis" for Justices of the Peace, he then holding that office in Middlesex County, and the following year *moved his press from Woodbridge to Burlington for the accommodation of the author of the History of New Jersey (Smith)*, but on the completion of the work it was returned to the former place.

Twice was Mr. Parker brought before the Assembly of New York for printing matter reflecting upon some of the "pillars of the State," and obliged to give up the authors, to pay fines, be confined, &c., but, although he may have been rendered more cautious, it is doubtful if his sentiments in favor of the rights of the people were changed by such logic. It would seem that he was ever an opponent to the oppression of the "higher powers," which in his day was too apt to be exercised.

[41] Thomas, in his History of Printing, states that he printed these laws in 1752; the first volume was given to the public in that year, but all the copies the writer has seen bear the imprint of "Wm. Bradford, Printer to the King's Most Excellent Majesty, &c."

He died July 2d, 1770. He had been long an invalid and obliged to retire from business, in a great measure, for a considerable time before his death, which occurred at Burlington while residing there for the benefit of his health.

He was a correct and neat printer, understanding his business perfectly, and at his death his contemporaries gave him credit for possessing a sound judgment and extensive knowledge, for industrious habits, integrity, benevolence of heart and fairness of character. His career was certainly one of great and extensive usefulness. Among other stations which he held to the satisfaction of his neighbors was that of Lay-reader to the Episcopal Congregation in Woodbridge, officiating several years on those Sundays when the Rev. Mr. Chandler of Elizabethtown was prevented from visiting the town by engagements elsewhere.

In a letter to the Secretary of the Society for the Propagation of the Gospel, dated Sept. 22d, 1764, he says:—

> "It pleased Providence to have given me ability to perform the service. I freely undertook it, and as I supposed to the general satisfaction of the congregation. I have continued it as well as my poor ability would permit to the present time, and I can say for myself it has been a real pleasure to me to see any of my endeavors acceptable or any way apparently useful in propagating true religion and piety. I neither wish nor hope for any other reward in this life, as it will be more than a compensation if I meet with any in the next—for though I can trust to the promises of the blessed Jesus, yet I at best fall far short of my duty. It hath pleased God to gather and increase the Church here a little, though the chief of us being old can't hope long to continue: notwithstanding our children, we hope, are growing up in the same path."

Mr. Parker was for some years Postmaster in New York, performing its duties while carrying on his business in that city, which of itself, one would think, would have been sufficient to engross all his time—for no one, unacquainted with the avocations of a printer in those days, can form an idea of the time which was devoted to the service of his customers. If a man had a horse or cow to sell, a house to let, a vessel to freight, a servant to hire, &c., &c., he referred to the printer, and it is amusing to look over the columns of the Post Boy and see the strange variety of employments, pursuits, wants and notices to which Mr. Parker was made a party. At the time of his death he was Comptroller and Secretary of the Post-Office for the Northern District of the British Colonies, and held several local offices.

Great respect was manifested towards his remains on their way from Burlington to Woodbridge for burial. The New York Journal of July 5, 1770, states that "his remains were attended for five miles out of Burlington by a considerable number of gentlemen of that place, and at Amboy met by a like number who attended the corpse to Woodbridge, where a numerous congregation assembled at his house, and about 6 o'clock he was interred near his parents, in the meeting-house yard. The service was performed by the Rev. Mr. Preston, Minister of the Church at Amboy."

The headstone of the father is yet standing, but there is nothing to designate the spot where the remains of the First Printer in New Jersey were deposited. Too often they to whom communities are indebted, as in the present instance, for public services and the exhibition of private virtues, sleep unhonored, while the marble and the epitaph commemorate the drone and the profligate.

Samuel F. Parker inherited the press and other apparatus of his father, but did not continue the business: he leased the establishment in New York and sold that in Woodbridge soon after his father's death. Some of his descendants are believed to be still in the vicinity of Woodbridge.

James Parker had one daughter, *Janet,* who became the wife of Gunning Bedford, Governor of Delaware, in 1796.

I am indebted to Thomas' History of Printing for many of these facts. The most light, however, is thrown upon Mr. Parker's character by his own newspapers and those of his contemporaries.

TOWN AFFAIRS.

The affairs of the town were managed, as in New England generally, at town meetings, called, at first, by personal notice to every freeholder by the Constable, or some person specially authorized, and afterward by a written notice placed on the meeting-house door. There were committees or townsmen appointed to look after the interests of the community on ordinary occasions, but they do not appear to have been chosen at first at any regular times. The other officers of the township, however, were always elected annually,[42] and the administration of the public affairs generally conformed to the mode prescribed by the General Assembly or to the established customs of the other settlements.

In several of their local regulations they set a good example to their neighbors, and in some they might be followed even by the legislators of the present day. As an indication of the spirit which animated the community the following document is given from the records :—

"Corporation of Woodbridge, April ye 17th, 1695.

"The ingadgement of all freeholders by irigenall rites and of all freemen which have been, are, or shall be so admitted in this town and Corporation.

Viz., As a good and usfull member of this intire body in gouerment and guidance I will be subject to all the Lawfull and Regguler motions thereof, And to ye utmost of my Skill and abillity I will move and act with it so as may most directly tend to its peace and prosperity. Its nakedness I will cover, its secrets I will not discouer, but its weakness I will support; And finally in word and deed according to abillity and its occasions att all times I will indeavor to prevent the euill and to promote ye good and just interest of this body; and each member thereof, on penielty of corection or expulsion as default may require. In testimony hereof wee under writter have subscribed our names."

There are only thirty-four signatures appended to this document, from which it is presumed not to have been generally agreed to.

In this year it was found necessary to make it obligatory upon all to attend the town meeting ; and in January, 1699,

[42] January 1st, 1687-8, was Sunday, but the usual meeting was held, but no business transacted, save the election of Deputies to the Assembly.

the fine for non-attendance was fixed at ninepence for every omission, and upon refusal to pay "every delinquent to be *turned out of the meeting-house* until he complies;" which, in some communities, would not have been considered a very grievous punishment.

In 1671 some apprehensions were entertained respecting the Indians, and a rate was levied to provide for an expedition against them: ten pounds of powder and twenty pounds of lead being the total quantity of war material required:—but there is no account given of the prosecution of the enterprise, or of any actual danger incurred.

In September, 1675, in accordance with an order of the Governor and Council, it was resolved to fortify the prison forthwith, by stockades of a half or whole tree, of "nine feet long at least," in the expectation of an attack from the natives, with the view of providing a place of safety for the women and children—but it was never occupied.

In April, 1690, a ranger of the woods was appointed to join similar persons from other neighboring towns, "in order" —using the words of the record—to prevent a danger (before it comes to our homes) threatened by the French and Indians." He was to be paid twenty shillings per week, and as "Mr. Lyon" was subsequently paid £1 5*s.*, "for his charges with the Indians" this year, the duty could not have been long performed. These are the only occurrences on record intimating the existence of any apprehended difficulty with the natives.

PRESBYTERIAN CONGREGATION.

The settlers of New Jersey from New England, accustomed to a government in which their civil and religious duties were closely commingled, naturally gave their early attention to the establishment of ministers in all their communities. The people of Woodbridge were not exceptions, although great difficulty seems to have been experienced in giving permanency to the residence among them of those called to the town.

The first movement towards obtaining the services of a

clergyman was on the 8th June, 1669, when a Committee was appointed to go to Newark, "as messengers from the town, to declare to Mr. Pierson, junior, that the inhabitants were all willing and desirous that he would be pleased to come up to them and help them in the work of the ministry;" and anticipating an acceptance, Robert Dennis was appointed to entertain him with "meat, drink and lodgings;" and when on the west side of the creek—called in the records Papiack creek—similar accommodations were to be afforded by John Smith the Constable.

The application to Mr. Pierson was, however, not favorably considered by him. The advanced age of his father, who was the Pastor of the Newark Congregation, rendered the services of an assistant necessary, and measures were in progress to secure the son in that capacity. The application from Woodbridge probably brought the matter to a conclusion, as the ensuing month Mr. Pierson was regularly employed as an assistant minister. This was a great disappointment to the Woodbridge people, and we find them the next year again exerting themselves to obtain a supply. Mr. Peck of Elizabethtown was, in July, 1670, to be applied to, or the committee, at their discretion, was to procure Mr. Samuel Treat "to preach six or seven months." On the 6th November a letter from Mr. Treat was laid before the town meeting, and twenty one pounds sterling was voted to that gentleman "for six months preaching." There is a tradition that he officiated for a while at that time, but he did not accept the invitation to become permanently settled, and a second application, made to him in January, 1672, was attended with no better success.

No further proceedings were had on the subject until July 2d, 1674, when the town resolved to agree with Mr. Benjamin Salsbury "to serve as Minister for the space of ——— months on trial." The agreement was entered into, but on the 27th Oct. the connection was thus summarily broken:—

"At a general town meeting it was passed by vote that the inhabitants of this town of Woodbridge are determined to use such means as to them shall seem meet to obtain a minister that may be suitable for them, and that *Mr. Benjamin Salsbury may be pleased to take notice that when his quarter's time is out he is free from any engagement from this town*, *that he may be at liberty to dispose of himself as he shall see good*, and Mr. Robert Dennis, Mr. John Bishop, Senr., and Mr. Samuel Dennis do deliver this to Mr. Salsbury as the mind of the town."

At this meeting a committee was appointed to agree with carpenters for erecting "a meeting-house 30 feet square and 15, 16 or 17 feet between joints;" and on 30th November a table, room, and other necessaries were directed to be provided for the comfortable entertainment of a minister when he should come on trial in the spring ensuing.

But where was a minister to be obtained? Five years had elapsed since their first endeavors to secure "help in the work of the ministry," but with the exception of the brief *season of trial* under poor Mr. Salsbury they had been without regular religious services. At this time, however, Samuel Dennis was selected to go North to procure a clergyman; and to defray his expenses, three thousand pipe staves were furnished by Robert Dennis, John Bloomfield and John Pike, junior—whether gratuitously or not is uncertain from the record—and placed in charge of the messenger, to be disposed of to the best advantage; he to account to the town for the proceeds, after deducting his expenses and reasonable wages while absent. There is nothing to be found indicative of a favorable result to this expedition.

In May following (1675) negotiations were resumed with "Mr. Jeremiah Peck"—the same, it is supposed, who declined their overtures in 1670. Again was the proposition unsuccessful, and another year passed away with the vacancy unsupplied, and apparently without farther efforts on the part of the inhabitants. In April, 1676, an application was directed to be made to Messrs. Richard Ball (or Hall) Senior and Junior, residing, it is presumed, in New England; but neither of these accepting, in January following (1677) a definite call was made to Mr. Ezekiel Fogg: he being assured for his encouragement the privileges of a freeholder and fifty pounds a year "to be paid in meat, peas, pork and (not above one fourth part in) Indian Corn, and beef at country prices." As the records contain no entries between this date and June, 1679, we have no certain information of the rejection of this liberal offer, but as the name of Fogg does not appear in the list of freeholders it is supposed to have fared no better than the offers previously made to others.

Though discouraged, the settlers were not in despair—disappointed in every quarter in America, they next turned their eyes towards England, and raised their voices for help to "Dr. Burns and Mr. Richard Baxter." Letters were addressed to those divines in July, 1679, desiring them to be instrumental in getting a minister for them, and "Captain Bound," an early trader between the two continents, was requested to deliver the letters and to aid, if necessary, in securing him a passage to America. Success at last rewarded these or similar exertions, for in September, 1680, Mr. John Allen commenced preaching among them, and fifty pounds was granted to him, and in November following voluntary subscriptions were directed to be taken for his permanent support. The meeting-house which it was resolved to build in October, 1674, was, by the 27th May, 1675, raised, and the frame approved of by the town, although *not* thirty feet square as originally contemplated; and a Committee was appointed to make the necessary arrangements to have it shingled and clap-boarded, and a floor laid; but the want of a minister seems to have prevented the observance of despatch in the complete execution of these plans, and it was not until December, 1680, or January, 1681, after Mr. Allen's arrival, that the house was actually floored. In October following it was directed to be plastered, "all but the South side, over the clapboards." In June, 1682, the process of completion was continued by "lathing and *daubing*" the building substantially within "as high as the plate beams;" and the "daubing" appears to have been made the employment of all in the town having suitable tools. Nails and hinges for two doors, yet wanting, were also provided, and a lock for the third. These, for the time, finished the additions to the edifice.

On the 1st January, 1681, the following entry appears on the records: "We the freeholders and inhabitants of Woodbridge having sent to England to have an honest, able, godly minister to Come over to vs to preach the word of God sinserly and faithfully—And Mr. John Alin by the providence of God being for that End Come amongst vs, and we having had Sum Experience of his good Abilities: are willing and doe hereby make Choise of him to be our Minister and desire to put ourselfs under his ministry According to the Rules of the gospel."

The satisfaction thus expressed was further manifested by admitting Mr. Allen, on 13th February, as a freeholder, and by granting him a house lot of ten acres; and, in September, 1682, a request was directed to be presented to the Governor and Council to induct him formally as their minister, in order that all the immunities of the station might devolve upon him.

From this time until January, 1686, we find no allusion to Mr. Allen, or the meeting house, but at the annual gathering of the freeholders in that month, a committee was appointed to negotiate with Mr. Archibald Riddell [43] to preach for them, which argues a dissolution of the connection between the town and Mr. Allen, although the name of that gentlemen appears in the records subsequently as still a resident. Mr. Riddell probably officiated until he left the country, in 1689; and not until November, 1692, do we find the employment of another referred to. On the first of that month, a committee was appointed "to write for a minister," and in March, 1694, a messenger was despatched to New England to obtain one in the person of Ephraim Andrews, who consented to go "provided the town doe furnish him with money sufficient for his jorney, and a hors to ride on." Ten pounds were raised for the purpose.

These measures, however, do not appear to have been successful, and not until October, 1695, do we find the town supplied. Mr. Samuel Shepard then appears as their minister at a salary of fifty pounds, and in May following, thirty acres of land, and a house were granted to him, provided he should return from New England, whither he was about to go—possibly for his family,— and permanently settle among them;

[43] See page 370.

conditions which he complied with.[44] The spiritual affairs of the town seem to have prospered under Mr. Shepard's care ;— if we may judge from improvements made in the temporalities, —the meeting-house galleries, which in May, 1686, were directed to be constructed, were finished—in 1697, sixty pounds were allowed the minister instead of fifty, he having been "at the charge of his diet the year past,"—and in July, 1698, the walls of the meeting-house were to be whitewashed, and a new pulpit built "forthwith."

In March, 1696, it is recorded that Wm. Webster "pretending that it was contrary to his conscience to pay any thing towards ye maintenance of a minister," Capt. John Bishop agreed to pay for him as long as he shall live. Kind Capt. Bishop was far more considerate of the spiritual interests of Wm. Webster, than of the temporal interests of Mr. Shepard, for we find the following year that the successful pleading of Webster led others to try a similar procedure, and the town found it necessary to ordain, that those refusing to pay Mr. S.'s rate, should have a distraining warrant issued against them. This may have checked the evil, but in February, 1670, it was found necessary to change the mode of raising Mr. Shepard's salary, making it depend upon voluntary subscriptions ; it having been previously provided for in the common rate levied for the general purposes of the town. At this time too, a committee was appointed to settle all differences with their "dissenting neighbors, the Quakers," in reference to their refusal to contribute towards the support of "the publique ministry."

More than five years had elapsed since Mr. Shepard had entered upon his ministerial functions in Woodbridge, and on April 10th, 1701, a committee were directed to confer with him upon the propriety of his being "ordained" as the minister of the town. What necessity existed for this I do not know, but, apparently to the surprise and regret of the people, difficulties arose in consequence, which, increased by the per-

[44] He was the son of Rev. Samuel Shepard of Rowley, Mass., and graduated at Harvard College in 1685.—*MS. Letter of Mr. L. M. Boltwood.*

25

tinacity with which female influence and prejudices will be sometimes exercised—resulted in Mr. Shepard's separation from the congregation.

The committee appointed to confer with their pastor, reported on the 24th, June, "that his wife is so advers to his Setling here, that tho he is otherwise willing to be ordained, he cannot admit of ordination to setle as a minister in this town; and it being moved to him, that his wife upon second thoughts might be persuaded, Mr. Shepard replyed, there is no hope of my wife's complyance with my setling here, and therefore I would advise you to look out for another." Unwilling to relinquish the benefits of his ministry, another committee were authorized to negotiate farther with him, but a month later (July 23d) they too reported that "his wife is utterly adverse to his setling here, and he concludes shee will so remaine if we should still wait longer for a change of her mind; and therefore adviseth us to have no farther dependence on him." Whereupon the necessary steps were taken to dissolve the connection and obtain another, but for many years, there is no indication on the records of their being supplied. How long Mr. Shepard remained an inhabitant is not known, but in January, 1702, he was requested to preach for the town until another minister should be obtained. He died in the year 1722 or 1723.

In 1707, the Rev. Nathaniel Wade was ordained and installed the Pastor of the congregation; [45] and the following entries in the Records of the Church in Mr. Wade's own writing are before me.

"January 29th, 1707–8. Was gathered the Church of Christ, in Woodbridge by Nath. Wade, Pastor. Present there were as Messengers, two from ye Church of Newark, and one from the Church of Elizabethtown; Theophilus Pierson, Jonahs Wood, Benjamin Price. The foundation of ye Church was laid first upon three persons who had been Communicants in other churches, viz: Sam'l Hail, John Pike, and Noah Bishop. The names of the church are as follows:

---

[45] "A short History" (MS.) in the Church Records states, that the Sacrament of the Lord's Supper was first administered by Mr. Wade, but this is a mistake—other errors are also contained in that history.

Admitted.		
January 29, 1707–8,	Sam'l Hail, Assistant.	Stephen Tuttle.
	John Pike, Assistant.	John Foard.
	Noah Bishop, Assistant.	
February 28, 1707-8,	Thomas Pike.	Richard Skiner, Assistant.
	John Ayers.	Joseph Gray.
June 6, 1708,	Lidea Bishop.	Francis Skiner.
June 20, 1708,	Mathew Fors.	
August 15, 1708,	Joseph Thorp.	Elizabeth Britton.
	Daniel Britton.	Sarah Fors.
	Richard Cutter.	Elizabeth Gray.
	Sarah Pike.	Lidea Pangborn.
August 20, 1708,	Sarah Holland.	Mark Pike.
	John Ilsley.	Mary Stilwell.
	John Jaques.	Susannah Jaques.
	John Skiner.	Desire Walker.
	Nath'l Pike.	Mehitable Butler.
	Mary Groves.	Hannah Freeman.
	Ann Skiner.	Mary Wade.
	Elizabeth Ilsley.	Ester Blumfield.
	Mary Cutter.	John Chaplin.
Oct. 31, 1708,	Benjamin Jones.	Daniel Dane.
	John Robinson.	Mary Curtis.
	Eliz'th Thorp.	Phebe Ayers.
	Nat'l Dunham.	
Dec. 26, 1708,	Mary Ayers.	Sarah Conger.
January 2, 1708–9,	William Sharp.	Mary Sharp.
Feb'y 27, 1708–9	Moses Ralph.	Hope Blumfield.
May 12, 1709,	John Conger.	Edward Wilkinson.
	Thomas Collier.	Mary Ralph.
	Mary Conger.	Sam'l Butler.
	Anna Thorp.	
June 26, 1709,	John Dille.	Joanna Pangborn.
	Eliza'th Foard.	Ruth Dille.
	Hannah Crowel.	Susannah Shippy.
September 4, 1709,	Peenelipoe Titus.	
Nov. 6, 1709,	Rebeckah Phylip.	Obediah Ayers.
Jan. 1, 1709–10,	Peter Pain.	Hannah Right.
	Joanna Ayers.	
June 25, 1710,	Benjamin Thorp.	John Scuder.
Sept. 10, 1710,	Hannah Collier.	Rebeckah Mills.
Oct. 3, 1710,	Joannah Jones.	

In 1711, for some cause not now known, Mr. Wade became disliked by a number of the people. They seceded and formed an Episcopal Congregation, the Rev. Mr. Vaughan of Elizabethtown visiting them at regular periods. Previous to this, Mr. Vaughan says in one of his letters, the people "born in New England and Scotland, had been bred in both places in the greatest prejudice and opposition to the Established Church of England."

The first notice of a settled clergyman thereafter, appears

in 1714, when "Mr. John Pierson, Clerk" is mentioned as having been called from Connecticut, but as the salary seems no longer to have been raised by a general rate upon the inhabitants, there is not the same frequency of allusion to the minister as in the earlier years of the settlement. In 1722 and 1723, Mr. Pierson is mentioned in the town records in connection with the parsonage grounds as "*our* present minister," although for 11 or 12 years there had been a congregation formed within the town, worshipping in their own edifice according to the forms of the Church of England,—a significant indication of what was "the religion of the State."

Mr. Pierson was the son of the Rev. Abm. Pierson, Jr., whom the town had called in 1669, and the grandson of the Rev. Abraham Pierson, the first minister of Newark. He continued in Woodbridge until 1752. In 1739, his salary was assured to him by mutual agreement among sixty individuals. He was one of the first trustees of the College of New Jersey, and died at Hanover, N. J., in 1770, in his 81st year; and in the 57th year of his ministry.[46]

He was dismissed from Woodbridge at his own request, and it is recorded of him that "he was justly reputed and esteemed a worthy and able minister, sound in the faith, and of exemplary conversation and conduct. He well supported the dignity of his office, and had but few equals in his day, in theological knowledge. It was in his time, and by his influence, that the congregation obtained a Royal Charter."[47]

Mr. Nathaniel Whitaker, a Licentiate of the Presbytery of New York, followed Mr. Pierson as a supply, and was subsequently called to the pastorate, which he accepted, December 10th, 1755, and was immediately ordained and installed. He continued to officiate until 1759 or 1760, when he resigned his charge.

Mr. Azel Roe was then selected as their preacher, and after being among them for a year or two, was, in the autumn

[46] Newark Daily Advertiser, Sept. 11, 1848.

[47] MS. account in Church Records; but see a subsequent page for a somewhat different picture.

of 1763, ordained, and installed pastor of the congregation. Some time during Mr. Whitaker's administration, a portion of the inhabitants residing in the southern part of the township formed a separate congregation, subsequently known as the Second Presbyterian Church of Woodbridge, and, eventually, as the Presbyterian Church at Metuchin. Mr. Roe officiated alternately in the two congregations very acceptably, and continued among them during the Revolution.

In 1790, the old congregation were no longer satisfied to share the labors of their pastor with another, and after considerable opposition, effected a separation from the Metuchin Society; and thereafter, until 1815, when he closed his long and faithful career in his 82d year, Mr. Roe continued to "go in and out" among them, respected and beloved, having been pastor of the same flock for about 54 years.

In April, 1803, a movement was made towards the erection of a new place of worship; and, so vigorously was the work prosecuted, it was finished and consecrated in December of the same year. It yet stands, in all respects a convenient and suitable edifice.

The Rev. Henry Mills was called in 1816, to succeed Mr. Roe, and remained in charge of the congregation until 1821. The next year the Rev. Wm. B. Barton was installed, and for thirty years was their faithful minister. During his administration, the number of members reached 242 (in 1843), and at the time of his death, April 7th, 1852, there were 160 in communion with the Church. His successor was the Rev. Wm. M. Martin, the present pastor. [48]

TRINITY CHURCH CONGREGATION.

The invitation given to Mr. Vaughan in 1711, from which originated the Congregation of Protestant Episcopalians in Woodbridge,[49] was as follows:

[48] The number of Church members at different periods was as follows: January, 1787—82; 1830—160; 1831—157; 1832—170; 1833—181; 1834—184; 1835—211; 1837—196; 1838—206; 1839—198; 1840—201; 1841—194; 1943—242; 1845—233; 1847—213; 1850—200; 1853—163.

[49] The Rev. George Keith, in h Journal, mentions Woodbridge as one

"Sir the unhappy difference between Mr. Wade and the people of Woodbridge, is grown to that height, that we cannot joyn with him in the worship of God as Xtians ought to do, it is the desire of some people here that if you think it may be for the Glory of God, and no damage to other Churches, that you would be pleased to afford us your help sometimes on the Sabbath days, according as you shall think convenient; we do it not with any intent to augment the difference among us, but rather hope that with the blessing of God, it may be a means for our better joyning together in setting up the true worship of our Lord Jesus Christ, here amongst a poor deluded people, this is the desire of your humble servants."

"Rich. Smith, John Ashton, Benj. Dunham,
Amos Goodwin, Gershom Higgins, Hen'y Rolph,
John Bishop, Will'm Bingle, George Eubancks.
Robert Wright,

A house was placed at the disposal of Mr. Vaughan, as a place of worship, by Benjamin Dunham, and for four or five years monthly services were regularly held. A convenient frame building was also put up and enclosed, but a stop was put to further proceeding, and to the growth of the congregation by the death of Mr. Dunham on 31st Dec., 1715, in the 35th year of his age,[50] and the transfer of Mr. Vaughan's services to Amboy and Piscataway.[51]

The ground upon which this edifice was erected is represented to have been a portion of the 200 acres providently set apart by the Proprietors for parsonage lands, but the Rev. Mr. Halliday, who occasionally officiated after the withdrawal of Mr. Vaughan, states in 1717, that the church was still without either floor or glass—and although divine service was sometimes performed in it afterwards, it was never finished, and eventually went to ruin.

Subsequently the visits of clergymen of the Established Church became less frequent, and finally ceased entirely; so that the Rev. Mr. Chandler, of Elizabethtown, on commencing missionary labors there in 1752, wrote to the Secretary of

of the places at which he officiated; and the entry records an instance of generous catholicity which deserves notice. "On Thursday, Dec. 30, 1702, preached in Woodbridge, at the Independent Meeting House, at the desire of Mr. Shepherd and some others there, on 1 Tim. 3, 16. After sermon Mr. Shepherd kindly entertained us at his house."

[50] His grave is in the rear of the present church.

[51] Mr. Vaughan's letter to the Secretary, Sept. 28, 1716.

the Society in England "they had not been visited by any of our clergy for upwards of twenty years." Some few of the congregation had during this period attended public worship at Amboy, but many connected themselves with other denominations. "Appearances now are much in favor of the church there," says Mr. Chandler—"and I have seldom had less than 200 hearers." He continued his visits monthly, the number of families professedly Episcopalians being about fifteen, and his audience generally numbering two hundred. In November, 1752, he wrote, that the Presbyterians had dismissed their minister, who had been with them for more than thirty years (the Rev. Mr. Pierson), in consequence of his being somewhat dull, and too feeble an antagonist of the Church, at the growth of which they were much disturbed.

TRINITY CHURCH, WOODBRIDGE.

Thus situated was the congregation for several years, excepting that the other engagements of Mr Chandler, did not long admit of his visiting Woodbridge oftener than once in six weeks; on intervening Sundays, James Parker, officiating as lay-reader, to the general satisfaction of the congregation.[52] In 1754, they erected a church—the specimen of minute architecture which is still standing, and of which a representation is given on the preceding page.

In 1760, the small-pox carried off many useful and reputable persons in the parish, much to the regret of their zealous missionary. "More than half of those who had the disease in the natural way died." Mr. Chandler himself took it in 1757, and did not entirely recover from its effects for three years.

In 1764, Woodbridge was placed in charge of the missionary at Amboy—the Rev. Mr. McKean visiting it once every three weeks—and continued thereafter connected with that parish, until the Revolution put a stop to all religious services in the town according to the forms of the English Established Church—Mr. Bingley reading the service while the Rev. Mr. Preston was the missionary, and absent at Amboy. The congregation then, as for some years before, numbering about 14 families, although the auditories were large.

The Charter of the congregation was granted, December 6th, 1769. Samuel Jaques and Samuel Tingley being named therein as Wardens, and David Alston, Thomas Haddon, Joseph Donham and Ebenezer Foster, Vestrymen.

In February, 1770, Mr. Preston wrote, that his regular induction into the parish as Rector was thought advisable, in order that he might properly present a claim for a due portion of the glebe set apart by the Proprietaries; but as affairs then stood he deemed it best to let the matter remain in abeyance, "till people"—he adds—"are grown a little cooler, so as to be able to distinguish that a trial of a matter of right is not an attack upon their principles; which I am afraid would hardly be the case at present." The question was again agitated in 1774, and the worthy missionary, averse to entering into a lawsuit, prevailed upon the Vestry to propose a compromise, but

[52] Mr. Parker, in a letter to the Secretary of the Society, dated September 1764, complains of the hostility of the "dissenters." "They claim that liberty of conscience for themselves," —he says—"which they don't seem willing to allow to others. We do not trouble them, but they will not eat their bread in quiet with us."

See also letter of Rev. Mr. Skinner, of March 27th, 1722–3.

possession being thought then as now " nine points in the law," no terms would be made by the Presbyterian congregation; and a project was on foot to raise a fund to meet the expense of prosecuting the claim in the Courts, when the confusion and distractions of the war ensued, and effectually stayed the proceedings. If the author has been rightly informed, no portion of the lands set apart for the support of the ministry has been enjoyed by the Episcopal congregation, excepting the lot upon which the Church edifice is erected.

After the Revolution, Woodbridge was only visited occasionally by missionaries of the Protestant Episcopal Church, and as a natural consequence, both the temporal and spiritual interests of the congregation suffered. In 1810, such was the dilapidated condition of the church, that the Convention of the Diocese appointed a Committee to see to its repair, which was done in the course of the year, through the agency of Mr. Daniel Terrill, of Elizabethtown. From that time till 1830, the Rev. James Chapman, of Perth Amboy, officiated from time to time; and during 1818 and 1819, the Rev. F. H. Cuming, also, gave the parish a portion of his services. From 1830 to 1840, the Rev. William Douglas had charge of it, in connection with St. James' Piscataway, and from 1840 to 1841, the Rev. Frederick Ogilby. From 1841 to 1842, the Rev. Hamble J. Leacock ministered in the parish, and from 1843 to the present time the Rev. James Chapman has performed missionary services within it, but the congregation has rather decreased in numbers, than otherwise, with the lapse of years.

TOWN SCHOOLS.

Although the allotment of a portion of the common lands for the benefit of Schools is evidence of the interest in education felt by the first settlers, yet there was no action on the part of the town to effect the establishment of a school until March, 1689, when James Fullerton was, by a resolution in town meeting, " to be entertained as Schoolmaster."

In February, 1694, however, there was no school, and John

Brown of Amboy, or any other person that might be suitable for that employ, was to be "discoursed with" by a Committee appointed for that purpose. The following month Mr. Brown was engaged at a salary of £24 sterling to keep a free school for the next year. Against this proceeding a protest was entered by John Conger, to which due weight will in all time to come be given, when it is stated that, on a subsequent page of the same records, the gentleman saves himself the trouble of writing his name by substituting therefor "his mark."

There may have been some cause for Mr. Conger's objection, for we find that in November of the same year the town was in treaty with John Boacker to teach for six months, on trial, he to keep "ye school this winter time until nine o'clock at night,"—says the record. He was in the discharge of the duties of the office in June following—but thereafter no mention is made of the schoolmaster for several years: but in December, 1701, a piece of land "about ten rods" was allowed for a school-house, "provided it did not prejudice the highway." This is presumed to have been the renowned edifice on Strawberry Hill.

Thereafter nothing appears on the records respecting the school until March, 1735, when measures were taken to make the school lands more productive, by the appointment of a special committee to lease and manage them; and such continued to be the mode of administration down to the present century. The first statement made of the amount of the fund which had accumulated for the use of schools, appears in March, 1761, when the sum of £321 11*s.* 11½*d.* is reported to be in the hands of the Committee, and from its rapid increase it is probable more attention was bestowed upon amassing the means, than upon disseminating the blessings of education.' In March, 1764, the fund was £434 7*s.* 9*d.*; in March, 1765, £465 5*s.* 3*d.*; in March, 1766, £533 8*s.* 2*d.*

At this time a vote was taken "whether or not it was best to take part of the money that was arisen from ye use and Profits of the School Land, and make use of it for ye Schooling of Poor People's children, and the Votes passed in the negative." In September, 1769, the fund had increased to

£740 ; in September, 1770, to £794 ; in September, 1771, to £850 ; in March, 1773, to £900 ; in March, 1774, to £985 4*s.* 10*d.* ; in March, 1775, to £1,063 14*s.* 11*d.* ; and in November, 1775, to £1,062 12*s.* 6*d.*

What was the character of the schools established in the town is not known, but it *would* have been "best," assuredly, to have expended some of the fund upon the education of "poor people's children," than to have kept it to be dissipated or squandered during the troubles of the Revolution ; which was the case, for in March, 1783, the fund was reduced to £480 10*s.* 5*d.*—a less amount than that on hand in 1766, when the above-mentioned vote "passed in the negative."

The inhabitants, however, appear to have learned something from experience, and, after 1789, the interest of the school fund in connection with the amount of tax assessed upon dogs, was appropriated for the schooling of poor children.

POOR RATES.

No regular assessment for the support of the poor seems to have been made prior to October, 1705, when £30 was authorized to be raised for that purpose. In 1707, £25, in 1711 and 1712, £30 each, and in 1714, £15 were the amounts appropriated, but the last-named sum was not raised until 1718. Subsequently a rate was established almost yearly, varying from £30 to £60, till 1751, and thereafter till the Revolution from £70 to £100, and in some years going as high as £200, as in 1764 and 1765, and in 1775, to £220 ; but this was to cover the expense also of copying the old town book, it being "in a Dangerous Situation by Reason of its being old and Mutch to Peases ; " but this probably was never done, as the old book still exists, although the lapse of time has tended to increase the number of its "pieces" materially. After the Revolution the appropriations for the poor were from £100 to £300, annually, but towards the close of the century 400 pounds were raised for their benefit. As was usual before the Revolution—and may be still in many places—the paupers were supported by contract in private families, and in one year, 1770, the announcement is made that "the poor are to be sold at public vendue."

A list of all those maintained by the town during the years 1797, 1798, 1799, 1800 and 1801, is before me, from which I take the following summary :

1797,	11	Paupers,	£184	4	0,	average	£16	14	1.
1798,	17	"	215	12	0,	"	12	13	7.
1799,	13	"	195	7	0,	"	15	0	7.
1800,	15	"	196	19	3,	"	13	2	8.
1801,	12	"	197	12	11,	"	16	19	5.
Total......	68		£989	15	2,	average,	£14	11	1.

During these years the poor were put out at auction to the lowest bidder, the person contracting for their maintenance being at all expense for clothing, medical attendance, funeral charges in case of death, &c. ; bonds being given to indemnify the township, and to deliver the paupers up at the close of the year well clad. As some of them were able to work, a premium would sometimes be paid for the services of those who claimed their maintenance from the town.

MISCELLANEOUS ITEMS.

The first grist-mill was erected in 1670–1, by Jonathan Dunham, under an agreement with the town, in which he engaged to furnish "two good stones of at least five feet over." He was admitted a freeholder, and certain grants of land were made to him in consideration of his erecting the mill. His toll to be one sixteenth. In 1705 another mill was erected by Elisha Parker ; in 1709 another by John Pike and Richard Cutter, and in 1710 one by Richard Soper.

The first saw-mill in the township was erected by Jonathan Bishop, on Rahawack River, in 1682.

In February, 1703, John Clake (or Cleak) "for his encouragement in fitting up a fulling-mill," received a grant for twenty acres on the southerly branch of the Rahawack.

It is difficult at the present day to realize the fact, that wolves should have given the inhabitants so much trouble as they seem to have done. There were town bounties established from time to time, varying from ten to twenty-five shillings for each head, and there are frequent entries of the names of claimants, among them that of John Ilsley appears most frequently. He is mentioned twice in 1693, four times in 1695, twice in 1696 and in 1697, twice in 1698, and three times subsequently. In February, 1671, there were "two wolf pits" constructed by Ephraim Andros and Thomas Auger, and their respective companies.

The first "ordinary" established, was by Samuel Moore in 1683, and he was authorized, when Rum could be had at three shillings, or two shillings and sixpence per gallon, to charge *three pence* the gill, *sixpence* the half pint, and *eighteen pence* the quart, and if he gave more he might raise the price.

In April, 1697, an ordinance was adopted against the running at large, unless sufficiently fettered, of all "fadges" more than a year old. What were fadges?

Previous to 1707, great regularity seems to have been observed in recording the proceedings of the Town; but subsequently they received less attention, and there are evident omissions. From 1714 to 1718, there was also, judging from the records, some irregularity in holding the usual meetings for the despatch of business,—but thereafter, although there was less attention given to minor matters (such as were probably confided to the discretion of committees, with powers rendering the action of the town upon them unnecessary), the meetings were held regularly,[53] until from 1775 to 1783, during which period they appear to have ceased, and also from 1784 to 1788.

Under date of July, 1712, John Pike and John Bishop, Justices, certify, that John Robison, when a child, had one of his ears partly bitten off "by a jade;" that they had known him from childhood, and that he had never been guilty of any crime to merit such punishment. They give him the certificate "to prevent any scandal that he may be liable unto by

[53] There is only one instance in the records of any disorganizing proceedings in the town; that was in March, 1764, when it is said, after the enumeration of sundry officers elected, "But ye meeting got into confusion and so broke up."

strangers in any place where the Providence of God shall cast him."

As almost all pasturage was in common in these early periods of the history of the province, great necessity existed for the due identification of cattle by their respective owners, and their marks were consequently duly recorded in the "town book"—their number calling for the exercise of some ingenuity in devising the requisite variety; thus we have for Elisha Parker's mark "A cross of the near Ear and a slit on the under side of the same;" for Richard Potter's "three holes in the left ear;" for Obadiah Ayres' "two half pennies on the under side of the off or right ear;" and for Samuel Moore's "a half penny on the under side of the right or off ear, and a slit across the upper side of the near or left ear."

At the period of the Revolution the position of Woodbridge among the other towns of the colony was far more important than at present, exceeding greatly in influence many which now are far ahead in the great race of progress. The "Sons of Liberty" of Woodbridge and Piscataway took the lead in 1765–6 in several of the prominent measures of the day, and it was through their interference mainly, that William Coxe of Philadelphia was led to decline the office of Stamp Distributor for New Jersey:—a deputation from them to that gentleman, while instructed to treat him with great deference and respect, bearing to him a communication to the effect that, a week's delay in resigning the office would render a visit from them in a body necessary, and produce results mutually disagreeable.

The town was then on the great thoroughfare between New York and Philadelphia, and the road which was travelled over by the worthies of that day retains for miles the characteristics it then possessed; so that when the octogenarian points along it and describes the passage through the place of Washington on his way to New York, to be inaugurated President, or details other events occurring on the route, it is comparatively easy to conjure up the scenery and the actors. The main features of the country, too, are unchanged; the pleasing undulations of the surface diversified with wood and meadow, exhibiting the good judgment of the early settlers in selecting the site for an agricultural community ; "the forms which the earth wore and the hues with which the air was beautified in ancient days, are still the same," in general appearance, however changed may be the denizens of the place.

It is manifest, however, that it is still within the domain of Time, and subject to the modifications which he is for ever working. Many objects that were wont to meet the eye of the traveller have disappeared, not the least among them being the famous Elm-tree, upon which the author's boyish eyes were wont to gaze in admiration, and which was noted the country round, both for its size and for its pointing out the village tavern ; and there was no one thoughtful enough to perpetuate its memory either by pencil or description. Perhaps the woodman, beneath whose axe it fell, felt less its loss than he who, a thousand miles off, read its obituary in a stray paragraph of a newspaper [54] —another link of the chain connecting the present with the past was severed,—the man's hold upon the days of his childhood was less secure.

The following was the population of Woodbridge Township at five decennial periods :—

Year	Class	Number	Total
In 1810	White—Males	1,980	
	" Females	1,903	
	"All other free persons"	134	
	Slaves	230	
	Total		4,247
In 1820	White—Males	1,863	
	" Females	2,051	
	"All other free persons"	220	
	Slaves	92	
	Total		4,226
In 1830	White—Males	1,770	
	" Females	1,887	
	Free Colored Persons	297	
	Slaves	15	
	Total		3,969

[54] Its destruction was thus announced in the newspapers of the day:—"The ancient Elm in Woodbridge, N. J., fronting the "Elm Tree Tavern," from its decayed state, has been cut down. The trunk was hollow, and measured 32 feet in circumference, capable of accommodating 15 men standing upright within. One limb measured 15 feet in circumference. About half a barrel of honey, of exquisite quality and flavor, was found in the tree." This was in 1837.

In 1840	White—Males - -	2,188	
	" Females - -	2,275	
	Free Colored Persons -	351	
	Slaves - - - - -	7	
	Total - - -		4,821
In 1850	White—Males - -	2,444	
	" Females - -	2,488	
	Free Colored Persons -	209	
	Total - -		5,141

Chapter XII.—Piscataway.

"* * * * It is sweet
To linger here, among the flitting birds
And leaping squirrels, wandering brooks and winds
That shake the leaves, and scatter as they pass
A fragrance from the cedars, thickly set
With pale blue berries. In these peaceful shades,—
Peaceful, unpruned, immeasurably old—
My thoughts go up the long dim path of years,
Back to the earliest days of liberty."

PISCATAWAY was settled under a grant, dated December 18th, 1666,[1] the grantees being John Martin,[2] Charles Gilman, Hugh Dun and Hopewell Hull; and on the 30th May, 1668, Robert Dennis, John Smith, John Gilman and Benjamin Hull, were announced as associates. They came principally from Piscataqua in New England, but were originally from Britain. They conferred upon their township the name of the place whence they came; it being known as Piscataqua for some time after the settlement.

The following are the names of those for whom land was surveyed up to 1690, with their respective quantities: [3]

[1] East Jersey, &c., p. 42.

[2] This Martin was the ancestor of the once celebrated Luther Martin, of Baltimore. In a pamphlet, entitled "Modern Gratitude,"—written and published by him in 1799, for the purpose of enlightening the public mind as to the circumstances connected with some domestic trials to which he was subjected—he gives all the particulars of his history. He says, "Two brothers of that family from which I derive my name were among the first settlers in East Jersey. They came immediately, I believe, from Piscataqua, in New England, with the ancestors of the Dunns, the Dunhams, the FitzRandolphs, the Mannings, the Bonhams, and other old and respectable families in that State. * * * * * Numerous yet are the persons who bear my name in New Jersey, to all of whom I am more or less distantly connected, and the descendants of the same family are to be found from the Hudson on the East, to the Spanish possessions on the West."

[3] These names are from the East Jersey Records, through the Elizabethtown Bill in Chancery, p. 37. The Town Records contain two lists which contain a few names not in the text, and there are some here given not included in those lists.

Name	Acres.	Name	Acres.
Alexander Adams	150	Thomas Gordon (of Amboy)	110
Thomas Bartlett	70	John Hendricks	120
Simon Brinley	90	Daniel Hendricks	195
Peter Billiow	210	Mary Higgins [7]	254
Nicholas Bonham [4]	122	Jediah Higging	80
Elizabeth Bonham	100	Thomas Higgins	53
Timothy Carter	63	George Jewel	95
Benjamin Clarke	275	Hopewell Hull	284
George Drake	424	Benjamin Hull [8]	498
Francis Drake (Capt.)	245	Samuel Hull	144
John Drake	30	Daniel Lepinton	129
Samuel Doty	252½	Thomas Lowry	70
Hugh Dun	138	John Langstaff	300
Benajah Dunham	103½	John Martin	334
Edmond Dunham	100	John Martin, junior	230
John FitzRandolph	225	Joseph Martin	60
Elizabeth FitzRandolph [5]	277	Jefery Maning (1678)	195
Benjamin FitzRandolph	130	Ann, his widow (1690)	200
Thomas FitzRandolph	106	Samuel Moore	280
Rehoboth Gannet	224	John Mullison	100
Henry Greenland [6]	384	Nicholas Mundaye	101½
Charles Gilman	340	Joshua Perine	30
John Gilman	300	Vincent Rognion [9]	154½
Matthew Giles	120	Walter Robinson	100
James Giles	280	John Smalley	118½
James Godfry	34½	John Smalley, junior	215

---

[4] Hence "Bonhamtown." He died in 1683.

[5] She is presumed to be the widow of Edward, and to have become, on the 30th June, 1685, the wife of Capt. John Pike, of Woodbridge.

[6] He is styled "Doctor" in 1678, and subsequently "Captain"—by which title he is designated as implicated in some disorderly proceedings in 1681, for which the General Assembly declared him incapable of holding office; an act, however, disallowed by the Proprietaries [see East Jersey, p. 80, *note*; Grants and Concess., pp. 228,280, 281.] He was probably the individual alluded to in the following extract from Coffin's History of Newbury, Mass., pp. 64, 66, 67: "1662, Doctor Henry Greenland and his wife Mary came to Newbury. He appears to have been a man of good education, but passionate, unprincipled, and grossly immoral. He, of course, soon became involved in difficulties with his neighbors, and caused great excitement among the sober citizens of the town, who had not been accustomed to such specimens of immorality as he had displayed before them." In March, for some gross offence against good morals, the Court sentenced him "to be imprisoned till next sessions of the court, then to be whipt or pay a fine of thirty pounds, and be bound to good behaviour." "One of the witnesses in his behalf testified that 'he had been a soldier and was a gentleman, and they must have their liberties.' Another asserted, that, as he was a stranger and 'a great man, it would be best not to make an uprore, but to let him goe away privately.'" In September following (1664) he was convicted, with one other, of an assault, for which he was again fined and bound to keep the peace. He appealed to the general court, but his sentence was confirmed, and he was ordered "to depart the jurisdiction, and not to practice physic or surgery." From 1666 to 1672 he resided in Kittery.

[7] Widow of Richard—a son, Eliakim, married a Newbold, of West Jersey.

[8] Innkeeper in 1677. The name and the business have continued connected to the present day.

[9] Soon converted into *Runyon*.

	Acres.		Acres.
Edward Slater - - -	464	Samuel Walker - - -	120
Michael Simmons - - -	$104\frac{1}{2}$	Andrew Worden - - -	67
Richard Smith - - -	164	George Winckfield - -	63
William Sutton [10] - - -	249	Robert Wright - - -	86

The following are some of the village dignitaries during the early years of the settlement :—

DEPUTIES TO THE GENERAL ASSEMBLY.

1675	John Gilman,	Hopewell Hull,
1684–86	George Drake,	Isaac Smalley,
1687	George Drake,	John Langstaff,
1692	George Drake,	Benjamin Clarke,
1693	Hopewell Hull,	John Drake,
" Sept.,	Thomas FitzRandolph, in place of H. Hull, deceased.	
1694–95	Thomas FitzRandolph,	Thomas Higgins,
1696–97	Cornelius Longfield,	Jediah Higgins,
1698	Samuel Walker,	Cornelius Longfield.

OVERSEERS OF THE HIGHWAYS.

1683	George Drake,	Hopewell Hull,
1684	Charles Gilman,	John Martin,
1686–7	George Drake,	Hopewell Hull,
1688	William Wright,	Thomas Higgins,
1689	Benjamin Clarke,	Benjamin Hull,
1690	Thomas Higgins,	Matthew Giles,
1692	Benjamin Clarke,	Jediah Higgins,
1695–6	John Drake, Thomas Grubs, Benajah Dunham,	
1698	John Field,	John Drake.

JUSTICES OF THE TOWN COURT.

May, 1688, Benjamin Clarke, George Drake, Charles Gilman.
(Their successors or predecessors are not mentioned.)

CONSTABLES.

1684 Hopewell Hull,	1692 Jabez Hendricks,
1685 Jediah Higgins,	1693 Wm. Sutton,
1686 Nicolas Mundaye,	1694 Benjamin James,
1687 Charles Gilman,	1695 Benjamin Clarke,
1688 Thomas FitzRandolph,	1696 John Drake,
1689 John Martin,	1697 Isaac Smalley,
1690 Joseph Martin,	1698 Thomas Grub.

SELECT MEN to manage the affairs of the town were first established in January, 1693. Those first selected were Captain Francis Drake, Thomas FitzRandolph, Benjamin Hull, Isaac Smalley, and Edward Slater.

---

[10] On the 25th Nov., 1682, William Sutton voluntarily gives his son Richard to James and Elizabeth Giles, until he shall be 21—they agreeing to do for him "as for their own."

TOWN CLERKS.

1684–87	Edward Slater,	1731–41	John Dunham,
1687–92	Isaac Smalley,	1741–50	John Stelle,
1692–97	Edward Slater,	1750	Reune Rugnion,
1705–11	Isaac Smalley,	1767	Ephraim Runyon,
1711–1714	John Mullison,	1777	Thompson Stelle,
1714 to 1731	Benajah Dunham,	1810	Reune Martin.

Overseers of the Poor were not chosen until 1709, John Drake and Hugh Dun being the first. The same year Chosen Freeholders were first selected, John Burrows and William Hudson being appointed.

The first recorded marriage by a "Minister of the Gospel," was on the 5th August, 1714,—Jonathan Dunham and Joan Piat being the happy couple. They were united by Mr. John Drake, whose services are occasionally referred to thereafter until 1737. Mr. Edmond Dunham is also mentioned in connection with marriages as "a Minister of the Gospel" from 1712 to 1732. The Rev. Gilbert Tennent officiated at a marriage in 1734. Only one or two marriages are *recorded* (in 1738–9) as having been sanctioned by the Rev. Benjamin Stelle, although in charge of the congregation for twenty years.

The Baptists appear to have been the first to establish religious services in Piscatáway. Some of the original settlers were of that persuasion,[11] and in 1683 they received an addition to their numbers by the arrival of a company from Tipperary in Ireland. Messrs. Drake and Dunham, and also Mr. Hugh Dunn, are said by Benedict to have preached in Piscataway prior to 1689, although unordained; but in the spring of that year the Rev. Thomas Killingworth visited the town, organized a congregation, and ordained Mr. Drake, who continued as their pastor thereafter until his death, in 1739. He bore an excellent character.[12] The Rev. Henry Lovell was associated with him towards the close of his career, but for some misconduct was expelled the society.

[11] Edwards says, that "tradition will allow of no more than six to have been professed Baptists, viz., Hugh Dunn, who was an exhorter; John Drake, afterwards their pastor; Nicholas Bonham; John Smalley; Edmond Dunham, afterwards minister of the Seventh-day Baptists; and John Randolph. It is not to be doubted but the said men had wives or sisters or daughters of the same way of thinking."

[12] He had three wives, by whom he had six sons: Isaac, Abraham, Francis, John, Benjamin and Samuel; and two daughters: Sarah and Rebecca.—*Edwards' Materials*, p. 25.

The successor of Mr. Drake was Benjamin Stelle, of French parentage, but born in New York—"a popular preacher and upright magistrate." He continued in charge of the congregation until his death in January, 1759, in his 76th year, having been assisted in his ministerial labors for several years by his son, Isaac Stelle, who continued to officiate for nearly twenty-three years after the death of his father, and died October 9th, 1781, in his 63d year, highly esteemed. In company with the Rev. Benjamin Miller, Mr. Stelle travelled much among the Baptists of America.[13]

The Rev. Reune Runyon succeeded Mr. Stelle in 1783, having been called to the ministry in 1771, when 30 years of age. He was ordained at Morristown, in March, 1772, where he remained until 1780. Mr. Runyon died in Nov., 1811; having been assisted in his labors part of the time by Henry Smalley.[14]

The Rev. James McLaughlin—then pastor of the Baptist Church at Kingwood, N. J.,—was called to succeed Mr. Runyon, and entered upon his duties in October, 1812. A portion of the congregation resided in New Brunswick, where a convenient meeting-house had been built two years before, and as there was no parsonage in Piscataway, Mr. McLaughlin took up his residence there, holding his services at both places—at Piscataway in the morning of each Lord's day, and in New Brunswick in the afternoon. On the 1st September, 1816, the members of the congregation residing in New Brunswick, twenty-three in number, were formed into a separate church.

Mr. McLaughlin continued to serve both congregations until his resignation, which was presented October 19th, 1817. He is remembered by many as a worthy man and excellent minister, grave in his deportment and unusually solemn in his pulpit addresses.

[13] Mr. Stelle married Christiana Clarkson, by whom he had six sons: Benjamin, John, Abel, Joseph, Oliver and Samuel; and one daughter, Mary. —*Edwards*, p. 27.

[14] He was "remarkable for dexterity in administering baptism." "On 30th June, 1786," says Edwards, "a gentleman held his watch in his hand till he had baptized 30 in 58 minutes." His wife was Ann Bray, by whom he had five daughters: Ann, Rachel, Charlotte, Matilda and Isabella; and three sons: Vincent, Daniel, Reune.—*Edwards*, p. 28.

The congregation was without a pastor about a year, but on the 1st October, 1818, the Rev. William Dodge, of Wilmington, Delaware, took it under his charge, and for nearly fourteen years continued its efficient and exemplary pastor, attracting the people to him by a happy union of dignity and affability in his deportment, his neatness of person and becoming walk and conversation; and though dead, still lives in the warm affections of many of his flock. During the pastorate of Mr. Dodge the congregation prospered materially. In February, 1825, it was determined to erect a new house of worship on the site of the old one,[15] and so vigorously was the building prosecuted, that in the following October it was dedicated. It cost $3,000. When he first entered upon his duties, Mr. Dodge resided in New Brunswick, as his predecessor had done, but in 1830 removed to a farm near the Piscataway meeting-house. On his resignation he removed to Newark, and became the pastor of the first Baptist Church there, in 1832.

The Rev. Daniel D. Lewis succeeded Mr. Dodge in June, 1833, and remained in charge of the congregation until his death, Sept. 27th, 1849, "having served the Church faithfully and successfully for more than sixteen years. His remains were interred in the yard near the house where he labored so long, and where he finished his course. A plain stone marks the place where they rest. He was a plain man, making no pretensions to learning or eloquence, diffident and retiring in his manners, but sound in the faith, and earnest in his delivery of the truth, seeking the honor of his Divine Master, and the peace and harmony of his people." [16] On April 1st, 1850, the Rev. Henry V. Jones, the present incumbent, accepted a call to the pastorate, removing from Newark, where he had had charge of the first Baptist Church.

Mr. Lewis, like his predecessors, had resided in New Brunswick, but shortly after his death, it was resolved to provide a parsonage within the town limits, which was accomplished by

[15] This old church was probably the one built in 1686. See Extracts from the Town Records on a following page.

[16] Letter from Mr. S. Smith of Piscataway; to whom I am under many obligations for information respecting the place and people, and particularly for the items in the text referring to the Baptist Congregation in late years.

purchasing a small farm of twenty acres and constructing thereon a new house, at an expense of $4,000. On the 1st January, 1851, the meeting-house erected in 1825 took fire and was entirely consumed; but with commendable zeal the people at once took measures to build another, and in January, 1852, a little more than a year after the destruction of the old one, a handsome new edifice, costing $7,500, was completed and dedicated; occupying the same spot which had been the site of the two former ones,

"Where, * * * in many a mould'ring heap,
Each in his narrow cell for ever laid,
The rude forefathers of the hamlet sleep"—

who were the worshippers within their walls; and their children, grandchildren and great grandchildren, constitute the congregation that now periodically assembles within the present meeting-house.

The first congregation in New Jersey of Seventh-day Baptists was gathered in Piscataway. The first members were originally of the regular Baptist Society, the first Association being formed in April, 1707, although they held religious services two years earlier.[17] The cause of the secession is stated by Edwards to have been owing to Mr. Edmond Dunham's admonishing Hezekiah Bonham for doing some servile work on Sunday, when Bonham required of him proof that the first day of the week was holy by divine institution. This Mr. Dunham could not do to his own satisfaction, after duly examining the point, and he consequently renounced the observance of the first in favor of the seventh day of the week: receiving the fourth commandment as an unchangeable law. This was about the year 1700 or 1701.

[17] The signers to the agreement were, Edmond Dunham, Mary Dunham, Benjamin Dunham, Dorothy Dunham, John FitzRandolph, Sarah FitzRandolph, Elizabeth FitzRandolph, Benjamin Martin, Margaret Martin, Jonathan Martin, Hannah Martin, Hugh Dunn, Elizabeth Dunn, Samuel Dunn, Hesther Dunn, Joseph Dunn, and Gershom Hull; and subsequently individuals from the families of the Dottas, Cummins, Wooders, Smalleys, Algers, Chandlers, &c.—*Edwards*, p. 130. At the time he wrote, in 1789, the congregation numbered 100.

Mr. Dunham continued the oversight of the church until his death, March 7th, 1734, in the 73d year of his age.[18] He was succeeded by his son, the Rev. Jonathan Dunham; preaching as a licentiate until 1745, when he was chosen pastor, and so continued until his death, March 11th, 1777, from small-pox, in his 86th year—leaving behind him an excellent character.

The next pastor was the Rev. Nathan Rogers, who assumed the care of the congregation in 1787 :—but with the succession during the present century I am unacquainted.

ST. JAMES' CHURCH.

As has been already stated,[19] the first regular religious services in Piscataway, according to the forms of the Church of England, were performed by the Rev. Mr. Brooks, whose labors in the Province commenced in 1704. He usually visited the place once a month, and some steps were taken towards the erection of a church.[20] Mr. Vaughan succeeded him in similar services, and subsequently Mr. Halliday officiated once a fortnight. At this time the building of a brick church "87 feet long, 23 wide, and 13 high on the side walls" was undertaken, and more than £100 subscribed ; a portion of which is stated to have been expended for materials, but no further progress was made.[21] Subsequently, about the year 1717, by the advice of Mr. Vaughan the frame of a timber church was put up, but the funds being exhausted, it remained in an unfinished state until 1724 ; at which time they received occasional visits from the Rev. Mr. Skinner of Perth Amboy ; who gives, as the number of communicants in that year, eighteen

[18] He married Elizabeth Bonham, by whom he had four sons: Benajah, Edmond, Jonathan and Ephraim; and three daughters: Elizabeth, Mary and Hannah.

[19] Page 213.

[20] Rev. George Keith, in his Journal, mentions officiating once in Piscataway, on Dec. 30, 1702.

[21] Communication to the Society from the Vestry, Dec. 24th, 1714. The most prominent man of the congregation at that time was John Barrow, one of the Wardens. The other Warden was Thomas Wetherel; the Vestry John Molleson, William Hodgson, Robert Webster, Charles Glover, Hopewell Hull, Henry Langstaff, Samuel Walker, John Jennings, William Olden, Samuel Royse.

or nineteen, and represents the congregation as increasing—the attendance being as large there as in Amboy. For more than thirty years, and probably until his death, did Mr. Skinner discharge his duties faithfully as a missionary to this flock. In 1747 he wrote, "My circuit from the first Sunday in May is from Amboy to South River, from thence to Piscataway, and from thence to Amboy, while the river is passable, or travelling possible; and indeed the extremes of heat and cold render the service at sixty years of age very hard to your most humble servant."

He had the satisfaction of seeing the congregation enlarge under his ministrations—stating in 1741 that his hearers generally numbered 200, and on Christmas Day, 1748, he reports the number of communicants to have been forty-five.

The parish subsequently passed into the charge of the missionaries stationed at New Brunswick—the Rev. Messrs. Wood, McKean and Cutting, who officiated there at different periods. The latter gentleman, who commenced his labors in 1764, appears to have been of a truly catholic spirit, living at New Brunswick and associating harmoniously with all denominations; in addition to his clerical functions, having under his care a few young gentlemen whom he prepared for College. His services at Piscataway were well attended, and he states that he was on the most friendly terms with the Baptist clergyman, by agreement with him, officiating every third Sunday in the month, when that gentleman's duties called him elsewhere. He met, however, with much to discourage him; so strong were the prejudices which education and association had engendered in those composing his congregation, on his proposing to them baptism, they preferred objections to sprinkling, and on offering to immerse them, they declined receiving the sign of the cross upon their foreheads; and what gave him great uneasiness was the divisions existing among them respecting land titles, one of the principal men of the congregation becoming very inimical to many, who wished Mr. Cutting to exercise ecclesiastical discipline upon him. "I remonstrated to them," says the missionary; "it was a matter of law and too intricate for me. In vain did I endeavor to convince them the Church had no business with disputes concerning property I offered every thing in my power to mediate matters, and at last brought the principal parties to agree to leave the affair to arbitration; the rest were still violent, and because I refused to do what I could not answer to God, my conscience and the Society, * * * they threatened to leave the Church: and the last communion some really absented themselves." This was in 1765; the next year he states with pleasure that the hostility of the parties was somewhat mollified, though he found it "more difficult to appease them when their temporal interest was concerned than when any scruples arose in their minds concerning religion."

Shortly after this the Rev. Abraham Beach succeeded Mr. Cutting at New Brunswick, and officiated occasionally at Piscataway until the Revolution. From the re-establishment of peace up to 1830, missionaries of the Protestant Episcopal Church, or clergymen from the nearest towns, visited the place only two or three times a year. In 1830 the congregation was placed, along with that of Trinity Church, Woodbridge, in charge of the Rev. Wm. Douglas, and so continued for ten years and until Mr. Douglas's removal to the West. In 1840 the Rev. Frederick Ogilby officiated occasionally; in 1841 and 1842 the Rev. Hamble J. Leacock; in 1843 and 1844 the Rev. Alfred Stubbs, of New Brunswick; in 1845 the Rev. James Chipchase; and from 1847 to 1855 the Rev. Isaac Smith, were either in charge of the parish or gave to it a portion of their time.

On the 19th June, 1835, the Church was entirely destroyed by a tornado, and the present edifice was erected at the expense of Joseph Foulke, Esq., of New York.

The following items are from the Town Records excepting the first, the authority for which is the Official Record at Trenton, Liber 4:—

November, 1681. Testimony was taken before Justices Vicars and Greenland, Piscataway, to the effect that Edward Slater had "uttered very pnishouse and Squerillousse words Rendering the Government of the provinse, the Governor and Counsell Odyouse in the Eyes and hearts of the people." Slater was in consequence imprisoned for riotous conduct, and not allowed bail; but in 1683 he obtained a verdict of £45 against Vicars, and £50 against Greenland for false imprisonment. At the same Court, March, 1683, Vicars was indicted for opposing and advising against the holding of Courts under the Act of the General Assembly, passed Oct., 1681, and for conniving, advising and abetting the issuing out of several commissions for holding special courts from Nov., 1681, to March, 1682, at Elizabethtown and elsewhere, and for exercising arbitary power over the inhabitants, and for dissolving the Assembly contrary to the Concessions in October, 1681.[2] He was again twice indicted in August, 1683, one of them stating that he was supposed to be an escaped criminal from England, and that he had taken upon himself, April 6, 1682, the office of Secretary and Register, and executed the duties for some months. In relation to his actions as a citizen, the grand jury in an indictment of nine counts, presented him "as a common nuisance and offence." He was found guilty, fined £100 sterling, and sentenced to Woodbridge Jail until paid, and required to give security for his good behavior. Slater evidently did not suffer in the estimation of his fellow townsmen by the persecution of Vicars and Greenland, which probably was the consequence of his course in the Assembly, in 1681, of which he was a member, although his name does not appear in the list of deputies on a preceding page.

October 26, 1683. Mr. Martin, Mr. Giles, Mr. Hull and Hopewell Hull chosen to be joined with John Gilman and Edward Slater, to treat with the Governor about the settlement of the township.

October 26, 1683. It was ordered there should be "a Cart Bridge by Higginses, a foot bridge by Rehobeth Gannet's, and a foot bridge at Stonybrook going to Greenlands."

January 1, 1683–4. Major Giles and Lieutenant Doty were appointed to visit the town magazine, and to report thereon to the townsmen at the next meeting.

April 2, 1684. H. Hull, G. Drake, John Langstaff and John Gilman to go and treat with Governor Lawrie about the quit rents and patents. Another Committee for similar purpose the next year—Gilman, Drake, Smalley and Slater.

January 1, 1684–5. H. Hull and J. Martin to run the lines and lay out the bounds between "Beaver Dam and Woodbridge line."

September 4, 1685. A bounty of twenty shillings authorized to be paid to any one killing a wolf in the township—renewed in 1696.

January 18, 1685–6. "Att the Towne Meetinge then agreed yt there should be a meetinge house built forthwith, the dimentions as followeth: Twenty foot wide, thirty foot Longe and Ten foot between joynts." John Gilman, H. Hull, John FitzRandolph, John Martin, senior, and Edward Slater appointed to agree with the workmen and look after the building. They were also ordered "to provide a house to meet in both for Towne meetings, Courts, and other publick businesse."

September 17, 1686. "Hopewell Hull and George Drake chosen to make ye bridge att John Pounds."

"Agreed yt every inhabitant of this Towne is to pay nine pence in silver towards ye buyinge of Nailes for ye Towne house."

December 10, 1686. Town rate fixed at £44 6*s*.

[2] See East Jersey &c., pp. 81, 192, and page 402 of this volume.

January, 1688–9. "It was agreed that there shall bee a Sled waye maide to the greate meadows and iff any man shall goe with a carte In the said sled waye shall paye ten shillings for so dowinge for each trespase."

January 1, 1689–90. Edward Slater, George Drake and Isaac Smalley were chosen "to Discorse hopwell hull a bout the finishen the towne house and If hopwell hull refuse to finish it that the above mentioned men have power to hire workmen to finish the saide houste."

March 2, 1690. Edmond Dunham to have ten shillings "for mending the buriall place and to set it up with good white-oacke or Chesnut stakes And bound with good Withes."

"Shingle Hill," "Turtle Hill," "Scotlands Bridge," are mentioned about this period.

January 1, 1691–2. "Considering ye season for getting out hay and that few attend att ye Towne meetinge, the said Towne meetinge was adjourned to the second day of february or Candlmas day."

January 1, 1692-3. "By virtue of a Warrant from ye Sheriff of the County of Middlesex, for making choise of debuties or representatives for ye succeeding year, the Inhabitants of this Towne meetinge att ye place appointed &c att ye day &c considering that itt was ye Lord's day or Sunday day, the meeting was adjourned by the consent of ye People then assembled none contradictinge and it is adjourned till tomorrow morninge att Eight o'clock precisely."

January 1, 1694–5. A Committee appointed to get the burial place fenced and a good gate made to it.

July 20, 1695. The Deputies of the town for the year to have 4 shillings a day.

January 1, 1695–6. A Pound established.

October 24, 1696. Robert Cole engaged to keep school in the town for one year, to be supported by voluntary subscriptions.

January 1, 1705. The Stocks, Burying place, Pound and the Town House were all to be substantially repaired, the latter to have "glaysed dores hanged and maid tite."

April 11, 1711. John Molleson was chosen Town Clerk, and in September he thus makes his first record:—

the
"Piscataway 13 of Suptember 1711

At the towne Meting then Choes William olding and James maning overseers for the puer and Isac Small and John Drak Seneor for the inshuing year asesers: which ofesess they argried execuit grates. The Raiets is to be resed by Discration of the assesers"

JOHN MOLLESON clark

"At the forsaid meting it is agried that the biring place shall be fensed suficient."

This entry the Town thought it advisable to confirm the following March, by having the substance of it repeated in plainer English.

March, 1712–13. The Freeholders were "to look after the building of a goal."

March 10, 1719. It was agreed that Benjamin Hull "should have the benefit of the burying yard for six shillings a year" * * and "Edmund Dunham was chosen to receive the money of the said Hull yearly for to keep until the fence of the said burying place wanted repairing"—which does not appear to have been the case until 1728.

"At the Same Town meeting it was agreed upon that when the Townsmen are gathered together at a Town meeting for to do any Town business, then they shall give in their minds in writing"—a requisition, which, judging from the clerical abilities of their chosen clerk, must have given the "townsmen" no little trouble.

May 16, 1732. *A specific sum* for the first time noticed as authorized to be raised for the relief of the poor—"fifteen pounds of Current Lawfull money at Eight Shillings per ounce."

A pair of Stocks to be made and kept in the usual place.

April, 1735, Poor rate 10 pounds; *November*, 1736, 20 pounds; *September*, 1752, 50 pounds; *December*, 1753, 60 pounds; *June*, 1755, 80 pounds; *November*, 1757, 50 pounds; *March*, 1759, 100 pounds; *April*, 1762, 150 pounds (8s. 9d. per ounce); *March*, 1763, 30 pounds; *March*, 1764, 200 pounds (proclamation money.)

March, 1764. It was agreed that Jersey Bills should pass among the inhabitants in all future contracts, in proclamation money, according to the laws of the province.

March, 1765. An arrangement authorized for boarding the poor at one place, with such person as would take them for the least sum.

February 7, 1766. Reune Runyon, Town Clerk and one of the Judges of Common Pleas, certifies that Jacob Martin, son of Joshua Martin, had appeared before him 'and said he had had the misfortune that morning to have a large piece bit off the back side of his left ear by a horse:' which relation he believed as he saw the ear bloody—a proper precaution when cropping was a common punishment.

March, 1766. £100 assessed for the poor.

April, 1766. The town poor put with John Dunn for one year at £48 11*s*. light money, to be paid quarterly.

March, 1767. "The taker of the poor to clothe the poor for the ensuing year"—"the poor set up to the lowest bidder," who was Jeremiah Dunn, at £120, but the bidding then adjourned until April, when they were put with John Dunn, at £49 16*s*. 6*d*. In *April*, 1768, they were put with him for £59 19*s*. 10*d*., light money; in 1769 at £40; in 1770 at £50 12*s*. 11*d*.; in 1771 at £48 15*s*.

May 25, 1767, £17 was assessed for the poor; *March*, 1768, £100; 1770, £80; 1771, £50; 1772, £80; 1773, £80; 1774, £70; 1775, £80; 1776, £90; 1777, £75; *March*, 1778, £175 Proc.; 1779, £150; 1780, £150; *January*, 1781, this sum not having been found sufficient £30 more authorized, "in spetia;" 1781, £100 lawful money; 1782, £40; 1783, £50; 1784, £50; 1785, £40; 1786, £60; 1787, £80; 1788, £130; 1789, £220; 1790, £160; 1791, £150; 1792, £120; 1793, £130; 1794, £130; 1795, £100; 1796, £120; 1797, £150; 1798, £140; 1799, £100; 1800, £150.

The following table gives the population of the township of Piscataway at five decennial periods:—

Year	Class	Number	Total
In 1810	White—Males	1,094	
	" Females	1,053	
	"Other free persons"	77	
	Slaves	251	
	Total		2,475
In 1820	White—Males	1,153	
	" Females	1,170	
	"Other free persons"	174	
	Slaves	151	
	Total		2,648

Year	Class	Number	Total
In 1830	White—Males	1,168	
	" Females	1,191	
	Free Colored Persons	249	
	Slaves	56	
	Total		2,664
In 1840	White—Males	1,250	
	" Females	1,277	
	Free Colored Persons	298	
	Slaves	3	
	Total		2,828
In 1850	White—Males	1,356	
	" Females	1,398	
	Free Colored Persons	221	
	Slaves	0	
	Total		2,975

APPENDIX.

NOTE A, PAGE 2.

THE word *Ompoge* or *Ambo* was probably a generic appellation, and became, in consequence, more easily attached to the name of PERTH, given to the settlement by the proprietaries: "Perth Ambo" being used instead of Perth-point; and hence the compound title.

Lieutenant W. Smyth, in his "Narrative of a Journey from Lima to Para," mentions avillage named *Ambo* by the natives, situated, like the ancient capital, at the confluence of two streams. May there not have been some similarity between the language of that branch of the American Aboriginal family and the language of the Delawares?

There are four towns or villages called Amboy in he United States, besides Perth Amboy and South Amboy in New Jersey: one is in the county of Lee, Illinois, having a population of 540 by the last census; one in the county of Hillsdale, Michigan, having a population of only 252; one in Oswego County, New York, having a population of 1,132; and one in Fulton County, Ohio, with a population of 460. I have taken some pains to trace the origin of their name, but with little success. The one in New York was so named by a company of citizens who accidentally met in a country store, Amboy being selected by a majority from a number mentioned, and the doings of the little self-constituted convention being published in the county newspaper, the name became confirmed. One of the persons present, from whom this information was received, was not aware that Amboy in New Jersey was thought of. Amboy in Ohio is thought to have derived its name from its ancient forerunner, through a Mr. Thomas Berry, who felt some interest in the place; and Amboy in Illinois owes its title to the impression made by the productions of its Jersey namesake upon one of the Commissioners appointed in 1845 to divide the county in which it is situated into townships. "Amoy" was a name proposed, and it immediately reminded the functionary alluded to (so says my informant, as from himself) of having visited Perth Amboy, New Jersey, in 1842, in his "clerical capacity," as a Mormon Elder; and retaining many pleasing recollections of fat oysters, good wives, and pretty women," he urged the adoption of Amboy as the name of the township, and his request was complied with. I have no information relative to the Amboy in Michigan.

NOTE B, PAGE 6.

JAMES, *Earl of Perth*, interested in East Jersey, and in whose honor the Capital of the province was named, succeeded to the title and estates of his father, in 1675, and was the fourth who had borne the title. Between the time of his accession and that of his connection with the New Jersey proprietors (which arose probably from the courtly associations of Robert Barclay and William Penn), he had filled several high stations; attaining in 1684 to that of Lord High Chancellor of Scotland, in which capacity he sanctioned the embarcation of George Scot and his unfortunate companions for the province the ensuing year, having been continued in the possession of all his offices on the accession of James II., and honored with the chief administration of affairs in Scotland as a reward for his stanch adherence to the Stuart family, and his adoption of the Roman Catholic religion.

The abdication of James in 1688, and subsequent retreat to France, led the Earl (who in 1687 had resigned his Earldom and several of his offices in favor of his son and heirs male) to seek a refuge there also; but his intentions becoming known, he was pursued by an armed boat, overtaken, stripped of all he had with him of value, and being brought back, was thrown into the common prison at Kirkaldy; and was subsequently removed to Stirling Castle, where he remained in confinement until 1693, being relieved on his giving bonds in the sum of £5,000 to leave the kingdom. Of the circumstances attending his capture and imprisonment, he has left a graphic account, in letters to his sister, which contain many touching expressions of the abandonment of friends and retainers. "Every thing," he says, "that was designed to do me good turned to my hurt, and death was wherever I turned my eye. * * * many have left me who professed they never would, and to say true, few have stuck by me."

On his release the Earl proceeded to Rome, and resided there for two years, but was sent for by his Sovereign, then at St. Germain, and received from him the title of Duke of Perth, was invested with the Order of the Garter, and had conferred upon him the offices of First Lord of the Bedchamber, Chamberlain to the Queen, and Governor of the Prince of Wales: empty honors it is true, but valuable as indications of regard from the fallen monarch. The Earl died at St. Germain, March 11th, 1716, aged 68, having survived James more than five years, and was buried in the chapel of the Scots college at Paris.

A contemporary says of the Earl that he was "passionately proud, told a story prettily, was of middle stature, with a quick look and brown complexion;" by other writers he has been pronounced timorous and wavering. His letters which have been published by the "Camden Society," show that he possessed no small share of Christian resignation, and a firm conviction that the cause in which he suffered was the cause of God. "I am in great quiet and peace," he wrote to his sister while imprisoned in Stirling Castle, "and I have not a wish but that the will of God is done in all that relates to me. Blessed are they who suffer for righteousness' sake, for theirs is the kingdom of Heaven." Of the sincerity of his conversion to the Romish faith these letters give abundant evidence, and he manifests an unbounded belief in all the relics, legends and mysteries of the times.

The Earl had several sons, one of whom, James, adhered to the fortunes of the exiled family of the Stuarts, was engaged in the rebellion of 1715, and by Act of Parliament was attainted. He had two sons, both of whom followed the example of their father and grandfather in continuing their adherence to the Stuarts, and were engaged in the rebellion of 1745. They were also attainted, but the eldest son died before the attainder came into effect, and the youngest was restored to the title in 1797; but dying in 1809 without male issue, the title became extinct; for although the Drummonds claimed it through John, the brother of the fourth Earl of Perth, it was not accorded to them by the English Parliament until June, 1853, when Queen Victoria assented to a bill reversing the attainder, and allowing the title of the Earl of Perth once more to be enjoyed by George, the fourth Duke of Melfort—the title conferred upon the Drummonds by James II. The Scottish estates, however, are in the possession of the Burrel family, through a daughter of the Earl, who died in 1809.

The rights of the Earl of Perth in East Jersey were conveyed to others, partly by himself in 1683 and 1684, and partly by his heir and assignee in 1704. For further information respecting the family, the reader is referred to the introduction to the Letters published by the Camden Society: East Jersey, under the Proprietors, p. 197, Macauley's England, II. p. 87, &c.

NOTE C, PAGE 73.

The following are extracts from the letters of Gronovius to Dr. Lewis Johnston, referred to in the text. They are given *verbatim*. From 1743 to 1754 Gronovius corresponded also with Bertram, the American Botanist:—

"LEYDEN, Feb. 22, 1735.

" * * * * * It happened in December, that I was at Rotterdam, where I find a friend, who hath a mind to stay all winter at London, to whom I have given a box with some of the officinall plants, which I hath dryed last summer; and some disputes of gentlemen that took their degree;—some orations of the professors, and a part of Albinus upon the Muscels." * * * * * "In the same room where you lived at Mr. Brandright is come a divine, being a Dutchman but from Scotch parents, so that he speaks the two languages; he is a regenerated, and hath got a place at Won'brugge, two hours from hence near Alphon, where formerly Mr. Blok was a pearson, whom *he* succeeded. Must ye not say how happy is my room? Dr. Bull a pretty Gentleman from Carolina, and who hath an exceeding good education, lived a great while with Him, but because he was not regenerated, it was enongh for Him, wen they saw one another to hear, Sir, your servant. That new superstitious and phantastic religion [has] increased here very much. I wish it never will come in that happy country where you are. * * * * * Boerhave hath printed nothing; but hath still his collegies as frequently as before, * * * * * people from abroad come frequently to Him." * * * * *

"I am very much obliged to you for the branches, and the fruit of the Cedar, I shall bee very glad to see them; they will bee a great ornament to my collection and garden. * * * * * The Bookseller, Vander Aa, who lived next the university is dead; his books which are in a great number will bee sold by auction; *if I can get the catalogue in time, I shall send them to you.* I am very much obliged to you for the good mind you have to send again a Cedar logg, and the Elk-skin, * * * * * *of the former log I have a very curious bufit, and other conveniences which are much admired by the people here.*

[He then tells him that having seen the son of the deceased bookseller, he has ascertained that the books would be sold in September, allowing time to learn Dr. Johnston's wishes respecting any work in the collection.] "About the Cicero of Grœvius. You must known that Grœvius never printed all Cicero's works, but only some of them which are in all eleventh volumes which are sold not long ago for fifty gilders. But Davisius hath printed which Grœvius hath omitted, so that those of Grœvius and Davisius make Cicero's work all together and the price of these of Davisius is uncertain, for hardly to be got.

The best Plato, is that apud Hennicum Stephanum, 3 vol., in folio, Ann 1758, grœce et Latine, en interpretatione Latina Job. Serrani—it is a very scarce book and when it is in an auction it always cometh to about 50 gilders. There is another edition of Plato by Ficinus, not much estimed, but printed with a large caracter, the price is about 6 gilders.

[Desires that 25 pounds of Candleberry wax or Barberry should be got for him. "I would try" he says "to make these candles of myself."] * * * I should desire you would send me the seeds of these greens which serveth for the kitchen and which you have not seen in Holland, as the fabœ, pisa, and particularly of those greens which are used by the Indians.

All this was written before the 20th of February. When this very morning, being the 21st, I received Mr. Santvoords box with the branches, and fruit of Cedar. I thank you kindly for them. * * * * I always thought that the Cedar was a coniferous plant but by your kindness I am wiser, and see clear that it is a berry bearing and belongst to the Iuniperus. I believe there are several sorts of pine trees and oaks in your country. * * * * * Mr. Santvoord hath sent to me several fine specimens of plants and trees which I have never seen before: amongst these where two specimens of oak trees, quite different from ours, and no doubt there are more. You should do me a great favour when the fruits of the oaks are ripe, to send a boy to gather them; I would try to make a walk of them in my garden. * * * * *

JOHN FREDERICK GRONOVIUS.

LEYDEN, August 29th, 1736.

[Acknowledges the receipt of the cedar, candleberry wax "Eland's skin" and a box of sassafras flowers.] "In the university is no change at all, except that the publicq garden is extended till the very ramparts; You remember when you went to Boerhave's chymistry, at the other side of the canal, there was a Racket play, which, and all the houses in the length to the ramparts are taken away, and in the Braughtness from the corner of the Derle Steg (where the gardener lived) to Boerhave's chymistry, so that she is three times larger as she was used to be before." [Albinus had finished his work on the muscles, and Boerhave intended publishing Swammerdam's works.]

* * * * * "I thank you kindly for the beans, which is a plant never seen in Holland, in my next letter I shall tell you the right name of it. The Stomach [Sumac?] seed is very welcome to, and seems to be very fresh, and no doubt a species of Alhohongi or Capsecum; next summer I hope to have it in flower when I shall easily determine the species." * * * * * "At the end of your letter you acquaint me of setting up a Botanic Library. I never would advise it; when you have Ray's Historia Plantarum, Tournefort's Institute, and Plukenet's Phytographia, it is sufficient. But I must tell you Botany has taken a quite other turn. You have heard how Ray Tournefort, Revini, and others quarreled about methods, all taken from the flowers and fruit. Now is come up one Dr. Linnæus, from Sweden, whose methode only consists in the stamina and pistilla; who hath not only invented this method about plants, but the same he hath done with the Lapidos and animals. Lawson and I printed it at our expenses, for ourselves, and our friends; I hope you will accept it and give it room in your Library." * * * * *

LEYDEN, August 26, 1736.

"I thank God I am by the Favour of good Friends come so far, that I get ever year a vast quantity of seeds of plants, which in Europe are quite lost; and particularly this year, I restored about 50 plants, which were in no public or private garden in Holland, the specimens of these you shall see with the next ship. * * * * I have a particular Friend living in the Virginy's at Gloucester County, on York river, whose name is Mr. John Clayton; that gentleman hath only by reading and looking in Tourneforts plates made himself a Botanist, and so far, that he hath collected more than 400 plants of which he sent me specimens, and of whom I send him the names, and synonymes." [Proposes to do the same for Dr. Johnston, and adds the price of some Botanical works. Ray's Historum Plantarum. 3 vols.folio, 20 guilders—Plukenet's works 50 to 60 guilders—Tournefort he presumes Dr. J. has.] * * * * * "All the other books are of no use to you, except those which Dr. Linnæus will publish, which I shall always send to you as soon as they are printed—wherefore I should persuade you now and then to read over the observations in Regnum vegitabile, and those pages of the Fundamenta Botanica of which I wrote in my first letter; for I am printing, with Linnæus, New Characters of all the genera plantarum which are known till this very day; in two months time it will be printed, when I shall by the first occasion present you a copy." * * * * * Lawson [an English gentleman, an acquaintance of Dr. J. who adds a postscript to one of these letters] is so charmed with the flowers of sassafras, that it is surprising. Yesterday he came to me with Gaunius to drink a tea of it, and they concluded with you that it must be an exceeding good anti-scorbutica."

October 12, 1736.

* * * * * "I am mightely obliged to Mr. Dubois [of New York] for several curious plants he brought with Him, and made a present of them to me; and by overlooking them I must conclude that the country you live in must be the finest in the world, for I see amongst these plants some which were thought only to grow in the healthiest of East Indies—Surinam and Guinea, and which grow in Europe."

May 26, 1737.

[Mr. Dubois established as a student at Leyden: mentions a case which Dr. Johnston had referred for the opinion of Boerhave—whose charge had been two pistoles.] "I send you here two copys of a plate which contains all the classes of the Systema Botanica of Linnæus." * * * * *

Sept. 3d, 1737.

[Sends Dr. J— Plukenet's works which cost 60 guilders.] * * * * "I hope this book will give you a good diversion and entertainment, most all the plants of your country you will find there, and I wish you could find a new genus which must be Johnstonia." [Promises to send by the next vessel a continuation of his and Linnæus' work—they had discovered some new genera among plants received from Virginia. Ray's work to be sent so soon as he could obtain it.]

LEYDEN, 11th November, 1739.

[Boerhave had died in the mean while.] "Boerhave's books are sold very dear, and next week his chymerical preparations—the corals which you remember were always standing in the gallery of the garden—every one hath thought these corals, besides two cases with insects and animals in liquor, would have been a legacy to the university, but he left no legacy at all. His papers and writings are in hands of his two cousins Kaw, the eldest, a physician at the Hague, who is at present reduced to such a low state, that for fear his creditors should make him hospes in the Gevanger poort at the Hague, he flyed to Vianea, where he liveth in great misery. His brother is in no better condition. Haller a learned man at Ottingen is printing Boerhave's Theory, and Dr. Van Sweeter the collegiani practicum." * * * * I remain,

Your most obedient servant,

JOH. FRED. GRONOVIUS.

INDEX.

*** References to Individuals are omitted when they occur in the notices of the Families of the same name.

A.

B.

G.

28

H.

I.

J.

K.

L.

M.

T.

U.

V.

W.

www.ingramcontent.com/pod-product-compliance
Lightning Source LLC
LaVergne TN
LVHW021130110826
845150LV00005B/987

* 9 7 8 1 4 2 5 5 4 9 3 9 8 *